DIAMONDS

OTHER BOOKS BY MICHAEL GERSHMAN

The Baseball Stadium Postcard Album (American League)

The Baseball Stadium Postcard Album (National League)

The Big Brother Book of Lists

Getting It Right the Second Time

The Score Board Book of Baseball Cards

Smarter Barter

CALENDARS

The Baseball Card Engagement Books (1987–1992)

The 1990 College Football Datebook

The 1989 NFL Datebook

The 1986 Stamp Calendar

1984 Big Brother Calendar

THE EVOLUTION
DIAMONDS
OF THE BALLPARK

MICHAEL GERSHMAN

HOUGHTON MIFFLIN COMPANY

Boston ◆ New York

For information about permission to reproduce
selections from this book, write to Permissions,
Houghton Mifflin Company, 215 Park Avenue
South, New York, New York 10003.

Library of Congress Cataloging-in-Publication Data
Gershman, Michael.
Diamonds : the evolution of the ballpark / Michael Gershman.
p.   cm.
Includes bibliographical references and index.
ISBN 0-395-61212-8
ISBN 0-395-73524-6 (pbk)
1. Baseball fields — United States — History. 2. Stadiums — United
States — History.   I. Title.
GV879.5.G47 1993 93-8025
796.357'06'873 — dc20 CIP

Printed in the United States of America

HOR 10 9 8 7 6 5 4 3 2

Book Design: Jennie Bush, Designworks, Inc.
Illustrations: Andrew Bartalotta
Photography: John Bunting and Rudolph Vetter
Chief photo researcher: Eliot Knispel

This book is dedicated

to two men—

GAVIN RILEY,

who opened my eyes

to the joys of ballpark research,

and my father,

DICK GERSHMAN,

who took me

out to the ball game.

Decades after a person has
stopped collecting bubble gum cards,
he can still discover himself collecting
ballparks . . .
their smells, their special seasons,
their moods.

—THOMAS BOSWELL

DIAMONDS

TIMELINE

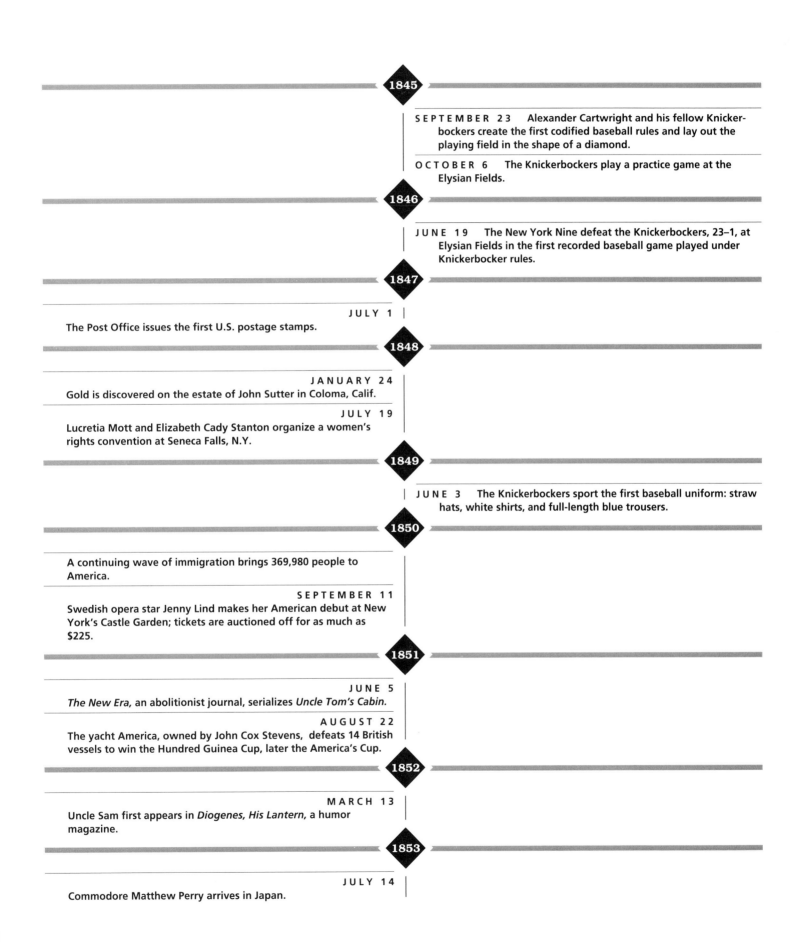

1845

SEPTEMBER 23 Alexander Cartwright and his fellow Knickerbockers create the first codified baseball rules and lay out the playing field in the shape of a diamond.

OCTOBER 6 The Knickerbockers play a practice game at the Elysian Fields.

1846

JUNE 19 The New York Nine defeat the Knickerbockers, 23–1, at Elysian Fields in the first recorded baseball game played under Knickerbocker rules.

1847

JULY 1
The Post Office issues the first U.S. postage stamps.

1848

JANUARY 24
Gold is discovered on the estate of John Sutter in Coloma, Calif.

JULY 19
Lucretia Mott and Elizabeth Cady Stanton organize a women's rights convention at Seneca Falls, N.Y.

1849

JUNE 3 The Knickerbockers sport the first baseball uniform: straw hats, white shirts, and full-length blue trousers.

1850

A continuing wave of immigration brings 369,980 people to America.

SEPTEMBER 11
Swedish opera star Jenny Lind makes her American debut at New York's Castle Garden; tickets are auctioned off for as much as $225.

1851

JUNE 5
The New Era, an abolitionist journal, serializes *Uncle Tom's Cabin.*

AUGUST 22
The yacht America, owned by John Cox Stevens, defeats 14 British vessels to win the Hundred Guinea Cup, later the America's Cup.

1852

MARCH 13
Uncle Sam first appears in *Diogenes, His Lantern*, a humor magazine.

1853

JULY 14
Commodore Matthew Perry arrives in Japan.

TIMELINE

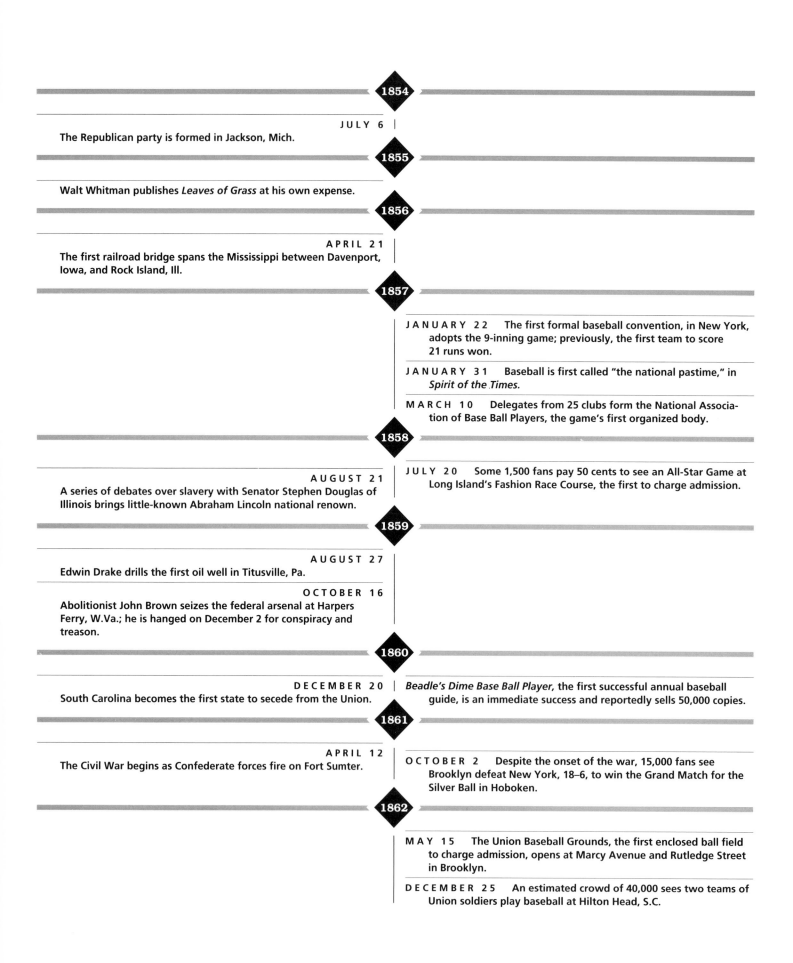

1854

JULY 6
The Republican party is formed in Jackson, Mich.

1855

Walt Whitman publishes *Leaves of Grass* at his own expense.

1856

APRIL 21
The first railroad bridge spans the Mississippi between Davenport, Iowa, and Rock Island, Ill.

1857

JANUARY 22 The first formal baseball convention, in New York, adopts the 9-inning game; previously, the first team to score 21 runs won.

JANUARY 31 Baseball is first called "the national pastime," in *Spirit of the Times.*

MARCH 10 Delegates from 25 clubs form the National Association of Base Ball Players, the game's first organized body.

1858

AUGUST 21
A series of debates over slavery with Senator Stephen Douglas of Illinois brings little-known Abraham Lincoln national renown.

JULY 20 Some 1,500 fans pay 50 cents to see an All-Star Game at Long Island's Fashion Race Course, the first to charge admission.

1859

AUGUST 27
Edwin Drake drills the first oil well in Titusville, Pa.

OCTOBER 16
Abolitionist John Brown seizes the federal arsenal at Harpers Ferry, W.Va.; he is hanged on December 2 for conspiracy and treason.

1860

DECEMBER 20
South Carolina becomes the first state to secede from the Union.

Beadle's Dime Base Ball Player, the first successful annual baseball guide, is an immediate success and reportedly sells 50,000 copies.

1861

APRIL 12
The Civil War begins as Confederate forces fire on Fort Sumter.

OCTOBER 2 Despite the onset of the war, 15,000 fans see Brooklyn defeat New York, 18–6, to win the Grand Match for the Silver Ball in Hoboken.

1862

MAY 15 The Union Baseball Grounds, the first enclosed ball field to charge admission, opens at Marcy Avenue and Rutledge Street in Brooklyn.

DECEMBER 25 An estimated crowd of 40,000 sees two teams of Union soldiers play baseball at Hilton Head, S.C.

TIMELINE

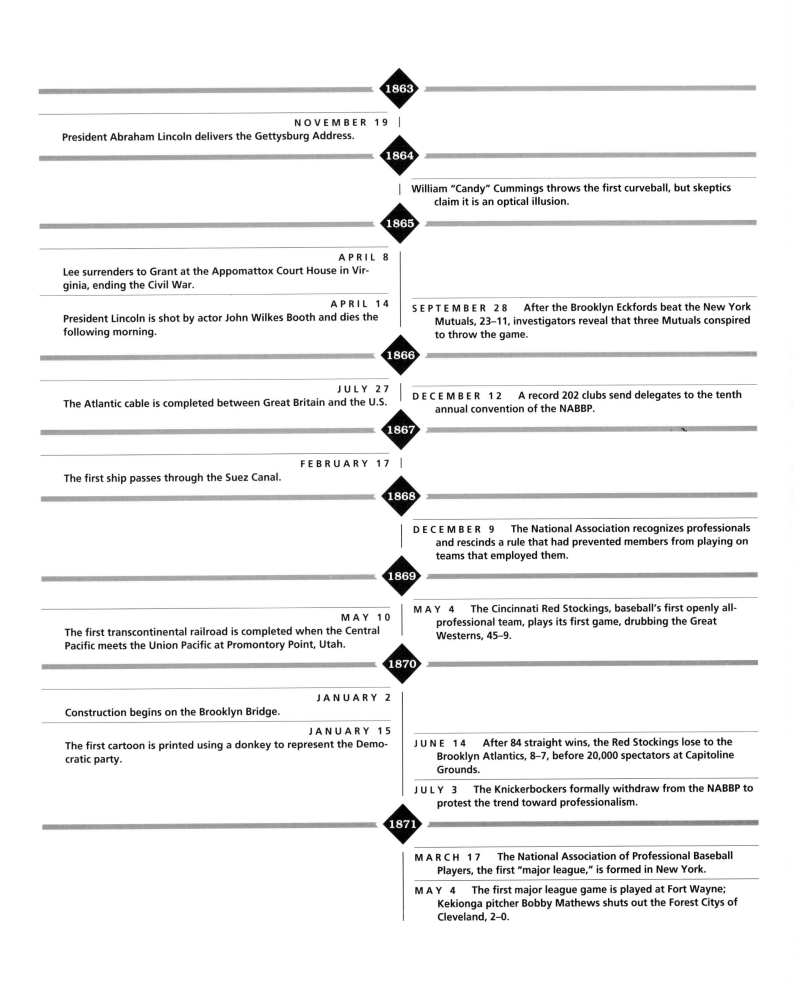

1863

NOVEMBER 19
President Abraham Lincoln delivers the Gettysburg Address.

1864

William "Candy" Cummings throws the first curveball, but skeptics claim it is an optical illusion.

1865

APRIL 8
Lee surrenders to Grant at the Appomattox Court House in Virginia, ending the Civil War.

APRIL 14
President Lincoln is shot by actor John Wilkes Booth and dies the following morning.

SEPTEMBER 28   After the Brooklyn Eckfords beat the New York Mutuals, 23–11, investigators reveal that three Mutuals conspired to throw the game.

1866

JULY 27
The Atlantic cable is completed between Great Britain and the U.S.

DECEMBER 12   A record 202 clubs send delegates to the tenth annual convention of the NABBP.

1867

FEBRUARY 17
The first ship passes through the Suez Canal.

1868

DECEMBER 9   The National Association recognizes professionals and rescinds a rule that had prevented members from playing on teams that employed them.

1869

MAY 10
The first transcontinental railroad is completed when the Central Pacific meets the Union Pacific at Promontory Point, Utah.

MAY 4   The Cincinnati Red Stockings, baseball's first openly all-professional team, plays its first game, drubbing the Great Westerns, 45–9.

1870

JANUARY 2
Construction begins on the Brooklyn Bridge.

JANUARY 15
The first cartoon is printed using a donkey to represent the Democratic party.

JUNE 14   After 84 straight wins, the Red Stockings lose to the Brooklyn Atlantics, 8–7, before 20,000 spectators at Capitoline Grounds.

JULY 3   The Knickerbockers formally withdraw from the NABBP to protest the trend toward professionalism.

1871

MARCH 17   The National Association of Professional Baseball Players, the first "major league," is formed in New York.

MAY 4   The first major league game is played at Fort Wayne; Kekionga pitcher Bobby Mathews shuts out the Forest Citys of Cleveland, 2–0.

TIMELINE

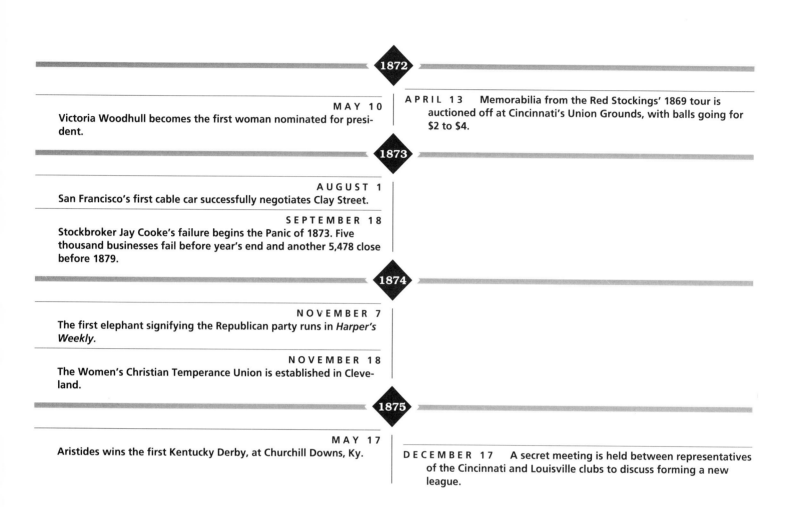

1872

MAY 10
Victoria Woodhull becomes the first woman nominated for president.

APRIL 13 Memorabilia from the Red Stockings' 1869 tour is auctioned off at Cincinnati's Union Grounds, with balls going for $2 to $4.

1873

AUGUST 1
San Francisco's first cable car successfully negotiates Clay Street.

SEPTEMBER 18
Stockbroker Jay Cooke's failure begins the Panic of 1873. Five thousand businesses fail before year's end and another 5,478 close before 1879.

1874

NOVEMBER 7
The first elephant signifying the Republican party runs in *Harper's Weekly*.

NOVEMBER 18
The Women's Christian Temperance Union is established in Cleveland.

1875

MAY 17
Aristides wins the first Kentucky Derby, at Churchill Downs, Ky.

DECEMBER 17 A secret meeting is held between representatives of the Cincinnati and Louisville clubs to discuss forming a new league.

C H A P T E R   O N E

Green Pastures

Since 1946, every NBA court has been exactly 94 feet long by 50 feet wide.

Since 1920, every NFL football field has been precisely 360 feet long by 160 feet wide.

Since 1871, every major league baseball field has been anywhere from, say, 180 to about 425 feet down the left field line, 390 to 635 in center, give or take a foot, and 196 to 402 or so in right.

The basketball court and football field allow for no variation in dimensions, but the ballpark varies markedly from city to city and even within a city. Consider the original Comiskey Park and Wrigley Field in Chicago. A pitcher, Ed Walsh, helped design Comiskey to be particularly tough on batters, as one might expect. Wrigley is a hitter's paradise, particularly when the wind is blowing out toward Lake Michigan.

These kinds of variations in and on the playing field have helped give baseball its character and set it apart from other professional sports. Constrained as he was by the rigid dimensions of the gridiron, Elroy "Crazy Legs" Hirsch made acrobatic catches in Los Angeles that could have been duplicated in Detroit, Green Bay, Philadelphia, or any NFL city; but Willie Mays's 1954 catch of Vic Wertz's drive could have happened only in New York, where the center fields at the time measured 461 (Yankee Stadium) and 483 (the Polo Grounds). All of Oscar Robertson's drives to the hoop produced two points in Syracuse, St. Louis, and San Francisco; the "Called Shot" Babe Ruth hit on October 1, 1932, in Wrigley Field might have been the "Called Out" in St. Louis, New York, or Philadelphia.

Ballparks are the "where" of baseball, and they

have indelibly shaped the action on the field since 1845, when the Knickerbocker Base Ball Club began playing a variation of "the New York game" of baseball. Baseball began as a pastoral game in what were, literally, limitless green pastures. Perhaps it is no coincidence that on June 19, 1846, the first recorded game took place in Hoboken, New Jersey, at a place known as the Elysian Fields — the "happy place" where the Greek gods and goddesses dispatched their favored humans "without tasting of death, to enjoy an immortality of bliss."

Bliss of any sort other than religious was frowned upon when America was first settled, and baseball might never have become the national pastime if the atmosphere maintained by Puritan leaders had prevailed. Sports and games were considered godless and frivolous on even the most joyous occasions. By 1732, sport had come up a peg or two socially, and three New Yorkers were allowed to lease a bowling green at the southern tip of Manhattan Island; yet lawn bowling ended when the Revolution began in 1775. Even after the war, sports and games were largely considered improper until the dawn of the nineteenth century.

The continuing disapproval of sports through the eighteenth century can be seen as an expression of national insecurity. The United States was a young country beset by financial woes internally and experienced enemies externally. Though independent, it still needed a defining moment, which came when, for the first time, America successfully defended itself as a sovereign nation, defeating Great Britain in the War of 1812.

Sports began to be looked on more positively in

The only known picture of the Cincinnati Red Stockings on the field (Case Commons) was taken before the Reds took on the Forest Citys of Cleveland (at right) in 1870. (Note the stylized FC on the Cleveland uniform in Charles Waldack's albumen photograph.) Case Commons was a typical wooden ballpark of the era and had very few seats (left). Spectators stood behind ropes or perched on the fences like the fans shown here.

5

Alexander Cartwright (center rear), one of baseball's prime movers, poses with his brother Alfred (right rear) and other Knickerbockers in the 1840s. In 1845, Cartwright was a teller at New York's Union Bank, where his superior was Daniel Ebbets, the father of Charles Hercules Ebbets, who built Ebbets Field.

America in the aftermath of victory. Games like soccer were played at American colleges in 1820, and laws against public horse racing were relaxed a year later. This change allowed the first racetrack — the Union Course — to be built on Long Island, New York. The first grandstands built solely for paying sports customers were at racetracks, and by the end of the decade, horse racing had become the original national pastime.

In 1829 *The Boy's Own Book,* published in England, recounted the rules for a children's game called rounders. Five years later, precisely the same rules were applied to "base" or "goal ball" in *The Book of Sports* by Robin Carver, published in America; however, the description was illustrated with a line drawing that may have shown baseball being played on Boston Common. This version used four stakes driven into the ground for bases (see diagram). The east corner was "first bound," and the other three proceeded counterclockwise at the corners. The pitcher stood on a grassy area defined by dotted lines. Five fielders, called scouts, were clumped between first and third, with one between each bound, much the way shortstops and second basemen are aligned today.

Watching such a game was a far cry from paying to be a spectator at a sports event because the choices were few and the premises insecure. Most

sports events were, literally, standing room only. There were no grandstands, no bleacher boards, no seats of any kind. At the time, the emphasis was on participation, not entertainment.

By the 1840s, horse racing, boxing, yachting, and track had become more popular but were still the preserve of gentlemen, i.e., the well-heeled. Cricket had a long run as a fad but never really had a chance here, because it was too slow and undemocratic. The role of national pastime would fall to baseball, based largely on the game yuppies of the period — the Knickerbocker Base Ball Club — played in New York City's Madison Square. It was a bucolic spot in the early 1840s, traversed by a brook favored by trout and deer, but already disfigured by urbanization. A glue factory had polluted Sunfish Pond so badly in the 1830s that it had to be drained and leveled with landfill. The Knicks moved to Murray Hill, but the New York & Haarlem Rail Road announced plans for a stable on the spot where they played, currently Thirty-fourth Street and Third Avenue.

The task of finding new grounds fell to Alexander Cartwright, a particularly imposing figure by the standards of 1845. He stood 6'2", had an athletic build, and had been a volunteer fireman with the Knickerbocker Engine Company; although it disbanded in 1843, he named his baseball club after it. Faced with being dispossessed, Cartwright urged his mates to flee New York's urban sprawl for the wide open spaces of Hoboken, New Jersey, and the Elysian Fields. They made their first trip in 1845 and stayed until 1852.

There are nearly as many detractors of Cartwright's contributions to baseball as there are debunkers of the Abner Doubleday myth. Some point out that Cartwright didn't set the bases 90 feet apart, instead using the inexact "forty-two paces" when a military pace measured either 2½ or 3 feet. Nevertheless, the Knicks transformed the game with four key changes: *(continued p. 11)*

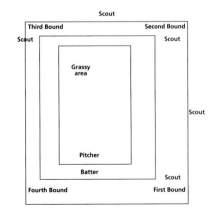

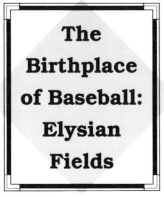

The Birthplace of Baseball: Elysian Fields

Baseball, the most democratic of games, was born in the Elysian Fields, an idyllic New Jersey pasture better suited to the rich.

The Fields were owned by Commodore John Cox Stevens, who founded the New York Yacht Club in 1844 and, five years later, piloted his yacht, *America,* to win the first Hundred Guinea Cup (later, the America's Cup). Since Stevens ran a ferry between Hoboken and Barclay Street, in downtown New York, he promoted Elysian Fields as a tourist attraction to sell more round-trip tickets at 13 cents a pop. It was an easy sell, because the Fields were "a place of surpassing beauty."

In 1902, William A. Shephard described them in retrospect:

About a mile and a half from the ferry, up the Jersey shore of the Hudson, along a road that skirted the river bank on one side and was hugged by trees and thicket on the other, brought one suddenly to an opening in the "forest primeval." This open spot was a level, grass-covered plain, some two hundred yards across, and as deep . . . a perfect greensward. Nature must have foreseen the needs of base ball, and designed the place especially for that purpose.

The site also had cultural cachet as a subject for the Hudson River School of painters, but developers added so many hotels, bars, and restaurants that the authors of *The Jersey Game* call it "the Disneyland of its day." (In 1843, Phineas T. Barnum staged a buffalo hunt here and roped in 30,000 paying customers.) In spite of commercialization, the Elysian Fields remained a choice site, and Cartwright and his friends played various forms of baseball there every Tuesday and Friday afternoon. On September 23, 1845, Cartwright drew up the first set of baseball rules with several of his fellow Knickerbockers.

They played what is still recognized as the first recorded baseball match on June 19, 1846. The ball had a rubber center, the catcher was called "the behind," and home plate was made, not of rubber but Hoboken slate. The Knicks were trounced, 23–1, by the New York Nine but graciously feted their conquerors at McCarty's Hotel.

On August 3, 1865, the first Grand Match for the Championship of the United States was held here between the Mutuals and the Atlantics before a crowd of between 15,000 and 20,000. On September 28, 1865, almost twenty years to the day since Cartwright set down his rules, the Fields became the site of baseball's first scandal. Set to play the Eckfords, the Mutuals were originally the bettors' choice at 5–3, but the Eckfords were favored by game time. Leading, 5–4, after four innings, the Mutuals began booting grounders and yielding passed balls. The Eckfords went on to win, 23–11, and several Mutual players were later suspended.

The Stevens family banned championship games at the Elysian Fields in 1867, and in 1869 the lower part of it was partitioned to accommodate sewers and streets for the expansion of Hoboken from 2,500 people in 1850 to more than 20,000. Less than fifty years after the Knicks first played ball, in 1893 a local history noted, "All of the old Elysian Fields have been swept away in the demand for building lots." A Maxwell House coffee plant was built on the site in 1938 and demolished in 1992.

This lithograph of Elysian Fields by Nathaniel Currier and James Merritt Ives is dated 1865 but appears to have been drawn earlier. The three basemen are attached to their respective stations as if manacled, rather than playing halfway off the bag in the modern style.

Hoboken's Elysian Fields, where the Knickerbockers played a modern form of baseball at least as early as 1845, was, in 1995, the site of a recently abandoned Maxwell House Coffee plant. A plaque across the street commemorates what is generally regarded as the Knickerbockers' first match game, on June 19, 1846. History records that the New York Nine trounced the Knickerbocker "muffins," 23–1. Cartwright, as umpire, fined James Whyte Davis sixpence for swearing.

In October 1859, *Harper's Weekly* ran a spread devoted to two games played at Elysian Fields, one cricket, the other baseball. Positions on the off side (team in the field) on the cricket pitch are clearly marked by posts but not on the crude baseball diamond. Note the carriages and large number of women. In *Playing for Keeps,* Warren Goldstein says, "Just as women's presence at club social events was taken to be a guarantor of ballplayers' maturity, or manliness, their attendance at games was considered evidence of baseball's worthiness, popularity, and respectability."

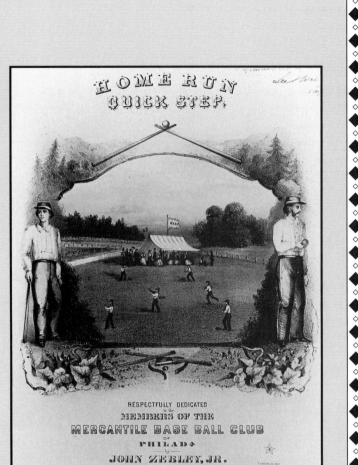

One of the best ways to comprehend the extent of the baseball craze in the early 1860s is to examine sheet music showing Union Army soldiers playing baseball on idealized fields (perhaps a way of momentarily forgetting the war). Both "Baseball Polka" and "Home Run Quick Step" feature players clad exclusively in Union caps. "Live Oak Polka," a paean to the Live Oak Base Ball Club of Rochester, New York, shows players wearing caps and adds a Live Oak resplendent in the home team's uniform.

1. Set a distance between bases which made the race to the bag so close that grounders became possibly exciting plays; it took skill to catch a small, hard-hit ball, then throw it across the diamond in time to nip a baserunner.

2. Made the game more demanding by making fielders throw at a small target — a fielder's hand — rather than the batsman's body, as earlier rules specified.

3. Suggested "retiring the side" on three outs. This change made the New York game infinitely faster than cricket. (Since all "hands" have to be retired in cricket, matches last four or five days even now).

4. Concentrated the action in a 90-degree quadrant by separating fair territory from foul, the defining first step in the evolution of the ballpark. In the long run, the foul line's greatest impact was on the spectators; confining the action made it easy to follow the ball and focus on the players.

A little more than two years after he had become intrigued with diamonds, Cartwright became obsessed with gold. When news of the strike at Sutter's Mill reached New York, he became a "forty-niner." But after a four-month journey to California, he quickly gave up digging for gold and struck out for another Elysian Field — Oahu — where he laid out Hawaii's first baseball diamond. The man most responsible for "inventing" the multibillion-dollar business of baseball never capitalized on it.

THE AGE OF CLUBS (1845–1865)

Social changes in the 1840s and 1850s accelerated the growth of sports:

1. Great waves of immigrants hit America, spurred initially by the Great Potato Famine in Ireland and later by Eastern Europeans fleeing social and religious persecution.

2. New Americans began migrating west, lessening the East's grasp on the nation's political and financial reins.

3. Workers taken to Mauch Chunk, Pennsylvania, to smelt iron or to make woolens in Lowell, Massachusetts, had no ties to the traditional arbiters of local style — the minister, schoolmaster, and banker. A growing industrial society created a need for a new social framework in the urban centers, which were filled by fraternal orders and ethnic clubs like the Ancient Order of Hibernians and B'nai B'rith.

Such groups began to use sports as a way of teaching English, demonstrating solidarity, publicizing the group, and attracting new members. The *New York Times* estimated that there were some 2,000 community teams in New England alone during the 1860s. In New York, the Brooklyn Eckfords were formed by Henry Eckford, a Scottish shipbuilder, and there were also the Manhattans (cops), Phantoms (barkeeps), and Aesculapians (doctors). In 1856, *Porter's Spirit of the Times* said that every available plot "within ten miles of the city [New York] was being used as a playing field."

With baseball fever gripping the city, the Knickerbockers were asked to organize a formal baseball group, and, after much prodding, they arranged a convention of baseball clubs on January 22, 1857, in New York. As a result, the first formal baseball organization of any kind, the National Association of Base Ball Players (NABBP), was established on March 10, with twenty-five clubs. That fall, the first baseball championship series was held: the Brooklyn Atlantics defeated the Eckfords, 2 out of 3 games, to become the first "world champions."

No fans paid to see those matches, but the idea soon occurred to would-be entrepreneurs. The first match at which an entry fee (50 cents) was charged was the first of a best-of-three All-Star Game between teams representing New York and Brooklyn on July 20, 1858. The "park" was, of all places, the Fashion Race Course in Newtown, Long Island. (Newtown is near Flushing Meadow, Queens, which means the park was less than three miles from Shea Stadium.)

Fifteen years after Cartwright laid out the first diamond, the elements required to make the ballpark a commercial venture were all in place:

◆ a line dividing players from spectators and concentrating the action in a small area (the Knickerbocker layout);

◆ a pool of talented players (the NABBP);

◆ fans willing to pay to see a game (the Fashion Race Course series).

This ad, which ran in the *Brooklyn Eagle* on May 15, played up the park's convenience to public transportation and its seats for women. Cammeyer shrewdly made admission free — at least initially — to increase attendance and word-of-mouth.

The First Enclosed Ballpark: Union Grounds

The true "father" of baseball may always remain a matter for debate, but there's no question that the father of the enclosed ballpark was a shrewd Brooklyn politician named William H. Cammeyer.

The heir to a successful leather business (and an intimate of New York's notorious mayor, William Marcy "Boss" Tweed), Cammeyer bought a plot of land in Brooklyn in 1861 and created the Union ice skating rink. Hoping to enhance a barely profitable seasonal operation, he tried to get the community to use his plot for pleasure boating and horseback riding but failed. Then Cammeyer looked at his ice pond and envisioned what was, in the terminology of the day, a ball grounds. Given baseball's popularity, even during the Civil War, Cammeyer decided to provide bench seating for the ladies (a first), confine gamblers to a separate "bettor's ring," and build "the game's finest playing field."

When it opened, on May 15, 1862, many fans preferred to stand outside the enclosure — even though admission was free. The grandstand was shaped like a horseshoe, and benches on three sides accommodated 1,500 people. The outfield fences were more than 500 feet from home plate. (Before the game, a band played "The Star-Spangled Banner," the first time music was ever performed at a ball game.)

Although tickets had been sold for the Brooklyn-Manhattan series four years earlier, Cammeyer's experiment marked not only the beginning of the ballpark but also the true beginning of professional baseball as a spectator sport. After that first day, he charged an entry fee, clearly drawing the line between the merely curious and those willing to pay to watch a game.

This distinction was not lost on the players. The Eckfords, Putnams, and Constellations — the three clubs that initially shared the grounds — were happy to practice without paying rent and enjoyed a clubhouse large enough to fit all three teams; however, as admissions rose, the players demanded a cut of the gate; Cammeyer eventually gave in. Predictably, he upped the entry price from a dime to a quarter when good clubs such as the Atlantics began using his ballyard.

The most important park of its day, Union Grounds routinely hosted big games, even when Brooklyn teams were not involved. The Cincinnati Red Stockings played the New York Mutuals here, and the first major league postseason championship game was held here on October 30, 1871. Before it was torn down, the place had served as home grounds for three National Association teams (the Mutuals, Eckfords, and Atlantics) and two National League teams (the Mutuals in 1876 and the Hartfords in 1877) and set the pattern for what fans would come to expect of a ballpark.

Inauguration of the Union Base Ball and Cricket Grounds — Grand Opening Game — 2,000 to 3,000 spectators present.

The project to establish the "Union Skating, Riding School, Base Ball, Gymnastic and Boating Association" as one of our permanent institutions having been abandoned on account of the hard times, the scheme of establishing the "Union Base Ball and Cricket grounds" was adopted in its stead, and through the energy of the officers of the association, this project has been carried into execution, and the inaugural game was played upon the grounds yesterday.

For some weeks past, laborers have been engaged in draining, leveling, sodding, and converting the lots occupied last winter as a skating rink into a ball ground. This project is particularly acceptable, as in laying out the grounds much labor and expense are being bestowed upon them, and this not only gave employment to unemployed laborers, but will eventually prove an ornament to that portion of the city in which they are located, and it is a fair specimen of the enterprise of our citizens, this being the first of the kind in Brooklyn. At the Central Park, N.Y., there are ball grounds on the same plan as those established here, and for the past year or two there have been numbers established in London and other European cities. The chief object of the Association is to provide a suitable place for ball playing, where ladies can witness the game without being annoyed by the indecorous behavior of the rowdies who attend some of the first-class matches. The buildings occupied last winter are left standing....

Near these a long wooden shed has been erected, capable of accommodating several hundred persons, and benches provided for the fair sex, and wherever their presence enlivens the scene, there gentlemanly conduct will follow. Indecorous proceedings will cause the offenders to be instantly expelled from the grounds....Several more acres have been added to the enclosure, which is fenced in with a board fence six or seven feet in height. On the southeast corner, a large and commodious clubhouse has been erected, containing accommodations for three clubs. The field is now almost a perfect level, covering at least six acres of ground, all of which is well drained, rolled, and in a few weeks will be in splendid condition. Yesterday it was in a fine state, but rain was needed to make it suitable for playing, the ground being dry and dusty. Several flag staffs have been put up, from which floated the banners of the clubs, o'er shadowed by the nation's ensign. The Eckford, Putnam, and Constellation Clubs have engaged the grounds for the season — each having the use of them two days in the week....From 2 o'clock until long after the game commenced there was one continuous stream of visitors, filling up the ladies' shed and every available seat on the ground; even then several hundred had to stand. There were representatives present from almost every club in the city, besides several from New York.... The embankments outside the enclosure also were occupied with spectators, on foot and in carriages; the concourse, it is estimated, amounted to 8000 persons. At 3 o'clock the music arrived and the proceeding commenced, opening by playing the "Star Spangled Banner."

— **Brooklyn Eagle,** May 16, 1862

When William Cammeyer bought land at Marcy and Rutledge streets in Brooklyn in 1861, he initially created a skater's haven, Union Pond (above). This *Harper's* illustration charmingly captures the spirit of the pond, which failed financially. In its stead, Cammeyer created Union Grounds, the first enclosed ballpark, in 1862. When the Philadelphia Athletics played the Brooklyn Resolutes on June 15, 1865, an estimated 6,000, "the most numerous assemblage yet seen on the Union grounds," saw the contest (below). Note the Athletic flag waving from a hexagonal pagoda in center field, the Resolute flag down the right field line, and the umpire (in top hat) watching from foul territory. The Athletics won, 39–14.

Even though baseball was largely confined to the Northeast and upper Midwest, Union Grounds was, by 1868, the most famous ball grounds in the country. It is featured here on the cover of an 1868 edition of the *New York Clipper.* Clearly, after only six years, the field had evolved into something more like what we call a ballpark than earlier illustrations show.

Six months after the war ended and Lincoln was assassinated, baseball was bigger than ever. When two Brooklyn teams, the Atlantics and the Eckfords, played at Union Grounds in October, the field was lined with a crowd that exceeded 10,000. In its report, *Frank Leslie's Illustrated Newspaper* compliments the players and spectators and editorializes against professionalism: "The time has arrived for contests for the championship to be ignored and discouraged by all those who do not want to see the game made a means of livelihood."

In October 1865, the Atlantics journeyed to the City of Brotherly Love to take on Philadelphia at Athletics Park (above). Note the elaborate marquee at center, the antics of the crowd, and the primitive grandstand at far right. A year later, the same teams met at Athletics Park to play a championship game (below). Spectators paid the astronomical sum of $1 to watch. The stiff admission is probably why, although the park doesn't look crowded, the area was mobbed. Ed Doyle, in his monograph on Philadelphia ballparks, says, "The newspapers claimed there were 20,000 people in the area in trees, on roof tops, on trucks, and in second floor windows."

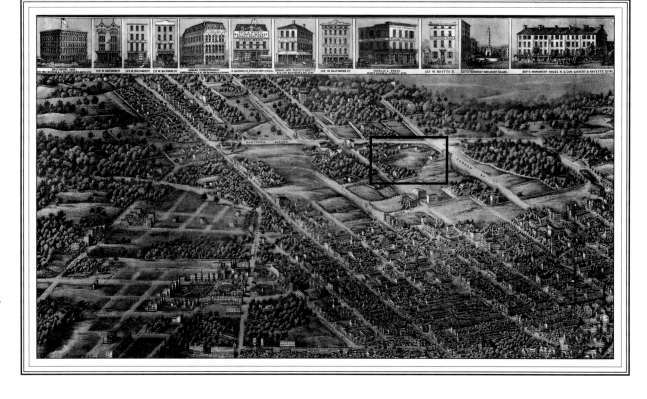

By the 1860s, ballparks began showing up on official documents like city maps, which were often lined with drawings of prominent buildings. A keen observer can see Madison Avenue Grounds, Baltimore's first ballpark, on E. Sachse's *Grand View of Baltimore City*, drawn in 1869. Notice the flagpole and bleachers along third base.

Further evolution of the enclosed ballpark had to await the end of the Civil War, but baseball thrived during the conflict. An estimated 40,000 saw two Union teams play at Hilton Head, South Carolina, in 1862. In 1863, Acting Major Otto Boetticher, an artist, depicted Union soldiers playing baseball in a Confederate prison camp at Salisbury, North Carolina. On the way home from Appomattox, the 133rd New York Volunteers took time out to play the Washington Nationals behind the White House.

THE AGE OF TEAMS (1866–1870)

After the Civil War, baseball took another quantum leap in popularity. The National Association's 97 members in 1865 more than doubled a year later, to 202. National newspapers like *Harper's Weekly* and *Frank Leslie's Illustrated Weekly* began devoting more space to baseball, spurred in part by the telegraph, which charged for delivering baseball news.

The growth of the railroads made intercity travel easier and baseball rivalries inevitable. In *The Creation of American Team Sports*, George Kirsch says:

Intercity competition provided most of the excitement that fanned baseball fever. Traditions of local pride, urban rivalries, and city boosterism spurred hometown clubs and newspapers to seek glory for their nines and communities. . . . Winning nines could propel quiet country towns and sleepy villages into the limelight.

In the Midwest, competition was rife to see which city — Cincinnati, St. Louis, or Chicago — would become the area's dominant metropolis. When the Louisville Base Ball Club journeyed to Cincinnati in July 1867 to play the Red Stockings on the brand-new Union Cricket and Base Ball Grounds, they found a space that had been improved at a cost of $10,000, a huge sum at the time. A new fence enclosed the eight-acre site, which was manicured like the finest lawns. The park featured a "beautiful two-story pavilion with a verandah and raised seats for the accommodation of the ladies."

By 1868 the move toward professionalism — spurred by intercity rivalry and paid admissions — had become inexorable. As Harold Seymour points out, the top clubs (all of them in thriving cities) were divvying up gate receipts of $100,000 in 1868; that figure reflects upwards of 300,000 paid admissions at 25 and 50 cents. The climactic moment came on December 9, 1868, when the National Association realized that its ban on hiring players had become moot and officially recognized two classes, professionals and amateurs. Ten clubs began compensating players and, aided by the new transcontinental railroad, the Cincinnati Red Stockings became the first openly all-professional team.

In less than thirty years, rounders — a game British children played — had become baseball — a sport American adults *paid* to watch. The financial success William Cammeyer had enjoyed by enclosing Union Grounds created income for baseball — admissions — and, in turn, fostered a new type of ballplayer — the openly paid professional. It also upgraded baseball's audience by getting rid of the "riff-raff," who couldn't, or wouldn't, spend a quarter to see a game. Chadwick wrote that the 25-cent admission charge was "not relished by the masses but, by the respectable portion of the community, it is regarded as a considerable improvement, as by means of the increased price hundreds of blackguard boys and roughs generally are kept out."

Harry Wright and the First Big Red Machine

Harry Wright, the cricketer who had embraced baseball, was fully behind the professional movement, saying, "It is well worth 50 cents to see a good game of base ball, and when the public refuse to pay that, then good bye base ball. They do not object to paying 75 cents to $1.50 to go to the theater. . . . We must make the games worth witnessing and there will be no fault found with the price of admission. A good game is worth 50 cents, a poor one is dear at 25 cents."

Sportswriter Henry Chadwick called Wright "the Father of Professional Baseball" with good reason. Although born to cricket, Harry was exposed to baseball at the Elysian Fields and was drawn to it immediately. He played and coached both sports in New York and Philadelphia, moved to Cincinnati in August 1865 as player-coach of the Union Cricket Club (UCC), and helped form the Cincinnati Base Ball Club the following summer. Early in 1867, his club moved to the Union Cricket Grounds and merged with the UCC. When Wright, at the suggestion of club president George Ellard, added scarlet hose to the uniform, the team became known as the Red Stockings.

By 1868, the Red Stockings were mostly pros; several were salaried, and nearly all the others were compensated with a share of the gate receipts. When the NABBP revoked its rule preventing members from playing against professionals, the way was clear for Wright and Cincinnati businessmen to transform the Red Stockings into a totally professional outfit.

Aaron B. Champion, a 26-year-old lawyer who was well connected, organized the new team, raised $11,000 through a stock issue to beautify Union Grounds, and floated another $15,000 to find the best players money could buy. When he was finished, baseball's first all-pro team included only one hometown boy.

To put these figures in perspective, laborers earned $2 a day then, and spacious houses could be rented for less than $500 a year. Accordingly, a salary of even $800 a year was a powerful inducement for players to move from New York and New Jersey. The *National Chronicle* said, "Had the Cincinnati Base Ball Club depended upon home talent it would never have been heard from outside its own locality."

Champion saw the team as a way of promoting Cincinnati and arranged a tour that took his team to Fort Wayne, Boston, New York, and San Francisco. All in all, the 1869 Reds won 59 games and tied 1, playing before 200,000 people. After paying all salaries and travel expenses, the team finished the year $1.26 in the black. But, as Champion reminded everyone, "Glory, they've advertised the city — advertised us, sir, and helped our business, sir."

The Red Stockings won 24 straight in 1870 before meeting the Atlantics on Brooklyn's Capitoline Grounds. The teams battled to a 5–5 tie after nine innings; the Atlantics left the field, but Harry Wright wanted to play on, and the umpire fetched the Brooklynites. After a scoreless tenth, the Red Stockings scored twice in the top of the eleventh. With one Atlantic out and a man on third, Joe Start hit a drive to right, and Cal McVey knelt to take it on one hop. But several fans jumped onto his back and, in the ensuing confusion, Start got to third; the tying run scored on Bob Ferguson's single to right, and he scored the winning run on a twice-botched ground ball.

Fans "cheered and swung their hats, and yelled, and shouted, and danced, til it seemed as if they would go wild," according to the *Clipper.* "The club that had been regarded as the Invincible had been beaten for the first time in two years." Champion sent a telegram home: ATLANTICS 8, CINCINNATIS 7. THE FINEST GAME EVER PLAYED. OUR BOYS DID NOBLY, BUT FORTUNE WAS AGAINST US. ELEVEN INNINGS PLAYED. THOUGH BEATEN, NOT DISGRACED.

But in *Baseball in Cincinnati,* Joseph S. Stern, Jr., captured the feeling that followed the loss: "With this first defeat the heart also went out of the ball club. The holy crusade was over; something snapped." After a second loss, Champion resigned and the fickle fans turned away. Disturbed at this turn of events, Harry Wright decided to abandon Porkopolis (Cincinnati) for Beantown (Boston), taking to the Hub of the Universe his brother, Gould, and McVey. He also took the Red Stockings, which became the name of Boston's National Association team and, ultimately, the present American League team. On November 20, 1870, the Cincinnati Baseball Club officially disbanded. A few months later, on March 17, 1871, the first major league, the National Association of Professional Baseball Players, was formed with teams in thirteen cities.

PLAYER	POSITION	HOME	SALARY
George Wright	Shortstop	Washington	$1,400
Harry Wright	Center field	New York	1,200
Asa Brainard	Pitcher	New York	1,100
Fred Waterman	Third base	New York	1,000
Charles Sweasy	Second base	Newark	800
Charles Gould	First base	Cincinnati	800
Douglas Allison	Catcher	Jersey City	800
Andrew Leonard	Left field	Newark	800
Calvin McVey	Right field	Indianapolis	800
Richard Hurley	Substitute	Indianapolis	800

While Union Grounds was justly famous, Brooklyn had another standout ballpark, also a former ice skating ground, called Capitoline Grounds. Named after one of Rome's Seven Hills, it was the home field of the Brooklyn Atlantics, and in June 1870, they ended the Red Stockings' fabulous winning streak here, as this illustration shows. Two months later, on August 16, pitcher Fred Goldsmith proved conclusively that a baseball curved here, throwing an "inshoot" between two 8-foot stakes, one between the pitcher's box and the plate, the other to the right of the plate.

Just as *GQ* might shoot a spring fashion layout at Yankee Stadium, Butterick, the pattern company, used Union Grounds (the hexagonal pagoda) as a background for its new spring uniforms in 1870. As Warren Goldstein notes, "Like the fences around enclosed grounds, the ropes that kept back spectators, and the foul lines on the field, uniforms were boundaries between what was baseball and what was not, between who belonged on the playing field and who did not."

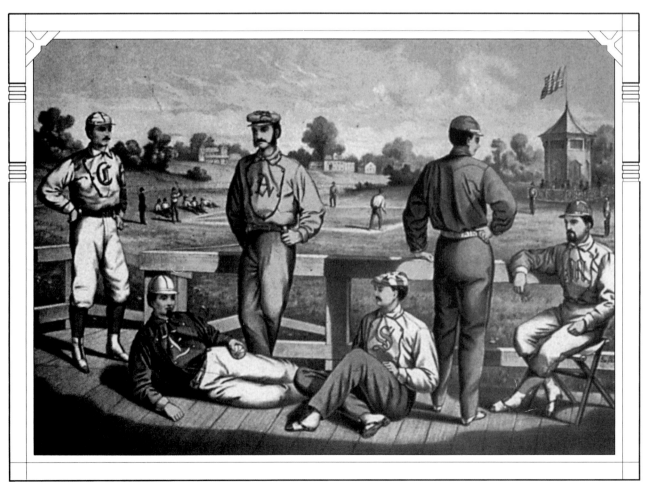

Enclosed ballparks and an admission charge had provided

◆ regular pay to support the players.

◆ revenue for the owners (later supplemented by food, drinks, and souvenirs).

◆ protection for women and children, increasing the potential audience.

◆ greater entertainment value based on comfort and, later, reserved seating.

THE FIRST LEAGUE: THE NATIONAL ASSOCIATION (1871–1875)

An 1870 *New York Times* article described how eighteen players were paid: two were appointed to political office, nine were given salaries, and the other seven were compensated solely with a share of the gate. At the end of the season, the NABBP proposed restrictions against professionalism at its November meeting; the move failed by a vote of 17–9, and the stage was set in America for professional baseball.

On St. Patrick's Day, 1871, representatives of nine clubs formed the National Association of Professional Baseball Players (NA) in New York. With good weather approaching, the organizers slapped together a loose confederation in a single day. Each club paid a franchise fee of $10 to buy the championship pennant, awarded to the winner of the most five-game series; clubs scurried to build ball grounds and made their own schedules.

All nine parks were built of wood and, in this era before trolleys, were generally located where land was cheap. Rockford, for instance, took an existing fairgrounds and didn't even cut down a cluster of

Original National Association Teams and Parks

Boston Red Stockings	South End Grounds
Chicago White Stockings	Union Base-Ball Grounds (Lake Park)
Cleveland Forest Citys	National Association Grounds
Fort Wayne Kekiongas	Hamilton Field
New York Mutuals	Union Grounds
Philadelphia Athletics	Athletics Park (Jefferson Street Grounds)
Rockford Forest Citys	Fairgrounds Park
Troy Haymakers	Haymakers' Grounds
Washington Olympics	Olympics Grounds

five trees around third base. But Athletics Park boasted the first press box, "a reporters' stand . . . sufficiently elevated to be out of the reach of strong foul balls that may chance their way." Similarly, the operators of Cleveland's National Association Grounds pioneered the reserved seat, after a fashion. Fans paid $6 for a single seat at 15 home games or could buy a pair of ducats — "only ten dollars for yourself, your lady, and your carriage." (Of course, the carriage *was* the reserved seat; instead of sitting on a plank, ticket holders parked their buggies and sat in specified locations behind first or third base.)

Chicago's Lake Park, known variously as Lake Street Dumping Ground, White Stocking Park, and Union Base-Ball Grounds, was built on a city dump near Lake Michigan within walking distance of the business district. Capacity was 7,000; a season ticket cost $15 and entitled patrons to be

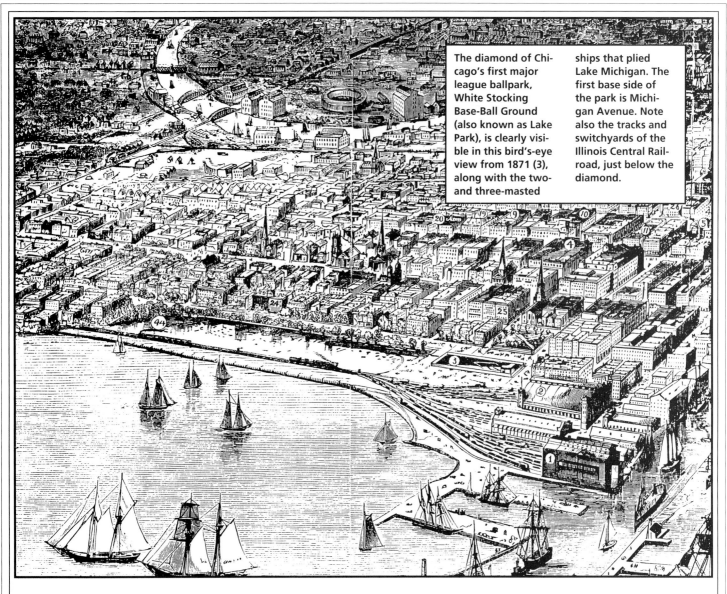

The diamond of Chicago's first major league ballpark, White Stocking Base-Ball Ground (also known as Lake Park), is clearly visible in this bird's-eye view from 1871 (3), along with the two- and three-masted ships that plied Lake Michigan. The first base side of the park is Michigan Avenue. Note also the tracks and switchyards of the Illinois Central Railroad, just below the diamond.

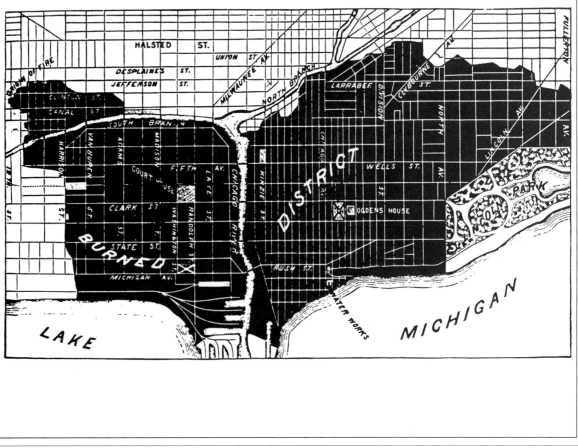

Just as the White Stockings were putting on a stretch run to win the first National Association pennant, the Great Chicago Fire burned down their ballpark, seen here as the blank rectangle below the cross-hatched rectangle at the left center of the illustration. The Illinois Central tracks are depicted by the forking lines at the bottom in this representation of the fire's effects. Damage was estimated at $196 million; 17,450 buildings were consumed, 250 people were killed, and 98,000 were rendered homeless. The original Emancipation Proclamation was also lost in the blaze.

a six-day bike race. I told him bike fans preferred ham and cheese, but he insisted."

What we now call the hot dog was named in 1905 by Hearst cartoonist Thomas A. Dorgan, who signed his drawings TAD. A Polo Grounds regular, Dorgan drew a cartoon animating the sausage by placing an elongated dachshund on a bun. Flexner says that the dachshund was "a facetious symbol for things German in the early 1900s" and adds that "many people suspected the mixed meats in the sausage contained dog meat, or worse." When Dorgan heard a vendor yell, "Get a red-hot dachshund sausage on a roll," he was inspired to dub the concoction "the hot dog," and the name stuck. (After his father's death, Frank Stevens was indeed given credit for inventing the hot dog. When his daughter, Alice, wed James Titus, whose mother was a Gulden, the *Daily News* headlined the event, "Hot Dog Marries the Mustard.")

The company Harry started also cleans arenas and K mart stores on a contract basis and has helped design Arby's, Holiday Inns, and Florida's Gulfstream Park. In 1992, the company's clients ranged from the Central Park Zoo and Churchill Downs to the Astrodome, Candlestick Park, Fenway Park, and Shea Stadium. These days, Joseph B. Stevens, Jr., Harry's grandson and the company's retired chairman, keeps his hand in

HARRY STEVENS

by adding to the company's collection of programs and scorecards. He says, "I just paid $21,500 for a scorecard; in 1905, my grandfather sold it for a dime."

This illustration of a natty Harry M. Stevens ran in an 1896 edition of the *New York Clipper.*

THE BALLPARK FIRES OF 1894

The illumination provided by numerous early attempts at night baseball were pale compared with the light of the fires that bedeviled ballparks in the 1890s. The parks in St. Louis had six fires during the decade, and at least twenty others around the country burst into flame during the otherwise Gay Nineties. One way to appreciate the extent of the problem is to review insurance maps of the period, which list in great detail all the fire-fighting equipment in ballparks and other public buildings.

Of course, ballparks had already had their share of disasters. High winds stripped the grandstand roof from the original Polo Grounds in 1884, and fire destroyed most of the stands at Washington

Park in 1889 — fortunately while the Bridegrooms were on the road. After a Louisville-Syracuse Sunday game in Three Rivers, New York, in 1890, part of a grandstand collapsed, causing injuries but no fatalities. Fire also destroyed most of the Louisville Colonels' ballpark in 1892, but the bleachers survived and a game was played there two days later.

The fires of 1894 were far more treacherous. Ballparks in Baltimore, Boston, Chicago, and Philadelphia all had fires, and hundreds of thousands of dollars of property was lost. It was rumored in the sporting press that the fires were being set deliberately, and some went so far as to hint that Sabbatarians were not above using arson to stop Sunday baseball, which had officially been adopted by the league in 1892.

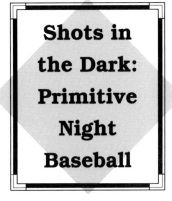

Shots in the Dark: Primitive Night Baseball

Defeating darkness had been an American priority at least since 1757, when Benjamin Franklin designed whale oil street lamps for Philadelphia, the city that introduced gas streetlights in 1796. Baltimore was lit by coal gas in 1816, and arc lights, activated by passing charges between carbon electrodes, came into general use around 1850. Electric lighting took a quantum leap forward on October 21, 1879, when Thomas Edison's carbonized filament of cotton burned for forty hours; less than a year later, the first baseball game was played under lights — on a peninsula jutting into the Atlantic Ocean.

The Northern Electric Light Company had recently been formed in Boston, a city proud of its Red Stockings, National League champs in 1877 and 1878. Looking for publicity, Northern Electric invited the employees of the Jordan Marsh and R. H. White department stores to play baseball under its lights on September 2, 1880, at Nantasket Beach in nearby Hull.

By game time, 8 P.M., Northern Electric had put three 100-foot-high wooden towers around a crude diamond. As David Pietrusza notes in *Lights On!*, each pole supported thirty-six lamps with carbonized cotton filaments. Two engines and three generators yielded 30,000

candlepower of light. (In 1992, Hubbell Lighting relit Pittsburgh's Three Rivers Stadium; each of the park's *six hundred* lights averaged 2 *million* candlepower.)

The *Boston Post* reported that the carbon arc lamps produced "a clear, pure, bright light . . . very strong and yet very pleasant to the sight." However, the players complained to the *Boston Transcript* that "the light was not sufficient, was too much like moonlight." The *Boston Daily Globe* said unequivocally that "it was a failure."

A second serious attempt at night ball occurred three years later in Fort Wayne; again, the motivating force was a local entrepreneur of electricity. Charles Jenney of the Jenney Electric Light Company staged a game between professionals from Quincy, Illinois, of the Northwestern League and a team from Methodist College on June 3, 1883. League Park hosted the seven-inning game (won by the pros, 19–11). Jenney provided seventeen huge arc lamps of 4,000 candlepower each, an amount equal to 4,857 gas burners. One lightstand was placed behind the pitcher's mound, three were attached to the front of the grandstand, and the others lined the baselines and outfield.

Although a historic event for Fort Wayne, the *Gazette* was forced to admit that "players had to shield their eyes with their caps when they faced the light." The competing *Fort Wayne News* was even less impressed, commenting wryly, "The

outlines of persons standing at the bases were so dim that it was suggested that it would do well to electrify the players too." *Sporting Life* gave the national view as it complained, "When a ball became dirty it could not be seen," but concluded, "With between twenty-five and thirty lights there is no question but what electric ball playing is an assured success."

Another lighting nonevent involved a scheme that has to rank among baseball's looniest — using water fountains to light a baseball diamond. As noted, Erastus Wiman had bought the New York Metropolitans of the American Association mostly because he also owned the ferry running between Manhattan and Staten Island. To fatten the gate, Wiman tried to institute night baseball at St. George's.

After several failed attempts using electric lights alone, he was encouraged to try a different approach by an aide of Edison's, one Mr. Johnson. Mr. Johnson visited the grounds and was struck by another tourist attraction, the illuminated fountains. After conducting some experiments, he was "entirely confident of ultimate success" and thought that "base ball by electric light will eventually be an established fact at Staten Island."

After conferring with Edison, Mr. Johnson proposed "to line the outside of the diamond, foul lines and extremes of the outfield with electric lights placed beneath the ground and projecting, by means of powerful

---

The fire at Chicago's West Side Grounds on August 5, a Sunday, was particularly tragic. Some 500 people were seriously injured — but not by fire. In a game two years earlier, fans had streamed onto the field to curse the umpire, who then awarded the game to the opposition. To prevent this from happening again, Chicago enclosed the West Side bleachers in barbed wire. In the seventh inning of that Sunday game, after Cap Anson had struck out, fire erupted:

> The crowd was between the growing fire and the . . . barbed fence. Men began to clamber up these wires like rats in a cage. . . . The first few got through easily. Others tried to slip between

the wires and hung there, entangled fast in the barbs.

Cub players George Decker, Jimmy Ryan, and Walt Wilmot tried to force the wire open with their bats; eventually, the pressure of the crowd pushed open the staples holding the wire. A young eyewitness said that the fire had been started by a cigar stub: "The grass took fire, the fire creeping in under the pavilion . . . it would have been easy for anyone to have stamped out the flame if anyone could have got over the barrier without trouble; but as the barrier was a barbed wire fence no one tried to get through it til the fire became dangerous."

reflectors, the rays upward through covering plates of corrugated glass." Johnson's scheme never got off the drawing board.

One of the century's last attempts to toss around the old melon by moonlight was also less than serious but involved two Hall of Famers, Ed Barrow and Honus Wagner. In 1896, thirteen years before his face appeared on that celebrated T-206 baseball card, Wagner had worked his way up from Warren (Pa.) of the Iron-Oil League and played for Paterson (N.J.) of the Atlantic League, which Barrow then managed.

Paterson was about to meet Wilmington in a July Fourth doubleheader, and business was slow. In his autobiography, *My Fifty Years in Baseball,* Barrow said, "Crowds had been poor and we needed a shot in the arm of some kind." The answer, as it would be during the Depression, was night baseball. On July 2, Wilmington's management installed arc lights at Union Street Grounds, the city's ballpark, and announced a novel tripleheader, regulation morning and afternoon games followed by a nighttime exhibition game. The *Wilmington Evening Journal* announced that "white balls, very similar to a tennis ball only larger, will be used. They are made specially for such an occasion."

Perhaps Wilmington was satiated with baseball by nightfall; a mere 200 fans showed up for the festivities. It was just as well. The *Wilmington Morning News* observed, "The game

Nineteenth-Century Night Games

YEAR	DATE	SITE	CITY
1880	September 2	Nantasket Beach	Hull, Mass.
1883	June 2	League Park (Jailhouse Flats)	Fort Wayne, Ind.
1888	August 21	Tinker Park	Indianapolis
1888	September 6	Tinker Park	Indianapolis
1891	August 8	Twickerham Grounds	Seattle
1893	July 2	Athletic Park	Los Angeles
1896	July 4	Union Street Grounds	Wilmington, Del.
1897	June 30	Beach Park	Galveston, Tex.
1897	July 16	Clyde Park	San Antonio, Tex.

was the most unique and comical ever seen here. The ball became lost so often and so many runs were made that they were not counted." Barrow said, "You could hardly see the outfielders. For improved visibility we used an indoor baseball [a softball]. All during the game the spectators were shouting and jeering and jumping on the field."

Wagner, who was known to stretch a truth or two, said in 1924 that he played in the night game, although Paterson used the same eight position players for both the morning and afternoon games. Wagner said that he came to bat in the sixth inning. In line with the general hilarity of the proceedings, Morris "Doc" Amole, Wilmington's pitcher, had a Fourth of July surprise for him. When Wagner took a mighty cut at

a fastball, it exploded, thanks to a hidden firecracker. He said, "The crowd didn't get any laugh, though. Instead, they got sore and made a rush on the box office to get their money back. . . . I'll never forget the way those fellows [Barrow et al.] scooted down the street to escape that crowd and save what little money was taken in. That was the end of night baseball."

SOUTH END GROUNDS AND BAKER BOWL

The 1894 ballpark fires raised the owners' consciousness about providing accessible escape routes for fans and prompted them to use steel and concrete in building their parks. Two classic ballparks rose from the ashes of their wooden predecessors in 1894, Baker Bowl in Philadelphia and Boston's South End Grounds.

South End Grounds was struck by fire on May 15, 1894, during a game between the Beaneaters and the Orioles. It was clearly the result of a prank, as reported in the *Boston Post:*

Boys set fire to some rubbish under seats at the Boston ball grounds yesterday. The flames spread rapidly, and in less than three hours ran over 12 acres of territory. The base ball grand stand and bleachers, a large school house, an engine house, and 164 wooden buildings were destroyed. . . . The loss is variously estimated at from $300,000 to $1,000,000.

It started in the right field bleachers and destroyed the park in just one hour. Afterward, it was discovered that owner Arthur Soden, a notorious pennypincher who charged the players' wives

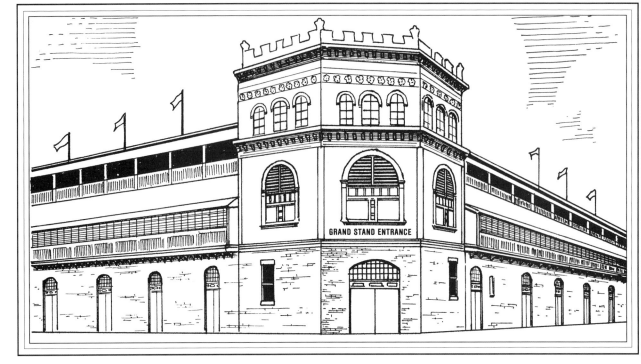

If South End Grounds in Boston was a reminder of Camelot, then the rebuilt Baker Bowl in Philadelphia was baseball's answer to Runnymede. Even though the interior featured the first cantilever design, the exterior looked more like a castle or an armory, complete with turrets and battlements. This illustration is the Baker Bowl Philadelphians prefer to remember, not the seedy and sadly unkempt "Dump on the Hump" of the 1920s and 1930s.

Railroad tracks have long offered a kind of physical shorthand to define (and divide) social classes. Philadelphia's Baker Bowl, on Lehigh and Huntingdon, was originally on the same side of the tracks as Columbia Park, the first American League park in town; later, Connie Mack would move to Shibe Park, across the tracks at Somerset and Lehigh. In Boston in 1910, the tracks of the New York, New Haven & Hartford Railroad separated the city's two ballparks. South End Grounds, the home of the NL Bean-eaters (Braves), was on the east side, while the AL Pilgrims (Red Sox) were on the west side. Even farther west was the still-undeveloped Fenway, a marshy area to which the Sox moved in 1912. South of the National League bailiwick lay Third Base, the saloon owned by Michael "Nuf Ced" McGreevy.

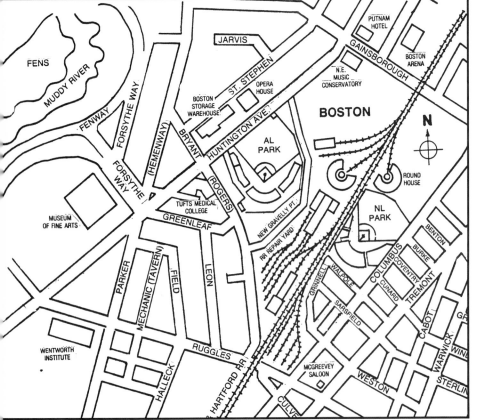

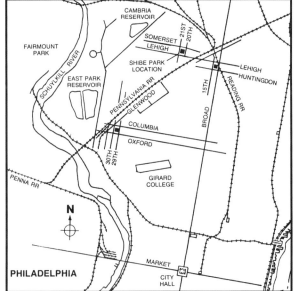

After the fires of 1894, owners tried to assure potential patrons that their ballparks were substantial places. One way was to use advertising puffery to make the parks look safer than they actually were. One of the first parks to appear on a program cover was Cincinnati's League Park, in 1896. Contrast this piece of PR wizardry with a shot of the park's rickety-looking right field fence. Sure enough, the park burned to a crisp in 1901 and rose again, phoenix-like, in 1902, as the Palace of the Fans.

for their tickets, had underinsured the park, and there was not nearly enough money to recreate the fabulous pavilion. Instead, while the Braves played at Congress Street Grounds, a single-decked park replaced what may have been the most ornate baseball stadium ever built.

Baker Bowl also began its long life (fifty-one years) as a turreted medieval castle, a building that would have been more at home in Runnymede than three miles north of Independence Hall in North Philadelphia. The home of the Quakers (later Phillies), it was successively known as National League Park, Philadelphia Baseball Grounds, and Huntingdon Street Grounds, for its eastern boundary.

Like Boston's South End Grounds, it was rebuilt in a far more conventional style after being con-sumed by fire. The Quakers' owner, Al Reach, had the debris cleared quickly and hired three shifts of mechanics to restore the park. For ten days, the Phils played home games at the University of Pennsylvania's athletic field; they played again on Huntingdon Street twelve days after the fire. Reach immediately began making plans for a replacement that was ambitious, elaborate — and fireproof. In so doing, he created the first modern ballpark.

Where South End Grounds and West Side Grounds were rebuilt in wood, Baker Bowl used steel and brick in 1894; it was also the first ball-park to feature cantilever construction, something of a defining moment for the future of ballparks. Using cantilevered concrete supports, architects could eliminate the columns that made for "obstructed view seating." (Future generations

When Brooklyn's National League team moved to Eastern Park, in 1891, it became known as the Trolley Dodgers because of the maze of streetcar tracks patrons had to negotiate to reach the park. A bit out of the way for Man-hattan fans, Eastern Park had a substantial double-decked grandstand, conical spires like South End Grounds, and was at its best covered with bunting, as here, on Opening Day in 1894.

As noted, parks became part of the marketing mix in the 1890s. This sketch of a Giants-Orioles Temple Cup game at the Polo Grounds in 1894 was widely distributed as a poster, with cameos of players and team officials. At the end of the grandstand, along the third base line, is the original brick and mortar High Bridge, which was partly rebuilt in steel after the turn of the century. Why does Baltimore have five infielders? Good question.

Home Field Advantage: Oriole Park

The 1890s will always be remembered as the time the original *National League* Baltimore Orioles ran roughshod over their opponents. What is less well documented is the role that Oriole Park, their home field, played in their success under Ned Hanlon.

In May 1892, Hanlon arrived in Baltimore to manage the Orioles. Blessed with a keen appreciation of talent, he traded for no less than four players who turned out to be Hall of Famers — Joe Kelley, Hughie Jennings, Dan Brouthers, and Wee Willie Keeler — and brought Baltimore several pennants in the bargain. Hanlon was also a strategist of note, and his minions, John McGraw, Keeler, and Jennings, popularized the hit-and-run, the squeeze play, and other elements of "inside baseball." (Years later, Billy Martin, Hanlon's lineal strategic descendant — Hanlon to McGraw to Casey Stengel to Martin — renamed it "Little Ball.")

Little Ball suited the Orioles, who were, with the exception of Brouthers, a smallish lot. Jennings stood 5′8½″, McGraw topped out at 5′7″, and Willie Keeler was wee indeed at 5′4½″. Accordingly, Hanlon felt

justified in making sure that the park was carefully prepared to use inside baseball against visiting giants. Under his direction, Orioles groundskeeper Thomas J. Murphy used every part of the field to give the home team the edge. He

• loaded up the foul lines. Unlike the emaciated foul lines one saw at other parks, the lines at Union Park were lavishly decorated with chalk. Perhaps that's why so many of the Oriole bunts seemed to roll back into fair territory.

• let the outfield grass grow. This conscientious organic approach often paid dividends to O's outfielders, who sometimes found a spare ball or two in the outfield grass.

• packed the dirt around home plate. Rather than scatter ordinary soil around the plate, Murphy made sure that any Orioles attempting "Baltimore chops" were rewarded with acrobatically high bounces off the fine, firm, fully packed clay.

• "customized" the pitcher's mound. Murphy mixed soap shavings with the dirt on the mound, causing opposing servers to wonder why their control was off a tad after they wiped their hands.

Whatever little advantages Murphy couldn't supply through Mother Nature came from other quarters. Orioles would shortcut from first to third when the sole umpire's back was turned, and Harold Seymour says they would barge into catchers and even try to jostle first basemen holding on to throws. Third sacker McGraw was particularly expert at getting in the way of runners or holding their belts to slow their progress. (One day, Louisville slugger Pete Browning foiled the strategy by loosening his, leaving McGraw holding the sash.)

In *The Home Team,* James Bready mentions that often when an Oriole runner reached third safely, the third base coach would suddenly break for the plate, hoping to induce the opposing hurler to throw the ball away, allowing the real baserunner to score or at least upset the moundsman. The fans, too, became part of the action by shouting as opposing fielders tried to catch balls or by shining mirrors into the eyes of opposing batsmen. Modern Oriole rooters at Camden Yards refrain from such shenanigans, making the game fairer but, alas, a bit less interesting.

would see cantilevered loge seats and luxury boxes push the average fan farther from the field of play.)

The invitation to Opening Day described the building process:

> The new structure is mainly of brick and steel, containing no wood or other inflammable material except the platform and seats . . . nine platforms of the upper deck project beyond any post into the air, and over the head of those below.

The new Philadelphia Ball Park opened on May 2, 1895, with roughly the dimensions it would carry until the Phillies left in 1938. Left field was 341 feet from home plate, center was 408, and right was 279½ feet from home plate and topped by a 40-foot wall, a distance that Chuck Klein and other left-handed hitters would later exploit. In 1895, two left-handed Phils, outfielder Sam Thompson and catcher Jack Clements, finished first and third in homers, a good example of fitting one's personnel to the park. Meanwhile, other teams were finding more inventive ways to get the edge at home.

MONOPOLY AND SYNDICATE BASEBALL

Using every edge, the Orioles won three straight National League pennants from 1894 through 1896 and narrowly missed a fourth in 1897; however, attendance, which had been hovering around 250,000, nosedived to 123,000 in 1898 despite another second-place finish.

Baltimore owner Harry Von der Horst decided to move his stars to a more populous city by swapping half of his franchise. Von der Horst and his manager, Ned Hanlon, gave 50 percent of their club to Ferdinand Abell and Charles Ebbets for half of the Trolley Dodgers.

It should have come as no surprise in the Age of the Robber Barons that baseball, too, would succumb to interlocking directorates of ownership. The practice grew unchallenged throughout the decade. Harold Seymour's findings on cross-ownership as of March 1900 are summarized in the table on the next page.

Robison, the Cleveland trolley operator and owner of the National League Spiders, is a particu-

As parks became fancier, simplicity gave way to gimmickry. Sportsman's Park in St. Louis was once an oasis of baseball, as seen in this drawing from 1892. By 1898, however, it had become a joke park. The wings of the grandstand had been severely truncated. An elevated stand, formed by seven round columns, wasn't meant for baseball but was designed instead to give those seated on top a great view of the Shoot-the-Chutes roller-coaster. This addition led the *Sporting News* to lament "the prostitution of a ballpark" (see Chapter 1).

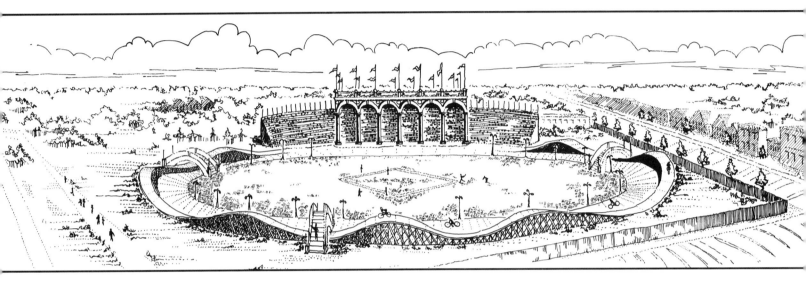

Conflicts in National League Ownership, March 1900

NAME	CLUB(S) OWNED	STOCKHOLDER IN
Ferdinand Abell	Baltimore (40%)	
	Brooklyn (40%)	New York
John T. Brush	Cincinnati	New York
Charles Ebbets		Baltimore (10%)
		Brooklyn (10%)
Ned Hanlon		Baltimore (10%)
		Brooklyn (10%)
Frank Robison	Cleveland	
	St. Louis	
Arthur Soden	Boston (33⅓%)	New York (principal minority stockholder)
Albert Spalding	Chicago	New York
Harry Von der Horst	Baltimore (40%)	
	Brooklyn (40%)	

larly noxious example. On April 24, 1898, Spain declared war on the United States, and the Spanish-American War drew fans from the ballparks. Cleveland, with a population of only 261,353 in 1890, was particularly affected, so Robison decided to move his trolleys and ballplayers to St. Louis (pop. 451,770). While retaining ownership of the Spiders, he bought the competing St. Louis Cardinals after the 1898 season. On April 3, 1899, Robison stocked the Cardinals with former Cleveland players — including Cy Young and Jess Burkett, renamed Sportsman's Park League Park and called the Cardinals the Perfectos.

Every other team gave Cleveland excess players to fill out its roster; it didn't help. The 1899 Cleveland Spiders were — collectively — a 20-game winner, and their 134 losses set a major league record for ineptitude. The Spiders were so bad and attendance was so low for their 24 home games that they also set a major league low for season attendance — 6,088. Called the Exiles, Misfits, Castoffs, Wanderers, Forsakens, and worse by Cleveland's baseball fans, they were the Team Without a Park for the entire month of September and finished it 1–27.

Not surprisingly, the National League dropped Cleveland before the 1900 season, but help was on the way. Ban Johnson, the commissioner of the minor Western League, had major league ambitions and told haberdasher Jack Kilfoyl and Charles Somers to buy the Grand Rapids franchise. Before the 1901 season, the partners would transfer the team to Cleveland, which became part of a new major league circuit. The decade that began with the unsuccessful debut of the Players League ended with the dramatic launching of the American League.

TIMELINE

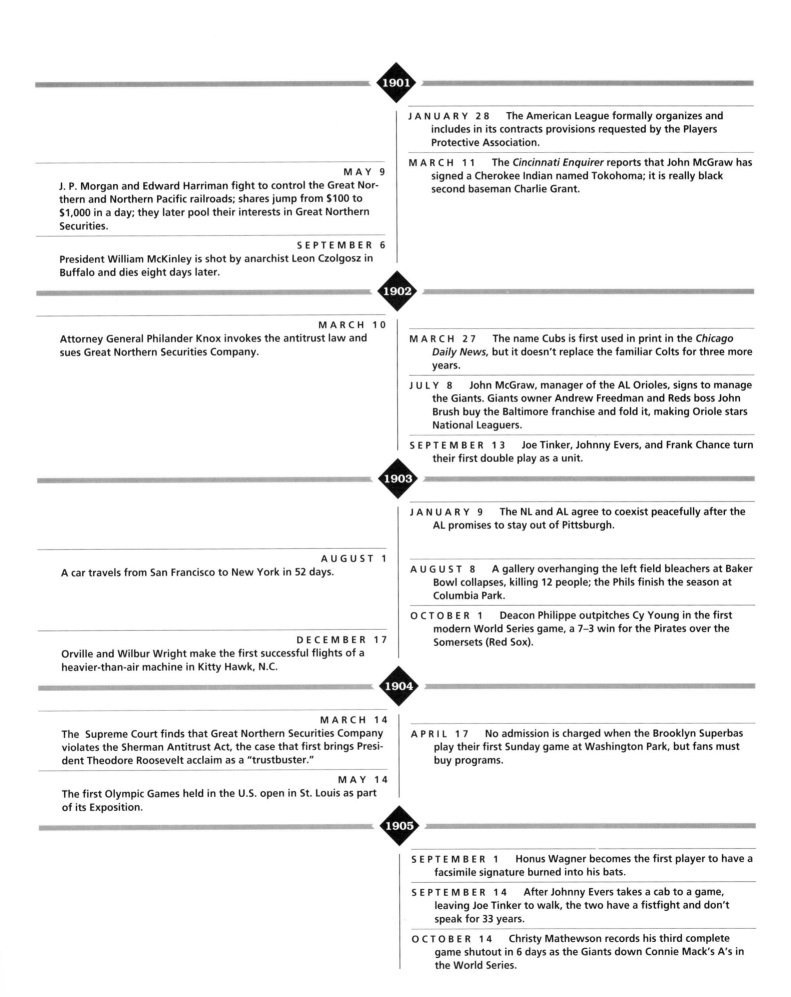

1901

JANUARY 28   The American League formally organizes and includes in its contracts provisions requested by the Players Protective Association.

MARCH 11   The *Cincinnati Enquirer* reports that John McGraw has signed a Cherokee Indian named Tokohoma; it is really black second baseman Charlie Grant.

MAY 9
J. P. Morgan and Edward Harriman fight to control the Great Northern and Northern Pacific railroads; shares jump from $100 to $1,000 in a day; they later pool their interests in Great Northern Securities.

SEPTEMBER 6
President William McKinley is shot by anarchist Leon Czolgosz in Buffalo and dies eight days later.

1902

MARCH 10
Attorney General Philander Knox invokes the antitrust law and sues Great Northern Securities Company.

MARCH 27   The name Cubs is first used in print in the *Chicago Daily News,* but it doesn't replace the familiar Colts for three more years.

JULY 8   John McGraw, manager of the AL Orioles, signs to manage the Giants. Giants owner Andrew Freedman and Reds boss John Brush buy the Baltimore franchise and fold it, making Oriole stars National Leaguers.

SEPTEMBER 13   Joe Tinker, Johnny Evers, and Frank Chance turn their first double play as a unit.

1903

JANUARY 9   The NL and AL agree to coexist peacefully after the AL promises to stay out of Pittsburgh.

AUGUST 1
A car travels from San Francisco to New York in 52 days.

AUGUST 8   A gallery overhanging the left field bleachers at Baker Bowl collapses, killing 12 people; the Phils finish the season at Columbia Park.

OCTOBER 1   Deacon Philippe outpitches Cy Young in the first modern World Series game, a 7–3 win for the Pirates over the Somersets (Red Sox).

DECEMBER 17
Orville and Wilbur Wright make the first successful flights of a heavier-than-air machine in Kitty Hawk, N.C.

1904

MARCH 14
The Supreme Court finds that Great Northern Securities Company violates the Sherman Antitrust Act, the case that first brings President Theodore Roosevelt acclaim as a "trustbuster."

APRIL 17   No admission is charged when the Brooklyn Superbas play their first Sunday game at Washington Park, but fans must buy programs.

MAY 14
The first Olympic Games held in the U.S. open in St. Louis as part of its Exposition.

1905

SEPTEMBER 1   Honus Wagner becomes the first player to have a facsimile signature burned into his bats.

SEPTEMBER 14   After Johnny Evers takes a cab to a game, leaving Joe Tinker to walk, the two have a fistfight and don't speak for 33 years.

OCTOBER 14   Christy Mathewson records his third complete game shutout in 6 days as the Giants down Connie Mack's A's in the World Series.

TIMELINE

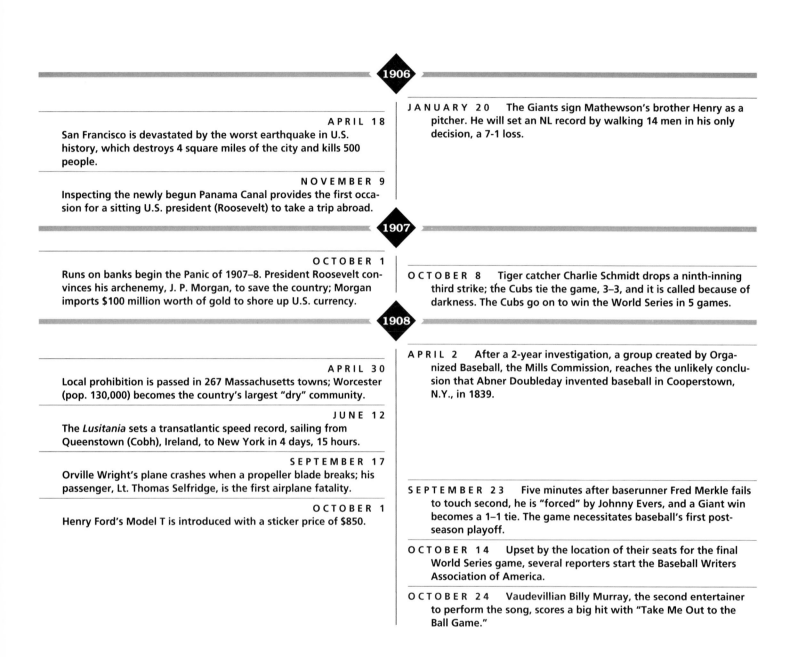

1906

APRIL 18

San Francisco is devastated by the worst earthquake in U.S. history, which destroys 4 square miles of the city and kills 500 people.

NOVEMBER 9

Inspecting the newly begun Panama Canal provides the first occasion for a sitting U.S. president (Roosevelt) to take a trip abroad.

JANUARY 20   The Giants sign Mathewson's brother Henry as a pitcher. He will set an NL record by walking 14 men in his only decision, a 7-1 loss.

1907

OCTOBER 1

Runs on banks begin the Panic of 1907–8. President Roosevelt convinces his archenemy, J. P. Morgan, to save the country; Morgan imports $100 million worth of gold to shore up U.S. currency.

OCTOBER 8   Tiger catcher Charlie Schmidt drops a ninth-inning third strike; the Cubs tie the game, 3–3, and it is called because of darkness. The Cubs go on to win the World Series in 5 games.

1908

APRIL 30

Local prohibition is passed in 267 Massachusetts towns; Worcester (pop. 130,000) becomes the country's largest "dry" community.

JUNE 12

The *Lusitania* sets a transatlantic speed record, sailing from Queenstown (Cobh), Ireland, to New York in 4 days, 15 hours.

SEPTEMBER 17

Orville Wright's plane crashes when a propeller blade breaks; his passenger, Lt. Thomas Selfridge, is the first airplane fatality.

OCTOBER 1

Henry Ford's Model T is introduced with a sticker price of $850.

APRIL 2   After a 2-year investigation, a group created by Organized Baseball, the Mills Commission, reaches the unlikely conclusion that Abner Doubleday invented baseball in Cooperstown, N.Y., in 1839.

SEPTEMBER 23   Five minutes after baserunner Fred Merkle fails to touch second, he is "forced" by Johnny Evers, and a Giant win becomes a 1–1 tie. The game necessitates baseball's first post-season playoff.

OCTOBER 14   Upset by the location of their seats for the final World Series game, several reporters start the Baseball Writers Association of America.

OCTOBER 24   Vaudevillian Billy Murray, the second entertainer to perform the song, scores a big hit with "Take Me Out to the Ball Game."

C H A P T E R   F O U R

The Birth of the American League

A new major league was born in 1901 with the help of some heavyweight midwives. Five Hall of Famers — Charles Comiskey, Clark Griffith, Connie Mack, John McGraw, and, most important, Byron Bancroft "Ban" Johnson — all played key roles in founding the new circuit.

After graduating from Marietta College in 1887, Johnson became a sportswriter for the *Cincinnati Commercial-Gazette.* In 1892, the newly reformed Western League needed a president, and John T. Brush, who owned the Western League Indianapolis Indians as well as the Cincinnati Reds, had been given a say in deciding just who it should be.

Brush had not suffered gladly Johnson's journalistic barbs about the Reds' ineffective management. (They were barely above .500 at the time.) Although writers say Brush wanted to "get him [Johnson] out of the way," he was surely aware that Johnson could be a formidable opponent. Caught on the horns of a dilemma, Brush fretted over his decision but never did completely resolve his conflict. He was supposed to go to a conference empowered to name the new president, but, according to historian Lee Allen, he missed the train. The other delegates, assuming that Brush supported Johnson, elected him president. The missed train, like the nail for which a shoe and eventually a kingdom were lost, had major ramifications: Johnson ultimately transformed the minor Western League into the major American League, which soon rivaled the National League, in which Brush owned a club.

It was no small task. Three out of every four professional baseball teams in the nineteenth century went belly up in two years or less. According to *Mudville's Revenge,* "Between 1869 and 1900 over 850 professional franchises were launched; 650 of them went out of business in two years or less, and only 50 lasted six years or more." No minor league had ever escalated to major league status; none had even tried. All three attempts at a second major league — the American Association, Union Association, and Players League — had failed.

When Johnson was named president of the Western League on November 20, 1893, he inherited a league patterned after the Western Association, never a moneymaker. His "domain" was a very mixed bag of large cities and small towns — Detroit, Grand Rapids, Indianapolis, Kansas City, Milwaukee, Minneapolis, Sioux City, and Toledo.

To his credit, Johnson compressed them into a highly organized league. So that franchises wouldn't constantly change cities, he asked for 51 percent of every team's stock, which he kept in his office safe. Johnson also understood that the public wanted hard-fought, well-run games. He backed his umpires completely in disputes with both players and fans and was noticeably successful in outlawing gambling in league parks, something that eluded the National League.

In 1895, the league got a double lift when Sioux City moved to St. Paul and Johnson brought Comiskey in to run the team. Later that season, Johnson gained more respect at Brush's expense. Brush would ostensibly "sign" players to the Reds, then send them to Indianapolis, an early variant of the farm system. After Johnson slapped his hand a few times, Brush tried to remove him from office; instead, Brush was forced to sell his stock in Indianapolis.

By 1896 the Western League was judged "the strongest minor ever," and it only improved when Connie Mack took over Milwaukee a year later. Johnson began thinking about going major but had

On October 12, 1907, Mordecai "Three Finger" Brown shut out the Tigers, 2–0, at Bennett Park in Detroit to give the Cubs their first world championship. This picture doesn't begin to explain how Bennett Park evolved into Tiger Stadium. In fact, the wooden grandstand was removed over the winter of 1911–1912 and a concrete and steel horseshoe erected in its place.

While owners like Charles Comiskey and Ben Shibe would later be associated with forward-looking parks, their first American League fields were unremarkable in any way. South Side Park (top), the predecessor of Comiskey, was notable only for its vast outfield distances, which yielded just 2 homers in 1904, 3 in 1906, and 4 in 1909. Columbia Park, the A's home before Shibe Park, is set apart only by its elevated press box.

to delay his plans when the United States entered the Spanish-American War. Baseball attendance slumped, and the national pastime lost ground to both the bicycle craze and a renewed interest in horse racing.

After the 1899 season, Johnson named his circuit the American League to give it a national character. At the same time the National League decided to buy out the owners of its deadwood franchises but keep would-be leagues out of those cities by maintaining the empty ballfields. In March 1900, Louisville's owners got a measly $10,000 while Frank Robison raked in $25,000 for the Cleveland franchise he'd so willfully denuded (see Chapter 3); Van der Horst, Hanlon, and company took in $30,000 for Baltimore, and Washington's George Wagner topped all the other owners, walking away with $46,500.

When it became clear that the National League would drop Cleveland, Johnson snapped up that territory with the backing of local coal magnate Charles Somers. In March 1900, he expanded into Chicago as well. In exchange, the American League

◆ assented to honor the National Agreement.

◆ reimbursed the NL for improvements to League Park, its abandoned field in Cleveland.

◆ allowed Chicago owner James Hart to pick two American League players.

◆ agreed not to build a park in Chicago north of 35th Street. (Confined to the stockyards, Johnson built South Side Park at 39th Street and Wentworth Avenue.)

The American League now comprised Buffalo, Chicago, Cleveland, Detroit, Indianapolis, Kansas City, Milwaukee, and Minneapolis, all growing and all but the last former NL cities.

More important, the National League players began to create significant problems for management. On June 10, 1900, delegates from every team met in New York to form the Protective Association of Professional Baseball Players (PAPBP). Pittsburgh catcher Charles "Chief" Zimmer was elected president and Chicago pitcher Clark Griffith named vice president. At a second meeting, Buffalo attorney Harry Leonard, a former first baseman, won over the delegates by asking for wages higher than the $2,500 limit, medical coverage for on-the-field injuries, an arbitration system for settling disputes, and freedom from being shuttled to the minor leagues at the owners' whim.

Braves owner Arthur Soden was one of a three-man committee delegated to deal with the PAPBP

If Columbia Park and South Side Park were undistinguished, Oriole Park in Baltimore and League Park in Cleveland were even less notable. Oriole Park (above), used for just a single year (1901) as an American League park, had a wooden scoreboard and an outfield fence to match. The photo below shows Cy Young, baseball's winningest pitcher (511 victories), delivering in full overhand motion at League Park. In its wooden version, the place looked temporary, a feeling reinforced by the blizzard of signs in the outfield. There are no coaches' boxes, and the infield grass just seems to meander up the third base line.

at the annual postseason league meeting. However, Soden pocketed their proposal and never presented or even read it. When Zimmer, Jennings, and Griffith found out, they released a statement to the Associated Press advising players not to sign with their old clubs. Simultaneously, Johnson had gone to New York seeking recognition of his league as a major; the NL owners slipped out a side door to avoid meeting with him.

By rejecting both parties, the National League succeeded only in driving them together. Johnson made common cause with the players' union by vowing that he would not enforce an arbitrary salary limitation and agreeing that American Leaguers could not be farmed out without their consent. Although the Protective Association never formally recognized the new league, it did enhance Johnson's cause in a practical way by giving the players good reason to jump their National League teams.

Buoyed by this cooperation, Johnson announced in February 1901 that the AL was going to be a major league, with teams in Cleveland, Chicago, Milwaukee, Louisville, Boston, Baltimore, Philadelphia, and Washington. He said, "The National League has taken for granted that no one had a right to expand without first getting its permission. . . . If we had waited for the National League to do something for us, we would have remained a minor league forever."

In seven years, Johnson had transformed a clutch of struggling minor league franchises into a major league. Aside from Detroit and Milwaukee, which had franchises when he took over, he had traded up magnificently, a feat that can be best appreciated by looking at the chart below.

The parks, however, were not uniformly major league, and only Cleveland's League Park had, in fact, been used as an NL park. The year-old South Side Park in Chicago and Lloyd Street Grounds in Milwaukee were holdovers from Johnson's Western League days. Lloyd Street had the typical racetrack grandstand and a rickety wooden outfield fence with wooden supports. It was used as a major league park for just a single season because this original Milwaukee Brewers team became the St. Louis Browns in 1902 (and the Baltimore Orioles in 1954).

South Side had been used in 1900, when Johnson first invaded Chicago. One of the few cricket pitches used for major league baseball, it had been the home of Comiskey's former St. Paul Saints, known briefly as the Invaders; however, management grafted the successful White Stockings name onto them that first year, and it was shortened to White Sox in 1904. That year, and in 1907 as well, the Sox hit no homers at home, leading to their nickname, the Hitless Wonders.

THE TIGERS' LAIR: BENNETT PARK

The new American League parks were all made of wood. Despite the publicity Baker Bowl had received for its steel construction, the AL owners lacked the money for steel, so wood was used to build Columbia Park in Philadelphia, at a cost of just $7,500.

Fortunately, one of those original wooden American League parks — Bennett Park in Detroit — was later rebuilt on the same site in steel and concrete, and the site on which it sat is, at this writing, still being used for major league baseball as Tiger Stadium. The corner of Michigan and Trumbull is now, by a wide margin, the oldest continuous address in American professional sports.

In 1894 Detroit, which had been NL territory and the home of the Wolverines, joined the Western League and played in Boulevard Park at Helen Avenue and Champlain Street (now Lafayette Boulevard), close to the city's eastern boundary. In 1895,

Original American League Parks

WESTERN LEAGUE 1894	AMERICAN LEAGUE 1901	ORIGINAL PARK
Detroit Creams	Baltimore Orioles	Oriole Park
Grand Rapids Gold Bugs	Boston Somersets	Huntington Avenue Grounds
Indianapolis Hoosiers	Chicago White Sox	South Side Park
Kansas City Blues	Cleveland Bluebirds	League Park
Milwaukee Brewers	Detroit Tigers	Bennett Park
Minneapolis Millers	Milwaukee Brewers	Lloyd Street Grounds
Sioux City Huskers	Philadelphia Athletics	Columbia Park
Toledo Swamp Angels	Washington Senators	American League Park

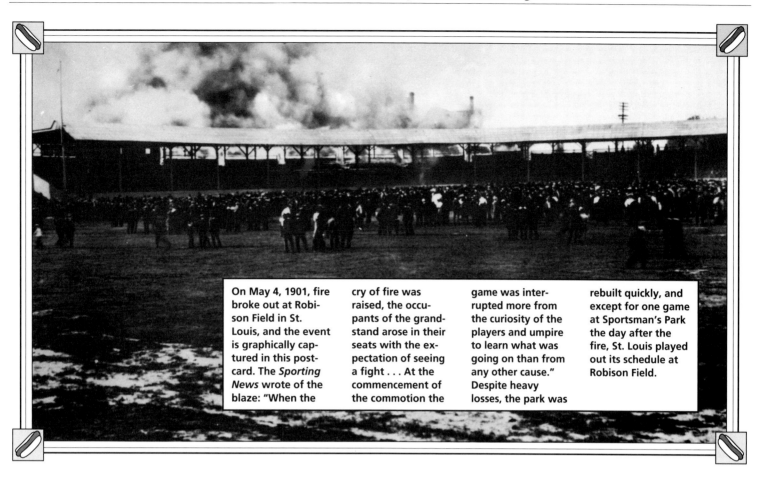

On May 4, 1901, fire broke out at Robison Field in St. Louis, and the event is graphically captured in this postcard. The *Sporting News* wrote of the blaze: "When the cry of fire was raised, the occupants of the grandstand arose in their seats with the expectation of seeing a fight . . . At the commencement of the commotion the game was interrupted more from the curiosity of the players and umpire to learn what was going on than from any other cause." Despite heavy losses, the park was rebuilt quickly, and except for one game at Sportsman's Park the day after the fire, St. Louis played out its schedule at Robison Field.

the players adopted brown and black striped stockings, and a headline writer for the *Detroit Free Press* began referring to them as the Tigers.

Tiger owner Arthur Van Der Beck moved the team to Michigan and Trumbull, the former site of an old hay market, in 1896. What was originally called the Haymarket or Woodbridge Grove (for the farm of William Woodbridge, a U.S. senator and governor of Michigan) came to be known as Bennett Park after Tiger catcher Charlie Bennett, one of the outstanding catchers of his day and the first man to test the reserve clause. Tragically, his career was cut short in 1893 when he slipped, waiting for a train, and fell under the wheels; his left foot was amputated at the ankle and his right leg at the knee.

Bennett Park was part of Detroit's Sixth Ward, an Irish neighborhood known as Corktown. Along the outfield walls, National Avenue in left and Cherry Avenue in right, entrepreneurs erected "wildcat bleachers," where the price of the seat varied with the importance of the game; admission to ordinary games went for a nickel but escalated to 15 cents for an important game and 50 cents for a World Series game. Tiger management tried to challenge this practice in court but always lost. Later, the view was blocked with huge, 40-foot-high strips of canvas; the bleachers were eventually proclaimed a hazard by the fire marshal and torn down.

Like all the other American League parks of the day, the 5,000-seat Bennett Park had been built in a hurry. Van Der Beck covered the cobblestones of the old hay market with a layer of topsoil that was a mere 2 inches at its height; other patches went completely uncovered, giving new meaning to the expression "bad hop." Any fielder could explain away an error with "It hit a cobble." According to *Queen of Diamonds*, the infield was dragged once a week rather than twice a day, the seam between dirt and grass was "more like a ledge," and the outfield turned marshy at the gentlest rain.

Faults and all, the park opened on April 28, 1896. The popular Bennett caught the ceremonial first pitch and repeated the feat at every home opener through 1926. (He died in February 1927.) During this first game, it was discovered that the afternoon sun glared directly into the eyes of the right fielders; the plate was reoriented in 1910.

Bennett Park officially became an American League park on April 20, 1900, when the Tigers were no-hit by Buffalo's Morris "Doc" Amole, the same man who had allegedly thrown the firecracker pitch to Honus Wagner (see Chapter 3). A year later, the park was ready for the majors; shallow bleachers were installed in the outfield, increasing the capacity to 8,500, but an overflow crowd necessitated seating fans in the outfield, making routine fly balls ground rule doubles.

The Tigers trailed the Milwaukee Brewers, 13–4, going into the bottom of the ninth. Four ground rule doubles sandwiched around an infield hit and a single produced five runs with nobody out. Detroit cut the deficit to three runs and loaded the bases, but a ground out and a strikeout had them down to their last lick. William "Kid" Gleason bunted toward third and reached first on an error; then James "Ducky" Holmes beat out an infield hit, making it a one-run game. Finally, Frank "Pop" Dillon lofted a fly down the left field line and two runs scored, giving the Bengals a 14–13 win and Bennett Park an unforgettable major league debut.

Although it had an imposing warehouse running from left field to left center (see p. 100), Boston's Huntington Avenue Grounds was as unprepossessing as other early American League parks, particularly when seen from the first base side (above). A clue to its lack of popularity can be found on the cover of the program for fans at a 1908 benefit game for Cy Young; the park is simply "Boston American League Grounds." At the time, just about any ballpark was called American or National League Grounds. Parks had as many as three names then — one used by newspapers, another by fans, and a third by the club itself.

ALL UP FOR "CY"
BOSTON AMERICAN
LEAGUE GROUNDS
AUG, 13, 1908

(VERY) DEEP CENTER: HUNTINGTON AVENUE GROUNDS

Johnson's lust for power led him to believe that having a team in Boston was absolutely vital to the American League's future, but there was neither a team nor a park three months before the season started. He was finally able to twist the arm of Charles Somers to finance another team besides the Indians. After Somers put up the franchise money, Johnson sent Connie Mack and the "Heavenly Twins" — Beaneater outfielder Hugh Duffy and the retired Tommy McCarthy — to scout possible ballpark sites.

The neighborhood they investigated was a natural for three Irish lads (Mack was born McGillicuddy). A working poor Irish district on the road to Roxbury, "the Village" was within walking distance of the Fens, a swampy area destined to house a ballpark. The Village could already boast one park — South End Grounds (see Chapters 2 and 3). The South End was defined by the yards of the

New York, New Haven, and Hartford Railroad, and its tracks separated one part of the Village from the other.

Mack and his colleagues wanted a spot on the other side of the tracks from the South End. What they found was a former circus lot, complete with a "Shoot the Chutes" pool hard by a pickle factory, several breweries, stables, and chemical odors created by the United Drug Company. Red Sox historian Ed Walton described the site in a 1989 Fenway Park scorecard:

> The lot's biggest drawback was a deep pond which was at the base of chutes used by kids as a water slide during the warmer months and for skating in the winter. This 300,000 square feet of filled, sprawling empty lot . . . was no more than an expansive wasteland made up of heavily weeded bumps and lumps.

Wasteland or no, ground was broken on March 12, 1901, and two months later, the lot had been transformed into three light gray cement grand-

Some attendance figures from the first decade of the twentieth century are hard to believe. Take this Labor Day game between the Giants and Braves at the Polo Grounds. Even though the Giants had a 15-game lead over the Cubs and had already announced their intention *not* to play a World Series with the American League champs (the Boston Pilgrims), an overflow crowd of 38,000 flocked to see their heroes, ringing the entire outfield.

The Great Beantown Massacre

George "Rube" Waddell played a hand in one of baseball's screwiest incidents at Huntington Avenue.

The first time he saw Rube Waddell pitch, Connie Mack was told that before the third inning started, Waddell would walk into the bleachers and have a fan cut half an inch from the red undershirt he always wore; the superstitious Waddell did just that and also shut out Mack's Milwaukee team on two hits, fanning thirteen.

That incident made an impression on Mack that Waddell's wildest behavior could never quite destroy. When Waddell wrestled alligators, sparred with heavyweight champ Jim Jeffries (risking his good left arm), abandoned a major league game to play marbles with children, and walked out of a bases-loaded situation to chase a fire engine, Mack would just grin and bear it.

It would figure then, that putting a natural screwball like Waddell in a ballpark in a bustling commercial neighborhood like Huntington Avenue was bound to produce something unusual. That something occurred on August 11, 1903, and might be called the Great Beantown Massacre. Charles Dryden, for years Philadelphia's leading baseball writer, reported the game between the Somersets and Waddell's Athletics.

After noting that the Somersets had won, 5–1, Dryden added:

In the seventh inning, Rube Waddell hoisted a long foul over the right field bleachers that landed on the roof of the biggest bean cannery in Boston. In descending, the ball fell on the roof of the engine room and jammed itself between the steam whistle and the stem of the valve that operates it. The pressure set the whistle blowing. It lacked a few minutes of five o'clock, yet the workmen started to leave the building. They thought quitting time had come.

The incessant screeching of the bean-factory whistle led engineers in neighboring factories to think fire had broken out and they turned on their whistles. With a dozen whistles going full blast, a policeman sent in an alarm of fire.

Just as the engines arrived, a steam cauldron in the first factory, containing a ton of beans, blew up. The explosion dislodged Waddell's foul fly and the whistle stopped blowing, but that was not the end of the trouble. A shower of scalding beans descended on the bleachers and caused a small panic. One man went insane. When he saw the beans dropping out of a cloud of steam, the unfortunate rooter yelled, "The end of the world is coming and we will all be destroyed."

An ambulance summoned to the supposed fire conveyed the demented man to his home. The ton of beans proved a total loss.

stands, each seating 799 people, and a 300-foot-long covered lobby where fans could gather during rain delays. On May 8, the Somersets (named for their benefactor) beat Philadelphia, 12–4, before a capacity crowd of 11,500; star pitcher Cy Young not only got credit for the win but also tripled, singled, and stole a base.

The first home of the Red Sox was the most misshapen of all the big league ballparks. Fans are fond of remembering the center fields of the Polo Grounds (505) and Yankee Stadium (490) at their deepest, but both pale next to the Herculean 635 feet on Huntington Avenue in 1908. In modern terms, imagine a center field as deep as the left field lines of Cleveland Stadium (320) and Milwaukee's County Stadium (315) combined.

Nevertheless, Huntington Avenue was a home run park for pull hitters. In 1903, the Somersets hit 35 homers, a figure the other seven clubs combined could only double. (It is tempting to speculate that the Red Sox owners' traditional lust for power hitters began on Huntington Avenue.)

As time went on, the park's drawbacks became more evident. The outfield was one of the most challenging in major league history, since it featured hip-high weeds and was dotted with slippery patches of sand left over from the circus. In addition to being vast, center field sloped uphill and was made even more treacherous by the presence of a sizable tool shed in deep center. As for the stands, an Associated Press article states that Huntington's "wooden seats were rickety, soot from trains in neighboring yards filled the area, and the saloon next door was a beacon for bored players — during the games."

FIT FOR A KING: THE PALACE OF THE FANS

Faced with strong opposition for the first time since the early days of the American Association, the National League responded with a two-pronged strategy. Since Johnson had expanded eastward, the NL assigned the Kansas City and Minneapolis franchises to a new Western League, effectively making him fight a war on two fronts for players and fans. Second, the Nationals encouraged the formation of a new American Association to further siphon off money and players from the Americans.

In 1902, as part of the counterattack, Reds' owner (and future boss of the Giants) John Brush decided to rebuild the grandstand at League Park in a grand way. Influenced by the Columbian Exposition of 1893, which had reintroduced America to classical architecture, Brush created the first "baseball palace." Charles Comiskey and Philip

Although it was used for just one major league game, a Sunday meeting between the Yankees and Tigers in July 1904, Wiedenmayer's Park in Newark, New Jersey, was later used as a home field by the Yankees' famous farm team, the Newark Bears, and the Negro National League Newark Eagles in the 1930s and 1940s.

Shibe would later try to emulate Brush's flamboyance, but neither came close. One may question some of his choices, but Brush clearly created the first major league ballpark with a distinct architectural style, then added the final marketing touch by naming it the Palace of the Fans,

The Reds had been using this location for eighteen years, since 1884. Having lost their lease on Bank Street to the short-lived Union Association Outlaw Reds, the then–American Association Reds moved to a location half a mile away, an abandoned brickyard on the corner of Findlay Street and Western Avenue.

With the demise of the Union Association in 1884, the Reds prospered. Brush bought the team in 1891 and made two changes for the better. In 1894, he moved home plate to what had previously been the right field corner so that batters could avoid the afternoon sun. On a hot Sunday in 1892, the sun had been so blinding that a game with Boston was canceled, the only major league set-to foreshortened by an excess of sunshine. A year later, after slugger James "Bug" Holliday, twice a home run champ, complained that he couldn't see the ball because of a big white sign in center field, Brush painted it black to become the first owner to provide hitters with a dark background, the so-called batter's eye.

On the night of May 28, 1900, a fire burned most of the grandstand and was hurriedly replaced with temporary seating so that the Reds could finish their schedule. Brush moved home plate, again putting the sun in the batters' eyes. But this time a roof was put over the old bleachers to provide some shade. This makeshift grandstand served through the end of the 1901 season.

That winter, the park was rebuilt mostly of steel and concrete, and when the fans entered on Opening Day, April 17, 1902, what they saw more nearly resembled a Greek temple, a library, or a bank than the old League Park. From the main entrance, on Findlay Street, they saw a triangular pediment with CINCINNATI engraved on it in large letters. As if that weren't enough, the Palace had Corinthian columns instead of the old Y-shaped supports. Each one had been carved by hand with vaguely Egyptian detailing.

Of course, all these frills were designed to make money, and nothing addressed that goal more directly than the wide, semicircular concrete opera boxes, which were marketed as Fashion Boxes. These boxes overhung what would normally have been dugouts. Sadly, in the rush to please the paying customers, management had omitted them, so the players had to make do by sitting on park benches.

Nine years after the Columbian Exposition, the Beaux-Arts style of architecture was still very much in vogue. When Reds owner John Brush built his Palace of the Fans in 1902, he wanted to attract the Queen City's well-heeled burghers. To Brush, a department store magnate in Indianapolis, the Palace was to be a monument to his "making it in the big city." That is why the ballpark, formerly a democratic venue, had opera boxes to seat beer-swilling patrons. The semicircular concrete boxes were anchored by Corinthian columns to a frieze that had "Cincinnati" chiseled on it, as if it were a bank. For all its grandeur, the park lacked dressing rooms for the players. Accordingly, players got into uniform at their hotel or rooming house and arrived at the park in horse-drawn wagons, giving disgruntled fans a chance to pelt them with fruit.

349 CINCINNATI BASE BALL PARK GRAND STAND.

This photo shows the Polo Grounds from the vantage point of Coogan's Bluff in 1905. Naturally, the standees didn't pay to get in. In this view, we can see only about a third of the curving grandstand that gave the park its distinctive bathtub shape.

On the same level as the fashion boxes, next to the players' benches, was a stretch of seats — actually an elongated bar — called Rooters' Row, which extended along the first and third base lines level with the field. Even though they weren't in ritzy boxes, the fans on Rooters' Row could see their heroes up close, all the time nursing beer served by waiters. (Twelve glasses cost only $1.) Proximity, frustration, and inebriation combined to heap torrents of abuse on the players, but the arrangement lasted for ten years.

Four months after the Palace opened, Brush sold the club to Julius and Max Fleischmann, of the gin and yeast family, and political bosses George B. Cox and August "Garry" Herrmann. Cox headed what Lee Allen called "possibly the most corrupt government that ever infested a municipality." Brush was reluctant to sell until Cox told him, "If you don't sell the club to us, we're going to build a street in the city that will run right through the ball park."

Apparently Cox was better at threatmaking than housekeeping. The park began to deteriorate and, according to Michael Benson in *Ballparks of North America*, the building inspector was making formal complaints to Cox in 1907. "Girders were cracked.

Supports were decayed. Floors were unsafe. Fences needed rebuilding. A whole bleacher platform was defective." The park burned in 1911 and, Benson says, "when it reopened the place had lost its pillars and looked a lot more like the Crosley Field it was to become."

THE TRUCE OF 1903

John Brush and John McGraw, the two men who hated Ban Johnson with a passion, were ultimately responsible for cementing the final jewel in Johnson's crown — New York.

In the beginning of 1902, Johnson was planning to invade New York. McGraw was managing the American League Baltimore Orioles but resisted the leash with which Johnson bridled all his managers. Brush was running the National League as part of a troika named shortly before the 1902 season but knew his days in Cincinnati were numbered, as Boss Cox had made clear. Brush and McGraw conspired with Giant owner Andrew Freedman to keep Johnson out of New York and bring McGraw to New York to manage the Giants.

McGraw had advanced Baltimore $7,000 to meet expenses; when the club couldn't repay him, he

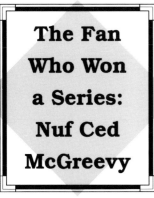

The Fan Who Won a Series: Nuf Ced McGreevy

In 1903, when the Somersets and Pirates played the first modern World Series, the hero wasn't Cy Young or Honus Wagner but a baseball-mad Boston saloonkeeper named Michael "Nuf Ced" McGreevy.

McGreevy owned one of the established landmarks in the Village, a Columbia Avenue alehouse called Third Base. ("The last stop before you steal home.") Whenever a dispute arose on the diamond, the parties would turn to McGreevy for the last word on the subject. He would end his sermons, "Enough said," which eventually became "Nuf Ced." The nickname was such an identifier that it was set in tile on the floor of his saloon.

Although McGreevy and his adoring patrons later became identified indelibly with the Somersets (Pilgrims, Red Sox), they were originally Beaneater boosters, National League fans. In the same way that the HIT SIGN, WIN SUIT sign at Ebbets Field later vaulted Abe Stark to the borough presidency of Brooklyn, the sign on the left field wall at South End Grounds, HOW CAN YOU GET HOME WITHOUT REACHING 3RD BASE?, made celebrities of McGreevy and his colorful crew. They became known collectively as the Royal Rooters, affected lightning-producing bean-pot badges, and composed (and loudly sang) baseball parodies of popular tunes.

With their enthusiastic backing, the Boston National League entry won championships in 1891, 1892, 1897, and 1898; however, management was not content with artistic success alone. The money-mad Arthur Soden boosted ticket prices in 1901, the year the American League put an entry in Beantown to contend for the hearts and minds of its fans. When former Beaneater heroes such as Hall of Famer Jimmy Collins and Chick Stahl left to join the new Somersets, McGreevy et al. moved with them.

These new Bostonians proved to be as formidable as the Beaneaters and won the American League pennant in 1903, but the Pirates took 3 of the first 4 games. In Game 5, played at Pittsburgh's Exposition Park, McGreevy and company serenaded the Iron City fans with a parody of a popular song called "Tessie."

Legend has it that the Rooters' spirited singing upset the Pirates so badly that the Somersets won three straight on the road and took Game 8 at home to become champs. According to Glenn Stout in the *Sox Fan News* (August 1986), "The Rooters were widely hailed in the press as the difference in the Series, and Nuf Ced McGreevy became a legend." He went to spring training every year thereafter, hunted with star pitcher Cy Young, and even signed a non-binding Red Sox contract as a "non-playing player."

His favored status took a tumble at the end of the 1912 World Series. By that time the Sox had moved to the Fens, built Fenway Park, and led the Giants, 3 games to 2. Better yet, warming up on a cold New England day they had Smoky Joe Wood, the dominant pitcher in baseball, who was coming off a 34–5 season and was nearly unbeatable at home.

The fans filed in, but the Royal Rooters were nowhere to be seen. When McGreevy and his friends did

appear — complete with a brass band — they were (deservedly) shocked to discover that their regular seats had been sold by impatient members of management.

Undaunted, McGreevy led the charge up the left field foul line to Duffy's Cliff (the incline named for Red Sox outfielder George "Duffy" Lewis). Once ensconced there, the Rooters refused to budge — even after mounted police tried to remove them forcibly. Eventually, management allowed the Rooters to roost on the gangplank in front of the left field stands.

Wood, thoroughly undone by the forty-five-minute delay, gave up seven hits in the first inning, and New York won, 11–4. Although the Red Sox won the next day to take the Series, this incident soured many on the Royal Rooters. McGreevy's influence faded further when Third Base moved and ended completely when Prohibition pushed it into foul territory in 1923. Before he was through, however, Michael McGreevy made his mark more than many players. Nuf Ced.

---

asked for and got his freedom. On July 8, McGraw announced that he had negotiated his release from the Orioles and had signed to manage the Giants for $11,000. What he didn't state was his plan to bring the Orioles to New York en masse. Brush briefly bought control of the Orioles and "released" pitcher Joe "Iron Man" McGinnity, catcher Roger Bresnahan, and two other players, who all signed with the Giants; on August 9, Brush sold the Reds

and, a month later, bought the Giants. The Orioles, left with only five players, were forced to forfeit a game to St. Louis and their franchise to the league.

After Freedman sold his Giant stock, he was appointed a director of New York City's Interborough Rapid Transit Construction Company, which built the IRT subway line. Johnson wanted to build a ballpark between 142nd Street and 145th Street and Lenox Avenue, near a proposed IRT subway

After deliberately avoiding a World Series in 1904, John McGraw's Giants played the A's in 1905 and beat them as Christy Mathewson threw three complete-game shutouts in six days. The next year, McGraw's men appeared in uniforms proclaiming them World's Champions. This team shot shows Mathewson leaning against the first post from the left at Cincinnati's Palace of the Fans. To his immediate left are John McGraw, then Roger Bresnahan. It is clear how high the curved boxes were, almost twice the height of the average Giant.

stop. AL officials urged John B. MacDonald of the IRT to buy the site and lease it to the club. Mac-Donald got an approval from his boss, August Belmont II, but Freedman scuttled the plan, forcing the league to seek another site.

Johnson swallowed his scruples and made a deal with a pair of shady characters and a front man. For $18,000, he sold the Baltimore franchise to Joseph Gordon, a beard for "Big Bill" Devery, one of Manhattan's biggest gamblers, and Frank Farrell, who owned 250 pool halls and nearly as many politicians. The deal resulted in the establishment of Hilltop Park, the New York Yankees' first home.

The previous December, the National League had adopted a resolution to "seek a peaceful settlement of the so-called baseball war." At the time, Johnson was in New York, completing his deal with Gordon, and the resolution was brought to him. The two sides met on January 9, 1903, at Cincinnati's Grand Hotel and made an agreement that

◆ settled territorial rights and ownership.

◆ recognized the reserve clause in both leagues' contracts.

◆ sought cooperation in scheduling games (to avoid conflicts).

◆ decided that "neither circuit could be changed without the consent of a majority of the clubs in each league."

A year after McGraw left Baltimore and Brush abandoned Cincinnati to make their marks in Manhattan, their worst enemy, Ban Johnson, had put a competing club in Washington Heights. Ironically, it was the only point in Manhattan big enough for a ballpark and high enough to look down on Coogan's Bluff. Nevertheless, the settlement of 1903 created a structure that survived with sixteen clubs in the same cities for exactly fifty years.

THE YANKEES' FIRST HOME: HILLTOP PARK

Nearly a year before the settlement, Farrell and Devery had found a site for a ballpark two blocks east of the Hudson River — a lot that ran from 165th Street to 168th Street between Broadway and Fort Washington Avenue in Washington Heights, the highest point on Manhattan Island.

Arranging to lease it for ten years from the New York Institute of the Blind, they spent $200,000 just to excavate the rocky terrain. Workmen replaced 12,000 cubic yards of rock, blasted a natural rockpile where the grandstand was to be, and used most of 30,000 cubic yards of rocks and earth to fill in a swamp at the Broadway edge of the field.

When all was said and done, Farrell and Devery had built a 16,000-seat park for $75,000, the last

Pitchers Practice at Cincinnati Ball Park.

If this postcard view of the Palace of the Fans is taken at face value, the owners didn't have much regard for the well-being of their stars in 1907. The player crouching in front of the target — fully exposed to bad hops or errant throws — is Honus Wagner, who was on his way to winning his fifth of eight batting titles.

time a big league park was built for five figures. On Opening Day, April 30, 1903, it was officially called American League Park and the team was to be known as the Highlanders, at Gordon's request; the Gordon Highlanders were the best-known regiment in the British army. However, newspapers soon referred to the park by its lofty location, and, by extension, the team became known sporadically as the Hilltoppers.

The park was in poor condition, as Marc Okkonen explains in *Yankee* magazine:

> The swamp in right field was not yet filled and had to be roped off, creating an abnormally short distance from home plate. The outfield was unsodded dirt and and sloped unevenly down toward the fences. The unfinished grandstand was little more than a huge bleacher — unpainted with only the roof supports in place and no roof.

> The players had to dress at their hotels because the clubhouse wasn't finished either, and anything hit past the swamp in right was a ground rule double. (A bit later in the home stand, a heavy rain created a gully in right; rightfielder "Wee Willie" Keeler was forced to stand on a wooden platform placed over the impromptu ravine.)

The march of "progress" brought Hilltop a parking lot in 1906 and a co-tenant in 1911 when the

Polo Grounds burned. It is fun to speculate on just how thrilled Brush and McGraw must have been to ask to rent the ballpark they'd fought so hard to keep from being built.

The original lease was up after the 1912 season. The team officially became the Yankees in 1913 and moved into the Polo Grounds, signing another ten-year lease from 1913 through 1922; when it expired, the new owners built Yankee Stadium. Hilltop Park was torn down in 1914, and the site is now occupied by Columbia-Presbyterian Medical Center, which was built in 1928.

THE GREATEST PENNANT RACES OF ALL TIME

Angus Abbott, an Englishman, wrote in 1904,

> The Americans have a genius for taking a thing, examining its every part, and developing each part to the utmost. This they have done with our game of rounders, and from a clumsy, primitive pastime, have so tightened its joints and put such a fine finish on its points that it stands forth a complicated machine of infinite exactitude.

If keen competition is a measure of infinite exactitude, that machine reached one of its high points in 1908 when seven teams in two leagues were still

battling tooth-and-nail for the pennants two days before the season ended. The effect of these races, which involved both Chicago teams as well as clubs in Cleveland, Detroit, New York, Pittsburgh, and St. Louis, was to make baseball front-page news across the country and spur owners to quickly build bigger ballparks.

The American League race had been tight all year, with the Tigers, Indians, Browns, and White Sox duking it out. The Indians were 11 games under .500 on September 6, then won 16 of their next 18 to make it a three-cornered race, and the Browns went on a tear as well; on September 24, just 2½ games separated the four teams. Then the Tigers swept the Senators in 4 straight while the Cleveland Naps (for Napoleon Lajoie) won 3 of 4 from the A's.

Cleveland had to beat the White Sox at League Park to have a chance. On Friday, October 2, Addie Joss of the Naps faced Ed Walsh, who had pitched and won both ends of a doubleheader three days earlier. Walsh was masterful, giving up only four hits and allowing a single run. Joss was even better — perfect, in fact — mowing down all 27 Chicago batters he faced. Sadly, the Naps lost the next day, 3–2, and were held to a tie, a win, and a loss by St. Louis; when Detroit's Bill Donovan beat Chicago, 7–0, on the last day of the season, Detroit won the pennant by ½ game over Cleveland and 1½ games over Chicago. The Naps argued that Detroit should make up a rained-out game, but the protest went unheeded; however, both leagues quickly

adopted a rule that rained-out games affecting the pennant should be replayed.

The Cubs, Giants, and Pirates had also been in a dogfight for the National League pennant. On Monday, July 20, Pittsburgh was a game ahead of the Giants and 1½ ahead of Chicago. The day before, the *Chicago Tribune* ran its "Inquisitive Fans" column of letters. One of them read:

In the last half of the ninth, with the score tied, two men out and a runner on third, the batter hits to left and the runner scores. The batter, seeing the runner score, stops between home and first. The ball is thrown to the first baseman, who touches his base before the batter reaches it. Can the runner score on this?

The *Trib*'s answer was "No. Run cannot score when third out is made before reaching first." When the Cubs and Giants took a nosedive in August, the letter was forgotten; the Pirates led New York by 3 and Chicago by 6. Then it was Pittsburgh's turn to slip, and by August 24 their lead was just a ½ game over the Giants and 3½ over the Cubs.

On August 30, as the Cubs and Giants were ready to do battle at West Side Park in Chicago, electric scoreboards were posted at the corner of Madison and Dearborn streets, and 10,000 people watched every play while an equal number observed a recreation at the Illinois Central Railroad station. Although Sunday ball was still illegal in New York, an electric diamond outside Madison

A panorama of Baker Bowl in 1904 gives a good view of the medieval turrets that anchored both ends of the grandstand. The tracks of the Philadelphia and Reading Railroad ran in a tunnel under the field from right to right center and gave the outfield its nickname, "the Hump." Note the alleyway between the mound and the plate and the triangular chalk lines behind it. Signs on the outfield walls admonish fans to use no insulting or other improper language or conduct.

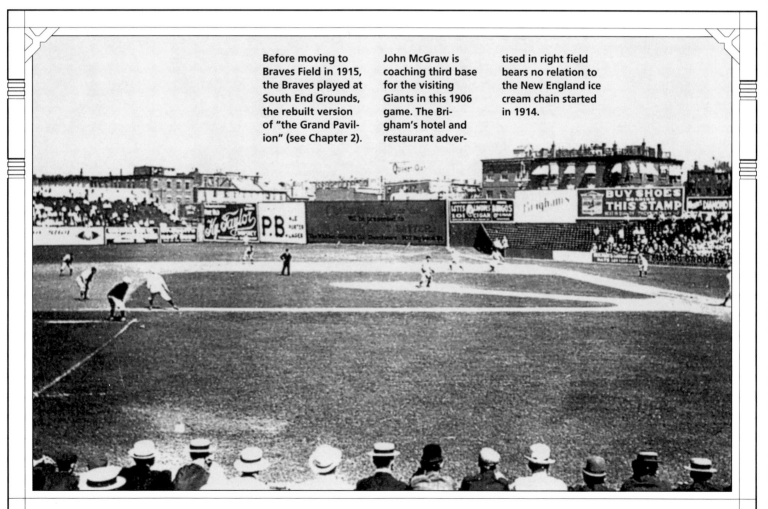

Before moving to Braves Field in 1915, the Braves played at South End Grounds, the rebuilt version of "the Grand Pavilion" (see Chapter 2). John McGraw is coaching third base for the visiting Giants in this 1906 game. The Brigham's hotel and restaurant advertised in right field bears no relation to the New England ice cream chain started in 1914.

Holiday double-headers always drew huge crowds, and this July 4, 1907, twin bill at New York's Hilltop Park was no exception (top). Hilltop had only 16,000 seats, but a crowd that *Sporting Life* estimated at 20,000 showed up for the two games. If they were ever bored, the fans sitting in left field could look out at the Hudson River (above).

Square Garden gave the play-by-play, and the *New York Times* reported:

> Thousands of businessmen temporarily gave up business to devote themselves to baseball. . . . Steady processions departed offices to hunt the nearest source of information . . . even in hospitals the baseball tidings were carried to patients. Everything was sidetracked for the latest news from the baseball war.

The news got hotter on September 4 when the Cubs lost to Pittsburgh, 1–0, in ten innings at Exposition Park but lodged a protest, claiming the run should not have scored. With one out in the bottom of the tenth, the Pirates loaded the bases; outfielder John "Chief" Wilson singled to short center, and Fred Clarke scored the winning run. Buc first baseman Warren Gill, who had reached first when hit by a pitch, turned and started for the clubhouse. Cub second baseman Johnny Evers, seeing Gill head off the field, called for the ball and touched second with it. Evers then charged umpire Hank O'Day and told him that the side had

been retired and that Clarke's run didn't count, but Chicago protested in vain.

In *The Unforgettable Season*, G. H. Fleming surmises that the earlier letter to the editor may have given Evers the idea. He says, "Not only Evers but other members of the Chicago team, including Slagle and Tinker, did not immediately head for the clubhouse but held their ground as if anticipating Gill's infraction."

Of course, nineteen days later another opposing runner, this time Fred Merkle of the Giants, also failed to touch second base. Evers again touched the base to "force" him before Harry "Moose" McCormick could score; O'Day ruled the game a tie, and league president Harry Pulliam upheld him on October 3. Pulliam ruled that the Cubs and Giants would play off the tie game, if necessary, to settle the pennant race. While the *Pittsburgh Press* printed extras on Sunday to keep up with the news, the *Chicago Tribune* actually *sold* tickets at Orchestra Hall, for 25 cents, 50 cents, and $1, so fans could see an electrical recreation of the playoff game.

This view of the Polo Grounds is taken from behind first base up to the apartment houses overlooking Coogan's Bluff. An unidentified Red has just crossed the bag, apparently heeding the warning in the coaches' box to "Stop." This bit of arcana is not explained, nor are the circles behind first and second that resemble nothing so much as manhole covers. Note also the wooden fences in right center.

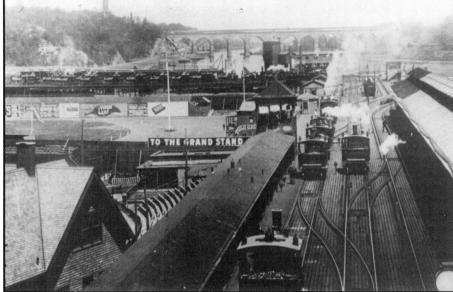

The Polo Grounds was the most interesting of the three New York ballparks in the era before concrete. Cars from the Eighth Avenue IND line clattered by the Polo Grounds and descended below street level for maintenance. As Lawrence Ritter has observed in *Lost Ballparks*, it was "the only major league ballpark where the most convenient way to get to upper-deck grandstand seats was by walking *down* rather than up." Note the sign "To the grand stand," coal cars on the railroad tracks at right, and the original High Bridge in the background over the Harlem River.

Opening Day was a special occasion in the early 1900s, particularly after the jingoism that infected the nation after the Spanish-American War. Red, white, and blue bunting was the order of the day, and fans were expected to dress up for the occasion. Ticket prices were fairly high, as at this 1907 opener at Washington Park in Brooklyn. For the price of a grandstand seat, Brooklynites could buy four wax cylinder recordings (early records) from Sears, Roebuck and still have change.

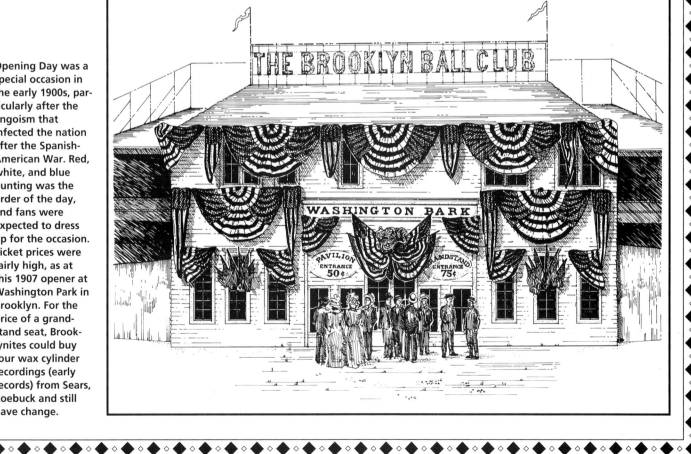

ALONG WATER STREET. PITTSB[...]
FOUR SQUARES FROM JUNCTION O[...]
ALLEGHENY AND MONONGAHE[...]

[...]ATING AT THE ENTRANCE TO
BASE BALL PARK. ALLEGHENY.

Exposition Park was a Pittsburgh fixture from 1882 and was used by American Association, Players League, National League, and Federal League teams. However, its location along the Allegheny River caused problems. When floodwaters submerged the city in 1902, a July Fourth morning-afternoon doubleheader was played even though at least a foot of water covered the outfield. A ground rule, passed just for that day, made all balls hit to the outfield automatic singles. With 10,000 fans looking on, both games were played, and the ball was dried after every pitch.

SMOKEY CITY.

On October 8, the *New York Evening Telegram* reported that

> the largest crowd ever gathered in the world for a sporting event — fully a quarter of a million people — were surging in and around the Polo Grounds. . . . From the press box the skyline everywhere was human heads. They were located on grandstand, roofs, fences, "L" structures [elevated railways], electric light poles and in the distance on smokestacks, chimneys, advertising signs, and copings of apartment houses.

Lest one think that this was hyperbole, listen to W. J. Lampton of the *New York Times*: "If 35,000 were inside, 35,000,000 were outside. . . . Never before in the history of the game have there been so many to see a game who didn't see it."

The Cubs won the playoff game, 4–2, and Mordecai Centennial "Three Finger" Brown won that game and 2 more in the World Series as the Cubs tamed the Tigers in 5 games. But the significance of the events of 1908 were to vault baseball to new heights of popularity. That summer a songwriter named Jack Norworth, who had never been to a game in his life, wrote "Take Me Out to the Ball Game." That fall James Buchanan Duke, the czar of the American Tobacco Company, decreed that his cigarettes would now be sold with cards of baseball players; eighty-three years later, hockey star Wayne Gretzky and Los Angeles Kings owner Bruce McNall paid $451,000 for one of them, featuring Honus Wagner.

The significance of that season for ballparks can best be summed up by a column W. A. Phelon wrote in *Sporting Life* on August 8:

> Baseball is only in its infancy . . . and it looks as though ball parks now in existence would be all too small for the multitudes ten years from now. . . . On some grounds — like the Cub park, for instance — the limit has been reached in seating capacity. The solution: I have a photograph of the grandstand at Epson, the great English race course. It has six decks, rising high in the air. Six decks — just think of it! A six-decked stand . . . would hold 60,000 — and the day is not far distant when 60,000 people will be at baseball games. Yes.

Yes indeed, Mr. Phelon.

TIMELINE

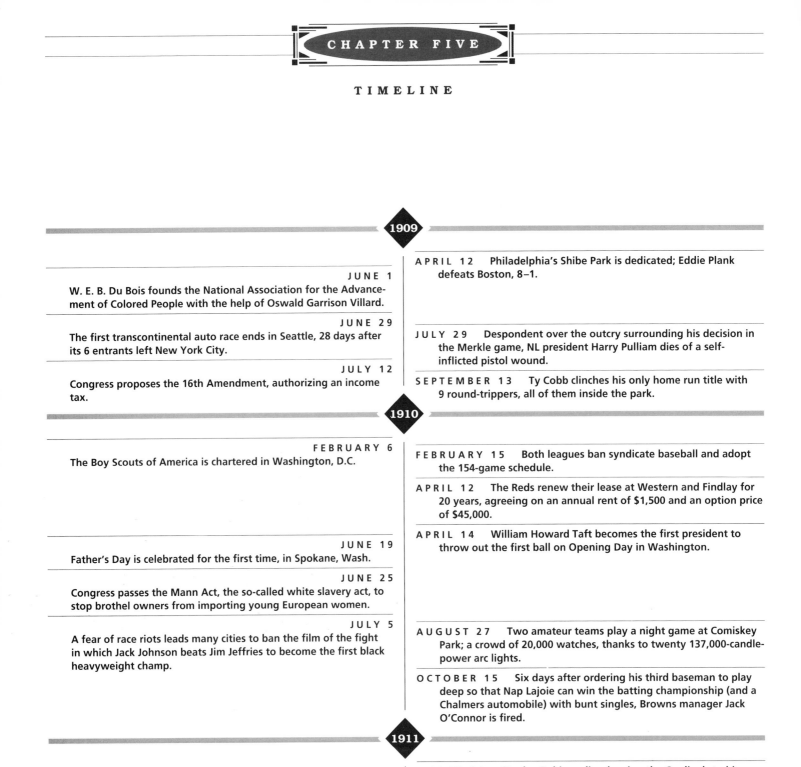

1909

JUNE 1
W. E. B. Du Bois founds the National Association for the Advancement of Colored People with the help of Oswald Garrison Villard.

JUNE 29
The first transcontinental auto race ends in Seattle, 28 days after its 6 entrants left New York City.

JULY 12
Congress proposes the 16th Amendment, authorizing an income tax.

APRIL 12   Philadelphia's Shibe Park is dedicated; Eddie Plank defeats Boston, 8–1.

JULY 29   Despondent over the outcry surrounding his decision in the Merkle game, NL president Harry Pulliam dies of a self-inflicted pistol wound.

SEPTEMBER 13   Ty Cobb clinches his only home run title with 9 round-trippers, all of them inside the park.

1910

FEBRUARY 6
The Boy Scouts of America is chartered in Washington, D.C.

JUNE 19
Father's Day is celebrated for the first time, in Spokane, Wash.

JUNE 25
Congress passes the Mann Act, the so-called white slavery act, to stop brothel owners from importing young European women.

JULY 5
A fear of race riots leads many cities to ban the film of the fight in which Jack Johnson beats Jim Jeffries to become the first black heavyweight champ.

FEBRUARY 15   Both leagues ban syndicate baseball and adopt the 154-game schedule.

APRIL 12   The Reds renew their lease at Western and Findlay for 20 years, agreeing on an annual rent of $1,500 and an option price of $45,000.

APRIL 14   William Howard Taft becomes the first president to throw out the first ball on Opening Day in Washington.

AUGUST 27   Two amateur teams play a night game at Comiskey Park; a crowd of 20,000 watches, thanks to twenty 137,000-candle-power arc lights.

OCTOBER 15   Six days after ordering his third baseman to play deep so that Nap Lajoie can win the batting championship (and a Chalmers automobile) with bunt singles, Browns manager Jack O'Connor is fired.

1911

MARCH 25
The Triangle Shirt Waist Company, in New York City, catches fire, and 146 people, mostly young women, die in the sweatshop.

MAY 30
The first Indianapolis 500 auto race is won by Ray Harroun in 6 hours, 42 minutes, and 8 seconds, an average speed of 74.59 mph.

MARCH 24   Stanley Robison dies, leaving the Cardinals to his niece, Helene Hathaway Britton, who becomes the first female big league club owner.

APRIL 4   Automaker Hugh Chalmers agrees to drop the batting title idea and, instead, awards new cars to the Most Valuable Player in each league.

MAY 29   En route from St. Louis, the Pennsylvania Railroad carries the Cubs the 191 miles from Columbus to Pittsburgh in 215 minutes (88 mph).

OCTOBER 5   The National Commission sells movie rights to the World Series for $3,500 but cancels the deal when the players ask for a share.

a six-day bike race. I told him bike fans preferred ham and cheese, but he insisted."

What we now call the hot dog was named in 1905 by Hearst cartoonist Thomas A. Dorgan, who signed his drawings TAD. A Polo Grounds regular, Dorgan drew a cartoon animating the sausage by placing an elongated dachshund on a bun. Flexner says that the dachshund was "a facetious symbol for things German in the early 1900s" and adds that "many people suspected the mixed meats in the sausage contained dog meat, or worse." When Dorgan heard a vendor yell, "Get a red-hot dachshund sausage on a roll," he was inspired to dub the concoction "the hot dog," and the name stuck. (After his father's death, Frank Stevens was indeed given credit for inventing the hot dog. When his daughter, Alice, wed James Titus, whose mother was a Gulden, the *Daily News* headlined the event, "Hot Dog Marries the Mustard.")

The company Harry started also cleans arenas and K mart stores on a contract basis and has helped design Arby's, Holiday Inns, and Florida's Gulfstream Park. In 1992, the company's clients ranged from the Central Park Zoo and Churchill Downs to the Astrodome, Candlestick Park, Fenway Park, and Shea Stadium. These days, Joseph B. Stevens, Jr., Harry's grandson and the company's retired chairman, keeps his hand in

by adding to the company's collection of programs and scorecards. He says, "I just paid $21,500 for a scorecard; in 1905, my grandfather sold it for a dime."

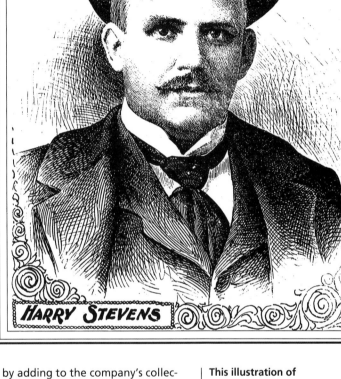

This illustration of a natty Harry M. Stevens ran in an 1896 edition of the *New York Clipper*.

THE BALLPARK FIRES OF 1894

The illumination provided by numerous early attempts at night baseball were pale compared with the light of the fires that bedeviled ballparks in the 1890s. The parks in St. Louis had six fires during the decade, and at least twenty others around the country burst into flame during the otherwise Gay Nineties. One way to appreciate the extent of the problem is to review insurance maps of the period, which list in great detail all the fire-fighting equipment in ballparks and other public buildings.

Of course, ballparks had already had their share of disasters. High winds stripped the grandstand roof from the original Polo Grounds in 1884, and fire destroyed most of the stands at Washington

Park in 1889 — fortunately while the Bridegrooms were on the road. After a Louisville-Syracuse Sunday game in Three Rivers, New York, in 1890, part of a grandstand collapsed, causing injuries but no fatalities. Fire also destroyed most of the Louisville Colonels' ballpark in 1892, but the bleachers survived and a game was played there two days later.

The fires of 1894 were far more treacherous. Ballparks in Baltimore, Boston, Chicago, and Philadelphia all had fires, and hundreds of thousands of dollars of property was lost. It was rumored in the sporting press that the fires were being set deliberately, and some went so far as to hint that Sabbatarians were not above using arson to stop Sunday baseball, which had officially been adopted by the league in 1892.

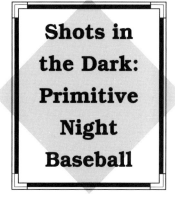

Shots in the Dark: Primitive Night Baseball

Defeating darkness had been an American priority at least since 1757, when Benjamin Franklin designed whale oil street lamps for Philadelphia, the city that introduced gas streetlights in 1796. Baltimore was lit by coal gas in 1816, and arc lights, activated by passing charges between carbon electrodes, came into general use around 1850. Electric lighting took a quantum leap forward on October 21, 1879, when Thomas Edison's carbonized filament of cotton burned for forty hours; less than a year later, the first baseball game was played under lights — on a peninsula jutting into the Atlantic Ocean.

The Northern Electric Light Company had recently been formed in Boston, a city proud of its Red Stockings, National League champs in 1877 and 1878. Looking for publicity, Northern Electric invited the employees of the Jordan Marsh and R. H. White department stores to play baseball under its lights on September 2, 1880, at Nantasket Beach in nearby Hull.

By game time, 8 P.M., Northern Electric had put three 100-foot-high wooden towers around a crude diamond. As David Pietrusza notes in *Lights On!,* each pole supported thirty-six lamps with carbonized cotton filaments. Two engines and three generators yielded 30,000

candlepower of light. (In 1992, Hubbell Lighting relit Pittsburgh's Three Rivers Stadium; each of the park's *six hundred* lights averaged 2 *million* candlepower.)

The *Boston Post* reported that the carbon arc lamps produced "a clear, pure, bright light . . . very strong and yet very pleasant to the sight." However, the players complained to the *Boston Transcript* that "the light was not sufficient, was too much like moonlight." The *Boston Daily Globe* said unequivocally that "it was a failure."

A second serious attempt at night ball occurred three years later in Fort Wayne; again, the motivating force was a local entrepreneur of electricity. Charles Jenney of the Jenney Electric Light Company staged a game between professionals from Quincy, Illinois, of the Northwestern League and a team from Methodist College on June 3, 1883. League Park hosted the seven-inning game (won by the pros, 19–11). Jenney provided seventeen huge arc lamps of 4,000 candlepower each, an amount equal to 4,857 gas burners. One lightstand was placed behind the pitcher's mound, three were attached to the front of the grandstand, and the others lined the baselines and outfield.

Although a historic event for Fort Wayne, the *Gazette* was forced to admit that "players had to shield their eyes with their caps when they faced the light." The competing *Fort Wayne News* was even less impressed, commenting wryly, "The

outlines of persons standing at the bases were so dim that it was suggested that it would do well to electrify the players too." *Sporting Life* gave the national view as it complained, "When a ball became dirty it could not be seen," but concluded, "With between twenty-five and thirty lights there is no question but what electric ball playing is an assured success."

Another lighting nonevent involved a scheme that has to rank among baseball's looniest — using water fountains to light a baseball diamond. As noted, Erastus Wiman had bought the New York Metropolitans of the American Association mostly because he also owned the ferry running between Manhattan and Staten Island. To fatten the gate, Wiman tried to institute night baseball at St. George's.

After several failed attempts using electric lights alone, he was encouraged to try a different approach by an aide of Edison's, one Mr. Johnson. Mr. Johnson visited the grounds and was struck by another tourist attraction, the illuminated fountains. After conducting some experiments, he was "entirely confident of ultimate success" and thought that "base ball by electric light will eventually be an established fact at Staten Island."

After conferring with Edison, Mr. Johnson proposed "to line the outside of the diamond, foul lines and extremes of the outfield with electric lights placed beneath the ground and projecting, by means of powerful

The fire at Chicago's West Side Grounds on August 5, a Sunday, was particularly tragic. Some 500 people were seriously injured — but not by fire. In a game two years earlier, fans had streamed onto the field to curse the umpire, who then awarded the game to the opposition. To prevent this from happening again, Chicago enclosed the West Side bleachers in barbed wire. In the seventh inning of that Sunday game, after Cap Anson had struck out, fire erupted:

The crowd was between the growing fire and the . . . barbed fence. Men began to clamber up these wires like rats in a cage. . . . The first few got through easily. Others tried to slip between

the wires and hung there, entangled fast in the barbs.

Cub players George Decker, Jimmy Ryan, and Walt Wilmot tried to force the wire open with their bats; eventually, the pressure of the crowd pushed open the staples holding the wire. A young eyewitness said that the fire had been started by a cigar stub: "The grass took fire, the fire creeping in under the pavilion . . . it would have been easy for anyone to have stamped out the flame if anyone could have got over the barrier without trouble; but as the barrier was a barbed wire fence no one tried to get through it til the fire became dangerous."

reflectors, the rays upward through covering plates of corrugated glass." Johnson's scheme never got off the drawing board.

One of the century's last attempts to toss around the old melon by moonlight was also less than serious but involved two Hall of Famers, Ed Barrow and Honus Wagner. In 1896, thirteen years before his face appeared on that celebrated T-206 baseball card, Wagner had worked his way up from Warren (Pa.) of the Iron-Oil League and played for Paterson (N.J.) of the Atlantic League, which Barrow then managed.

Paterson was about to meet Wilmington in a July Fourth doubleheader, and business was slow. In his autobiography, *My Fifty Years in Baseball,* Barrow said, "Crowds had been poor and we needed a shot in the arm of some kind." The answer, as it would be during the Depression, was night baseball. On July 2, Wilmington's management installed arc lights at Union Street Grounds, the city's ballpark, and announced a novel tripleheader, regulation morning and afternoon games followed by a nighttime exhibition game. The *Wilmington Evening Journal* announced that "white balls, very similar to a tennis ball only larger, will be used. They are made specially for such an occasion."

Perhaps Wilmington was satiated with baseball by nightfall; a mere 200 fans showed up for the festivities. It was just as well. The *Wilmington Morning News* observed, "The game

Nineteenth-Century Night Games

YEAR	DATE	SITE	CITY
1880	September 2	Nantasket Beach	Hull, Mass.
1883	June 2	League Park (Jailhouse Flats)	Fort Wayne, Ind.
1888	August 21	Tinker Park	Indianapolis
1888	September 6	Tinker Park	Indianapolis
1891	August 8	Twickerham Grounds	Seattle
1893	July 2	Athletic Park	Los Angeles
1896	July 4	Union Street Grounds	Wilmington, Del.
1897	June 30	Beach Park	Galveston, Tex.
1897	July 16	Clyde Park	San Antonio, Tex.

was the most unique and comical ever seen here. The ball became lost so often and so many runs were made that they were not counted." Barrow said, "You could hardly see the outfielders. For improved visibility we used an indoor baseball [a softball]. All during the game the spectators were shouting and jeering and jumping on the field."

Wagner, who was known to stretch a truth or two, said in 1924 that he played in the night game, although Paterson used the same eight position players for both the morning and afternoon games. Wagner said that he came to bat in the sixth inning. In line with the general hilarity of the proceedings, Morris "Doc" Amole, Wilmington's pitcher, had a Fourth of July surprise for him. When Wagner took a mighty cut at

a fastball, it exploded, thanks to a hidden firecracker. He said, "The crowd didn't get any laugh, though. Instead, they got sore and made a rush on the box office to get their money back. . . . I'll never forget the way those fellows [Barrow et al.] scooted down the street to escape that crowd and save what little money was taken in. That was the end of night baseball."

SOUTH END GROUNDS AND BAKER BOWL

The 1894 ballpark fires raised the owners' consciousness about providing accessible escape routes for fans and prompted them to use steel and concrete in building their parks. Two classic ballparks rose from the ashes of their wooden predecessors in 1894, Baker Bowl in Philadelphia and Boston's South End Grounds.

South End Grounds was struck by fire on May 15, 1894, during a game between the Beaneaters and the Orioles. It was clearly the result of a prank, as reported in the *Boston Post:*

Boys set fire to some rubbish under seats at the Boston ball grounds yesterday. The flames spread rapidly, and in less than three hours ran over 12 acres of territory. The base ball grand stand and bleachers, a large school house, an engine house, and 164 wooden buildings were destroyed. . . . The loss is variously estimated at from $300,000 to $1,000,000.

It started in the right field bleachers and destroyed the park in just one hour. Afterward, it was discovered that owner Arthur Soden, a notorious pennypincher who charged the players' wives

If South End Grounds in Boston was a reminder of Camelot, then the rebuilt Baker Bowl in Philadelphia was baseball's answer to Runnymede. Even though the interior featured the first cantilever design, the exterior looked more like a castle or an armory, complete with turrets and battlements. This illustration is the Baker Bowl Philadelphians prefer to remember, not the seedy and sadly unkempt "Dump on the Hump" of the 1920s and 1930s.

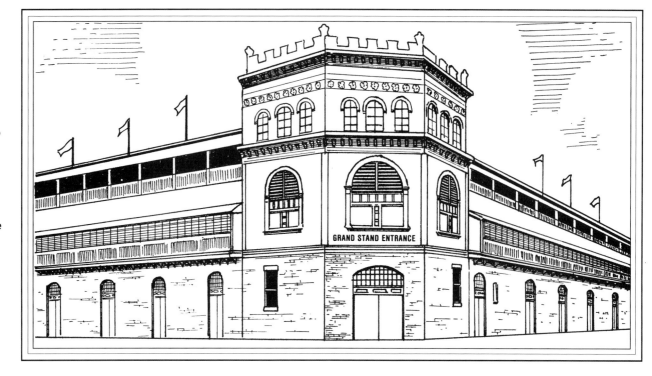

Railroad tracks have long offered a kind of physical short-hand to define (and divide) social classes. Philadelphia's Baker Bowl, on Lehigh and Huntingdon, was originally on the same side of the tracks as Columbia Park, the first American League park in town; later, Connie Mack would move to Shibe Park, across the tracks at Somerset and Lehigh. In Boston in 1910, the tracks of the New York, New Haven & Hartford Railroad separated the city's two ballparks. South End Grounds, the home of the NL Bean-eaters (Braves), was on the east side, while the AL Pilgrims (Red Sox) were on the west side. Even farther west was the still-undeveloped Fenway, a marshy area to which the Sox moved in 1912. South of the National League bailiwick lay Third Base, the saloon owned by Michael "Nuf Ced" McGreevy.

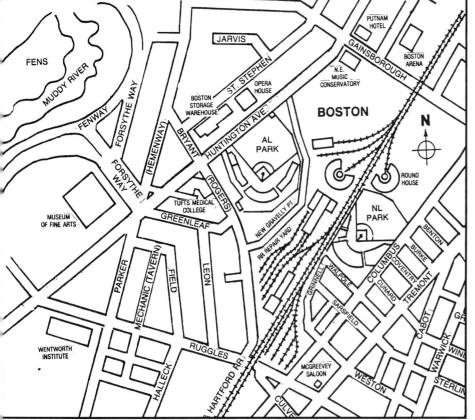

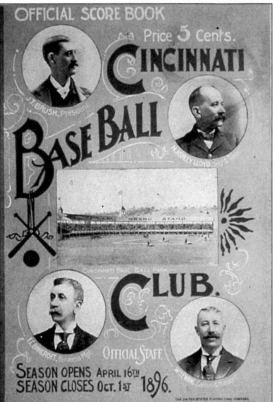

After the fires of 1894, owners tried to assure potential patrons that their ballparks were substantial places. One way was to use advertising puffery to make the parks look safer than they actually were. One of the first parks to appear on a program cover was Cincinnati's League Park, in 1896. Contrast this piece of PR wizardry with a shot of the park's rickety-looking right field fence. Sure enough, the park burned to a crisp in 1901 and rose again, phoenix-like, in 1902, as the Palace of the Fans.

for their tickets, had underinsured the park, and there was not nearly enough money to recreate the fabulous pavilion. Instead, while the Braves played at Congress Street Grounds, a single-decked park replaced what may have been the most ornate baseball stadium ever built.

Baker Bowl also began its long life (fifty-one years) as a turreted medieval castle, a building that would have been more at home in Runnymede than three miles north of Independence Hall in North Philadelphia. The home of the Quakers (later Phillies), it was successively known as National League Park, Philadelphia Baseball Grounds, and Huntingdon Street Grounds, for its eastern boundary.

Like Boston's South End Grounds, it was rebuilt in a far more conventional style after being con-

sumed by fire. The Quakers' owner, Al Reach, had the debris cleared quickly and hired three shifts of mechanics to restore the park. For ten days, the Phils played home games at the University of Pennsylvania's athletic field; they played again on Huntingdon Street twelve days after the fire. Reach immediately began making plans for a replacement that was ambitious, elaborate — and fireproof. In so doing, he created the first modern ballpark.

Where South End Grounds and West Side Grounds were rebuilt in wood, Baker Bowl used steel and brick in 1894; it was also the first ballpark to feature cantilever construction, something of a defining moment for the future of ballparks. Using cantilevered concrete supports, architects could eliminate the columns that made for "obstructed view seating." (Future generations

When Brooklyn's National League team moved to Eastern Park, in 1891, it became known as the Trolley Dodgers because of the maze of streetcar tracks patrons had to negotiate to reach the park. A bit out of the way for Manhattan fans, Eastern Park had a substantial double-decked grandstand, conical spires like South End Grounds, and was at its best covered with bunting, as here, on Opening Day in 1894.

As noted, parks became part of the marketing mix in the 1890s. This sketch of a Giants-Orioles Temple Cup game at the Polo Grounds in 1894 was widely distributed as a poster, with cameos of players and team officials. At the end of the grandstand, along the third base line, is the original brick and mortar High Bridge, which was partly rebuilt in steel after the turn of the century. Why does Baltimore have five infielders? Good question.

Home Field Advantage: Oriole Park

The 1890s will always be remembered as the time the original *National League* Baltimore Orioles ran roughshod over their opponents. What is less well documented is the role that Oriole Park, their home field, played in their success under Ned Hanlon.

In May 1892, Hanlon arrived in Baltimore to manage the Orioles. Blessed with a keen appreciation of talent, he traded for no less than four players who turned out to be Hall of Famers — Joe Kelley, Hughie Jennings, Dan Brouthers, and Wee Willie Keeler — and brought Baltimore several pennants in the bargain. Hanlon was also a strategist of note, and his minions, John McGraw, Keeler, and Jennings, popularized the hit-and-run, the squeeze play, and other elements of "inside baseball." (Years later, Billy Martin, Hanlon's lineal strategic descendant — Hanlon to McGraw to Casey Stengel to Martin — renamed it "Little Ball.")

Little Ball suited the Orioles, who were, with the exception of Brouthers, a smallish lot. Jennings stood 5'8½", McGraw topped out at 5'7", and Willie Keeler was wee indeed at 5'4½". Accordingly, Hanlon felt justified in making sure that the park was carefully prepared to use inside baseball against visiting giants. Under his direction, Orioles groundskeeper Thomas J. Murphy used every part of the field to give the home team the edge. He

• loaded up the foul lines. Unlike the emaciated foul lines one saw at other parks, the lines at Union Park were lavishly decorated with chalk. Perhaps that's why so many of the Oriole bunts seemed to roll back into fair territory.

• let the outfield grass grow. This conscientious organic approach often paid dividends to O's outfielders, who sometimes found a spare ball or two in the outfield grass.

• packed the dirt around home plate. Rather than scatter ordinary soil around the plate, Murphy made sure that any Orioles attempting "Baltimore chops" were rewarded with acrobatically high bounces off the fine, firm, fully packed clay.

• "customized" the pitcher's mound. Murphy mixed soap shavings with the dirt on the mound, causing opposing servers to wonder why their control was off a tad after they wiped their hands.

Whatever little advantages Murphy couldn't supply through Mother Nature came from other quarters. Orioles would shortcut from first to third when the sole umpire's back was turned, and Harold Seymour says they would barge into catchers and even try to jostle first basemen holding on to throws. Third sacker McGraw was particularly expert at getting in the way of runners or holding their belts to slow their progress. (One day, Louisville slugger Pete Browning foiled the strategy by loosening his, leaving McGraw holding the sash.)

In *The Home Team,* James Bready mentions that often when an Oriole runner reached third safely, the third base coach would suddenly break for the plate, hoping to induce the opposing hurler to throw the ball away, allowing the real baserunner to score or at least upset the moundsman. The fans, too, became part of the action by shouting as opposing fielders tried to catch balls or by shining mirrors into the eyes of opposing batsmen. Modern Oriole rooters at Camden Yards refrain from such shenanigans, making the game fairer but, alas, a bit less interesting.

would see cantilevered loge seats and luxury boxes push the average fan farther from the field of play.)

The invitation to Opening Day described the building process:

The new structure is mainly of brick and steel, containing no wood or other inflammable material except the platform and seats . . . nine platforms of the upper deck project beyond any post into the air, and over the head of those below.

The new Philadelphia Ball Park opened on May 2, 1895, with roughly the dimensions it would carry until the Phillies left in 1938. Left field was 341 feet from home plate, center was 408, and right was 279½ feet from home plate and topped by a 40-foot wall, a distance that Chuck Klein and other left-handed hitters would later exploit. In 1895, two left-handed Phils, outfielder Sam Thompson and catcher Jack Clements, finished first and third in homers, a good example of fitting one's personnel to the park. Meanwhile, other teams were finding more inventive ways to get the edge at home.

MONOPOLY AND SYNDICATE BASEBALL

Using every edge, the Orioles won three straight National League pennants from 1894 through 1896 and narrowly missed a fourth in 1897; however, attendance, which had been hovering around 250,000, nosedived to 123,000 in 1898 despite another second-place finish.

Baltimore owner Harry Von der Horst decided to move his stars to a more populous city by swapping half of his franchise. Von der Horst and his manager, Ned Hanlon, gave 50 percent of their club to Ferdinand Abell and Charles Ebbets for half of the Trolley Dodgers.

It should have come as no surprise in the Age of the Robber Barons that baseball, too, would succumb to interlocking directorates of ownership. The practice grew unchallenged throughout the decade. Harold Seymour's findings on cross-ownership as of March 1900 are summarized in the table on the next page.

Robison, the Cleveland trolley operator and owner of the National League Spiders, is a particu-

As parks became fancier, simplicity gave way to gimmickry. Sportsman's Park in St. Louis was once an oasis of baseball, as seen in this drawing from 1892. By 1898, however, it had become a joke park. The wings of the grandstand had been severely truncated. An elevated stand, formed by seven round columns, wasn't meant for baseball but was designed instead to give those seated on top a great view of the Shoot-the-Chutes roller-coaster. This addition led the *Sporting News* to lament "the prostitution of a ballpark" (see Chapter 1).

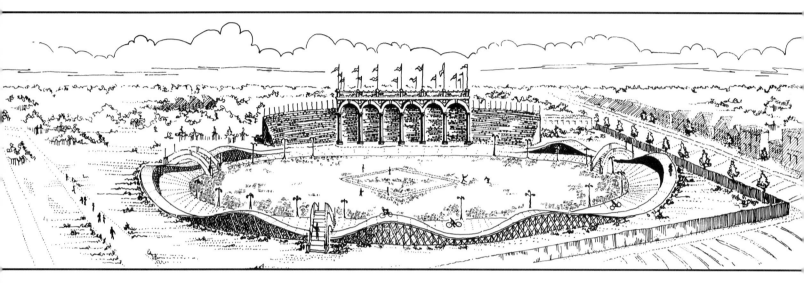

Conflicts in National League Ownership, March 1900

NAME	CLUB(S) OWNED	STOCKHOLDER IN
Ferdinand Abell	Baltimore (40%)	
	Brooklyn (40%)	New York
John T. Brush	Cincinnati	New York
Charles Ebbets		Baltimore (10%)
		Brooklyn (10%)
Ned Hanlon		Baltimore (10%)
		Brooklyn (10%)
Frank Robison	Cleveland	
	St. Louis	
Arthur Soden	Boston (33⅓%)	New York (principal minority stockholder)
Albert Spalding	Chicago	New York
Harry Von der Horst	Baltimore (40%)	
	Brooklyn (40%)	

larly noxious example. On April 24, 1898, Spain declared war on the United States, and the Spanish-American War drew fans from the ballparks. Cleveland, with a population of only 261,353 in 1890, was particularly affected, so Robison decided to move his trolleys and ballplayers to St. Louis (pop. 451,770). While retaining ownership of the Spiders, he bought the competing St. Louis Cardinals after the 1898 season. On April 3, 1899, Robison stocked the Cardinals with former Cleveland players — including Cy Young and Jess Burkett, renamed Sportsman's Park League Park and called the Cardinals the Perfectos.

Every other team gave Cleveland excess players to fill out its roster; it didn't help. The 1899 Cleveland Spiders were — collectively — a 20-game winner, and their 134 losses set a major league record for ineptitude. The Spiders were so bad and attendance was so low for their 24 home games that they also set a major league low for season attendance — 6,088. Called the Exiles, Misfits, Castoffs, Wanderers, Forsakens, and worse by Cleveland's baseball fans, they were the Team Without a Park for the entire month of September and finished it 1–27.

Not surprisingly, the National League dropped Cleveland before the 1900 season, but help was on the way. Ban Johnson, the commissioner of the minor Western League, had major league ambitions and told haberdasher Jack Kilfoyl and Charles Somers to buy the Grand Rapids franchise. Before the 1901 season, the partners would transfer the team to Cleveland, which became part of a new major league circuit. The decade that began with the unsuccessful debut of the Players League ended with the dramatic launching of the American League.

TIMELINE

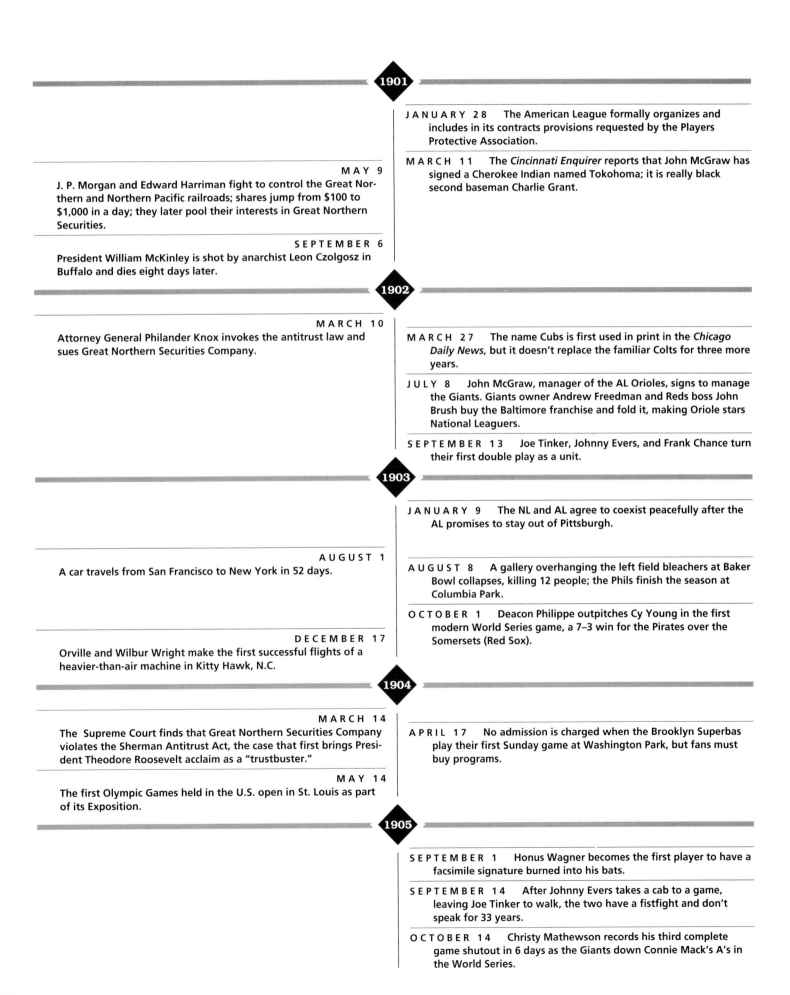

1901

JANUARY 28   The American League formally organizes and includes in its contracts provisions requested by the Players Protective Association.

MARCH 11   The *Cincinnati Enquirer* reports that John McGraw has signed a Cherokee Indian named Tokohoma; it is really black second baseman Charlie Grant.

MAY 9
J. P. Morgan and Edward Harriman fight to control the Great Northern and Northern Pacific railroads; shares jump from $100 to $1,000 in a day; they later pool their interests in Great Northern Securities.

SEPTEMBER 6
President William McKinley is shot by anarchist Leon Czolgosz in Buffalo and dies eight days later.

1902

MARCH 10
Attorney General Philander Knox invokes the antitrust law and sues Great Northern Securities Company.

MARCH 27   The name Cubs is first used in print in the *Chicago Daily News,* but it doesn't replace the familiar Colts for three more years.

JULY 8   John McGraw, manager of the AL Orioles, signs to manage the Giants. Giants owner Andrew Freedman and Reds boss John Brush buy the Baltimore franchise and fold it, making Oriole stars National Leaguers.

SEPTEMBER 13   Joe Tinker, Johnny Evers, and Frank Chance turn their first double play as a unit.

1903

JANUARY 9   The NL and AL agree to coexist peacefully after the AL promises to stay out of Pittsburgh.

AUGUST 1
A car travels from San Francisco to New York in 52 days.

AUGUST 8   A gallery overhanging the left field bleachers at Baker Bowl collapses, killing 12 people; the Phils finish the season at Columbia Park.

OCTOBER 1   Deacon Philippe outpitches Cy Young in the first modern World Series game, a 7–3 win for the Pirates over the Somersets (Red Sox).

DECEMBER 17
Orville and Wilbur Wright make the first successful flights of a heavier-than-air machine in Kitty Hawk, N.C.

1904

MARCH 14
The Supreme Court finds that Great Northern Securities Company violates the Sherman Antitrust Act, the case that first brings President Theodore Roosevelt acclaim as a "trustbuster."

APRIL 17   No admission is charged when the Brooklyn Superbas play their first Sunday game at Washington Park, but fans must buy programs.

MAY 14
The first Olympic Games held in the U.S. open in St. Louis as part of its Exposition.

1905

SEPTEMBER 1   Honus Wagner becomes the first player to have a facsimile signature burned into his bats.

SEPTEMBER 14   After Johnny Evers takes a cab to a game, leaving Joe Tinker to walk, the two have a fistfight and don't speak for 33 years.

OCTOBER 14   Christy Mathewson records his third complete game shutout in 6 days as the Giants down Connie Mack's A's in the World Series.

TIMELINE

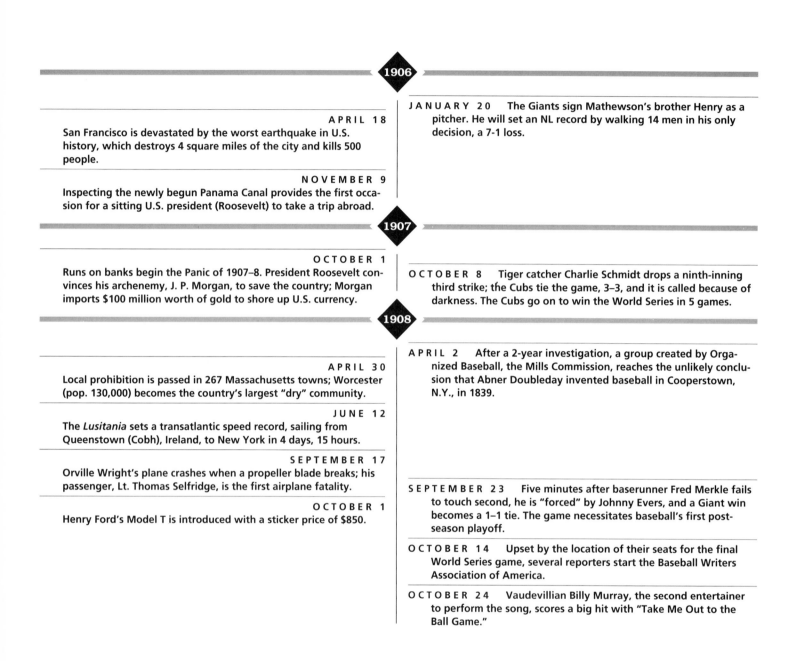

1906

APRIL 18
San Francisco is devastated by the worst earthquake in U.S. history, which destroys 4 square miles of the city and kills 500 people.

NOVEMBER 9
Inspecting the newly begun Panama Canal provides the first occasion for a sitting U.S. president (Roosevelt) to take a trip abroad.

JANUARY 20   The Giants sign Mathewson's brother Henry as a pitcher. He will set an NL record by walking 14 men in his only decision, a 7-1 loss.

1907

OCTOBER 1
Runs on banks begin the Panic of 1907–8. President Roosevelt convinces his archenemy, J. P. Morgan, to save the country; Morgan imports $100 million worth of gold to shore up U.S. currency.

OCTOBER 8   Tiger catcher Charlie Schmidt drops a ninth-inning third strike; the Cubs tie the game, 3–3, and it is called because of darkness. The Cubs go on to win the World Series in 5 games.

1908

APRIL 30
Local prohibition is passed in 267 Massachusetts towns; Worcester (pop. 130,000) becomes the country's largest "dry" community.

JUNE 12
The *Lusitania* sets a transatlantic speed record, sailing from Queenstown (Cobh), Ireland, to New York in 4 days, 15 hours.

SEPTEMBER 17
Orville Wright's plane crashes when a propeller blade breaks; his passenger, Lt. Thomas Selfridge, is the first airplane fatality.

OCTOBER 1
Henry Ford's Model T is introduced with a sticker price of $850.

APRIL 2   After a 2-year investigation, a group created by Organized Baseball, the Mills Commission, reaches the unlikely conclusion that Abner Doubleday invented baseball in Cooperstown, N.Y., in 1839.

SEPTEMBER 23   Five minutes after baserunner Fred Merkle fails to touch second, he is "forced" by Johnny Evers, and a Giant win becomes a 1–1 tie. The game necessitates baseball's first postseason playoff.

OCTOBER 14   Upset by the location of their seats for the final World Series game, several reporters start the Baseball Writers Association of America.

OCTOBER 24   Vaudevillian Billy Murray, the second entertainer to perform the song, scores a big hit with "Take Me Out to the Ball Game."

C H A P T E R   F O U R

The Birth of the American League

A new major league was born in 1901 with the help of some heavyweight midwives. Five Hall of Famers — Charles Comiskey, Clark Griffith, Connie Mack, John McGraw, and, most important, Byron Bancroft "Ban" Johnson — all played key roles in founding the new circuit.

After graduating from Marietta College in 1887, Johnson became a sportswriter for the *Cincinnati Commercial-Gazette.* In 1892, the newly reformed Western League needed a president, and John T. Brush, who owned the Western League Indianapolis Indians as well as the Cincinnati Reds, had been given a say in deciding just who it should be.

Brush had not suffered gladly Johnson's journalistic barbs about the Reds' ineffective management. (They were barely above .500 at the time.) Although writers say Brush wanted to "get him [Johnson] out of the way," he was surely aware that Johnson could be a formidable opponent. Caught on the horns of a dilemma, Brush fretted over his decision but never did completely resolve his conflict. He was supposed to go to a conference empowered to name the new president, but, according to historian Lee Allen, he missed the train. The other delegates, assuming that Brush supported Johnson, elected him president. The missed train, like the nail for which a shoe and eventually a kingdom were lost, had major ramifications: Johnson ultimately transformed the minor Western League into the major American League, which soon rivaled the National League, in which Brush owned a club.

It was no small task. Three out of every four professional baseball teams in the nineteenth century went belly up in two years or less. According to *Mudville's Revenge,* "Between 1869 and 1900 over 850 professional franchises were launched; 650 of them went out of business in two years or less, and only 50 lasted six years or more." No minor league had ever escalated to major league status; none had even tried. All three attempts at a second major league — the American Association, Union Association, and Players League — had failed.

When Johnson was named president of the Western League on November 20, 1893, he inherited a league patterned after the Western Association, never a moneymaker. His "domain" was a very mixed bag of large cities and small towns — Detroit, Grand Rapids, Indianapolis, Kansas City, Milwaukee, Minneapolis, Sioux City, and Toledo.

To his credit, Johnson compressed them into a highly organized league. So that franchises wouldn't constantly change cities, he asked for 51 percent of every team's stock, which he kept in his office safe. Johnson also understood that the public wanted hard-fought, well-run games. He backed his umpires completely in disputes with both players and fans and was noticeably successful in outlawing gambling in league parks, something that eluded the National League.

In 1895, the league got a double lift when Sioux City moved to St. Paul and Johnson brought Comiskey in to run the team. Later that season, Johnson gained more respect at Brush's expense. Brush would ostensibly "sign" players to the Reds, then send them to Indianapolis, an early variant of the farm system. After Johnson slapped his hand a few times, Brush tried to remove him from office; instead, Brush was forced to sell his stock in Indianapolis.

By 1896 the Western League was judged "the strongest minor ever," and it only improved when Connie Mack took over Milwaukee a year later. Johnson began thinking about going major but had

On October 12, 1907, Mordecai "Three Finger" Brown shut out the Tigers, 2–0, at Bennett Park in Detroit to give the Cubs their first world championship. This picture doesn't begin to explain how Bennett Park evolved into Tiger Stadium. In fact, the wooden grandstand was removed over the winter of 1911–1912 and a concrete and steel horseshoe erected in its place.

While owners like Charles Comiskey and Ben Shibe would later be associated with forward-looking parks, their first American League fields were unremarkable in any way. South Side Park (top), the predecessor of Comiskey, was notable only for its vast outfield distances, which yielded just 2 homers in 1904, 3 in 1906, and 4 in 1909. Columbia Park, the A's home before Shibe Park, is set apart only by its elevated press box.

to delay his plans when the United States entered the Spanish-American War. Baseball attendance slumped, and the national pastime lost ground to both the bicycle craze and a renewed interest in horse racing.

After the 1899 season, Johnson named his circuit the American League to give it a national character. At the same time the National League decided to buy out the owners of its deadwood franchises but keep would-be leagues out of those cities by maintaining the empty ballfields. In March 1900, Louisville's owners got a measly $10,000 while Frank Robison raked in $25,000 for the Cleveland franchise he'd so willfully denuded (see Chapter 3); Van der Horst, Hanlon, and company took in $30,000 for Baltimore, and Washington's George Wagner topped all the other owners, walking away with $46,500.

When it became clear that the National League would drop Cleveland, Johnson snapped up that territory with the backing of local coal magnate Charles Somers. In March 1900, he expanded into Chicago as well. In exchange, the American League

◆ assented to honor the National Agreement.

◆ reimbursed the NL for improvements to League Park, its abandoned field in Cleveland.

◆ allowed Chicago owner James Hart to pick two American League players.

◆ agreed not to build a park in Chicago north of 35th Street. (Confined to the stockyards, Johnson built South Side Park at 39th Street and Wentworth Avenue.)

The American League now comprised Buffalo, Chicago, Cleveland, Detroit, Indianapolis, Kansas City, Milwaukee, and Minneapolis, all growing and all but the last former NL cities.

More important, the National League players began to create significant problems for management. On June 10, 1900, delegates from every team met in New York to form the Protective Association of Professional Baseball Players (PAPBP). Pittsburgh catcher Charles "Chief" Zimmer was elected president and Chicago pitcher Clark Griffith named vice president. At a second meeting, Buffalo attorney Harry Leonard, a former first baseman, won over the delegates by asking for wages higher than the $2,500 limit, medical coverage for on-the-field injuries, an arbitration system for settling disputes, and freedom from being shuttled to the minor leagues at the owners' whim.

Braves owner Arthur Soden was one of a three-man committee delegated to deal with the PAPBP

If Columbia Park and South Side Park were undistinguished, Oriole Park in Baltimore and League Park in Cleveland were even less notable. Oriole Park (above), used for just a single year (1901) as an American League park, had a wooden scoreboard and an outfield fence to match. The photo below shows Cy Young, baseball's winningest pitcher (511 victories), delivering in full overhand motion at League Park. In its wooden version, the place looked temporary, a feeling reinforced by the blizzard of signs in the outfield. There are no coaches' boxes, and the infield grass just seems to meander up the third base line.

at the annual postseason league meeting. However, Soden pocketed their proposal and never presented or even read it. When Zimmer, Jennings, and Griffith found out, they released a statement to the Associated Press advising players not to sign with their old clubs. Simultaneously, Johnson had gone to New York seeking recognition of his league as a major; the NL owners slipped out a side door to avoid meeting with him.

By rejecting both parties, the National League succeeded only in driving them together. Johnson made common cause with the players' union by vowing that he would not enforce an arbitrary salary limitation and agreeing that American Leaguers could not be farmed out without their consent. Although the Protective Association never formally recognized the new league, it did enhance Johnson's cause in a practical way by giving the players good reason to jump their National League teams.

Buoyed by this cooperation, Johnson announced in February 1901 that the AL was going to be a major league, with teams in Cleveland, Chicago, Milwaukee, Louisville, Boston, Baltimore, Philadelphia, and Washington. He said, "The National League has taken for granted that no one had a right to expand without first getting its permission. . . . If we had waited for the National League to do something for us, we would have remained a minor league forever."

In seven years, Johnson had transformed a clutch of struggling minor league franchises into a major league. Aside from Detroit and Milwaukee, which had franchises when he took over, he had traded up magnificently, a feat that can be best appreciated by looking at the chart below.

The parks, however, were not uniformly major league, and only Cleveland's League Park had, in fact, been used as an NL park. The year-old South Side Park in Chicago and Lloyd Street Grounds in

Milwaukee were holdovers from Johnson's Western League days. Lloyd Street had the typical racetrack grandstand and a rickety wooden outfield fence with wooden supports. It was used as a major league park for just a single season because this original Milwaukee Brewers team became the St. Louis Browns in 1902 (and the Baltimore Orioles in 1954).

South Side had been used in 1900, when Johnson first invaded Chicago. One of the few cricket pitches used for major league baseball, it had been the home of Comiskey's former St. Paul Saints, known briefly as the Invaders; however, management grafted the successful White Stockings name onto them that first year, and it was shortened to White Sox in 1904. That year, and in 1907 as well, the Sox hit no homers at home, leading to their nickname, the Hitless Wonders.

THE TIGERS' LAIR: BENNETT PARK

The new American League parks were all made of wood. Despite the publicity Baker Bowl had received for its steel construction, the AL owners lacked the money for steel, so wood was used to build Columbia Park in Philadelphia, at a cost of just $7,500.

Fortunately, one of those original wooden American League parks — Bennett Park in Detroit — was later rebuilt on the same site in steel and concrete, and the site on which it sat is, at this writing, still being used for major league baseball as Tiger Stadium. The corner of Michigan and Trumbull is now, by a wide margin, the oldest continuous address in American professional sports.

In 1894 Detroit, which had been NL territory and the home of the Wolverines, joined the Western League and played in Boulevard Park at Helen Avenue and Champlain Street (now Lafayette Boulevard), close to the city's eastern boundary. In 1895,

Original American League Parks

WESTERN LEAGUE 1894	AMERICAN LEAGUE 1901	ORIGINAL PARK
Detroit Creams	Baltimore Orioles	Oriole Park
Grand Rapids Gold Bugs	Boston Somersets	Huntington Avenue Grounds
Indianapolis Hoosiers	Chicago White Sox	South Side Park
Kansas City Blues	Cleveland Bluebirds	League Park
Milwaukee Brewers	Detroit Tigers	Bennett Park
Minneapolis Millers	Milwaukee Brewers	Lloyd Street Grounds
Sioux City Huskers	Philadelphia Athletics	Columbia Park
Toledo Swamp Angels	Washington Senators	American League Park

On May 4, 1901, fire broke out at Robison Field in St. Louis, and the event is graphically captured in this postcard. The *Sporting News* wrote of the blaze: "When the cry of fire was raised, the occupants of the grandstand arose in their seats with the expectation of seeing a fight . . . At the commencement of the commotion the game was interrupted more from the curiosity of the players and umpire to learn what was going on than from any other cause." Despite heavy losses, the park was rebuilt quickly, and except for one game at Sportsman's Park the day after the fire, St. Louis played out its schedule at Robison Field.

the players adopted brown and black striped stockings, and a headline writer for the *Detroit Free Press* began referring to them as the Tigers.

Tiger owner Arthur Van Der Beck moved the team to Michigan and Trumbull, the former site of an old hay market, in 1896. What was originally called the Haymarket or Woodbridge Grove (for the farm of William Woodbridge, a U.S. senator and governor of Michigan) came to be known as Bennett Park after Tiger catcher Charlie Bennett, one of the outstanding catchers of his day and the first man to test the reserve clause. Tragically, his career was cut short in 1893 when he slipped, waiting for a train, and fell under the wheels; his left foot was amputated at the ankle and his right leg at the knee.

Bennett Park was part of Detroit's Sixth Ward, an Irish neighborhood known as Corktown. Along the outfield walls, National Avenue in left and Cherry Avenue in right, entrepreneurs erected "wildcat bleachers," where the price of the seat varied with the importance of the game; admission to ordinary games went for a nickel but escalated to 15 cents for an important game and 50 cents for a World Series game. Tiger management tried to challenge this practice in court but always lost. Later, the view was blocked with huge, 40-foot-high strips of canvas; the bleachers were eventually proclaimed a hazard by the fire marshal and torn down.

Like all the other American League parks of the day, the 5,000-seat Bennett Park had been built in a hurry. Van Der Beck covered the cobblestones of the old hay market with a layer of topsoil that was a mere 2 inches at its height; other patches went completely uncovered, giving new meaning to the expression "bad hop." Any fielder could explain away an error with "It hit a cobble." According to *Queen of Diamonds,* the infield was dragged once a week rather than twice a day, the seam between dirt and grass was "more like a ledge," and the outfield turned marshy at the gentlest rain.

Faults and all, the park opened on April 28, 1896. The popular Bennett caught the ceremonial first pitch and repeated the feat at every home opener through 1926. (He died in February 1927.) During this first game, it was discovered that the afternoon sun glared directly into the eyes of the right fielders; the plate was reoriented in 1910.

Bennett Park officially became an American League park on April 20, 1900, when the Tigers were no-hit by Buffalo's Morris "Doc" Amole, the same man who had allegedly thrown the firecracker pitch to Honus Wagner (see Chapter 3). A year later, the park was ready for the majors; shallow bleachers were installed in the outfield, increasing the capacity to 8,500, but an overflow crowd necessitated seating fans in the outfield, making routine fly balls ground rule doubles.

The Tigers trailed the Milwaukee Brewers, 13–4, going into the bottom of the ninth. Four ground rule doubles sandwiched around an infield hit and a single produced five runs with nobody out. Detroit cut the deficit to three runs and loaded the bases, but a ground out and a strikeout had them down to their last lick. William "Kid" Gleason bunted toward third and reached first on an error; then James "Ducky" Holmes beat out an infield hit, making it a one-run game. Finally, Frank "Pop" Dillon lofted a fly down the left field line and two runs scored, giving the Bengals a 14–13 win and Bennett Park an unforgettable major league debut.

Although it had an imposing ware-house running from left field to left center (see p. 100), Boston's Huntington Avenue Grounds was as unprepossessing as other early American League parks, particularly when seen from the first base side (above). A clue to its lack of popularity can be found on the cover of the program for fans at a 1908 benefit game for Cy Young; the park is simply "Boston American League Grounds." At the time, just about any ballpark was called American or National League Grounds. Parks had as many as three names then — one used by newspapers, another by fans, and a third by the club itself.

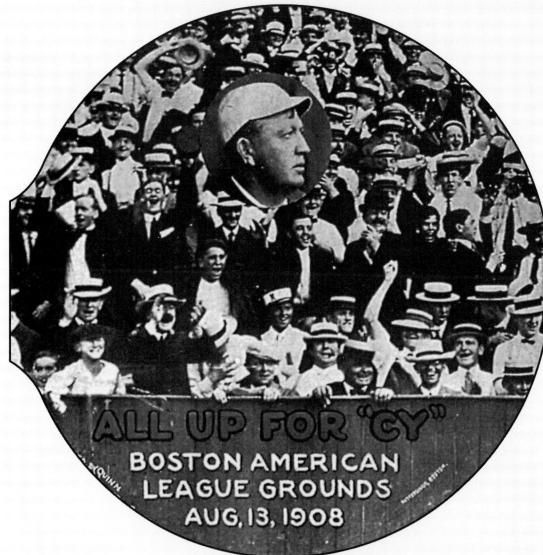

ALL UP FOR "CY"

BOSTON AMERICAN
LEAGUE GROUNDS
AUG, 13, 1908

(VERY) DEEP CENTER: HUNTINGTON AVENUE GROUNDS

Johnson's lust for power led him to believe that having a team in Boston was absolutely vital to the American League's future, but there was neither a team nor a park three months before the season started. He was finally able to twist the arm of Charles Somers to finance another team besides the Indians. After Somers put up the franchise money, Johnson sent Connie Mack and the "Heavenly Twins" — Beaneater outfielder Hugh Duffy and the retired Tommy McCarthy — to scout possible ballpark sites.

The neighborhood they investigated was a natural for three Irish lads (Mack was born McGillicuddy). A working poor Irish district on the road to Roxbury, "the Village" was within walking distance of the Fens, a swampy area destined to house a ballpark. The Village could already boast one park — South End Grounds (see Chapters 2 and 3). The South End was defined by the yards of the

New York, New Haven, and Hartford Railroad, and its tracks separated one part of the Village from the other.

Mack and his colleagues wanted a spot on the other side of the tracks from the South End. What they found was a former circus lot, complete with a "Shoot the Chutes" pool hard by a pickle factory, several breweries, stables, and chemical odors created by the United Drug Company. Red Sox historian Ed Walton described the site in a 1989 Fenway Park scorecard:

> The lot's biggest drawback was a deep pond which was at the base of chutes used by kids as a water slide during the warmer months and for skating in the winter. This 300,000 square feet of filled, sprawling empty lot . . . was no more than an expansive wasteland made up of heavily weeded bumps and lumps.

Wasteland or no, ground was broken on March 12, 1901, and two months later, the lot had been transformed into three light gray cement grand-

Some attendance figures from the first decade of the twentieth century are hard to believe. Take this Labor Day game between the Giants and Braves at the Polo Grounds. Even though the Giants had a 15-game lead over the Cubs and had already announced their intention *not* to play a World Series with the American League champs (the Boston Pilgrims), an overflow crowd of 38,000 flocked to see their heroes, ringing the entire outfield.

The Great Beantown Massacre

George "Rube" Waddell played a hand in one of baseball's screwiest incidents at Huntington Avenue.

The first time he saw Rube Waddell pitch, Connie Mack was told that before the third inning started, Waddell would walk into the bleachers and have a fan cut half an inch from the red undershirt he always wore; the superstitious Waddell did just that and also shut out Mack's Milwaukee team on two hits, fanning thirteen.

That incident made an impression on Mack that Waddell's wildest behavior could never quite destroy. When Waddell wrestled alligators, sparred with heavyweight champ Jim Jeffries (risking his good left arm), abandoned a major league game to play marbles with children, and walked out of a bases-loaded situation to chase a fire engine, Mack would just grin and bear it.

It would figure then, that putting a natural screwball like Waddell in a ballpark in a bustling commercial neighborhood like Huntington Avenue was bound to produce something unusual. That something occurred on August 11, 1903, and might be called the Great Beantown Massacre. Charles Dryden, for years Philadelphia's leading baseball writer, reported the game between the Somersets and Waddell's Athletics.

After noting that the Somersets had won, 5–1, Dryden added:

In the seventh inning, Rube Waddell hoisted a long foul over the right field bleachers that landed on the roof of the biggest bean cannery in Boston. In descending, the ball fell on the roof of the engine room and jammed itself between the steam whistle and the stem of the valve that operates it. The pressure set the whistle blowing. It lacked a few minutes of five o'clock, yet the workmen started to leave the building. They thought quitting time had come.

The incessant screeching of the bean-factory whistle led engineers in neighboring factories to think fire had broken out and they turned on their whistles. With a dozen whistles going full blast, a policeman sent in an alarm of fire.

Just as the engines arrived, a steam cauldron in the first factory, containing a ton of beans, blew up. The explosion dislodged Waddell's foul fly and the whistle stopped blowing, but that was not the end of the trouble. A shower of scalding beans descended on the bleachers and caused a small panic. One man went insane. When he saw the beans dropping out of a cloud of steam, the unfortunate rooter yelled, "The end of the world is coming and we will all be destroyed."

An ambulance summoned to the supposed fire conveyed the demented man to his home. The ton of beans proved a total loss.

---

stands, each seating 799 people, and a 300-foot-long covered lobby where fans could gather during rain delays. On May 8, the Somersets (named for their benefactor) beat Philadelphia, 12–4, before a capacity crowd of 11,500; star pitcher Cy Young not only got credit for the win but also tripled, singled, and stole a base.

The first home of the Red Sox was the most misshapen of all the big league ballparks. Fans are fond of remembering the center fields of the Polo Grounds (505) and Yankee Stadium (490) at their deepest, but both pale next to the Herculean 635 feet on Huntington Avenue in 1908. In modern terms, imagine a center field as deep as the left field lines of Cleveland Stadium (320) and Milwaukee's County Stadium (315) combined.

Nevertheless, Huntington Avenue was a home run park for pull hitters. In 1903, the Somersets hit 35 homers, a figure the other seven clubs combined could only double. (It is tempting to speculate that the Red Sox owners' traditional lust for power hitters began on Huntington Avenue.)

As time went on, the park's drawbacks became more evident. The outfield was one of the most challenging in major league history, since it featured hip-high weeds and was dotted with slippery patches of sand left over from the circus. In addition to being vast, center field sloped uphill and was made even more treacherous by the presence of a sizable tool shed in deep center. As for the stands, an Associated Press article states that Huntington's "wooden seats were rickety, soot from trains in neighboring yards filled the area, and the saloon next door was a beacon for bored players — during the games."

Fit for a King: The Palace of the Fans

Faced with strong opposition for the first time since the early days of the American Association, the National League responded with a two-pronged strategy. Since Johnson had expanded eastward, the NL assigned the Kansas City and Minneapolis franchises to a new Western League, effectively making him fight a war on two fronts for players and fans. Second, the Nationals encouraged the formation of a new American Association to further siphon off money and players from the Americans.

In 1902, as part of the counterattack, Reds' owner (and future boss of the Giants) John Brush decided to rebuild the grandstand at League Park in a grand way. Influenced by the Columbian Exposition of 1893, which had reintroduced America to classical architecture, Brush created the first "baseball palace." Charles Comiskey and Philip

Although it was used for just one major league game, a Sunday meeting between the Yankees and Tigers in July 1904, Wiedenmayer's Park in Newark, New Jersey, was later used as a home field by the Yankees' famous farm team, the Newark Bears, and the Negro National League Newark Eagles in the 1930s and 1940s.

Shibe would later try to emulate Brush's flamboyance, but neither came close. One may question some of his choices, but Brush clearly created the first major league ballpark with a distinct architectural style, then added the final marketing touch by naming it the Palace of the Fans,

The Reds had been using this location for eighteen years, since 1884. Having lost their lease on Bank Street to the short-lived Union Association Outlaw Reds, the then–American Association Reds moved to a location half a mile away, an abandoned brickyard on the corner of Findlay Street and Western Avenue.

With the demise of the Union Association in 1884, the Reds prospered. Brush bought the team in 1891 and made two changes for the better. In 1894, he moved home plate to what had previously been the right field corner so that batters could avoid the afternoon sun. On a hot Sunday in 1892, the sun had been so blinding that a game with Boston was canceled, the only major league set-to foreshortened by an excess of sunshine. A year later, after slugger James "Bug" Holliday, twice a home run champ, complained that he couldn't see the ball because of a big white sign in center field, Brush painted it black to become the first owner to provide hitters with a dark background, the so-called batter's eye.

On the night of May 28, 1900, a fire burned most of the grandstand and was hurriedly replaced with temporary seating so that the Reds could finish their schedule. Brush moved home plate, again putting the sun in the batters' eyes. But this time a roof was put over the old bleachers to provide some shade. This makeshift grandstand served through the end of the 1901 season.

That winter, the park was rebuilt mostly of steel and concrete, and when the fans entered on Opening Day, April 17, 1902, what they saw more nearly resembled a Greek temple, a library, or a bank than the old League Park. From the main entrance, on Findlay Street, they saw a triangular pediment with CINCINNATI engraved on it in large letters. As if that weren't enough, the Palace had Corinthian columns instead of the old Y-shaped supports. Each one had been carved by hand with vaguely Egyptian detailing.

Of course, all these frills were designed to make money, and nothing addressed that goal more directly than the wide, semicircular concrete opera boxes, which were marketed as Fashion Boxes. These boxes overhung what would normally have been dugouts. Sadly, in the rush to please the paying customers, management had omitted them, so the players had to make do by sitting on park benches.

Nine years after the Columbian Exposition, the Beaux-Arts style of architecture was still very much in vogue. When Reds owner John Brush built his Palace of the Fans in 1902, he wanted to attract the Queen City's well-heeled burghers. To Brush, a department store magnate in Indianapolis, the Palace was to be a monument to his "making it in the big city." That is why the ballpark, formerly a democratic venue, had opera boxes to seat beer-swilling patrons. The semicircular concrete boxes were anchored by Corinthian columns to a frieze that had "Cincinnati" chiseled on it, as if it were a bank. For all its grandeur, the park lacked dressing rooms for the players. Accordingly, players got into uniform at their hotel or rooming house and arrived at the park in horse-drawn wagons, giving disgruntled fans a chance to pelt them with fruit.

CINCINNATI BASE BALL PARK GRAND STAND.

This photo shows the Polo Grounds from the vantage point of Coogan's Bluff in 1905. Naturally, the standees didn't pay to get in.

In this view, we can see only about a third of the curving grandstand that gave the park its distinctive bathtub shape.

On the same level as the fashion boxes, next to the players' benches, was a stretch of seats — actually an elongated bar — called Rooters' Row, which extended along the first and third base lines level with the field. Even though they weren't in ritzy boxes, the fans on Rooters' Row could see their heroes up close, all the time nursing beer served by waiters. (Twelve glasses cost only $1.) Proximity, frustration, and inebriation combined to heap torrents of abuse on the players, but the arrangement lasted for ten years.

Four months after the Palace opened, Brush sold the club to Julius and Max Fleischmann, of the gin and yeast family, and political bosses George B. Cox and August "Garry" Herrmann. Cox headed what Lee Allen called "possibly the most corrupt government that ever infested a municipality." Brush was reluctant to sell until Cox told him, "If you don't sell the club to us, we're going to build a street in the city that will run right through the ball park."

Apparently Cox was better at threatmaking than housekeeping. The park began to deteriorate and, according to Michael Benson in *Ballparks of North America*, the building inspector was making formal complaints to Cox in 1907. "Girders were cracked.

Supports were decayed. Floors were unsafe. Fences needed rebuilding. A whole bleacher platform was defective." The park burned in 1911 and, Benson says, "when it reopened the place had lost its pillars and looked a lot more like the Crosley Field it was to become."

THE TRUCE OF 1903

John Brush and John McGraw, the two men who hated Ban Johnson with a passion, were ultimately responsible for cementing the final jewel in Johnson's crown — New York.

In the beginning of 1902, Johnson was planning to invade New York. McGraw was managing the American League Baltimore Orioles but resisted the leash with which Johnson bridled all his managers. Brush was running the National League as part of a troika named shortly before the 1902 season but knew his days in Cincinnati were numbered, as Boss Cox had made clear. Brush and McGraw conspired with Giant owner Andrew Freedman to keep Johnson out of New York and bring McGraw to New York to manage the Giants.

McGraw had advanced Baltimore $7,000 to meet expenses; when the club couldn't repay him, he

The Fan Who Won a Series: Nuf Ced McGreevy

In 1903, when the Somersets and Pirates played the first modern World Series, the hero wasn't Cy Young or Honus Wagner but a baseball-mad Boston saloonkeeper named Michael "Nuf Ced" McGreevy.

McGreevy owned one of the established landmarks in the Village, a Columbia Avenue alehouse called Third Base. ("The last stop before you steal home.") Whenever a dispute arose on the diamond, the parties would turn to McGreevy for the last word on the subject. He would end his sermons, "Enough said," which eventually became "Nuf Ced." The nickname was such an identifier that it was set in tile on the floor of his saloon.

Although McGreevy and his adoring patrons later became identified indelibly with the Somersets (Pilgrims, Red Sox), they were originally Beaneater boosters, National League fans. In the same way that the HIT SIGN, WIN SUIT sign at Ebbets Field later vaulted Abe Stark to the borough presidency of Brooklyn, the sign on the left field wall at South End Grounds, HOW CAN YOU GET HOME WITHOUT REACHING 3RD BASE?, made celebrities of McGreevy and his colorful crew. They became known collectively as the Royal Rooters, affected lightning-producing bean-pot badges, and composed (and loudly sang) baseball parodies of popular tunes.

With their enthusiastic backing, the Boston National League entry won championships in 1891, 1892, 1897, and 1898; however, management was not content with artistic success alone. The money-mad Arthur Soden boosted ticket prices in 1901, the year the American League put an entry in Beantown to contend for the hearts and minds of its fans. When former Beaneater heroes such as Hall of Famer Jimmy Collins and Chick Stahl left to join the new Somersets, McGreevy et al. moved with them.

These new Bostonians proved to be as formidable as the Beaneaters and won the American League pennant in 1903, but the Pirates took 3 of the first 4 games. In Game 5, played at Pittsburgh's Exposition Park, McGreevy and company serenaded the Iron City fans with a parody of a popular song called "Tessie."

Legend has it that the Rooters' spirited singing upset the Pirates so badly that the Somersets won three straight on the road and took Game 8 at home to become champs. According to Glenn Stout in the *Sox Fan News* (August 1986), "The Rooters were widely hailed in the press as the difference in the Series, and Nuf Ced McGreevy became a legend." He went to spring training every year thereafter, hunted with star pitcher Cy Young, and even signed a non-binding Red Sox contract as a "non-playing player."

His favored status took a tumble at the end of the 1912 World Series. By that time the Sox had moved to the Fens, built Fenway Park, and led the Giants, 3 games to 2. Better yet, warming up on a cold New England day they had Smoky Joe Wood, the dominant pitcher in baseball, who was coming off a 34–5 season and was nearly unbeatable at home.

The fans filed in, but the Royal Rooters were nowhere to be seen. When McGreevy and his friends did

appear — complete with a brass band — they were (deservedly) shocked to discover that their regular seats had been sold by impatient members of management.

Undaunted, McGreevy led the charge up the left field foul line to Duffy's Cliff (the incline named for Red Sox outfielder George "Duffy" Lewis). Once ensconced there, the Rooters refused to budge — even after mounted police tried to remove them forcibly. Eventually, management allowed the Rooters to roost on the gangplank in front of the left field stands.

Wood, thoroughly undone by the forty-five-minute delay, gave up seven hits in the first inning, and New York won, 11–4. Although the Red Sox won the next day to take the Series, this incident soured many on the Royal Rooters. McGreevy's influence faded further when Third Base moved and ended completely when Prohibition pushed it into foul territory in 1923. Before he was through, however, Michael McGreevy made his mark more than many players. Nuf Ced.

asked for and got his freedom. On July 8, McGraw announced that he had negotiated his release from the Orioles and had signed to manage the Giants for $11,000. What he didn't state was his plan to bring the Orioles to New York en masse. Brush briefly bought control of the Orioles and "released" pitcher Joe "Iron Man" McGinnity, catcher Roger Bresnahan, and two other players, who all signed with the Giants; on August 9, Brush sold the Reds and, a month later, bought the Giants. The Orioles, left with only five players, were forced to forfeit a game to St. Louis and their franchise to the league.

After Freedman sold his Giant stock, he was appointed a director of New York City's Interborough Rapid Transit Construction Company, which built the IRT subway line. Johnson wanted to build a ballpark between 142nd Street and 145th Street and Lenox Avenue, near a proposed IRT subway

After deliberately avoiding a World Series in 1904, John McGraw's Giants played the A's in 1905 and beat them as Christy Mathewson threw three complete-game shutouts in six days. The next year, McGraw's men appeared in uniforms proclaiming them World's Champions. This team shot shows Mathewson leaning against the first post from the left at Cincinnati's Palace of the Fans. To his immediate left are John McGraw, then Roger Bresnahan. It is clear how high the curved boxes were, almost twice the height of the average Giant.

stop. AL officials urged John B. MacDonald of the IRT to buy the site and lease it to the club. MacDonald got an approval from his boss, August Belmont II, but Freedman scuttled the plan, forcing the league to seek another site.

Johnson swallowed his scruples and made a deal with a pair of shady characters and a front man. For $18,000, he sold the Baltimore franchise to Joseph Gordon, a beard for "Big Bill" Devery, one of Manhattan's biggest gamblers, and Frank Farrell, who owned 250 pool halls and nearly as many politicians. The deal resulted in the establishment of Hilltop Park, the New York Yankees' first home.

The previous December, the National League had adopted a resolution to "seek a peaceful settlement of the so-called baseball war." At the time, Johnson was in New York, completing his deal with Gordon, and the resolution was brought to him. The two sides met on January 9, 1903, at Cincinnati's Grand Hotel and made an agreement that

◆ settled territorial rights and ownership.
◆ recognized the reserve clause in both leagues' contracts.
◆ sought cooperation in scheduling games (to avoid conflicts).
◆ decided that "neither circuit could be changed without the consent of a majority of the clubs in each league."

A year after McGraw left Baltimore and Brush abandoned Cincinnati to make their marks in Manhattan, their worst enemy, Ban Johnson, had put a competing club in Washington Heights. Ironically, it was the only point in Manhattan big enough for a ballpark and high enough to look down on Coogan's Bluff. Nevertheless, the settlement of 1903 created a structure that survived with sixteen clubs in the same cities for exactly fifty years.

THE YANKEES' FIRST HOME: HILLTOP PARK

Nearly a year before the settlement, Farrell and Devery had found a site for a ballpark two blocks east of the Hudson River — a lot that ran from 165th Street to 168th Street between Broadway and Fort Washington Avenue in Washington Heights, the highest point on Manhattan Island.

Arranging to lease it for ten years from the New York Institute of the Blind, they spent $200,000 just to excavate the rocky terrain. Workmen replaced 12,000 cubic yards of rock, blasted a natural rockpile where the grandstand was to be, and used most of 30,000 cubic yards of rocks and earth to fill in a swamp at the Broadway edge of the field.

When all was said and done, Farrell and Devery had built a 16,000-seat park for $75,000, the last

Pitchers Practice at Cincinnati Ball Park.

If this postcard view of the Palace of the Fans is taken at face value, the owners didn't have much regard for the well-being of their stars in 1907. The player crouching in front of the target — fully exposed to bad hops or errant throws — is Honus Wagner, who was on his way to winning his fifth of eight batting titles.

time a big league park was built for five figures. On Opening Day, April 30, 1903, it was officially called American League Park and the team was to be known as the Highlanders, at Gordon's request; the Gordon Highlanders were the best-known regiment in the British army. However, newspapers soon referred to the park by its lofty location, and, by extension, the team became known sporadically as the Hilltoppers.

The park was in poor condition, as Marc Okkonen explains in *Yankee* magazine:

> The swamp in right field was not yet filled and had to be roped off, creating an abnormally short distance from home plate. The outfield was unsodded dirt and and sloped unevenly down toward the fences. The unfinished grandstand was little more than a huge bleacher — unpainted with only the roof supports in place and no roof.

The players had to dress at their hotels because the clubhouse wasn't finished either, and anything hit past the swamp in right was a ground rule double. (A bit later in the home stand, a heavy rain created a gully in right; rightfielder "Wee Willie" Keeler was forced to stand on a wooden platform placed over the impromptu ravine.)

The march of "progress" brought Hilltop a parking lot in 1906 and a co-tenant in 1911 when the Polo Grounds burned. It is fun to speculate on just how thrilled Brush and McGraw must have been to ask to rent the ballpark they'd fought so hard to keep from being built.

The original lease was up after the 1912 season. The team officially became the Yankees in 1913 and moved into the Polo Grounds, signing another ten-year lease from 1913 through 1922; when it expired, the new owners built Yankee Stadium. Hilltop Park was torn down in 1914, and the site is now occupied by Columbia-Presbyterian Medical Center, which was built in 1928.

THE GREATEST PENNANT RACES OF ALL TIME

Angus Abbott, an Englishman, wrote in 1904,

The Americans have a genius for taking a thing, examining its every part, and developing each part to the utmost. This they have done with our game of rounders, and from a clumsy, primitive pastime, have so tightened its joints and put such a fine finish on its points that it stands forth a complicated machine of infinite exactitude.

If keen competition is a measure of infinite exactitude, that machine reached one of its high points in 1908 when seven teams in two leagues were still

battling tooth-and-nail for the pennants two days before the season ended. The effect of these races, which involved both Chicago teams as well as clubs in Cleveland, Detroit, New York, Pittsburgh, and St. Louis, was to make baseball front-page news across the country and spur owners to quickly build bigger ballparks.

The American League race had been tight all year, with the Tigers, Indians, Browns, and White Sox duking it out. The Indians were 11 games under .500 on September 6, then won 16 of their next 18 to make it a three-cornered race, and the Browns went on a tear as well; on September 24, just 2½ games separated the four teams. Then the Tigers swept the Senators in 4 straight while the Cleveland Naps (for Napoleon Lajoie) won 3 of 4 from the A's.

Cleveland had to beat the White Sox at League Park to have a chance. On Friday, October 2, Addie Joss of the Naps faced Ed Walsh, who had pitched and won both ends of a doubleheader three days earlier. Walsh was masterful, giving up only four hits and allowing a single run. Joss was even better — perfect, in fact — mowing down all 27 Chicago batters he faced. Sadly, the Naps lost the next day, 3–2, and were held to a tie, a win, and a loss by St. Louis; when Detroit's Bill Donovan beat Chicago, 7–0, on the last day of the season, Detroit won the pennant by ½ game over Cleveland and 1½ games over Chicago. The Naps argued that Detroit should make up a rained-out game, but the protest went unheeded; however, both leagues quickly adopted a rule that rained-out games affecting the pennant should be replayed.

The Cubs, Giants, and Pirates had also been in a dogfight for the National League pennant. On Monday, July 20, Pittsburgh was a game ahead of the Giants and 1½ ahead of Chicago. The day before, the *Chicago Tribune* ran its "Inquisitive Fans" column of letters. One of them read:

> In the last half of the ninth, with the score tied, two men out and a runner on third, the batter hits to left and the runner scores. The batter, seeing the runner score, stops between home and first. The ball is thrown to the first base-man, who touches his base before the batter reaches it. Can the runner score on this?

The *Trib*'s answer was "No. Run cannot score when third out is made before reaching first." When the Cubs and Giants took a nosedive in August, the letter was forgotten; the Pirates led New York by 3 and Chicago by 6. Then it was Pittsburgh's turn to slip, and by August 24 their lead was just a ½ game over the Giants and 3½ over the Cubs.

On August 30, as the Cubs and Giants were ready to do battle at West Side Park in Chicago, electric scoreboards were posted at the corner of Madison and Dearborn streets, and 10,000 people watched every play while an equal number observed a recreation at the Illinois Central Rail-road station. Although Sunday ball was still illegal in New York, an electric diamond outside Madison

A panorama of Baker Bowl in 1904 gives a good view of the medieval turrets that anchored both ends of the grandstand. The tracks of the Philadelphia and Reading Railroad ran in a tunnel under the field from right to right center and gave the outfield its nickname, "the Hump." Note the alleyway between the mound and the plate and the triangular chalk lines behind it. Signs on the outfield walls admonish fans to use no insulting or other improper language or conduct.

Before moving to Braves Field in 1915, the Braves played at South End Grounds, the rebuilt version of "the Grand Pavilion" (see Chapter 2). John McGraw is coaching third base for the visiting Giants in this 1906 game. The Brigham's hotel and restaurant advertised in right field bears no relation to the New England ice cream chain started in 1914.

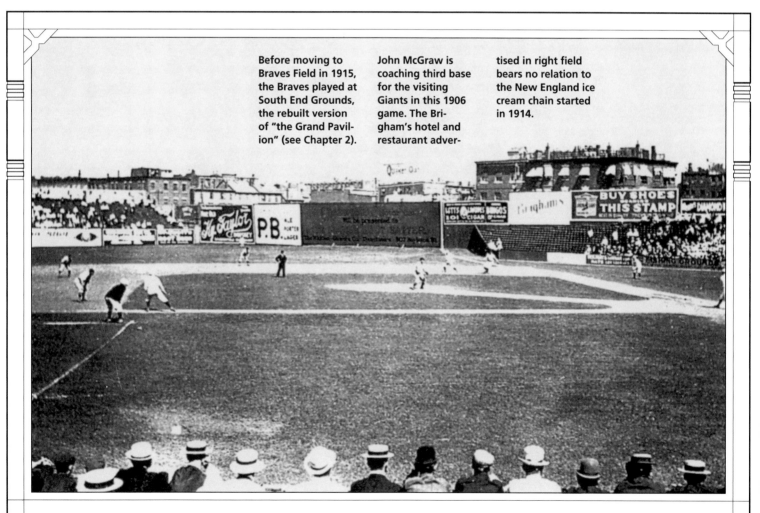

Holiday double-headers always drew huge crowds, and this July 4, 1907, twin bill at New York's Hilltop Park was no exception (top). Hilltop had only 16,000 seats, but a crowd that *Sporting Life* estimated at 20,000 showed up for the two games. If they were ever bored, the fans sitting in left field could look out at the Hudson River (above).

Square Garden gave the play-by-play, and the *New York Times* reported:

> Thousands of businessmen temporarily gave up business to devote themselves to base-ball. . . . Steady processions departed offices to hunt the nearest source of information . . . even in hospitals the baseball tidings were carried to patients. Everything was sidetracked for the latest news from the baseball war.

The news got hotter on September 4 when the Cubs lost to Pittsburgh, 1–0, in ten innings at Exposition Park but lodged a protest, claiming the run should not have scored. With one out in the bottom of the tenth, the Pirates loaded the bases; outfielder John "Chief" Wilson singled to short center, and Fred Clarke scored the winning run. Buc first baseman Warren Gill, who had reached first when hit by a pitch, turned and started for the clubhouse. Cub second baseman Johnny Evers, seeing Gill head off the field, called for the ball and touched second with it. Evers then charged umpire Hank O'Day and told him that the side had

been retired and that Clarke's run didn't count, but Chicago protested in vain.

In *The Unforgettable Season,* G. H. Fleming surmises that the earlier letter to the editor may have given Evers the idea. He says, "Not only Evers but other members of the Chicago team, including Slagle and Tinker, did not immediately head for the clubhouse but held their ground as if anticipating Gill's infraction."

Of course, nineteen days later another opposing runner, this time Fred Merkle of the Giants, also failed to touch second base. Evers again touched the base to "force" him before Harry "Moose" McCormick could score; O'Day ruled the game a tie, and league president Harry Pulliam upheld him on October 3. Pulliam ruled that the Cubs and Giants would play off the tie game, if necessary, to settle the pennant race. While the *Pittsburgh Press* printed extras on Sunday to keep up with the news, the *Chicago Tribune* actually *sold* tickets at Orchestra Hall, for 25 cents, 50 cents, and $1, so fans could see an electrical recreation of the playoff game.

This view of the Polo Grounds is taken from behind first base up to the apartment houses overlooking Coogan's Bluff. An unidentified Red has just crossed the bag, apparently heeding the warning in the coaches' box to "Stop." This bit of arcana is not explained, nor are the circles behind first and second that resemble nothing so much as manhole covers. Note also the wooden fences in right center.

The Polo Grounds was the most interesting of the three New York ballparks in the era before concrete. Cars from the Eighth Avenue IND line clattered by the Polo Grounds and descended below street level for maintenance. As Lawrence Ritter has observed in *Lost Ballparks*, it was "the only major league ballpark where the most convenient way to get to upper-deck grandstand seats was by walking *down* rather than up." Note the sign "To the grand stand," coal cars on the railroad tracks at right, and the original High Bridge in the background over the Harlem River.

Opening Day was a special occasion in the early 1900s, particularly after the jingoism that infected the nation after the Spanish-American War. Red, white, and blue bunting was the order of the day, and fans were expected to dress up for the occasion. Ticket prices were fairly high, as at this 1907 opener at Washington Park in Brooklyn. For the price of a grandstand seat, Brooklynites could buy four wax cylinder recordings (early records) from Sears, Roebuck and still have change.

Exposition Park was a Pittsburgh fixture from 1882 and was used by American Association, Players League, National League, and Federal League teams. However, its location along the Allegheny River caused problems. When floodwaters submerged the city in 1902, a July Fourth morning-afternoon doubleheader was played even though at least a foot of water covered the outfield. A ground rule, passed just for that day, made all balls hit to the outfield automatic singles. With 10,000 fans looking on, both games were played, and the ball was dried after every pitch.

SMOKEY CITY.

On October 8, the *New York Evening Telegram* reported that

the largest crowd ever gathered in the world for a sporting event — fully a quarter of a million people — were surging in and around the Polo Grounds. . . . From the press box the skyline everywhere was human heads. They were located on grandstand, roofs, fences, "L" structures [elevated railways], electric light poles and in the distance on smokestacks, chimneys, advertising signs, and copings of apartment houses.

Lest one think that this was hyperbole, listen to W. J. Lampton of the *New York Times*: "If 35,000 were inside, 35,000,000 were outside. . . . Never before in the history of the game have there been so many to see a game who didn't see it."

The Cubs won the playoff game, 4–2, and Mordecai Centennial "Three Finger" Brown won that game and 2 more in the World Series as the Cubs tamed the Tigers in 5 games. But the significance of the events of 1908 were to vault baseball to new heights of popularity. That summer a songwriter named Jack Norworth, who had never been to a game in his life, wrote "Take Me Out to the Ball Game." That fall James Buchanan Duke, the czar of the American Tobacco Company, decreed that his cigarettes would now be sold with cards of baseball players; eighty-three years later, hockey star Wayne Gretzky and Los Angeles Kings owner Bruce McNall paid $451,000 for one of them, featuring Honus Wagner.

The significance of that season for ballparks can best be summed up by a column W. A. Phelon wrote in *Sporting Life* on August 8:

Baseball is only in its infancy . . . and it looks as though ball parks now in existence would be all too small for the multitudes ten years from now. . . . On some grounds — like the Cub park, for instance — the limit has been reached in seating capacity. The solution: I have a photograph of the grandstand at Epson, the great English race course. It has six decks, rising high in the air. Six decks — just think of it! A six-decked stand . . . would hold 60,000 — and the day is not far distant when 60,000 people will be at baseball games. Yes.

Yes indeed, Mr. Phelon.

TIMELINE

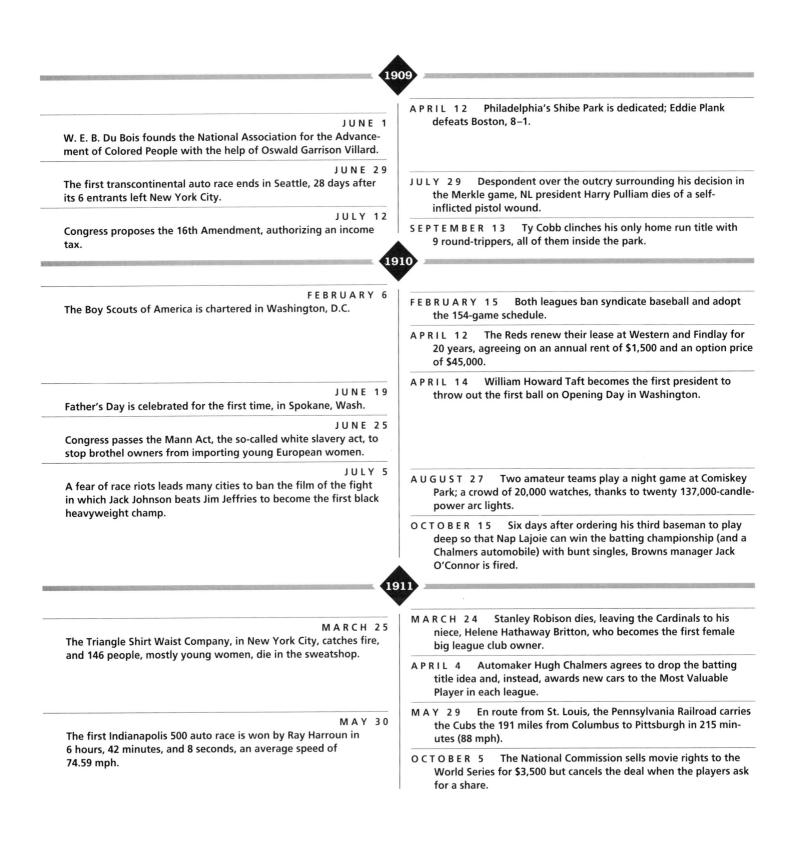

1909

JUNE 1
W. E. B. Du Bois founds the National Association for the Advancement of Colored People with the help of Oswald Garrison Villard.

JUNE 29
The first transcontinental auto race ends in Seattle, 28 days after its 6 entrants left New York City.

JULY 12
Congress proposes the 16th Amendment, authorizing an income tax.

APRIL 12 Philadelphia's Shibe Park is dedicated; Eddie Plank defeats Boston, 8–1.

JULY 29 Despondent over the outcry surrounding his decision in the Merkle game, NL president Harry Pulliam dies of a self-inflicted pistol wound.

SEPTEMBER 13 Ty Cobb clinches his only home run title with 9 round-trippers, all of them inside the park.

1910

FEBRUARY 6
The Boy Scouts of America is chartered in Washington, D.C.

JUNE 19
Father's Day is celebrated for the first time, in Spokane, Wash.

JUNE 25
Congress passes the Mann Act, the so-called white slavery act, to stop brothel owners from importing young European women.

JULY 5
A fear of race riots leads many cities to ban the film of the fight in which Jack Johnson beats Jim Jeffries to become the first black heavyweight champ.

FEBRUARY 15 Both leagues ban syndicate baseball and adopt the 154-game schedule.

APRIL 12 The Reds renew their lease at Western and Findlay for 20 years, agreeing on an annual rent of $1,500 and an option price of $45,000.

APRIL 14 William Howard Taft becomes the first president to throw out the first ball on Opening Day in Washington.

AUGUST 27 Two amateur teams play a night game at Comiskey Park; a crowd of 20,000 watches, thanks to twenty 137,000-candle-power arc lights.

OCTOBER 15 Six days after ordering his third baseman to play deep so that Nap Lajoie can win the batting championship (and a Chalmers automobile) with bunt singles, Browns manager Jack O'Connor is fired.

1911

MARCH 25
The Triangle Shirt Waist Company, in New York City, catches fire, and 146 people, mostly young women, die in the sweatshop.

MAY 30
The first Indianapolis 500 auto race is won by Ray Harroun in 6 hours, 42 minutes, and 8 seconds, an average speed of 74.59 mph.

MARCH 24 Stanley Robison dies, leaving the Cardinals to his niece, Helene Hathaway Britton, who becomes the first female big league club owner.

APRIL 4 Automaker Hugh Chalmers agrees to drop the batting title idea and, instead, awards new cars to the Most Valuable Player in each league.

MAY 29 En route from St. Louis, the Pennsylvania Railroad carries the Cubs the 191 miles from Columbus to Pittsburgh in 215 minutes (88 mph).

OCTOBER 5 The National Commission sells movie rights to the World Series for $3,500 but cancels the deal when the players ask for a share.

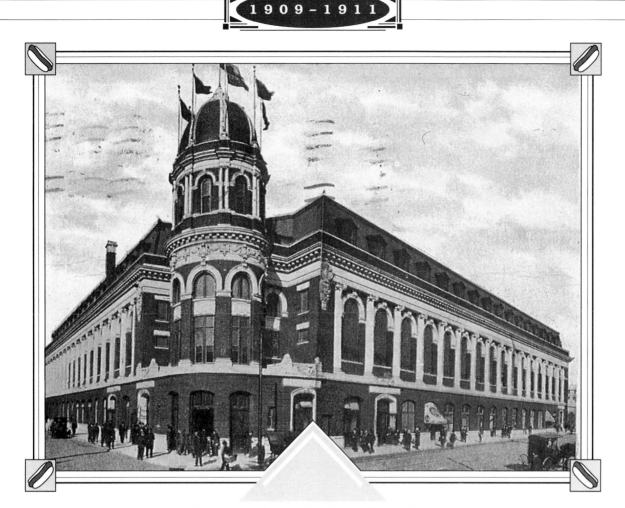

C H A P T E R   F I V E

Steeling Home

The use of reinforced concrete as a building material coincided quite nicely with the memorable two-league pennant races of 1908.

Always ahead of his time, Frank Lloyd Wright had used reinforced concrete in 1906 to build the Unity Temple in Oak Park, Illinois. Wright knew reinforced concrete was less expensive than stone and more durable than steel, which, used alone, could easily crack. Placing rods in concrete shaped by wooden forms reduced the amount of steel needed, increased the strength of the steel used, and fireproofed it as well.

The American League owners particularly took note, because its first-generation parks, dating from 1901, had been swiftly built affairs constructed mainly of wood. By 1909, however, the league was an equal partner in Organized Baseball, and something more permanent was in order. Entrepreneurial owners like the Athletics' Ben Shibe and White Sox boss Charles Comiskey wanted to build parks far greater in capacity, fancier (to attract the more well-heeled fan), and more stable than Columbia Park in Philadelphia or South Side Park in Chicago.

From 1909 through 1911, AL teams built spanking new parks in three cities — Comiskey Park in Chicago, Shibe Park in Philadelphia, and Griffith Stadium in Washington; in two other cities, the existing parks were enlarged to more than double their seating capacity — League Park in Cleveland and Sportsman's Park in St. Louis. At the same time, only one National League park, the Polo Grounds, was rebuilt after a fire; it was left to Barney Dreyfuss, who owned the Pirates, to be the National League's visionary, while A's owners Connie Mack and Ben Shibe served that purpose in the American League. These owners built the first concrete and steel ballparks in their respective leagues; both were in Pennsylvania; both were "born" in the same year, 1909, underwent major renovation in the same year, 1925, and "died" in the same year, 1970.

CONCRETE PROPOSAL: SHIBE PARK

On Monday, April 12, 1909, the first new ballpark built solely of steel and concrete opened its doors on Lehigh Avenue between 20th and 21st streets in Philadelphia.

What Philadelphians saw on that spring day was a dignified palace reminiscent of a bank or a library, with masses of pennants, ornamental

It would be difficult to imagine a more magnificent exterior for a ballpark than that of Philadelphia's Shibe Park in 1909. Built in the French Renaissance style, the park featured decorative concrete trim over every archway and window, more "gingerbread" than in any other park. The crowning touch was the cupola on the third floor which housed Connie Mack's office. Note also, on this promotional postcard, the car and carriage, eloquent reminders that, despite the change from wood to steel and concrete inside, the outside remained in transition, halfway between horse power and horsepower.

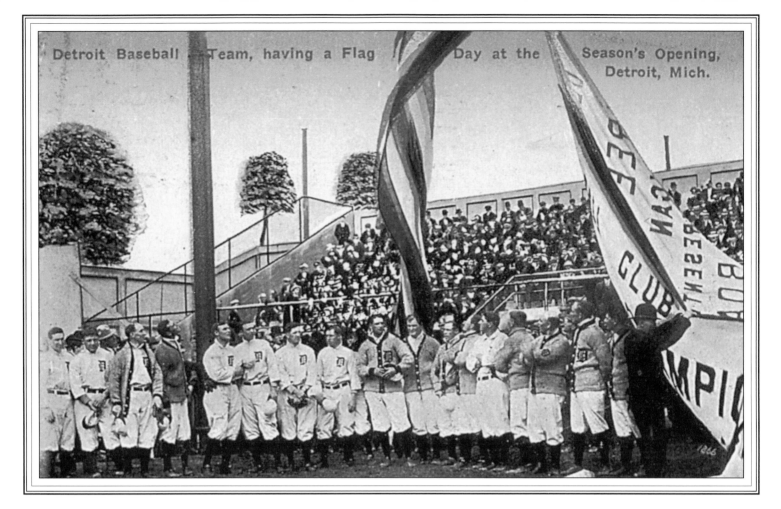

Detroit Baseball Team, having a Flag Day at the Season's Opening, Detroit, Mich.

scrollwork, and a fabulous French Renaissance cupola, which housed Connie Mack's office. Moreover, this wonder was not in Chestnut Hill or any other high-toned part of town but smack in the heart of North Philadelphia, in a neighborhood once known as Swampoodle for its tendency to get mushy in wet weather. The irony of putting the first modern baseball stadium in an area better known for its noisy truck gardens, pigs, horses, and ice wagons was lost on its residents at the time, but we can readily appreciate it today.

Shibe Park was built at a cost of $300,000. (In contrast, the wooden Columbia Park had cost $7,500, one fortieth as much, eight years earlier.) The park had sod transplanted from Columbia Park, parking spaces for 400 cars, and seats for 23,000. The double-decked grandstand hugged the infield in a half-hexagon, and open single-decked bleachers continued down the rest of both foul lines. The dimensions were generous: left field was 378 feet from the plate, right a smaller 340; at 515 feet, center field was more than twice as far from the plate as the right field line of the Polo Grounds in its later days (257 feet).

On Opening Day, the *Philadelphia Inquirer* reported that 30,162 people, "the greatest crowd that has ever witnessed a baseball game," paid to enter while "5,000 others gained admission by invitation, by scaling the high walls, or pressing into the grounds when the gates were rushed by surging crowds."

Using tactics that Whitey Herzog would successfully revive seven decades later, Mack built his first juggernaut of a team (four pennants in five years) by fitting it to the ballpark. Given the original dimensions, Mack built himself a succession of

winners using speed, defense, and left-handed power. In 1910, the A's pitchers had an ERA of 1.79 and yielded just 441 runs in 155 games to lead the league. In 1911 Danny Murphy, a converted second baseman, led all outfielders with an unbelievable 34 assists, and Frank "Home Run" Baker cranked out an even dozen homers to top the league.

In 1924 and 1925, Mack had arguably the greatest talent-scouting years of any manager in baseball history. He brought to spring training in 1924 Max "Camera Eye" Bishop, who had a lifetime on-base percentage of .423, and Hall of Famer Al Simmons, who posted a lifetime batting average of .334. A year later he added three other Hall of Famers: Gordon "Mickey" Cochrane (.320 lifetime), Robert "Lefty" Grove (300 wins), and Jimmie Foxx (534 home runs).

In 1925, management unveiled what it called Greater Shibe Park. Mack double-decked and covered the bleachers down the foul lines, rebuilt the grandstand, which enclosed the entire playing surface except for right field, and pared the dimensions back in all fields — 334 in left, 468 in center, and 334 in right — to get in step with the modern power game and the advent of the lively ball. After coming close to the Yankees in 1928, the A's breezed to three straight pennants in 1929, 1930, and 1931.

After his second great run of stars, Mack once again disposed of them and attendance tumbled. In the midst of a Depression and a World War, no significant changes were made to Shibe Park, and Mack also lost his touch in discovering great ballplayers. The A's became not only a tail-ender but, along with the Senators and the Browns, a

The Twentieth Street Irregulars

Something in the American psyche fervently appreciates getting something for nothing, and baseball fans are no exception. From the sport's earliest days, rooters have breached any obstacle — rickety walls, barbed wire fences, precarious perches on billboards or telephone poles — to see games for free. The tradition, which started with Union Grounds in 1862, is still being assiduously continued at Wrigley Field in Chicago; fans who own multistory houses on North Sheffield Avenue entertain during games, and one has even posted a sign saying "495," the distance from home plate to his rooftop bleachers.

But these modern "wildcat bleachers," complete with microwave ovens and big-screen TVs, can't compare with the way the residents of North Philadelphia profited from their proximity to the ballpark. These Twentieth Street Irregulars probably made greater profits than Mack and Shibe (with decidedly smaller volume), offering parking, food and drink, and seats nearly as good as any in the park.

Although Philadelphians had used Twentieth Street's unobstructed view as far back as 1911, Bruce Kuklick describes in *To Every Thing a Season* how Shibe's wildcat bleachers became a cottage industry in the late 1920s:

> Neighbors hired lusty barkers to advertise the attractions of their seats over Shibe Park bleachers. Mothers made lemonade to sell to thirsty rooters and dispatched the kids to buy hot dogs from street vendors for a nickel. Back in their houses, the kids would sell them for a dime.

John J. Rooney, a psychology professor at LaSalle, wrote in a 1984 *Philadelphia Magazine* that the establishment of the automobile amounted to a personal bonanza: "I would simply sit out on my front step well before game time and wait for a car to park in my territory." Rooney would wave the motorist into the space, then ask, " 'Want me to watch your car, Mister?' Usually I'd get a nickel or a dime when the game was over." The Rooneys redid their living room on game days. As Rooney explains:

> Because of Shibe Park's low right-field fence [12 feet], you could see the field from our front bedroom and we equipped it with a set of portable bleachers. . . . To permit a better view, all four windows were removed and stored in the basement.

Other neighbors followed suit. When the A's won the pennant in 1929, the Twentieth Street entrepreneurs prepared to spring into action for the World Series; then a neighbor learned that tax collectors were planning to close the wildcat bleachers down completely unless tenants paid $50 per house. As word spread, the price was negotiated down to $35 and $30, and Rooney's father even got them to accept $20:

> The $20 that we paid in taxes was quickly recouped threefold from our paying customers. We got even more income when one of the cameramen from the Pathé News Newsreel Service asked what we would charge to let him film the home games of the World Series from our roof. "Twenty dollars," was Dad's quick reply. . . . We soon made similar arrange-

ments with Fox Movietone News and Universal News.

When the A's repeated in 1930, wooden bleachers were erected along most of Twentieth Street, and a block committee, deciding that solidarity was the order of the day, fixed prices. Kuklick says, "During the World Series estimates were that 3,000 people per game collected in the houses, paying from $7 to $25 per head." As the Depression deepened, though, such fancy prices were far too much of a good thing. After the 1931 Series, Rooney's father and his neighbors dropped their prices to a quarter and still managed to draw fans away from the park.

The A's management, which had long considered the wildcat bleachers an unfair drain on revenues, finally did something about it. In 1935 Jack Shibe, Ben's son and the A's new co-owner, added 38 feet of corrugated green metal to the existing fence, totally closing off the rooftop view; he simultaneously got an ordinance passed which prevented homeowners from building higher stands. The Twentieth Street fans felt that the fence had been built solely from spite, and the resulting "spite fence," also known as "the Great Tin Monster," was the subject of several unsuccessful legal challenges.

For years afterward, parents complained indignantly about the way the A's bosses had taken away their "golden eggs." The most unforgiving of all told their children to avoid Shibe, because "Connie Mack built that spite fence so you couldn't see the games from across the street." Had enough of them faithfully attended games at Shibe, the A's might not have had to move to Kansas City.

symbol of futility. (The Phils began playing at Shibe in 1938 and were equally futile.)

In 1953, Shibe Park was renamed Connie Mack Stadium to honor the Grand Old Man of Baseball and, it was hoped, to transform the feeling for him into increased ticket sales. Two years later, after the A's had moved to Kansas City, Phillies owner Robert Carpenter II made repairs that the Macks had had to put off. The sod was replaced and pro-

tected from the fans after games and, for the first time, Carpenter began selling signboard space to carry advertising. The park was painted, and the scoreboard in front of the right field wall was replaced with a hand-me-down, the old 60-foot-high Yankee Stadium scoreboard.

By the 1960s, no amount of paint could hide the signs of age in the Grand Old Lady of Lehigh Avenue, and Philadelphia began planning a new home for the Phillies. The voters approved a $25 million bond issue in November 1964, and construction started on what became Veterans Stadium on October 2, 1967 (see Chapter 9).

When the last game was played at Shibe, on October 1, 1970, management had tried to anticipate problems with souvenir hunters by giving away 62 prizes in a postgame drawing, including the home plate rake, left field distance sign (334), pitching rubber, and Jim Bunning's locker seat. In addition, every fan got a souvenir seat slat on entering. Lowell Reidenbaugh relates what happened later in *Take Me Out to the Ball Park:*

> The slats turned to clubs in the hands of exuberant marauders. Ripping, slashing, crushing, the fans made a shambles of the old park. One muscular miscreant succeeded in detaching a toilet bowl and toted it triumphantly from the park. Some brought saws and hammers to the park. In the melee that followed the end of the game, fans ripped up souvenir sod and thirty-five people had their heads bashed with souvenir slats of wood.

Home plate survived fans' attempts to dislodge it and was taken to Veterans Stadium. On August 20, 1971, the first year the Phillies played at the Vet, a fire started by youngsters heavily damaged the vacated stadium, and the grandstand roof collapsed. By 1974 Shibe was a junkyard, six acres of weeds.

A city judge had ordered Phils owner Robert Carpenter III to raze the park; when he refused, the city did it for him. As things turned out, the last ball thrown at Connie Mack Stadium was made of steel and weighed three tons. In a poignant piece of symbolism, while the 1976 All-Star Game was being played at Veterans Stadium, Shibe Park was being demolished and eventually became the site of the Deliverance Evangelistic Church. Nevertheless, parts of it are still part of baseball; some of its seats are still in use at War Memorial Stadium in Greensboro, North Carolina, and Duncan Park in Spartanburg, South Carolina.

Dreyfuss's Folly: Forbes Field

Unlike Ben Shibe and Connie Mack, Barney Dreyfuss had no baseball background, but he was a shrewd businessman.

A German immigrant, Dreyfuss had worked his way up by cleaning barrels at a distillery in Louisville, Kentucky, eventually becoming its general manager. Since his boss also owned the National League's Louisville Colonels, Dreyfuss became the team's general manager, too, and saw at first hand just how big a business baseball was becoming. When the Colonels were dropped from the league in 1900, Dreyfuss decided to stay in baseball; he bought the Pittsburgh Pirates and transferred his team — including Honus Wagner — to Pittsburgh.

Rather than pay for high-priced property, the canny Dreyfuss chose to buy land cheap, intending to lavish most of his money on appointments for the new park. With the help of his fellow industrialist and friend Andrew Carnegie, Dreyfuss purchased seven acres opposite the Carnegie Library in Schenley Farms, later Schenley Park. Because it was so far from the thick of things — a ten-minute trolley ride from downtown — skeptics dubbed the spot Dreyfuss's Folly. Nevertheless, ground was broken on March 1, 1909, and a ravine that divided the property was quickly filled in. The first National League park built from scratch of concrete and steel required 40 train carloads of ornamental iron, 70 of seats, 110 of cement, 130 of structural steel, and 650 of sand and gravel.

Forbes Field opened not four months later, on June 30, 1909. Although reporters urged Dreyfuss to name the park after himself, he instead named it after a hero of the French and Indian War, the Scotch Brigadier General John Forbes. His nickname, "Old Ironsides," fit the concrete and steel park perfectly.

There was much to comment on that was new:

◆ ramps — to help speed fans to and from their seats.

◆ elevators — to get well-heeled fans to the luxury boxes on the third deck, "making them accessible for those who do not like to mount stairs or inclines."

◆ rooms for the umpires as well as a visiting clubhouse provided with the same lockers, baths, and clothes-drying apparatus as those in the home clubhouse.

◆ color — to distinguish the park from present and future competitors. The exterior was a buff-colored terra cotta with the monogram PAC (for Pittsburgh Athletic Company) spelled out in square blocks with numerous green panels for contrast. The steelwork was painted a lighter green, and the roof was covered with red-tinted slate.

◆ no signs — to keep the park's pastoral setting free of commercials. Except for ads for war stamps during World War I and war bonds during World War II, Dreyfuss's masterpiece remained pristine at a cost William Benswanger, his son-in-law, estimated as more than $1 million in revenue.

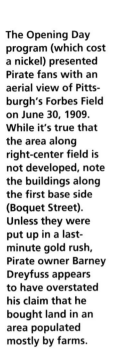

The Opening Day program (which cost a nickel) presented Pirate fans with an aerial view of Pittsburgh's Forbes Field on June 30, 1909. While it's true that the area along right-center field is not developed, note the buildings along the first base side (Boquet Street). Unless they were put up in a last-minute gold rush, Pirate owner Barney Dreyfuss appears to have overstated his claim that he bought land in an area populated mostly by farms.

Since Shibe Park and Forbes Field, the first steel and concrete parks in their respective leagues, were built in the same year, one might have expected the two Pennsylvania cities to be more in tune architecturally. Instead, Shibe Park, with its French Renaissance inspiration, seems more of a piece with the old South End Grounds (see Chapter 2), whereas the exterior of Forbes Field shows far more modern influences. Note the vertical columns of cross-hatched diamonds that resemble steel latticework and delineate each window and the diamonds beneath each one that differentiate the upper from the lower deck.

COPR. THE PICTORIAL NEWS CO. N.Y.

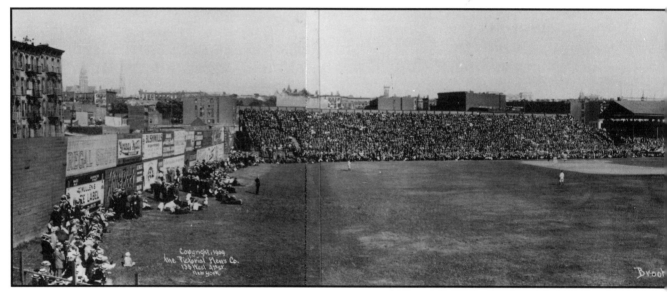

Copyright, 1909
The Pictorial News Co.
136 West 41st
New York

Brook

Comparing these postcard views of Forbes Field in Pittsburgh and Washington Park in Brooklyn speaks volumes about the differences between wooden and steel and concrete parks. The grandstand at Washington Park in 1909 (above) represents only a slight improvement over the Saratoga grandstand from 1867, even in this panoramic view (right), while the differences between the two contemporary parks are far more striking. The double-decking and sheer mass of Forbes Field (above right) make the Brooklyn park seem flimsy by comparison.

Dreyfuss was lavish in his spending and expected fans to be equally lavish in theirs, charging $1.25 for box seats and $1 for reserved grandstand seats. He also wanted his ballplayers to earn home runs. According to the *Forbes Field 60th Anniversary Picture Album,* Dreyfuss "hated cheap home runs and vowed he'd have none in his park." The original outfield distances — 360 in left, 462 in center, and 376 in right — were in keeping with the dimensions of the day and the owner's prejudices. (The first time a drive cleared the right field roof was May 25, 1935, when Babe Ruth hit his last home run as a Brave.) Precisely because of its generous dimensions, Forbes turned out to be a haven for triples and *inside-the-park* home runs. Yet, throughout its useful life, Forbes would be one of the toughest major league parks to hit home runs *out of.*

One of the park's other anomalies was its backstop. The average major league backstop is some 60 feet from home plate. Forbes's, however, was 110 feet. Despite this tremendous plus for the defense, it is one of the park's mysteries that, in the course of more than 4,000 games, no major league pitcher was able to throw a no-hitter there.

On Opening Day, it consisted of a roofed double-decked grandstand that curved around home plate and extended some 30 feet past first and third bases. On the roof was a third deck — the $1.25 seats for the rich, the high, the well-born.

From the start, it was clear that Dreyfuss's Folly would turn out to be Dreyfuss's Windfall. Although the park's capacity was originally 25,000, a crowd of 30,338 saw the Cubs beat the Buccos, 3–2, on Opening Day. According to *Take Me Out to the Ball Park*, Dreyfuss said, "One friend bet me a $150 suit

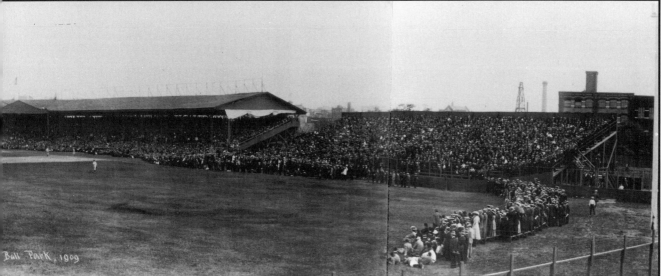

Ball Park, 1909

we would never fill the park, but we filled it five times the first two weeks."

Just as Connie Mack found a clutch of Hall of Famers in the mid-1920s, the Pirates also discovered Paul "Big Poison" Waner and Lloyd "Little Poison" Waner, Harold "Pie" Traynor, and Hazen "Kiki" Cuyler. As attendance increased, the right field grandstand was extended into the right field corner and well into fair territory. Since the addition reduced the outfield dimension from 376 to 300 feet, Dreyfuss erected a 28-foot-high screen to limit the home runs.

In 1938, Benswanger constructed a new press box on the roof of the grandstand behind home plate in anticipation of winning another pennant. The Pirates had a 3½-game lead over the Cubs in late September, but Chicago cut the margin by 2 games. On September 28, with two out in the bot-

tom of the ninth, the score tied, 5–5, and dusk falling, Charles "Gabby" Hartnett hit his famous "Homer in the Gloamin' " at Wrigley Field, and the Cubs went on to win the pennant. The press box, a symbol of Pirate frustration, became known thereafter as the Crow's Nest.

After World War II, the Pirates tried to buy their way back into contention, in part by acquiring Hank Greenberg from the Tigers. In a move that would have made Dreyfuss turn over in his grave, the bullpens of both the home and visiting clubs were shifted from foul territory to the base of the scoreboard in left field and fenced in. This act effectively cut 30 feet off the distance from the plate (to 335), and it was hoped that "Greenberg Gardens" would help the Bucs' resurgence. Greenberg hit 25 homers and retired; however, another right-handed slugger, Ralph Kiner, set a team record by

COPY'T 1909 BY THE GEO. R. LAWRENCE CO., CHICAGO.

Albert Spalding's White Stockings (Cubs) played Sunday games at Chicago's West Side Grounds in 1893 to take advantage of the crowds attending the nearby Columbia Exposition and moved there permanently in 1894. Joe Tinker, Johnny Evers, and Frank Chance led the Cubs to three straight pennants here from 1906 to 1908; they stayed through the 1915 season before moving to Weeghman Park (Wrigley Field). The park, seen here in 1909, can always be spotted by the unique round areas at first base, third base, and home plate.

hitting 31 dingers at home in 1948 and won or tied for seven straight National League home run crowns (see Chapter 8).

In the 1950s, the park rapidly began to go downhill; one sportswriter called it "as joyless as a prison exercise yard." The Pirates played their last game at Forbes Field on June 28, 1970, two days short of its sixty-first birthday. Some seats were donated to the Cy Young Museum in Toledo, Roberto Clemente and longtime Pirate announcer Bob Prince bought some as souvenirs, and other Forbes memorabilia were installed at the Allegheny Club, the restaurant in Three Rivers Stadium. Scheduled for demolition, Forbes was damaged by one fire on Christmas Eve and completely destroyed by another seven months later.

The space was taken over by the University of Pittsburgh, which has preserved home plate in Lucite at its exact location, now the lobby of the Forbes Quadrangle building. Sections of the ivy-covered outfield wall have also been preserved, and a plaque marks the spot where Bill Mazeroski's homer ended the 1960 World Series.

THE OLD ROMAN'S EMPIRE: COMISKEY PARK

Nicknamed "the Old Roman" for his classical profile and noble mane of flowing white hair, Charles Comiskey took an abandoned garbage dump not far from Chicago's odoriferous stockyards and had the audacity to build what he called

the Baseball Palace of the World. Against the odds, he built a field that had an eighty-year run and was, at the time of its closing in September 1990, the oldest existing big league ballpark.

South Side baseball fans have seen it all: the underdog "Hitless Wonders," who nickel-and-dimed a World Series in 1906; "the Black Sox," who threw one in 1919; and "the Go-Go Sox," who nearly stole one in 1959. Comiskey showcased the talents of hurlers "Big Ed" Walsh, Eddie Cicotte, Ted Lyons, and Billy Pierce as well as middle infielders from Eddie Collins to Luke Appling to Luis Aparicio to Ozzie Guillen and outfielders from Joe Jackson to Bo Jackson. Comiskey unveiled the first as well as two other All-Star Games, numerous Negro League World Series games, and East-West All-Star Games.

It is astonishing that all of this action took place not far from the stench of the stockyards. Infielder Tony Cuccinello, who ended his career with the Sox, said the wind generally blew in at Comiskey; however, he said, "when you could smell the stockyards, that meant the wind was blowing out, blowing with the hitter."

But Comiskey was a pitcher's park. One pitcher, the Sox stopper and Hall of Famer "Big Ed" Walsh, became the only pitcher who was active in planning a ballpark. Walsh toured Forbes, Shibe, and other parks with Zachary Taylor Davis's colleague, architect Karl Vitzhum, to help design Comiskey Park.

Davis, who later designed Wrigley Field, approved of the basic design of Forbes Field and

Comiskey Park's archlike openings were in place on Opening Day, July 1, 1910 (above). Planned, at least in part, by Hall of Fame pitcher Ed Walsh, Comiskey was a pitcher's park right off the bat. In its first full decade, (1911–1920), 153 home runs were hit in 752 games (not 770 because of ties and the curtailed 1918 season). Although this card is titled South Side Ball Park (below), it shows Comiskey Park when it opened, from the right field corner.

On June 18, 1909,
the first modern
(post-1900) game of
night baseball was
played at the Palace
of the Fans in
Cincinnati. George
Cahill of Holyoke,
Mass., who also
created a pitching
machine, erected
five steel towers,
and lights were
strung for the game
between the Elks
lodges of Cincinnati
and nearby New-
port, Kentucky.
A crowd of 3,000
was on hand, as
were the Reds and
Phillies, who
stayed after their
afternoon game
to watch the
festivities.

adapted it to what was, at the time, the largest lot in the major leagues. Thus he created a double-decked grandstand curving around home plate 30 feet or so beyond the bases and detached single-decked pavilions continuing down the foul lines. The original dimensions were 362 feet down the foul lines (in reality old water hoses, squooshed flat and painted white) and 420 to straightaway center.

Few ballfields have gotten off to so unabashedly sentimental a start as Comiskey Park. During the winter of 1909–1910, Sox catcher Billy Sullivan went to Ireland and brought back, literally, a piece of the "auld sod." On St. Patrick's Day, 1910, Davis placed a solitary green brick on the sod, and it became the cornerstone of Comiskey Park.

As great a park as the original Comiskey was, it might have been grander and more innovative. The facade had originally been planned as an elab-orate Romanesque design, in keeping with the grandeur of Shibe Park as well as Comiskey's nick-name. However, Commy, widely known as a nickel-nurser, decided to save $350,000 and put up a plain red brick facade instead. Davis and Vitzhum had designed the upper deck to be can-tilevered, but Comiskey also vetoed that suggestion as too costly. Still, the final tab for the park was $550,000 for the building and $150,000 for the land, a mighty amount of money for a ballpark.

In 1919, South Siders watched their heroes waltz away with the pennant but drop 3 of 4 home games to the Reds and lose the best-of-nine Series, 5 games to 3. The following September, it was dis-covered that Comiskey Park had smelled not only because of the stockyards, but because seven of the eight Black Sox had thrown the Series; the Sox wouldn't return to the Fall Classic until 1959.

After the 1926 City Series, the original single-decked grandstand pavilions were double-decked, and the wooden bleachers in left and right were replaced by steel and concrete. What had been a pitcher's park in the dead-ball era was updated, and though the foul lines were reduced to 352, cen-ter field was enlarged to 440 feet, with 10-foot-high walls all around. The capacity increased to 52,000, giving more Sox fans an opportunity to watch Babe Ruth destroy their team. On August 16, 1927, Ruth became the first hitter to clear the roof at Comiskey, hitting #37 off right-hander Tommy Thomas in an 8–1 Yankee win.

Before the 1934 season, the infield was moved out 14 feet to give slugger Al Simmons a better shot at the fences in his second season with the Sox; however, this transformation failed, like most short-term changes. Simmons became a Tiger in 1936, and the plate was returned to its original location in 1937.

The big news at Comiskey after World War II was the coming of "Trader Frank" Lane as general man-ager in 1948; in six years, Lane traded, bought, or sold 298 players in 192 deals. He was also active

on the field. In 1949, he installed fences that cut the foul lines from 352 to 332; the night before the hard-hitting Yankees came to town, however, the fences miraculously disappeared. The league quickly passed "the Lane rule," mandating that fences could only be moved once a season.

When the equally flamboyant Bill Veeck took over, he too made changes, painting the exterior of Comiskey white and building the first exploding scoreboard. In August 1959, with the Sox in the thick of a pennant race, he acquired Ted Kluszewski for Harry "Suitcase" Simpson and minor league first baseman Bob Sagers. Big Klu helped bring the South Siders their first pennant in forty years and, although they lost to the Dodgers, drove in 10 runs, a record for a 6-game World Series.

Veeck sold the Sox to the Allyn family, who ran the team from 1961 through 1975, renamed the field White Sox Park once again to expunge the Comiskey name, and decided to "adapt" it to fit the players rather than the reverse. Following orders, the groundskeeping Bossard family (Roger, Gene, and Emil) tailored the park daily to revive the "home field advantage" given Oriole Park in the 1890s.

The mounds in the opposing bullpen were raised and lowered from what was, at the time, the standard height (10 inches) to upset the opposition's rhythm. The infield grass was left long in front of Chicago fielders with limited range but cut short in front of speedsters. Similarly, the outfield stayed long when the Pale Hose had speedy line drive hitters, turning singles into doubles; when the Sox outfield was lacking defensively, long grass turned potential opposing triples into doubles.

The Bossards added white paint to the water hoses on the foul lines to tilt foul balls fair when the Sox had skillful bunters. When sinkerballers pitched for the opposition, the area in front of the plate was mixed with clay and gasoline to help ground balls scoot through the infield; however, when the Sox had sinkerball specialists, that area became so full of water, it was called Camp Swampy. Sadly, all this creativity didn't win the Sox a pennant, although they finished second three straight times, 1963–1965. To cut costs, the Allyns unveiled the first AstroTurf infield in the American League (in an outdoor park, yet) on April 16, 1969.

When Veeck returned as owner in 1976, he immediately removed the AstroTurf but made the biggest mistake of his career on July 12, 1979. Held between halves of a twinight doubleheader, Disco Demolition Night turned into a riot; when the patrons tore up the field, the Sox had to forfeit the nightcap to the Tigers.

Comiskey was quiet after Veeck's departure in 1980. Amid threats to move to suburban Addison, Milwaukee (the Sox had played 20 games as the home team at County Stadium in 1968 and 1969), or St. Petersburg, it was clear that refur-

From Shibe Park's earliest days, the people who lived on 20th Street, which ran from right to right center outside the park, made money selling rooftop seats as renegade bleachers. While the practice grew more pronounced in the late 1920s, it's clear that business was booming as early as October 17, 1910, the opening game of that World Series. Philadelphia won, 4–1, as Albert "Chief" Bender yielded only an unearned run in the ninth inning.

The Naming of "Voom Voom" Veeck

Despite all his colorful additions to baseball, a pastime in which nicknames blossom like dandelions, promoter extraordinaire Bill Veeck never had a nickname until 1960. Consider that this is the flamboyant individual who

• invented Bat Day (and, by extension, all the other promotional days) by buying up the inventory of a failed sporting goods store in St. Louis.

• turned around Indian fan Joe Earley when he complained that fans never had "Nights" by holding "Joe Earley Night" and paying off his mortgage.

• brought Satchel Paige, at long last, into the major leagues and underlined his age by putting a rocking chair in the bullpen for him.

• allowed Browns fans to make decisions while manager Zack Taylor held aloft signs that said BUNT or HIT AWAY.

• brought James Thurber's story "You Could Look It Up" to life by hiring 3'7" Eddie Gaedel for one memorable at-bat in the major leagues.

Then Veeck built an exploding scoreboard at Comiskey Park. As Lawrence Ritter explains in *Lost Ball-parks,* it was designed as a theatrical set piece from the start:

> The scoreboard went into action whenever a White Sox player hit a home run. There were foghorns, a cavalry-charge bugle, crashing trains, fire engine sirens, the William Tell overture, a chorus whistling "Dixie," flashing strobe lights, and . . . a series of fireworks explosions, each louder and more colorful than the one before.

While the fireworks were supposed to be the main attraction, most fans have more detailed memories of the sounds the Monster made during its 32-second routine — belching foghorns, the charge of the light brigade, the sounds of fighter planes in battle, a steam calliope, choo-choo trains, and a woman screaming, "Fireman, save my child!" A reporter said, "It must have reminded an old soldier, who saw the London blitz, of the anti-aircraft [guns] going into action."

It was the sound generated by the scoreboard that finally gave Veeck his nickname, albeit a derivative one. In a front-page story about the Monster, the *Sporting News* called him "Voom Voom" Veeck, in mock tribute to Walter "Boom Boom" Beck. (The Phillies pitcher of the 1930s was also named for sounds, the first made when opposing batsmen thwacked his offerings, the second as they cannonaded off the walls at Baker Bowl.)

"Voom Voom," of course, loved all the attention his noisy Monster got and modestly allowed as how his inspiration for it was William Saroyan's play *The Time of Your Life.* He said, "There was a guy in there who didn't have a line of dialogue. He kept playing a pinball machine and finally he hit the jackpot. . . .

---

bishing Comiskey was becoming a losing proposition. On March 21, 1986, engineer Peter Krallitsch said, "Comiskey Park is nearing the end of its useful life."

Faced with losing the Sox or building a park, voters elected to build a new Comiskey Park in the old parking lot. The original Comiskey Park held its final game on September 30, 1990, a 2–1 win over the Mariners, and, for the last time at this address, organist Nancy Faust played, "Na na na na, na na na na, hey hey hey, good-bye." Chuck Comiskey, a Chicago real estate developer and the grandson of Charles Comiskey, told *USA Today*, "Nothing is forever. The ballpark has served us well. It deserves a rest."

OLD WINE, NEW BOTTLES

At the same time Comiskey Park was being built from scratch, Cleveland's League Park was being refurbished after nineteen years of operation.

League Park's problem, through most of its usable life span, was that it had the smallest seating capacity (21,414) of any big league park due to restrictions rooted in the nineteenth century. When the park was built, in 1891, the owners of a saloon and two houses refused to move or sell their properties. Consequently, the side of the park that ran from right to center field — Lexington Avenue — was truncated, making the park essentially a rectangle, with right field and left center as the short sides.

When the park was rebuilt early in 1910, the object was to increase the seating from a minuscule 9,000 to 18,000; it was accomplished by double-decking the park in steel and concrete (although the new left field bleachers had wooden benches). At a time when other right fields measured anywhere from 330 to 380 feet, right at League Park was a scant 290 feet from home plate. Cleveland owner Charles Somers had a 40-foot-high barrier built to cool off the left-handed Sam Crawford, who had led the league with homers in 1907; challenged, Crawford blasted one over the wall on his first visit of the season.

League Park was a place for fans of strange right fields, the first but not the last (Baker Bowl, Ebbets Field) to give spectators in right something extra. To American League outfielders, playing a ball off that wall was a bit like picking the right door on *Let's Make a Deal.* Balls could hit three different surfaces with five different outcomes: the concrete, from which balls came fairly zooming back; the screen, from which balls could either rebound nor-

The machine practically exploded. The American flag was unfurled; battleships fired guns; music blared. It was just so silly, you know, that it was unforgettably funny. I began to imagine something like that on a big scale, like a scoreboard."

Nicknamed "the Monster," and "the Thing," the board cost $300,000 (as much as an entire park fifty years earlier) and stood high above the bleachers in center, 130 feet in the air. Ten slender columns (which concealed the fireworks) flanked the scoreboard, each good for four explosions. Fortunately, one sportswriter noted, "the White Sox are not likely to press the gimmick to capacity in any 24 hours."

Naturally, the Monster gave players and managers a reason to tut-tut about Veeck's lack of decorum. Jimmy Piersall once threw a baseball at it, and Tiger manager Jimmy Dykes compared it to Disneyland, but it was Casey Stengel who came up with the perfect squelch. When the Yanks made their first trip to Comiskey with the Monster in place, Clete Boyer homered; after much scurrying in the dugout, every Yankee emerged carrying sparklers and waved them about triumphantly.

Veeck's erupting scoreboard was, of course, the spiritual ancestor of today's ubiquitous computerized "entertainment centers." When Diamond Vision came to Comiskey in 1982, Veeck's pinwheels were retained. By the 1990s, however, scoreboards had become dispensers of entertainment unrelated to baseball, promoting upcoming games and incoming souvenirs and posting daily horse races, subway games, music trivia quizzes, and other diversions for people who come to ballparks primarily to be entertained by secondary sources. All in all, it's a pretty pale imitation of Voom Voom Veeck's Magnificent Monster.

The Polo Grounds was imposing, and this exterior view shows the park in all its steel and concrete glory shortly after being rebuilt. Making allowances for the fanciful plane, this view is noteworthy for its perspective of Coogan's Bluff (at left) and the water tower (center). For a view of the water tower from a different perspective more than twenty years later, see p. 146.

The bifold postcard below gives the reader a panoramic view of Cleveland's League Park in all its wooden glory. Note that the outfield has no signage, an anomaly for the period. When League Park was rebuilt in concrete and steel, the postcard at right— complete with an up-to-the-minute horseless carriage — was used to sell season tickets. On Opening Day (bottom), April 23, 1910, American League president Ban Johnson threw out the first ball.

AMERICAN LEAGUE BAS BALL PARK. CLEVELAND, O

mally, glance off at an oblique angle, or drop straight down; the steel beams that protruded where the screen joined the concrete. Balls would bounce off these beams at crazy angles, and left fielders wound up chasing doubles hit to right field. Longtime Indian catcher Luke Sewell said, "The ball would hit them and rebound crazily and the fielders would chase the bounces and the batter would run and the fans would love it."

When the lively ball was adopted, in 1920, spectators at League Park would scale precarious footholds outside the Andrews Storage building, just beyond the right field fence, to glimpse left-handed sluggers like Babe Ruth and Lou Gehrig bombing long drives and breaking windows. (Harold Bossard, the Indians' groundskeeper, said

that every year the club had to replace twenty to thirty broken windows in Andrews Storage.)

In 1920, the Indians won the pennant, and seats were added which cut the center field distance from 460 to 420. On October 10, 26,884 fans at League Park, many behind ropes in the outfield, saw three World Series firsts. With the Indians and Robins (Dodgers) tied at 2 games apiece, the first three batters singled off Brooklyn's Burleigh Grimes; then Elmer Smith hit the first grand slam in Series history. In the fourth, Grimes gave up a 3-run shot hit by Jim Bagby, the first pitcher to homer in the Series. Clarence Mitchell relieved Grimes and later made some history himself. The first two Dodgers singled to lead off the fifth and Mitchell hit a bullet; shortstop Bill Wambsganss speared it,

touched second, and tagged Otto Miller to complete the first and only unassisted triple play in World Series history.

Two days later, the Indians won the Series, but it was their only championship at League Park, which was, briefly, Dunn Field. In 1929, construction began on what was originally called Cleveland Public Municipal Stadium, the city's unsuccessful attempt to attract the 1932 Olympics. On July 31, 1932, it became the Indians' new home. The club also played the entire 1933 season there; however, in 1934, the Indians used League Park on weekdays and Municipal Stadium (also called Lakefront Stadium) on weekends and holidays. They used Municipal Stadium exclusively from 1947 on.

League Park was razed in 1951 and replaced with a recreational complex, League Park Center. A two-story ticket booth from 1909 still stands, along with a portion of the first base–right field grandstand. League Park was accepted on the National Register of Historic Places in 1979.

SENATORIAL PRIVILEGE: GRIFFITH STADIUM

Two fires — one late in 1910, the other in the spring of 1911 — motivated the creation of two new parks, one in the nation's largest city, New York, the other in the nation's capital, Washington, D.C. By rights, the latter should have been the more memorable, given its national prominence. Instead, Griffith Stadium was unremarkable during its life-

Huntington Avenue Grounds was no great shakes aesthetically, but it may have influenced ballpark architecture nevertheless. Much of the initial oohing and aahing over Oriole Park at Camden Yards in Baltimore (p. 222) had to do with the B&O warehouse behind the right field fence. It's possible that the architects were aware of the Boston Storage Warehouse behind the left and left-center field stands at Huntington Avenue. Note the sign for "Nuf Ced" McGreevy's saloon and the Boston Opera House, built in 1910, at right.

time and has become the Rodney Dangerfield of ballparks since its demise.

One reason is that Washington's support of baseball has always been tepid, while New York's, for instance, was driven by the intense rivalry among the Dodgers, Giants, and Yankees. The Senators had no natural rivals from 1901 to 1953, and Philadelphia, just to the north, was a two-league town. When the A's lit out for Kansas City and Baltimore got the Orioles, in 1954, Washington had two chances to improve — losing a competitor two hours away and gaining a new interleague rival an hour away. Instead, attendance nosedived from 503,542 in 1954 to 425,238 in 1955 and stayed below 500,000 until Harmon Killebrew rescued the franchise.

Washington had originally been a National League city, which was why the Senators, an American League team, wound up at a place called National Park, at the intersection of Florida Avenue and Seventh Street N.W. They played there from 1892 to 1899, then lost their franchise. Because the National League retained rights to the site, the now–American League Senators moved to American League Park, on 14th and Bladensburg, from 1900 to 1902. After the leagues negotiated a peace, the Senators moved back to National Park but physically brought the grandstand from American League Park with them; although their owner, Clark Griffith, tried to rename the new place

American League Park, it was generally known as National Park until 1920, when it was formally renamed Griffith Stadium.

After a fire burned down the grandstand in 1911, Griffith built the core of a concrete and steel stadium in three weeks with the minuscule insurance settlement of $20,000. Left was a hefty 407 feet, and right was a mere 320 from the plate, but it was guarded by a concrete wall 30 feet high. Center was 421 and might have been longer had the owner of a large tree allowed it to be removed. Instead, the tree became a landmark, and "Meet me at the tree" became the equivalent in Washington of New York's "Meet me under the clock at the Biltmore."

On Opening Day, National Park had a double-decked roofed grandstand like Forbes Field surrounding home plate and the infield. The only difference was that the outfield pavilions down the first and third base lines were covered; open bleachers stretched from the left field foul pole to midcenter behind a concrete wall. In 1920, the single-decked stands between the foul poles and the outfield were double-decked; however, they were not connected to the area behind home plate because the original single-decked stands had been graded more steeply, giving the stadium an unfinished air for the remainder of its life.

After winning a pennant in 1933, the Senators became a perennial second-division club. Even though they became a better club in 1959 and 1960, drawing more than 600,000 and 700,000, respectively, the franchise was moved to Minnesota. Then Washington was voted a new franchise, and the "original" Senators, now the Minnesota Twins, beat the "expansion" Senators, 6–3, in the last major league game at Griffith Stadium. They later moved to RFK Stadium before becoming the Texas Rangers.

COOGAN'S BLUFF: THE POLO GROUNDS

Willie Mays made "the Catch" here.
Carl Mays beaned Ray Chapman here.
Murderers' Row was born here.
Fred Merkle failed to touch second here.
Matty threw his third straight Series shutout here.
The Shot Heard 'Round the World was fired here.

The Polo Grounds was the home field of the Giants and the Yankees in their glory days (and the Mets in their gory days). The third park to bear the name, this last Polo Grounds was tucked in a hollow beneath Coogan's Bluff in North Harlem, on Eighth Avenue between 157th and 159th streets. Home plate was directly below a thoroughfare known as the Speedway (now Harlem River Drive). The top of the bluff led down to the ticket booths.

When the Players League merged with the National League, the Giants took over the park, adding a wooden upper deck. In the mid-1890s, owner Andrew Freedman added bleachers in deep center that were called "cigar boxes," due to their size and shape. (When the park burned in 1911, they were the only seats left because they had not been attached to the grandstand.)

As noted, John Brush, an enemy of Ban Johnson's, bought the Giants in 1902 and refused to participate in a World Series during 1904 because nothing in the National League constitution made a postseason series mandatory. Brush missed out on the 1908 Series when the Giants lost the pennant due to Fred Merkle's baserunning blunder; however, during the pennant race, he began adding seats as quickly as possible, a total of 7,000 by season's end, and gave the Polo Grounds baseball's largest seating capacity.

Many of the people who filled the seats lived in New York's "silk stocking district." For their convenience, Brush took every measure to ensure their comfort. In June 1910, New York Telephone took out a large ad to inform executives that they could take care of business and watch baseball at the same time: "Instruct your office to call you at the Polo Grounds if you are needed. Then leave your name and seat number with the operator. . . . If [you are] called on the telephone, a messenger will summon you."

Had a watchman on an elevated train summoned help sooner, the Polo Grounds might not have burned. The Giants were out of town on April 14, and by the time the blaze was put out, $250,000 of damage had been done to the park, and Harry M. Stevens had lost $25,000 worth of food and supplies.

During the field's reconstruction, the Giants played at Hilltop Park, despite Brush's previous efforts to keep the Highlanders out of New York. Rebuilding went quickly, and by June, 16,000 seats were ready at Coogan's Bluff and others were added gradually; at the end of the season, Brush had a 34,000-seat park, once again the biggest in baseball.

He restored the park's distinctive bathtub shape, double-decking the park halfway down the left field foul line and continuing 40 feet past the right field foul pole. The box seats in the upper deck sported an Italian marble facade, and the end seats of the rows had decorative iron scrollwork (a nicety revived by Oriole Park at Camden Yards). The apex of the upper deck featured American eagles with their wings outstretched, "symbols of the National Game," according to *Baseball* magazine, suggesting "the perfect idealization of national manhood and womanhood," and a series of shields containing the coats of arms of each of the National League cities "spangled with a pattern of gold stars." The shield and seal of the United States were rendered in "a warm ivory yellow in relief upon a background of gray, picked out with tones of turquoise blue, delicate green, and some slight shades of vermilion and gold."

While it is easy to twit Brush on the opulence of his decorating, he did build a great ballpark, with the fan very much in mind. The upper deck overhung the lower by 23 feet, and the sightlines were excellent, particularly in left field. Depending on their trajectory, ordinary fly balls could become home runs in left. Although the field measured 279 feet in left and 257 in right, upper-deck shots had to travel only *258* feet in left and 259 in right, according to Ritter, given the 34-foot trajectory.

Of course, the short foul lines combined with the bathtub shape also meant long — very long — power alleys. Left center measured 447 left of

No park better illustrates the transition from wood to steel more markedly than the Polo Grounds. The elevated view (left) shows Coogan's Bluff with the usual nonpaying customers, Manhattan Field to the right, which the Giants had used as a home in 1889, and, across the river, the Bronx. After the park burned down in April 1911, this rendering (below) imagined a rounder park than what was actually created. When the park did reopen, it had the distinctive bathtub shape this last Polo Grounds retained until 1964. The new concrete and steel Polo Grounds looked its best on this foldout view, which first appeared in a newspaper supplement (bottom). Note the impressive screen behind home plate and the decorative work on both the lower and upper deck facades. Although owner John T. Brush did his utmost to rename the Giants' lair Brush Stadium, as on this 1911 World Series program (right), the name never stuck with the fans and was soon abandoned.

OFFICIAL SCORE CARD
WORLD'S CHAMPIONSHIP SERIES
NEW YORK GIANTS VS PHILA. ATHLETICS
CHAMPIONS OF THE NATIONAL LEAGUE
CHAMPIONS OF THE AMERICAN LEAGUE

JOHN T. BRUSH

BRUSH STADIUM
1·9·1·1
PRICE 10 CENTS

HARRY M. STEVENS
Publisher

the bullpen and 460 in front of the clubhouse steps; right center was 440 to the right of the bullpen and flared out another 9 feet to its left. Center was 433 when the park was built, 483 in most years thereafter.

The park was ideal for left-handed pull hitters, and the greatest of them all — Babe Ruth — loved it. The Yankees had become Brush's tenants in 1913 and signed a ten-year lease. When Ruth joined the team, in 1920, his home run total in his home park zoomed from 9 at Fenway to 29 in four more at-bats at the Polo Grounds. Even making allowances for the new lively ball, these figures are an amazing measure of the park's potential for a left-handed pull hitter. Ruth did even better in 1921, hitting 32 homers in 255 home at-bats; he said later, "I cried when they took me out of the Polo Grounds."

In 1921, for the first time, all World Series games were played in the same park. McGraw's men won New York's first Subway Series, the last of the best-of-nine contests, and repeated in 1922, the first Series broadcast on the radio. A year later the park was enclosed and capacity reached 54,555. With the dominance of the automobile, there was no longer any reason to leave the outfield open for the carriage trade. The original 15,000 bleacher seats were reduced to 5,500, and the stands in left and right center were converted to covered, double-decked grandstands; only 4,600 bleacher seats in center field remained uncovered — 2,300 on either side of the clubhouses.

The Polo Grounds had attained its ultimate shape, and Giant managers from McGraw onward learned that, in addition to stockpiling pull hitters, it made good sense to find excellent outfielders because the sharply angled concrete outfield walls meant abrupt bounces. Left field was especially difficult. As Fred Stein explains in *Giants Diary:* "The upper-deck facing extended well beyond the lower deck. This meant that, in cases where fly balls just

missed the upper deck, there was a split second during which the fielder lost sight of the ball."

In 1945, the Polo Grounds got a new tenant, but it wasn't a ball club. Groundskeeper Matty Schwab was given a rent-free apartment tucked away under the left field stands.

Matty had worked for his father, the groundskeeper in Cincinnati, and became the head man at Ebbets Field in 1938. Horace Stoneham asked him to work for the Giants, but Schwab couldn't see himself commuting an hour from Brooklyn every day. To clinch the deal, Stoneham built the Schwabs' apartment. When Bobby Thomson hit the home run that gave the Giants the pennant in 1951, Schwab was fond of saying, "The Shot Heard 'Round the World landed on my roof."

Three years later Schwab had a pretty fair view of "the Catch." In the first game of the 1954 World Series, the Indians and Giants were tied, 2–2, and Larry Doby and Al Rosen were on first and second with nobody out. Lefty Don Liddle replaced Sal Maglie to face lefty Vic Wertz; Wertz hit a long drive that appeared headed for the bleachers just right of dead center. Running with his head down, Willie Mays looked over his left shoulder, slowed down a bit to avoid hitting the wall, pulled the ball in like a football receiver 445 feet from the plate, then whirled and threw a strike to Davey Williams at second base, almost catching the astonished Rosen napping. (Marv Grissom then replaced Liddle, who returned to the bench and announced nonchalantly, "Well, I got my man.")

Less than three years later, on September 29, 1957, the Giants played their last home game in the Polo Grounds before moving to San Francisco. Within five years, baseball — of a sort — returned. At a cost of $250,000, the New York Mets refurbished the park. Casey Stengel, who had played in the Polo Grounds fifty years earlier, led the Amazin' Mets to 120 losses in their first season. The Polo Grounds was demolished in 1964, with the same wrecking ball that knocked down Ebbets Field.

TIMELINE

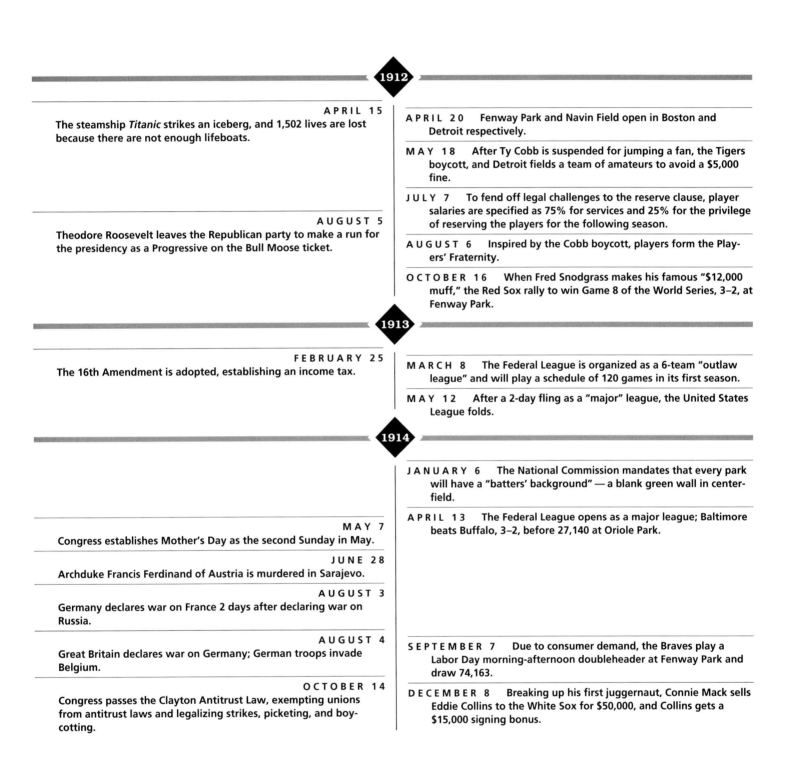

1912

APRIL 15
The steamship *Titanic* strikes an iceberg, and 1,502 lives are lost because there are not enough lifeboats.

AUGUST 5
Theodore Roosevelt leaves the Republican party to make a run for the presidency as a Progressive on the Bull Moose ticket.

APRIL 20 Fenway Park and Navin Field open in Boston and Detroit respectively.

MAY 18 After Ty Cobb is suspended for jumping a fan, the Tigers boycott, and Detroit fields a team of amateurs to avoid a $5,000 fine.

JULY 7 To fend off legal challenges to the reserve clause, player salaries are specified as 75% for services and 25% for the privilege of reserving the players for the following season.

AUGUST 6 Inspired by the Cobb boycott, players form the Players' Fraternity.

OCTOBER 16 When Fred Snodgrass makes his famous "$12,000 muff," the Red Sox rally to win Game 8 of the World Series, 3–2, at Fenway Park.

1913

FEBRUARY 25
The 16th Amendment is adopted, establishing an income tax.

MARCH 8 The Federal League is organized as a 6-team "outlaw league" and will play a schedule of 120 games in its first season.

MAY 12 After a 2-day fling as a "major" league, the United States League folds.

1914

JANUARY 6 The National Commission mandates that every park will have a "batters' background" — a blank green wall in centerfield.

APRIL 13 The Federal League opens as a major league; Baltimore beats Buffalo, 3–2, before 27,140 at Oriole Park.

MAY 7
Congress establishes Mother's Day as the second Sunday in May.

JUNE 28
Archduke Francis Ferdinand of Austria is murdered in Sarajevo.

AUGUST 3
Germany declares war on France 2 days after declaring war on Russia.

AUGUST 4
Great Britain declares war on Germany; German troops invade Belgium.

OCTOBER 14
Congress passes the Clayton Antitrust Law, exempting unions from antitrust laws and legalizing strikes, picketing, and boycotting.

SEPTEMBER 7 Due to consumer demand, the Braves play a Labor Day morning-afternoon doubleheader at Fenway Park and draw 74,163.

DECEMBER 8 Breaking up his first juggernaut, Connie Mack sells Eddie Collins to the White Sox for $50,000, and Collins gets a $15,000 signing bonus.

CHAPTER SIX

The entrance to Fenway Park hasn't changed much since the park opened in 1912. The windows, which had awnings, have been replaced by air conditioning units; mounted police have given way to motorists, and Jersey Street has been renamed Yawkey Way.

C H A P T E R   S I X

The Jewel Boxes

Baseball's three jewel boxes — Fenway Park, Ebbets Field, and Wrigley Field — were built, one a year, between 1912 and 1914. They constituted the second wave of what had started in 1909 with the introduction of reinforced concrete at Shibe Park and Forbes Field. Collectively, they were the coziest major league parks ever built from scratch.

The jewel boxes were the best ballparks from a fan's point of view because they were so close to the action, "you could see a pitcher sweat." They are the parks that have endured both in the flesh (Fenway and Wrigley) and in memory (Ebbets). All three had a relatively small seating capacity. (None *legally* held as many as 40,000.) They were also built on a human scale, built for baseball only, and built in harmony with their neighborhoods, where many of the players lived.

THE BEST PARK LEFT: FENWAY PARK

Some parks are hitter's parks. Some parks are pitcher's parks. Fenway is a writer's park.

Something in the air at Fenway leads writers to soar on wings of rhetoric in describing it. A Harvard professor once compared it to the pre-Christian bullring at Knossos, on the island of Crete. John Updike noted that "Fenway Park . . . is a lyric

little bandbox of a ballpark. Everything is painted green and seems in curiously sharp focus, like the inside of an old-fashioned peeping-type Easter egg."

Sportswriters in particular go to extremes. The *Boston Globe*'s Dan Shaughnessy wrote, "Fenway is only a ballpark the way the Sistine Chapel is only a church." And, setting a standard for exclamatory prose that may never be equaled, Joe Falls of the *Detroit News* was once unashamed to write, "I have often said that if I could have my choice of where I could die, it would be in the press box at Fenway Park on a fresh afternoon in June."

Longtime Red and White Sox catcher Carlton "Pudge" Fisk took a far more pragmatic approach. He said, "You can sit around and compare ballparks all you want, but no park in baseball compares to Fenway. If you want to come see 'a baseball game' — that's a generic term — and have a chance to see everything that baseball can provide, then Fenway is the place to see it."

Boston had had pro baseball for forty-one years by 1912, courtesy of George and Harry Wright (see Chapter 1). Fenway's predecessors in Boston — South End Grounds (actually in Roxbury, though near the South End), Dartmouth Street Grounds, the Union Association park (in Back Bay), and Congress Street Grounds, the Players League stand later used by the AA Reds and NL Beaneaters

Cincinnati's Palace of the Fans was torn down over the winter of 1911–1912 to make room for Redland Field. Patrons at a preseason banquet to toast the new park were given colored prints of an artist's rendition (top). Although the drawing suggests that right field is farther from home than left, the park was, in fact, symmetrical when first built (360 feet down each foul line). Trolley tracks were still prominent (center) despite the coming of the automobile, but the rendition doesn't give much of a hint of Redland's expanse. A postcard view (bottom) gives a much clearer impression of what was, when it opened, the largest big league ballpark in terms of area. This bifold postcard (below) was taken on Opening Day, April 11, 1912.

New Ball Park, Cincinnati, O. Opening Day, April 11, 1912. Attendance, 25,700.

In 1911, their last
year at Huntington
Avenue Grounds,
the Red Sox finished
24 games out of
first place. Just as
a new park inspired
the 1909 Pirates,
Fenway Park,
opened in 1912,
instantly became
the home of world
champions. When
the Red Sox ran
away with the pen-
nant, temporary
wooden stands
were shoehorned
in along the right
field line for the
World Series. The
grandstand along
first base was split
into two sections
(right) to bring the
fans closer to the
action. Had the first
base line been con-
tinued unbroken,
there would have
been fewer seats
behind first base.
(The split continues
to this day.)

(South Boston) — were all in more populous areas. Fenway Park sits on what had been stagnant, feculent fens — the marshes between the Muddy River and Stony Brook.

Frederick Law Olmsted, who designed New York's Central Park, drained the Fens between 1881 and 1885 as part of his "Emerald Necklace" of parks to surround Boston. By the turn of the century, the park idea had died, and the Fenway became the last of Boston's neighborhoods to be the product of filled-in land.

With the exception of Simmons College, the area was totally empty until 1902, but there was no doubt of its potential. It attracted the owners of the Boston and Albany Railroad, who laid tracks parallel to Lansdowne Street (which runs parallel to left and left center at Fenway), and John I. Taylor, whose family owned the Red Sox and the *Boston Globe.*

In addition, Taylor also owned the Huntington Avenue Grounds — but *not* the land under it, which he was forced to lease from the New York, New Haven, and Hartford Railroad. He wanted to sell the Sox but knew he could get a far better price by selling the team and a new park as a package. Since he owned a substantial interest in the Fenway Realty Company, Taylor sold himself some land in a cheap, undeveloped location next to the city's expanding streetcar lines, which served Ken-

more Square.

Writing about Taylor in the 1987 Red Sox yearbook, Glenn Stout says, "The enterprise was first and foremost a real estate venture; he used the ballpark to help draw attention to the surrounding area and enhance its value." Taylor's oft-quoted reason for renaming the marshland a park — "It's in the Fenway, isn't it?" — led Stout to write, "Even the park's name . . . served to promote real estate instead of baseball." Taylor broke ground for Fenway in September 1911; it is a measure of his shrewdness that he was able to sell the club to Washington manager Jimmy McAleer and Robert R. McRoy for $150,000 just three months later.

The new owners added their ideas to the design of the unbuilt park and changed it considerably. Osborn Engineering Company dispensed with the bleachers that were supposed to run from right field to center and installed a parking lot instead, a sign of the automobile's influence. The central grandstand was steel and concrete, as originally planned, but the bleachers in left and the right field pavilion were rendered in wood, even though they sat on concrete foundations.

Most fans have a tendency to think of Fenway as small and cramped, like the other jewel boxes. A look at this chart confirms that all three had dimensions comparable to the other steel and concrete parks of the era. All three, for instance, had

deeper center fields originally than Crosley Field, Griffith Stadium, and even the Polo Grounds. What made them seem small was the dead ball; the lively ball was unimagined when the jewel boxes were built, yet it came into play only six years after Wrigley, originally Weeghman Park, was built.

Fenway Park opened on April 20, 1912, although it wasn't finished or dedicated until May. Mayor John F. "Honey Fitz" Fitzgerald, President John F. Kennedy's maternal grandfather, threw out the first ball. A crowd of 27,000 was delighted to see Tris Speaker drive in the winning run as Boston beat the New York Highlanders (Yankees), 7–6, in eleven innings.

The park was quickly acclaimed as a great place to watch baseball. Fans came to see "the Golden Outfield" — Harry Hooper in right, Tris Speaker in center, and George "Duffy" Lewis in left. The seats

Original Dimensions of Parks Built from 1909 to 1914

YEAR	PARK	LEFT	CENTER	RIGHT
1909	Shibe Park	360	515	360
1909	Forbes Field	360	422	376
1910	Comiskey Park	362	420	362
1910	League Park	385	460	290
1911	Griffith Stadium	407	421	320
1911	Polo Grounds	277	433	257
1912	Redland Field	360	420	360
1912	Navin Field	345	467	370
1912	Fenway Park	321	488	314
1913	Ebbets Field	419	450	301
1914	Weeghman Park	310	440	356

were oak, and the red brick facade, done in the Tapestry style, seemed to be almost needlepointed and reminded onlookers of a New England sampler. Fans in the lower deck never had to worry about the upper deck's interfering with their view because there wasn't any (and still isn't).

Boston was the site of the World Series in four of the five years from 1914 through 1918. In 1914, George Stallings's Miracle Braves used Fenway as their home park since South End Grounds held little more than 10,000 and won 2 games from Connie Mack's Athletics. In 1915, the Sox beat Grover Cleveland Alexander's Phillies in 5 games. A year later, the Braves loaned the Sox Braves Field, the first superstadium (see Chapter 7), and Boston beat the Dodgers when Babe Ruth shut them out for thirteen straight innings.

In 1918, Red Sox owner Harry Frazee had put himself into debt putting *No, No, Nanette* together, so on December 26, 1919, he sold Babe Ruth to the Yankees for $125,000 and mortgaged Fenway Park for $350,000. Many impute the fact that the Sox haven't won a championship since to the Curse of the Bambino, a supernatural explanation for ineptitude rather than the more natural explanation — perennially so-so pitching (overall), a suspect defense, no team speed, and a lineup of right-handed sluggers that are vulnerable off their happy hunting ground.

Frazee sold the club in 1923 to Bob Quinn, the general manager of the St. Louis Browns. Quinn was no more flush than Frazee, and Fenway and the Sox both deteriorated, finishing last eight of the ten years he owned the club. When fire destroyed the bleachers along the left field line on May 8, 1926, Quinn pocketed the insurance money and never replaced them. On July 3, 1932, the Sox finally played their first Sunday game at Fenway. Sunday ball had become legal in Boston in 1929 but not at Fenway because it was near a church; the Sox played Sabbath games at Braves Field until the law was amended.

THE BEST PARK EVER: EBBETS FIELD

"Ebbets Field," says Michael Benson in *Ballparks of North America*, "was maybe the best ballpark ever." Perhaps that is an overstatement; maybe he just means it was the best-loved because the Dodgers were all Brooklyn had. In addition to the Pirates, Pittsburgh had Carnegie Tech, U.S.

Steel, and the Mellons; besides the Tigers, Detroit had the Lions, the Fords, and General Motors; Brooklyn had just the Dodgers, making Ebbets Field the borough's focal point, a shrine to Brooklynness. It was often chic not to like baseball in Philadelphia or Boston, but to be from Brooklyn and not *love* baseball was clearly impossible. Longtime Dodger announcer Red Barber was once offered a three-year contract to jump to the Yankees. He turned it down, saying, "I had roots. I love the borough, and it needed me. I loved the park."

The inspiration for Ebbets Field came from Dodger owner Charles Ebbets, who had started out as the ball club's bookkeeper in 1902, after the Dodgers-Orioles syndicate had peaked in baseball terms. (As Ebbets rose up the management ladder, Brooklyn was generally a second-division club.) When he became the owner, Ebbets wanted his own steel and concrete ballpark even though he had no money for one. That meant finding the cheapest land in Brooklyn, which lay between the bustling village of Flatbush and somewhat suburban Bedford.

Ebbets's site selection was brilliant; the area developed rapidly, and his park was eventually within three blocks of both the Franklin Avenue IRT and the Prospect Park BMT subways. Fans could walk easily from buses plying Flatbush Avenue, Reid Avenue, and Empire Boulevard, and the area was served by nine direct trolley lines that connected to thirty-two others. Motorists could also ride on such broad thoroughfares as Ocean and Bedford avenues to get to the park. Moreover, Wall Street and New York's City Hall were within twenty minutes, putting the park within easy reach of some four million people.

The site itself, however, was neither bustling nor suburban but a "malodorous four-and-a-half-acre slum." At its epicenter was "a large, gaping pit into which the shanty dwellers threw their fetid, stinking garbage." Local farmers found the pit a great place to feed their pigs; hence, the area became known as Pigtown.

Even in such an unprepossessing section, it took a while for Ebbets to consolidate the forty separate pieces of land necessary to build a ballpark. According to Benson, Ebbets had to buy up no less than twelve hundred parcels of land from fifteen different owners. He bought the first parcel in 1908, using various beards and dummy companies to disguise his intent. By 1911, however, he had already spent $200,000 and had run out of money before he had all the pieces. To make the park a

reality, he was forced to sell 50 percent of the team (for $100,000) to two contractors, Ed and Steve McKeever. (Ebbets Field ultimately cost $750,000.)

From a pitcher's standpoint, Ebbets Field had its downside. Foul territory was quite small, putting out of play balls that were caught in other parks. Then, of course, there were the dimensions, which made home runs out of fairly long fly balls to left field in the 1940s and 1950s. Finally, the bullpens were completely open areas along the foul lines, left field for visitors, right field for the Dodgers. Because there was no protection from line drives, a pitcher not warming up was always posted behind the bullpen catcher to watch for incoming missiles.

The original design had a double-decked grandstand that curved around home, continuing right to the foul pole in right field but only 30 or 40 feet past the third base line; wooden bleachers filled up the gap to the foul line; there were no outfield seats in fair territory. Aside from a short right field (301), the dimensions were generous: 419 to left

and 450 to center. The park opened on April 9, 1913, although nobody brought the key to open the park or a flag to salute or remembered to build a press box. (Ebbets removed two rows of seats from the upper deck behind home plate and roped off the area for the scribes; a proper press box wasn't built until 1929.)

In 1926, open wooden bleachers were installed in left field, cutting 35 feet off the distance from the fence to home plate. Ebbets assumed its final shape after the 1931 season, when a covered double-decked grandstand was extended from third base down to the left field corner and from there into center field. At the same time, the famous scoreboard was built in right field and topped with a fence that presented left-handed hitters with a target 40 feet high. Outfielder Floyd "Babe" Herman said, "You know that screen on top of the right-field fence? They put that there on account of me. I was breaking all the windows on the other side of Bedford Avenue."

It is rare to see a well-known ballpark with the playing field nearly complete but no hint at all of seats. This view of Ebbets Field was taken early in the winter of 1912–1913. Note the "keyhole" running from the pitcher's mound to home plate.

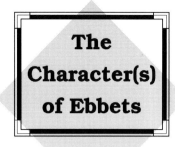

The Character(s) of Ebbets

Fans were a significant part of the experience at Ebbets. In *Mudville's Revenge,* Ted Vincent says, "I spent much of my youth in old Ebbets Field, and, in retrospect, my fondest memories are not of game-winning hits but of the fun Dodger fans had during the game." Of course, other parks had characters, too, like the Bleacher Bums at Wrigley Field. Sportsman's Park in St. Louis had Screechin' Screamin' Mary Ott berating visitors from behind first base, and Crosley Field in Cincinnati had Harry Thobe dancing a jig in a red-and-white-striped suit.

But where other parks had one character, Ebbets had a dozen. The first to come to public notice was Abie the Truck Driver, who named the Dodgers "the Bums." Abie would address individual Dodgers as "ya bum, ya" from the upper deck along the third base line. No matter how the Dodgers were doing, Abie let them know they were all bums in his book, and the heckling became a major irritant to the players. Finally "Uncle Robbie," manager Wilbert Robinson, offered Abie a free season pass to stop riding the home team, and the heckling ceased for a few days. Then Abie walked into Robinson's office and said, "You can keep the pass. I can't stand it anymore. They're still bums!" (Cartoonist Willard Mullin later immortalized the Dodgers with a single Emmet Kelly–like Bum, the team's unofficial logo until they left Brooklyn.)

Nearly every individual Dodger had a nickname, too. Harold Reese was "Pee Wee" (for his marble championships won as a boy). Johnny Jorgensen at third was "Spider," left fielder George Shuba was "Shotgun," Edwin Snider, in center, was "the Duke," and right field was patrolled at one time or another by Harold "Pistol Pete" Reiser, Fred "Dixie" Walker, and, of course "the Reading Rifle," Carl Furillo. (Walker was also "the Peepul's Cherce," Furillo was "Skoonj," short for the scungilli he loved to eat, and Reese and Reiser were, collectively, "the Gold Dust Twins.")

The fans at Ebbets were equally adept at nicknaming visiting players. Noticing that Bill Nicholson of the Cubs often fanned violently, creating huge masses of air, they named him "Swish." Stan Musial became "Musical" until the series he hit .625 against the Dodgers. A fan said, "Uh-oh. Here comes that man again." After that, Musial was "Stan the Man." In the late 1920s, Paul and Lloyd Waner terrorized the Dodgers, and a fan with a Brooklyn accent sadly noted, "Every time you look up those Waner boys are on base; it's always the little poyson on thoid and the big poyson on first." Translated into English, the Waners became "Little Poison" (Lloyd) and "Big Poison" (Paul).

The "Voice of Ebbets Field," the public address announcer in the 1940s and 1950s, was John "Tex" Rickard. (TV actor John Forsythe preceded him.) Rickard was renowned for his malapropisms, which included the announcement "A little boy has been found lost." On another occasion, fans had put brightly colored coats over the left field railing, and the batters complained that they were a distraction. When the umpires asked Rickard to do something, over the PA came his plaintive request, "Will the fans behind the rail in left field please remove their clothing?"

Even Ebbets's organist was a minor celebrity. One of the first popular baseball trivia questions was, "Who played for seventeen years for the Dodgers without making an error?" The answer, of course, was organist Gladys Gooding, who played "The Mexican Hat Dance" to induce the fans to clap and broke into "Follow the Dodgers" every time they took the field to start the game. At the end of the seventh game of the 1952 World Series, when Yankee outfielder Hank Bauer caught the last Dodger out, Gooding had the presence of mind to play a popular ballad from *South Pacific,* "This Nearly Was Mine."

If employees could be characters so could Ebbets Field's advertisers. The yellow sign at the base of the scoreboard in right field said, in black letters, HIT SIGN, WIN SUIT, and followed with an ad for the store of clothier Abe Stark, at 1514 Pitkin Avenue. (The sign made Stark so famous that he was elected borough president of Brooklyn.) Very few batters ever hit the sign, because it was at the base of the wall some 330 feet from home plate, and it was guarded by a succession of great right fielders that included Reiser, Walker, and Furillo. *Daily News* columnist Dick Young wrote a column about all the suits he figured Furillo had saved Stark. Embarrassed, Stark called the right fielder and measured him for a suit; then he hit him up for half a dozen autographed balls.

Ebbets Field assumed much of its character (and its characters) during the 1930s. Since rooting a bunch of bums to victory was self-defeating, the fans had to find other ways to amuse themselves. Eddie Battan rooted for the Brooks in a white pith helmet. Jack Pierce, cheering for "Cookie" Lavagetto from behind home plate, released balloons with Lavagetto's nickname on them and yelled, "Cooookie, Cooookie." Hilda Chester, who packed peanuts for Harry M. Stevens at New York racetracks, urged Duke and Dixie on with two cowbells and a foghorn voice.

Ebbets's best-known fans were the members of the homegrown band known as "the Sym-phoney." Its leader was welder Jack "Shorty" Laurice, but one of the surviving members — Jerry Martin, who played the snare drums — said Laurice "wasn't from our neighborhood" and was added to the band later by Dodger owner Walter O'Malley. Martin says the band was made up of fans from northern Williamsburg and names as original members Jo Jo Delio on cymbals, Paddy Palma, who manned the bass drum, and trumpeter Phil Cacavalle. Martin says, "In the beginning, we could never get in with all the instruments. The security cops would chase us. But, later, the fans started to like us, and Branch Rickey said, 'Let them come in and give them seats on the first-base side.' "

In Laurice's version, as related to Murray Schumach of the *New York Times,* the welder says he had the same seat for twenty-eight years, "section 8, row 12, on the aisle. I'm whistlin' through my megaphone like

It is easy to see the land as Charles Ebbets envisioned it: superficially a trash heap, with the ballpark dominating the area.

Just why the flag, in place in this photo, was removed for Opening Day is a subject for future generations to ponder.

always when I run into this guy, a drummer, and that was the beginning of the band." Whichever creation myth is correct, the Symphoney eventually resided in seats 1–8 in row 1, section 8, behind the Dodger dugout. It is also undeniable that the Sym-phoney's forte was enthusiasm rather than talent. Schumach says, "Sometimes the band sounds like a herd of elephants with whooping cough."

Yet fans who listened to its offerings never had to guess what the situation was on the field. Rallies were greeted with "Happy Days Are Here Again," and, when "Three Blind Mice" was played, it was to protest an umpire's call. If Eddie Stanky drew a base on balls, they'd break into "Oh, Oh, Oh, Would You Like to Take a Walk?" After being knocked out of the box, pitchers had to endure hearing "Who's Sorry Now?" or "Give Me Five Minutes More." The band played hardly at all during exciting games,

but, in the middle of a 12–3 laugher, it would break into "How Dry I Am" whenever a player strolled over to the water cooler.

Striking out an opposing batsman offered an occasion to play:

BAH DOMP BAH DOMP
BAH DOMP BAH DOMP
BAH DOMP BAH DAH DAH
BAH DOMP BAH DOMP

The tune has become known as "The Worm Crawls In," but its real name is "The Army Duff." When a visiting player fanned and returned to the bench, the Sym-phoney would play the tune and, when he sat down, give him a final raspberry-like "blat!" with the trumpet and bass drum at full volume. Opponents caught on and did their best to postpone the grand finale. Johnny Mize struck out once, pretended to sit, and, at the last possible moment, got up and became absorbed in his mitt, almost sat down again, and took a

drink. He repeatedly feigned sitting but never did. An inning later, he forgot the incident, finally sat, and got his "blat." The crowd cheered as lustily as if Duke or Campy had homered.

Even though the Sym-phoney was a band of volunteers, the musicians' union, at the height of its power, demanded that they be paid $100 a day. Worse yet, it threatened to picket if new owner Walter O'Malley didn't pay. In response, O'Malley decided to hold Music Appreciation Night on August 13, 1951. Anyone showing up with a musical instrument of any kind would be admitted to the left field bleachers for nothing. People came with ocarinas, two-man pianos, kazoos, stringless violins, and drums, drums, drums; defeated with humor, the union relented, and the Sym-phoney played at Ebbets Field until the Dodgers left.

114

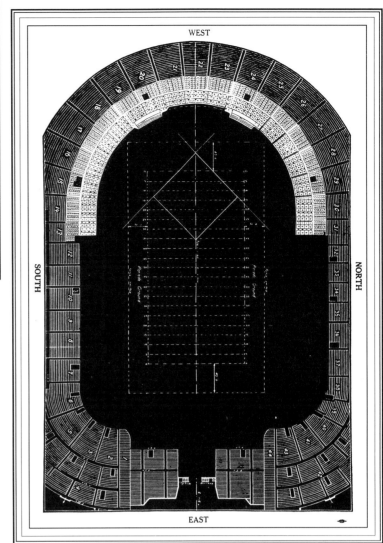

The Polo Grounds grew in stature as the Giants won pennants (but lost World Series) in 1911–1913. A long shot (left), taken during the 1913 fall classic, shows the architectural detailing on the third deck of the park, while a postcard (below left) displays the intricate scroll-work at the end of the second deck in right field. In 1913, the Polo Grounds also held the first Army-Navy football game played in New York (above). (President Woodrow Wilson attended.) A diagram shows how the field was used for both football and baseball.

THE FOUNDING OF THE FEDERAL LEAGUE

In 1958, Brooklyn had no functioning big league parks, but in 1914 it had two, thanks, in part, to a nationwide economic boom.

Unemployment, which had increased drastically after the Panic of 1907, from 2.8 to 8 percent, declined to 5.1 percent in 1909. The population had grown from 76 million people in 1900 to 92 million in 1910, helped by the arrival of the greatest number of immigrants in any ten-year period — 8,795,386 — more than three times as many as the later postwar boom, which welcomed 2.5 million immigrants from 1951 to 1960.

The United States was becoming the world's leading industrial power, and its citizens were using their newfound disposable income to make vaudeville, movies, legitimate theater, and horse racing big business. Baseball, once merely prosperous, was now riding a tidal wave of popularity. In 1903, the combined major leagues played to 2.7 million fans; five years later, after the frenzied pennant races of 1908, the total was 7.1 million.

Naturally, other entrepreneurs wanted part of the action, and no less than four other would-be major leagues never made it off the drawing board between 1910 and 1913. One of them was the Columbian League of 1912, the brainchild of John

T. Powers, who had created a Class D Wisconsin State League in 1904. A year later, Powers announced the formation of a new Columbian League, a *minor* league with three of the same cities that Ban Johnson's Western League had vacated around the turn of the century: Grand Rapids, Indianapolis, and Kansas City. A month later, Grand Rapids had disappeared, the circuit became the Federal League, and the lineup was Chicago, Cleveland, Covington, Kentucky (near Cincinnati), Indianapolis, Pittsburgh, and St. Louis.

The league was well organized for the times. Powers had gone out of his way not to antagonize Organized Baseball (O.B.) and, trying to avoid conflicts, drew up a schedule only after the major leagues had issued theirs. To ensure financial stability, each club had to deposit a $5,000 bond before the season opened. Moreover, each club had a manager with major league playing experience. Two standouts returned to the sites of their former greatness: Cy Young headed Cleveland's entry (dubbed the Green Sox for their youth), and Deacon Philippe bossed Pittsburgh's minions (nicknamed the Filipinos in his honor).

Although Cleveland played its home games at an amusement park (Luna Park), the other fields were more than adequate. Chicago and St. Louis used college stadiums: Chicago played on the baseball-hungry North Side, at DePaul University;

The Federal League was started by two entrepreneurs with snappy nicknames, equally snappy bowler hats, and the smug smiles of those "in the know" — "Fighting Jim" Gilmore, a hero of the Spanish-American War (left), and "Lucky Charlie" Weeghman, the owner of a chain of Chicago lunch-rooms.

and St. Louis used the ballfield at centrally located St. Louis University. Even though it was in Kentucky, just across the Ohio River, Covington was actually closer to downtown Cincinnati than Redland Field was. Indianapolis had Riverside Beach Park, and Pittsburgh played at Exposition Park, the selfsame turf Honus Wagner had ennobled with his presence.

On December 13, the league got its bellwether "name" player — Joe Tinker, once the shortstop in the Tinker-to-Evers-to-Chance trio of Cub infielders. Tinker had been traded to the Reds in 1912 and was ticketed to move on to Brooklyn in 1913; when he was refused a piece of the purchase price, he jumped to the Chicago Whales. Other signings followed, and in 1914 the Feds trotted out other names — Albert "Chief" Bender, Mordecai "Three Finger" Brown, and "Prince Hal" Chase.

The league got another boost when John Montgomery Ward, a pioneer of the Players League (see Chapter 2), signed on as business manager of the Brooklyn Tip-Tops. The Tip-Tops were owned by Robert Ward, whose bakery produced Tip-Top

bread and, Pietrusza says in *Major Leagues*, turned out an astronomical 249,992,325 loaves in 1913. That was enough bread to completely remodel Washington Park after building inspectors decided that simply expanding the old wooden grandstand wouldn't do. New parks were built in Baltimore, Buffalo (which tried to defray the costs by selling shares to the public in a series of newspaper ads), Chicago, and Indianapolis; Washington and Exposition parks were made over in concrete and steel.

Baltimore had the honor of holding the first Opening Day, on April 13, 1914, and Ned Hanlon, the creator of the Orioles' brand of hell-for-leather baseball, came out of retirement to help run the Terrapins (Balt-Feds). The Orioles of the International League had scheduled an exhibition game against John McGraw's Giants to draw spectators from the Feds. Instead, Hanlon's charges outdrew the Orioles by nearly 26,000 people and bested Buffalo in the first Federal League game played, 3–2. A smaller crowd, 20,000, attended Opening Day in Chicago — at a major league park still in use.

Original Federal League Parks and Outfield Dimensions

TEAM	PARK	CAPACITY	LEFT	CENTER	RIGHT
Baltimore Terrapins	Terrapin Park	15,000	300	450	335
Brooklyn Tip-Tops	Washington Park	18,800	300	400	275
Buffalo Blues	Federal Field	20,000	290	400	300
Chicago Whales	Weeghman Park	18,000	310	440	356
Indianapolis Hoo-feds	Greenlawn Park	20,000	375	400	310
Kansas City Packers	Gordon & Koppel Field	12,000	NA	NA	NA
Pittsburgh Stogies	Exposition Park	16,000	375	450	375
St. Louis Terriers	Handlan's Park	15,000	325	375	300

Terrapin Park, Federal League, Baltimore, Md.

Baltimore was "big league" again when the Feds came to town. The hometown Terrapins played at Terrapin Park (above), just across the street from Oriole Park. This exterior view (left) illustrates just how much builders of ballparks knew they had to allow for parking. Since it took roughly 90 square feet of space to park a 1914 car, supplying parking for 1,000 cars — 90,000 square feet — meant buying slightly more than two additional acres of land not to mention building materials and labor. These costs are one reason that only three new major league parks were built from 1915 to 1931.

Chicago Federal League Baseball Park

CLARK AND ADDISON STREETS

Home of the "Whales"

A somewhat man-
gled promotional
poster offers a
panoramic view of
Weeghman Park
from right field. It
was used in 1915
to advertise that
the Federal League
team in Chicago
was no longer the
Chi-Feds but the
Whales, making the
park "the Home of
the Whales." (Note
the logo, upper left
and right.)

THE FRIENDLY CONFINES: WRIGLEY FIELD

It is the only remaining Federal League ballpark, the only major league park built on Chicago's North Side, and the only park a player active in the salary-conscious 1990s — Andre Dawson — took a pay cut to play home games in.

Called both "the Bermuda Triangle of ballparks" and "the Peter Pan of ballparks," what was originally Weeghman Park has done more for wind than anyone with the possible exception of Margaret Mitchell. Except for Candlestick Park in San Francisco, Wrigley is affected by wind conditions more than any other major league park. The breeze, which does or does not blow in from Lake Michigan (three blocks to the northeast), is the great equalizer at Wrigley, like the Green Monster at Fenway Park. The wind giveth and the wind taketh away, adding an element of delicious uncertainty to any game played there. In 1922, the Cubs led the Phillies, 25–6, in the fourth inning; they held on to win, 26–23, with the bases loaded in the ninth.

Wrigley Field was built in 1914 by "Lucky Charlie" Weeghman, who bankrolled the Federal League Whales (Chi-Feds). Weeghman had gone to Chicago in 1892 and earned $8 a week as a waiter at King's Restaurant in the Loop. A few years later, he opened a lunchroom and maximized the space by having his customers sit in one-armed chairs. That business grew into a chain worth $8 million before World War I. Pressured by Fighting Jim Gilmore to

become involved with the Feds, Weeghman put up $25,000 for the Chicago franchise.

Chicago had originally grown south from the lake, then west. Accordingly, all its ballparks were on the South Side (South Side Park) or the West Side (West Side Park, West Side Grounds) except for DePaul University, which provided a field for the Federal League in 1913, when it was a minor league. Something of a visionary, Weeghman decided to build what was originally known as North Side Park on land that formerly housed the Chicago Lutheran Theological Seminary.

Weeghman hired architect Zachary Taylor Davis, who had designed Comiskey Park (see Chapter 5); he patterned Weeghman Park largely after the recently redone Polo Grounds in New York. A groundbreaking ceremony was held on March 4; just a month later, when the right field bleachers were completed, Weeghman was able to take Chicago reporters on an inspection tour of the park, which originally held 14,000. On April 19, more than 4,000 yards of soil and four acres of bluegrass were moved in to create the infield and the outfield. The $250,000 park opened, as scheduled, on April 23 despite a two-day work stoppage.

Big league ball on the North Side was a difficult concept for some Chicagoans. The area was so underdeveloped that Ring Lardner, then a *Chicago Tribune* columnist, wrote on Opening Day, "Many of our citizens will today visit the North Side for the first time." He added, "The North Side lacks the odors [from the stockyards] that have made the

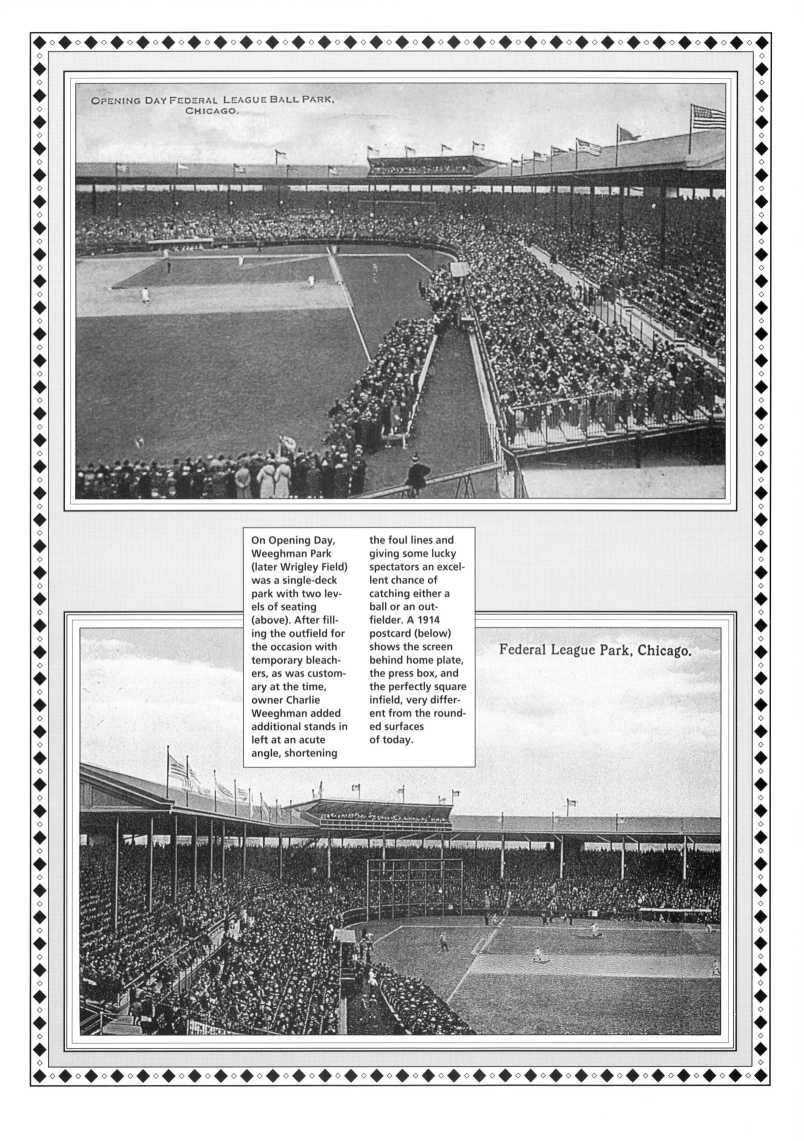

OPENING DAY FEDERAL LEAGUE BALL PARK,
CHICAGO.

On Opening Day, Weeghman Park (later Wrigley Field) was a single-deck park with two levels of seating (above). After filling the outfield for the occasion with temporary bleachers, as was customary at the time, owner Charlie Weeghman added additional stands in left at an acute angle, shortening the foul lines and giving some lucky spectators an excellent chance of catching either a ball or an outfielder. A 1914 postcard (below) shows the screen behind home plate, the press box, and the perfectly square infield, very different from the rounded surfaces of today.

Federal League Park, Chicago.

The Federal League asked to be included in the World Series, but the 1914 edition was a classic even without them, as Boston's Miracle Braves swept Connie Mack's A's. Game 1 drew 20,562 to Shibe Park — not to mention the crowds in the wildcat bleachers. (Although it's not possible for us to see the park from this angle, the wildcatters had no problem.) When the Series moved to Boston, the Braves played their home games at Fenway Park, with permission from the Red Sox. Wooden bleachers were added on Duffy's Cliff, in the left field corner (below right). The panoramic view of Fenway (above right) was taken during Game 3, won by the Braves, 5–4, in twelve innings.

South Side so popular." To make sure none of the citizenry became lost, Lardner thoughtfully provided travel tips.

Breaking new ground came easily to Weeghman. He became the first owner to let fans keep balls hit into the stands, and when patrons complained that strolling vendors spoiled their view, Lucky Charlie became the first ballpark magnate to install permanent concession stands. Although the other major leagues had outlawed Ladies Day, he reinstated it for the Feds. When nine homers were hit at Weeghman Park in the first 3 games, Lucky Charlie decided that the 310-foot left field wall was too close to the plate. On an off day, he had the front porch of a nearby house removed so that workmen could move the left field wall back 25 feet.

That fall, the Whales missed winning the pennant by just a game and a half. On the last Sunday of the season, the Whales took in 34,361 paid admissions; at the same time, the White Sox were drawing fewer than 3,500 at Comiskey Park, and the Cubs attracted fewer than 2,000 at West Side Grounds. In 1915, when his place was known as Whales Park, Weeghman expanded its capacity to 18,000. When the Federal League expired after the season (see Chapter 7), he was allowed to buy the Cubs, and his fellow owners looked forward to playing on the North Side.

In 1918, Lucky Charlie Weeghman's luck ran

out when commodity prices rollercoastered during World War I. Sugar that cost 22 cents a pound in May was worth just 3 cents in December, and Weeghman was forced to sell his controlling interest in the Cubs to William Wrigley, Jr., the heir to the Wrigley chewing gum fortune.

In 1922 and 1923, the entire grandstand and playing field were moved 60 feet southwest, toward the intersection of Clark and Addison. (The pitcher's mound of the 1990s is where home plate was in the early 1920s.) In the spring of 1923, the Cubs installed temporary bleachers to aid the would-be home runs of Lawrence "Hack" Miller, who had had many long drives pulled down just in front of Weeghman's redone fence. Miller's home runs increased from 12 to 20; when they dwindled to 4 and 2, the fence was gone and so was Miller.

The park became Wrigley Field in 1926, and the first major changes took place that winter. The left field bleachers were removed, the grandstand was double-decked to nearly double capacity to 38,396, and the playing area was lowered several feet. Extra bleachers were added outside the park in left and right field for the 1929 World Series, and the Cubs added a rope to hold back a standing room crowd in center field. The first Series game played at Wrigley was a classic. The Cubs featured free swingers like Lewis "Hack" Wilson and Riggs Stephenson. Instead of starting flamethrower

Robert "Lefty" Grove, A's manager Connie Mack chose a cunnythumb, 35-year-old Howard Ehmke, who had pitched in only 11 games all year. Ehmke yielded just an unearned run and set a Series record for strikeouts (13) as the A's won, 3–1.

The Cubs won a second pennant in 1932 and produced a Series game every bit the equal of 1929's. Before Game 3, on October 1, Babe Ruth said, "I'd play for half my salary if I could hit in this dump all the time." The Bambino homered in the first inning, flied deep to Kiki Cuyler in the second, and faced Charlie Root again with one out in the fifth. After taking two strikes and apparently pointing after each one, Ruth homered into the center field bleachers.

Journalists were convinced that he had "called his shot." The *Daily News*'s Paul Gallico wrote, "He pointed to the spot where he expected to send his rapier home." *New York Times* reporter John Drebinger wrote, "The Babe notified the crowd that the nature of his retaliation would be a wallop right out of the confines of the park." Others weren't sure. Yank shortstop Frank Crosetti said that Ruth "just happened to be pointing to center field." Manager Joe McCarthy said, "The gesture was meant for [Cub pitcher Guy] Bush. Ruth was going to foul one into the dugout, but when the pitch came up, big and fat, he belted it." When Ruth and Root met again on the movie set of *Pride of the Yankees*, Root asked if Ruth had indeed called his shot. Ruth said, "Of course not. But it made a hell of a story, didn't it?"

TIMELINE

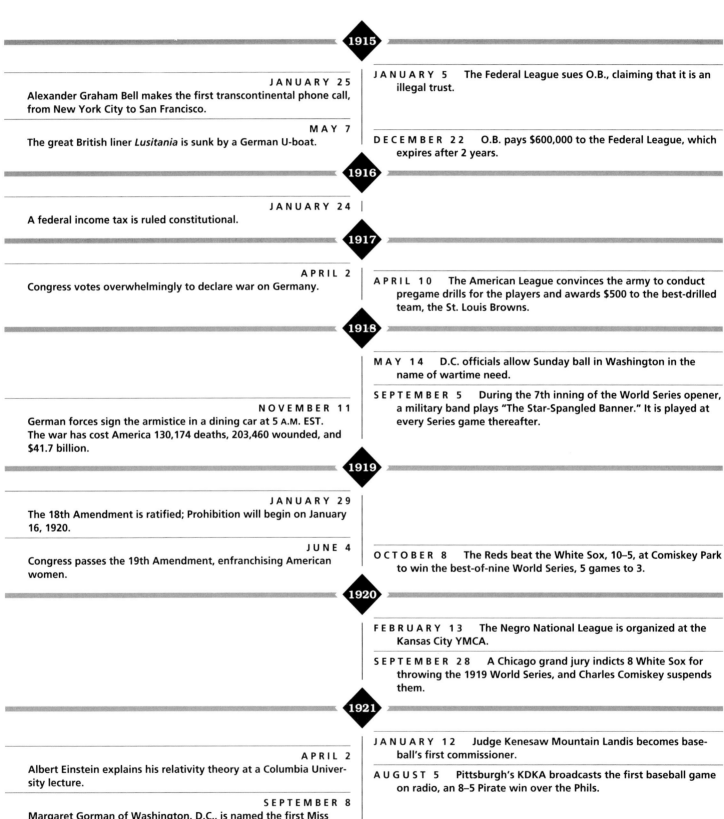

1915

JANUARY 25
Alexander Graham Bell makes the first transcontinental phone call, from New York City to San Francisco.

MAY 7
The great British liner *Lusitania* is sunk by a German U-boat.

JANUARY 5 The Federal League sues O.B., claiming that it is an illegal trust.

DECEMBER 22 O.B. pays $600,000 to the Federal League, which expires after 2 years.

1916

JANUARY 24
A federal income tax is ruled constitutional.

1917

APRIL 2
Congress votes overwhelmingly to declare war on Germany.

APRIL 10 The American League convinces the army to conduct pregame drills for the players and awards $500 to the best-drilled team, the St. Louis Browns.

1918

MAY 14 D.C. officials allow Sunday ball in Washington in the name of wartime need.

SEPTEMBER 5 During the 7th inning of the World Series opener, a military band plays "The Star-Spangled Banner." It is played at every Series game thereafter.

NOVEMBER 11
German forces sign the armistice in a dining car at 5 A.M. EST. The war has cost America 130,174 deaths, 203,460 wounded, and $41.7 billion.

1919

JANUARY 29
The 18th Amendment is ratified; Prohibition will begin on January 16, 1920.

JUNE 4
Congress passes the 19th Amendment, enfranchising American women.

OCTOBER 8 The Reds beat the White Sox, 10–5, at Comiskey Park to win the best-of-nine World Series, 5 games to 3.

1920

FEBRUARY 13 The Negro National League is organized at the Kansas City YMCA.

SEPTEMBER 28 A Chicago grand jury indicts 8 White Sox for throwing the 1919 World Series, and Charles Comiskey suspends them.

1921

APRIL 2
Albert Einstein explains his relativity theory at a Columbia University lecture.

SEPTEMBER 8
Margaret Gorman of Washington, D.C., is named the first Miss America.

JANUARY 12 Judge Kenesaw Mountain Landis becomes baseball's first commissioner.

AUGUST 5 Pittsburgh's KDKA broadcasts the first baseball game on radio, an 8–5 Pirate win over the Phils.

TIMELINE

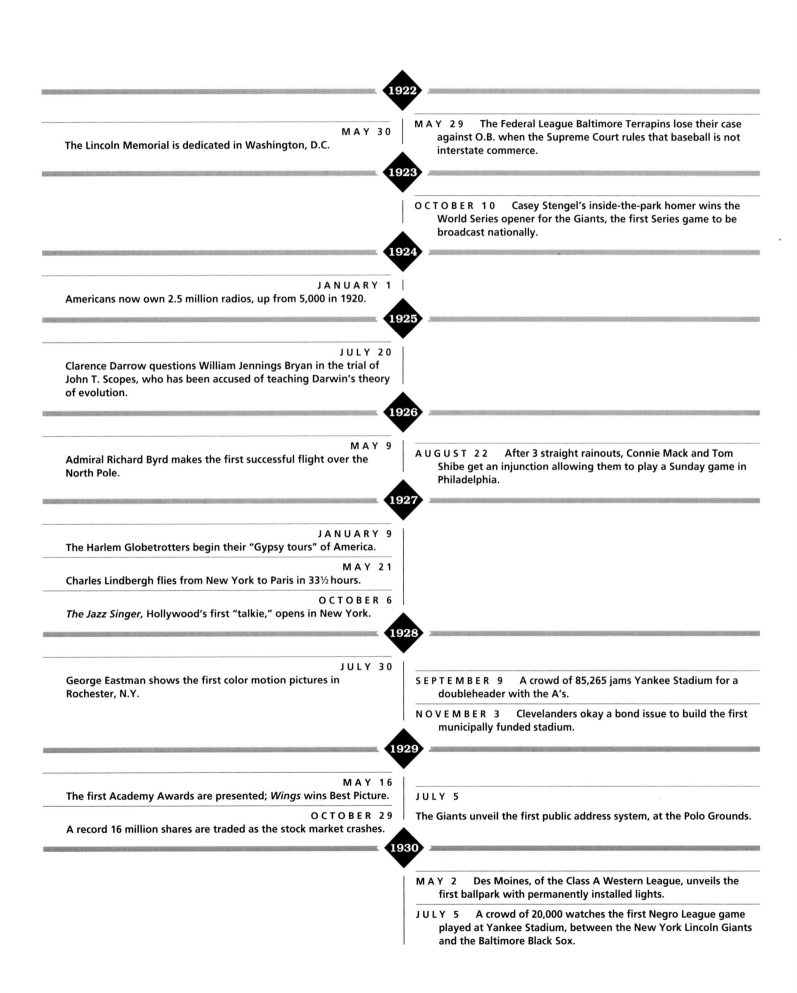

1922

MAY 29 The Federal League Baltimore Terrapins lose their case against O.B. when the Supreme Court rules that baseball is not interstate commerce.

MAY 30
The Lincoln Memorial is dedicated in Washington, D.C.

1923

OCTOBER 10 Casey Stengel's inside-the-park homer wins the World Series opener for the Giants, the first Series game to be broadcast nationally.

1924

JANUARY 1
Americans now own 2.5 million radios, up from 5,000 in 1920.

1925

JULY 20
Clarence Darrow questions William Jennings Bryan in the trial of John T. Scopes, who has been accused of teaching Darwin's theory of evolution.

1926

MAY 9
Admiral Richard Byrd makes the first successful flight over the North Pole.

AUGUST 22 After 3 straight rainouts, Connie Mack and Tom Shibe get an injunction allowing them to play a Sunday game in Philadelphia.

1927

JANUARY 9
The Harlem Globetrotters begin their "Gypsy tours" of America.

MAY 21
Charles Lindbergh flies from New York to Paris in 33½ hours.

OCTOBER 6
The Jazz Singer, Hollywood's first "talkie," opens in New York.

1928

JULY 30
George Eastman shows the first color motion pictures in Rochester, N.Y.

SEPTEMBER 9 A crowd of 85,265 jams Yankee Stadium for a doubleheader with the A's.

NOVEMBER 3 Clevelanders okay a bond issue to build the first municipally funded stadium.

1929

MAY 16
The first Academy Awards are presented; *Wings* wins Best Picture.

JULY 5
The Giants unveil the first public address system, at the Polo Grounds.

OCTOBER 29
A record 16 million shares are traded as the stock market crashes.

1930

MAY 2 Des Moines, of the Class A Western League, unveils the first ballpark with permanently installed lights.

JULY 5 A crowd of 20,000 watches the first Negro League game played at Yankee Stadium, between the New York Lincoln Giants and the Baltimore Black Sox.

TIMELINE

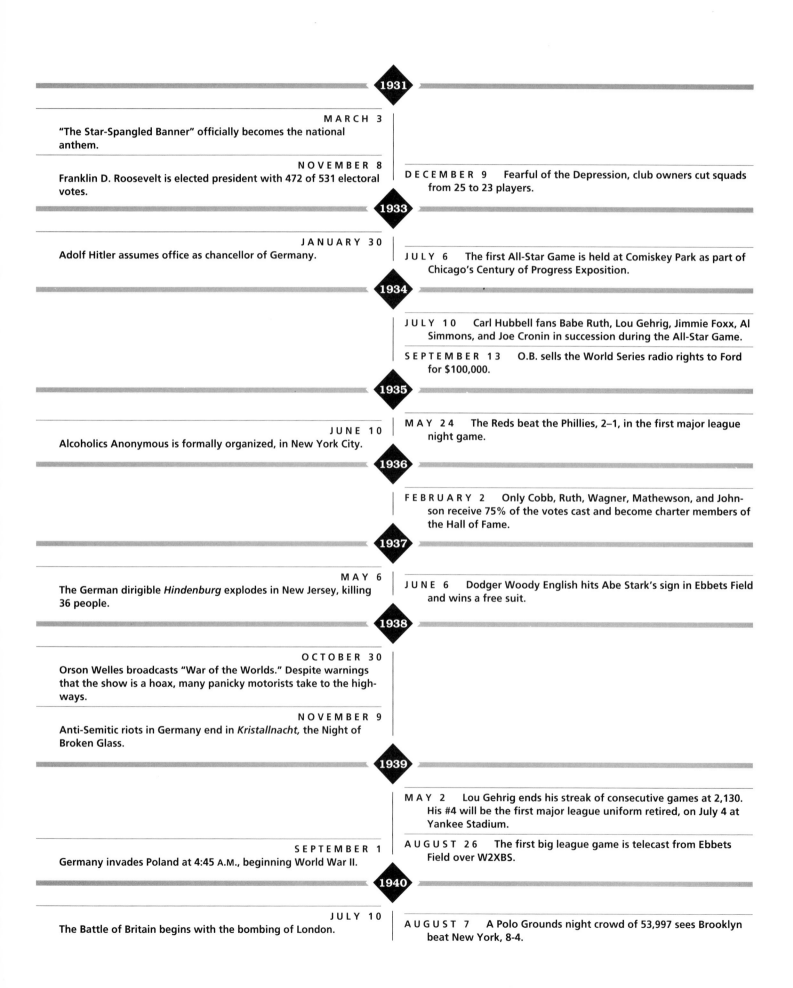

1931

MARCH 3
"The Star-Spangled Banner" officially becomes the national anthem.

NOVEMBER 8
Franklin D. Roosevelt is elected president with 472 of 531 electoral votes.

DECEMBER 9   Fearful of the Depression, club owners cut squads from 25 to 23 players.

1933

JANUARY 30
Adolf Hitler assumes office as chancellor of Germany.

JULY 6   The first All-Star Game is held at Comiskey Park as part of Chicago's Century of Progress Exposition.

1934

JULY 10   Carl Hubbell fans Babe Ruth, Lou Gehrig, Jimmie Foxx, Al Simmons, and Joe Cronin in succession during the All-Star Game.

SEPTEMBER 13   O.B. sells the World Series radio rights to Ford for $100,000.

1935

JUNE 10
Alcoholics Anonymous is formally organized, in New York City.

MAY 24   The Reds beat the Phillies, 2–1, in the first major league night game.

1936

FEBRUARY 2   Only Cobb, Ruth, Wagner, Mathewson, and Johnson receive 75% of the votes cast and become charter members of the Hall of Fame.

1937

MAY 6
The German dirigible *Hindenburg* explodes in New Jersey, killing 36 people.

JUNE 6   Dodger Woody English hits Abe Stark's sign in Ebbets Field and wins a free suit.

1938

OCTOBER 30
Orson Welles broadcasts "War of the Worlds." Despite warnings that the show is a hoax, many panicky motorists take to the highways.

NOVEMBER 9
Anti-Semitic riots in Germany end in *Kristallnacht,* the Night of Broken Glass.

1939

MAY 2   Lou Gehrig ends his streak of consecutive games at 2,130. His #4 will be the first major league uniform retired, on July 4 at Yankee Stadium.

SEPTEMBER 1
Germany invades Poland at 4:45 A.M., beginning World War II.

AUGUST 26   The first big league game is telecast from Ebbets Field over W2XBS.

1940

JULY 10
The Battle of Britain begins with the bombing of London.

AUGUST 7   A Polo Grounds night crowd of 53,997 sees Brooklyn beat New York, 8-4.

TIMELINE

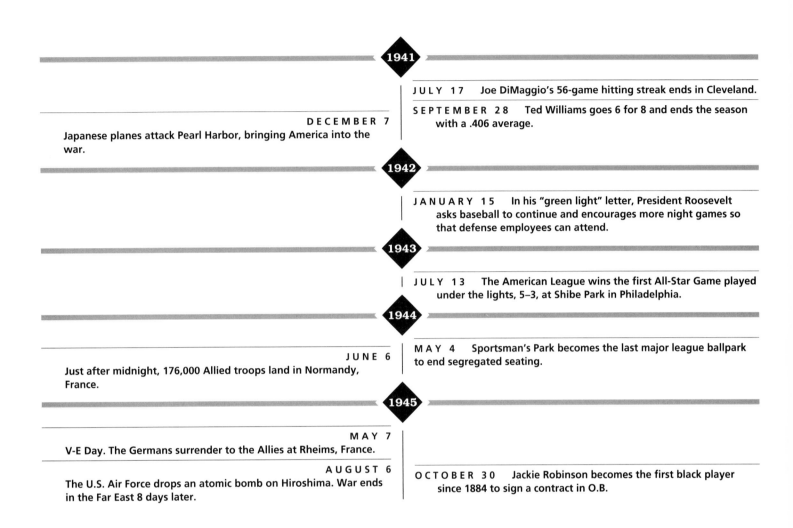

1941

JULY 17   Joe DiMaggio's 56-game hitting streak ends in Cleveland.

SEPTEMBER 28   Ted Williams goes 6 for 8 and ends the season with a .406 average.

DECEMBER 7
Japanese planes attack Pearl Harbor, bringing America into the war.

1942

JANUARY 15   In his "green light" letter, President Roosevelt asks baseball to continue and encourages more night games so that defense employees can attend.

1943

JULY 13   The American League wins the first All-Star Game played under the lights, 5–3, at Shibe Park in Philadelphia.

1944

MAY 4   Sportsman's Park becomes the last major league ballpark to end segregated seating.

JUNE 6
Just after midnight, 176,000 Allied troops land in Normandy, France.

1945

MAY 7
V-E Day. The Germans surrender to the Allies at Rheims, France.

AUGUST 6
The U.S. Air Force drops an atomic bomb on Hiroshima. War ends in the Far East 8 days later.

OCTOBER 30   Jackie Robinson becomes the first black player since 1884 to sign a contract in O.B.

The Miracle Braves deserted South End Grounds during the 1914 pennant race and played their home World Series games at Fenway Park. On October 12, Mayor John "Honey Fitz" Fitzgerald (in top hat), grandfather of President John F. Kennedy, posed for the camera with two Native Americans wearing headbands with the legend "Oh You Braves." Boston catcher Hank Gowdy, the first ballplayer to enlist during World War I, was snapped along with Braves owner James Gaffney (in bowler hat) and several Royal Rooters, colleagues of Nuf Ced McGreevy (see p. 75). The Braves subsequently built their own park — Braves Field, the first superstadium.

CHAPTER SEVEN

Superstadiums and Major Improvements

If baseball's best ballparks were built just before 1914, its biggest were built in the next eighteen years.

To understand just how big they actually were, consider the following: on September 9, 1928, in defiance of all fire regulations, Yankee Stadium held 85,265 fans. Even though the occasion was a doubleheader against the Philadelphia A's, with whom the Yanks were contending for the pennant, the crowd was, literally, more than *twice* as large as Ebbets Field *ever* held, legally or illegally.

The superstadium, to hold supercrowds, mirrored the growth of America as an economic (and later military) superpower with the approach of World War I. The millionth Ford rolled off the assembly line in 1915.

Cars weren't the only things that were moving. D. W. Griffith had just premiered *The Birth of a Nation*, the first great moving picture (despite its sympathetic treatment of the Ku Klux Klan, controversial even in 1915). Movie palaces holding a thousand people were sprouting up all over the place. If theaters in small towns could accommodate such crowds, then baseball could expand beyond the jewel box boundaries of Fenway Park, Ebbets Field, and Wrigley Field. Three superstadiums were built during this period: one to showcase

baseball's most popular slugger (Yankee Stadium in New York); one to bid for the summer Olympics (Municipal Stadium in Cleveland); and one big enough to supplant an entire eighteen-hole golf course (Braves Field in Boston).

THE HOME OF THE BRAVES: BRAVES FIELD

Originally the Red Stockings, the National League team in Boston became the Doves (for John Dovey in 1906) and the Rustlers (for William Russell in 1909). When James Gaffney, a contractor, bought the club in 1911, though, the team didn't become the Gaffers; instead, they were named Braves for, of all things, New York's Democratic organization. Gaffney was a member of Tammany Hall, which affected an Indian insignia; hence, its supporters became known as "braves" of Tammany Hall. The Tammany logo became that of the Braves, and Boston's team became the Braves. (Named in imitation of these Braves, the NFL's Boston Redskins eventually moved to Washington.)

Gaffney saw that, with fierce competition from the Red Sox's shiny new Fenway Park, the Braves would soon have to abandon the downtrodden South End Grounds. On December 1, 1912, he

Braves Field boasted a particularly attractive ticket booth. Hanging from the gold sign is a picture of Tamenund, an Indian chief from Bucks County, Pennsylvania, who was noted for his honesty. In the spring of 1789, a New York group opposing the new Federalist party named itself after Tamenund. Eventually, the group's headquarters became known as Tammany Hall, and Boston's ball club became known as the Braves after Tammany regular James Gaffney bought the club. The ticket booth Tamenund once adorned still exists as the Boston University police station.

bought the 13-acre Allston Golf Club on Commonwealth Avenue as the site for a ballpark; it became baseball's first superstadium.

Given Gaffney's inclinations as a baseball fan, the lot, measuring a heroic 850 by 675 feet, was just right. According to Bill Price in the 1978 *Baseball Research Journal*, Gaffney wanted the field large enough "to hit an inside-the-park home run in any of the three outfield directions." The original Braves Field was gargantuan, measuring 402 down the foul lines and a Bunyanesque 550 feet in deep center. Just in case distance alone wouldn't keep the number of out-of-the-park home runs down, the prevailing wind blew *in* from the Charles River; the year Braves Field opened, a total of just 8 home runs were hit, roughly one every 10 games, and all of them inside jobs.

Before building a new stadium, Gaffney brought in a new manager, George Tweedy Stallings, "a superstition-ridden zealot with the vocabulary of a camel driver." He brought the Braves home fifth in his first year. After the 1913 season, Gaffney arranged a trade with his brother-in-law, Cubs owner Charles F. Murphy, who was planning to fire Johnny Evers. Gaffney paid $25,000 for Evers and gave him a piece of the purchase price.

The Braves were still horrendous for the first half of the 1914 season. On the Fourth of July they were last, 15 games behind the Giants. Three days later they were trounced in Buffalo, 10–2, by the International League Bisons. Embarrassed by this pathetic showing against a team he'd managed for seven years, Stallings screamed, "By God, I'll get you out of last place if I have to break your necks!"

On the morning of July 18, the Braves were still last but beat the Reds with three ninth-inning runs to escape the cellar and improve their record to 36–43. On August 1 the surging Braves were fourth; by the 23rd, after Dick Rudolph, George "Lefty" Tyler, and "Seattle Bill" James had won 20 straight decisions among them, Boston was tied for first with New York.

With the Giants due in Boston for a Labor Day doubleheader, the by-then "Miracle Braves" decided to abandon South End Grounds, their home park of twenty-seven years. A symbolic move, it foreshadowed the building of Braves Field in the near future. Red Sox owner Joseph Lannin gave them permission to use Fenway Park, the only time a major league team smack in the middle of a pennant race felt compelled to move to a different location in its home town.

Boston split the doubleheader, won a single game the next day, 25 of their last 31 games, and

Washington Park, once the Dodgers' home, was resuscitated for the Federal League Tip-Tops. On Opening Day in 1915, the Feds' final season, the Tip-Tops opposed Buffalo; the other matchups are noted on the scoreboard. Note Buffalo's emblems and the Tip-Top sleeve patch worn by the Brooklyn players. On the billboard above, see that "Base Ball" is two words and that "Base Ball Players are all human."

ran away with the pennant by 10½ lengths. From July 4 until they clinched, on September 29, the Braves won 62 games out of 78, a .795 pace.

Having earned the dubious right to meet Connie Mack's A's in the World Series, Stallings told reporters, "I haven't scouted them. I don't care who they pitch. I predict a Boston victory in four straight." Stallings was proven a prophet yet again as the mighty A's scored a total of just 6 runs.

Now, with a championship team of miracle workers to fill all the seats, Gaffney surmised that it was precisely the right time to build his new park. Construction began on March 20, 1915, and by the time it opened five months later, Gaffney had become the first magnate to build a million-dollar ballpark, which required 750 tons of steel and 2,100 tons of cement. Curious fans arrived on the Commonwealth Avenue trolley, which paralleled the first base line and partially shielded riders from the elements. They saw what Gaffney trumpeted as "the world's largest ballpark ever," a field surrounded by a 10-foot cement wall and divided into four different seating sections:

◆ a covered single-decked grandstand, which seated 18,000, wrapped around home plate and extended down both foul lines.

◆ a pavilion in left field which seated 10,000. There was also a ground-level scoreboard in left, and opponents Johnny Rawlings and Bill Rariden were given home runs when their drives trickled through openings in it. Fans looking away from the action could see the Charles River and, just in front of it, the tracks of the Boston and Albany Railroad. Stories abound of home run balls that went over the fence, landed on trains, and were carried hundreds of miles.

◆ a similar uncovered pavilion in right field, also accommodating 10,000, running along (modestly named) Gaffney Street.

◆ the curious 2,000-seat bleachers in right center which, despite the 25-cent price, held a grand total of just 12 spectators one day. The best-known part of the park, it was known ever after as the Jury Box.

On Opening Day, August 18, 1915, more than 6,000 people were turned away, but at least 42,000 paid their way into the park, to date the largest crowd to see a baseball game. Traditionalists were pleased that the infield grass from South End Grounds had been moved to the new park, and everyone went home happy as Dick Rudolph beat the Cardinals, 3–1. As things turned out, however, the first team to use Braves Field as the home park in a World Series was the Red Sox; the Braves

finished second behind the Phillies. (The Red Sox never lost a World Series game at Braves Field, taking both games in 1915 and again in 1916. They used the park again for all their Sunday and holiday games from April 1929 to May 1932.)

Aside from Walter "Rabbit" Maranville, the Braves didn't develop any significant new talent for years; they became a second-division team, and attendance dropped. After a run of dismal seasons in the 1930s, the front office held a Name the Team contest in 1936; the winning entry was Bees. (Losers included Beacons, Bankrupts, and Sacred Cods.) Since the team was no longer the Braves, the park was officially renamed National League Field (also National League Ball Park); most fans, however, called it the Bee Hive from 1936 to 1940.

Management tried to spiff up the place in the 1940s, planting fir trees beyond the fence in center in an (unsuccessful) attempt to hide the huge clouds of smoke belching from the Boston and Albany locomotives in left and center. In 1946, lights were installed, the field was turned slightly toward right, and the grandstand seats were freshly painted for Opening Day. Unfortunately, they didn't dry in time, and thousands of fans left with green pants and red faces. (Braves management opened a "Paint Account" at a nearby bank and paid 5,000 claims at a cost of $6,000.)

Forty years after Boston's NL team became the Braves, they played their final home game on September 21, 1952, before just 8,822 fans. The following March they became the first major league team to move since the Baltimore Orioles became the New York Highlanders in 1903.

Braves Field was never used for big league baseball again. Eight years after the Braves left, it became the home of the AFL Boston Patriots and was used by the 1983 USFL Boston Breakers. The only remaining section from the original four components is the right field pavilion, but now it's a section of Nickerson Field and part of Boston University.

PEACE AND WAR

The superstadium craze started the same year the Federal League ended. Its first season had been profitable, and the Feds tried to increase their appeal by signing Walter Johnson and Rube Marquard; when both later returned to their original teams, the Feds filed an antitrust suit against O.B. in U.S. District Court for Northern Illinois, the jurisdiction of Judge Kenesaw Mountain Landis.

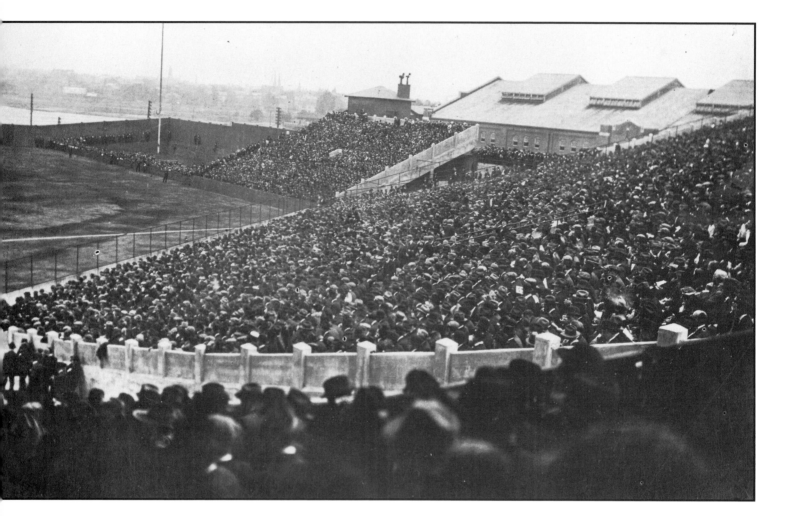

During the 1916 World Series, the Red Sox played their home games at Braves Field. On October 9, 47,373 fans set a major league attendance record. The game was a classic in which Babe Ruth held the Dodgers scoreless for 13 innings and the Red Sox won, 2–1, in 14 innings. Note the Charles River and the Jury Box in right center.

The Feds chose Landis's court because he had earned a reputation as a trustbuster by fining Standard Oil $29.2 million for illegal rebating; the company never paid a penny.

Unfortunately, the Feds' lawyers didn't realize the judge was a big baseball fan who saw no reason to change the foundations of the game. He said, "Both sides must understand that any blows at the thing called baseball would be regarded by this court as a blow to a national institution." According to *Major Leagues*, "Landis, a true ball fan, knew that if he rendered a decision based on the law it would go against Organized Baseball. This he was not prepared to do, and so he sat on the case for months."

The 1915 season got under way, and by its midpoint, Fed owners were cutting prices to the point where admission was a dime, a third of what a pound of coffee cost. Brooklyn's attendance flagged until one day the public was let in free to prove that there was "still interest in Federal League ball."

Despite these problems, the Feds discussed invading New York. "Fighting Jim" Gilmore grandly proclaimed, "We have drawn plans for a concrete

stadium to seat 55,000 persons — even bigger than Braves Field." It was announced in December that an $800,000 ballpark would be built at 145th Street between Lenox and Fifth avenues. Next, the Feds leased lavish offices in Manhattan and displayed a plan for the new stadium in a Fifth Avenue department store window. The gambit worked; in October peace talks were held, and on December 22 Landis dismissed the suit with the consent of both parties.

O.B. paid $600,000 for the dissolution of the Federal League, taking over the Fed parks in Brooklyn, Newark, and Pittsburgh for $400,000, $100,000, and $50,000 respectively over twenty years. Phil Ball, who owned the St. Louis Terriers, purchased the Browns, and Charlie Weeghman bought the Cubs with the National League kicking in $50,000. Kansas City and Buffalo got nothing, and Baltimore refused to accept a $50,000 settlement, leading to further litigation.

Only Weeghman Park remained a major league park. The International League Orioles moved into Terrapin Park after the Feds left, renamed it Oriole Park, and played there from 1916 to 1944. Washington Park, the site of General George Washing-

When Ban Johnson decreed that all American League teams put their players through military drills beginning in 1917, two prominent figures became platoon leaders. Yankees owner Colonel Jacob Ruppert, at left in a topcoat, put his team through their paces at the Polo Grounds, while Assistant Secretary of the Navy Franklin D. Roosevelt marched the Senators around Griffith Stadium (above). Note the detached covered bleachers in left field.

ton's last stand before his retreat to Trenton, was converted into a public market. In 1922, a neighborhood movement to save it as a "playground and national memorial," the first attempt to save a ballpark for historic reasons, failed dismally; in 1925, Brooklyn Edison took over the property and converted it into a warehouse.

The two-year war between O.B. and the Feds was over, but a more important conflict had started in 1914 when Archduke Francis Ferdinand, the crown prince of Austria, was assassinated at Sarajevo. Although the United States didn't enter the war until April 1917, its effect on baseball was felt immediately as attendance began to drop. Generally speaking, the teams playing well draw well, but that was not the case in 1917. Putting aside obvious nosedives such as the one that took the Dodgers from first to seventh, there were attendance losses even for average or good teams.

After deploring how international affairs had impinged on their pocketbooks in 1917, the owners announced at their annual meeting in December that they would conduct business as usual in 1918. When the *New York Times* commented that that policy was "not calculated to make us proud of baseball as an American institution," O.B. trimmed

Declining Attendance

TEAM	1916	PLACE	1917	PLACE
Chicago (NL)	453,685	5	360,218	5
New York (NL)	552,056	4	500,264	1
Philadelphia (NL)	515,365	2	354,428	2
Washington	177,265	7	89,682	5

its sails. The regular season was cut to 140 games per club, spring training was shortened, and sites closer to home were selected.

By the end of the 1918 season, major league attendance had plunged by more than 2 million again to barely over 3 million, the lowest figure of the twentieth century. On November 11, 1918, however, the armistice was signed, and the effect on baseball was as dramatic as the dip from 1916 to 1917: in 1919, attendance more than doubled to 6.5 million, and building a superstadium was no

longer a foolhardy idea. It particularly appealed to the Yankees, who had been badly outdrawn by their hosts, the Giants, in the first seven years of their tenancy.

THE HOUSE THAT RUTH BUILT: YANKEE STADIUM

In *Sleeping Arrangements*, Laura Cunningham recalls walking in the Bronx and, for the first time, seeing Yankee Stadium. She says, "The old stadium had a biblical look. I assumed it had been standing on 161st Street since before Christ. Years later, when I saw the actual Roman Coliseum, I couldn't suppress an inner gasp of recognition. 'Ahhhh! It's like Yankee Stadium.' "

It seems impossible that Yankee Stadium wasn't there before Christ, because so much baseball history has been made at 161st Street and River Avenue. Babe Ruth reinvented the game here, substituting power for finesse. Casey Stengel, who

Viewed from this angle, it's not difficult to understand why Babe Ruth cried when he was forced to leave the Polo Grounds for greener pastures across the Harlem River in the Bronx. Here is Ruth taking aim at the right field seats when they were 256 feet and change from home plate.

The old ballparks had gradual rakes, a nautical term taken from the slant or incline from the vertical, as a ship's mast. Architects spent much of the 1970s and 1980s designing grandstands that had steeper rakes because they were built without supporting posts. This exterior view of Ebbets Field (above), taken before 1920, shows how measured was the upward slope of both the upper and lower decks. When the 1920 World Series opened, on October 5, this same corner — Sullivan Place and Bedford Avenue — was bustling with commerce (left). Inside (below), late arrivals strolled to their seats, and vendors hawked their wares right on the field.

piloted the Boston Bees at their worst, became a "genius" here. Joe DiMaggio's 56-game hitting streak started here. Lou Gehrig said hello and good-bye here. Don Larsen was perfect here, and Roger Maris innocently angered the gods by breaking Ruth's record for home runs in a season here.

In 1913, when the Yankees moved into the Polo Grounds, New York was Giant territory. As can be seen from the table below, from 1913 to 1919, the Giants outdrew the Yankees every year except for the war-shortened 1918 season, when the Jints played only 56 home games to the Yanks' 67.

Then, with one stroke of a pen, the New York baseball world was turned upside down when the Yankees bought Babe Ruth from the Red Sox after the 1919 season.

In 1920, the Giants finished second, 7 games behind Wilbert Robinson's Dodgers, while the Yankees finished third, 3 games behind Tris Speaker's Indians. Ruth hit 29 majestic home runs at the Polo Grounds. (By comparison, American League runner-up George Sisler hit a total of only 19 — home *and* away.) The Yankees set a major league attendance record, becoming the first major league team to top a million in attendance in a season and reopening the idea of new superstadiums.

In 1921, the Giants served an eviction notice on the Yankees, effective after the following season. Giants owner John McGraw knew that there were no longer any lots as big as a golf course in Man-

hattan — at any price. "If we kick them [the Yankees] out, they won't be able to find another location on Manhattan Island. They'll have to move to the Bronx or Long Island. The fans will forget about them and they'll be through."

According to the *New York World-Telegram*'s Dan Daniel, the Yankee co-owners, Colonel Jacob Ruppert (who brewed Ruppert and Knickerbocker beers) and the extravagantly named Colonel Tillinghast L'Hommedieu Huston were first offered a lot in Long Island City, Queens, then made a deal for the Hebrew Orphan Asylum Grounds in Upper Manhattan; however, after a contract was drawn up, the asylum asked to be released, in part because alcohol would be consumed on the premises.

Colonel Huston, who was an engineer and architect, then devised a plan to build a stadium over the Pennsylvania Railroad tracks at Eighth Avenue and Thirty-second Street. The Pennsy was willing, but according to Daniel, "just as the deal was about to be closed, the War Department stepped in and killed it. The space was to be reserved indefinitely for anti-aircraft gun emplacements."

Finally, the colonels found a ten-acre plot in the Bronx, a corner of the William Waldorf Astor estate. The $600,000 lot, just across the Harlem River from the Polo Grounds, was served by the Lexington Avenue subway line. Working from plans prepared by the Osborn Engineering Company of Cleveland, the White Construction Company broke ground on May 5, 1922. The undertaking eventually involved

◆ 45,000 cubic yards of earth to grade the property, then the excavation of 25,000 cubic yards to lay the foundation.

◆ 2,200 tons of structural steel.

◆ 3,000,000 board-feet of lumber to form 28,000 cubic yards of concrete reinforced by 800 tons of steel.

◆ 13,000 cubic yards to form the playing field, topped by 116,000 square feet of sod trucked in from Long Island.

◆ 950,000 board-feet of Pacific Coast fir brought via the Panama Canal to erect the bleachers.

◆ 58,000 seats built on site, requiring 400,000 pieces of maple, 135,000 individual steel castings, and more than a million brass screws. Bolting the seats to the decks required drilling more than 90,000 holes in concrete.

White Construction did the job in 284 working days, completing America's first three-tier major league ballpark a month ahead of schedule.

The original park measured 295 feet to right, 281 to left, and 490 to dead center, which became known as Death Valley because it was death on

Giants-Yankees Attendance Before Ruth

YEAR	YANKEES	PLACE	GIANTS	PLACE
1913	357,551	7	630,000	1
1914	359,477	6 (T)	364,313	2
1915	256,035	5	391,850	8
1916	469,211	4	552,056	4
1917	330,294	6	500,264	1
1918	282,047	4	256,618	2
1919	619,164	3	708,857	2

Giants-Yankees Attendance After Ruth

YEAR	YANKEES	PLACE	GIANTS	PLACE
1920	1,289,422	3	929,609	2
1921	1,230,696	1	773,477	1
1922	1,026,134	1	945,809	1
1923	1,007,066	1	820,780	1

WRIGLEY FIELD
the Los Angeles Baseball Club, P. C. L.
Opening Day Sept. 29th, 1925.
Rogers Airport Photo.

The Pacific Coast League version of Wrigley Field (left) opened on September 29, 1925, in Los Angeles, but it wouldn't become a major league park until 1961. Comparing it with the Chicago original (below) reveals that the double-decked grandstands are nearly identical. A 1929 postcard shows Chicago's Wrigley eight years before the outfield got its ivy coating.

A NEW HOME OF THE AMERICAN LEAGUE BASEBALL CLUB OF NEW YORK
THE OSBORN ENGINEERING CO · CLEVELAND

Photography makes it possible to track Yankee Stadium from the initial sketch to the finished structure. The original model (above left) shows a structure with the third deck covered all the way around, but that idea never got off the drawing board. An early construction shot, taken on October 16, 1922 (below left), shows the framework for the famous copper frieze that became Yankee Stadium's signature. The next stage (right) shows the frieze two thirds finished and a bicycle track that was meant to create additional revenue. Riders on the Jerome Avenue IRT subway were able to monitor construction until the park was finished (below).

hitters who couldn't pull the ball. The first major league ballpark to be called a stadium, it deserved the name for its seating capacity alone (58,000). More than that, there was a feeling of great expanse, thanks perhaps to the three-deck construction. The vastness also created quiet, a grave dignity that no other ballpark has possessed before or since. It is a mark of Osborn's achievement that the players who performed regularly at the park — Lou Gehrig, Bill Dickey, Joe DiMaggio, quiet men with quiet pride — became reflections of it. Years later, Orioles pitching coach Ray Miller said of Yankee Stadium, "It's so big, so empty, and so silent that you can almost hear the sounds that aren't there."

Yankee Stadium opened on Wednesday, April 18, 1923, with all the pomp and circumstance befitting the new king of baseball stadiums. Before, the largest crowd to watch a baseball game had been the 47,373 at Game 2 of the 1916 World Series at Braves Field. According to the *New York Times*, there were 74,200 paying customers on Opening Day at Yankee Stadium and 25,000 more who "went home, convinced that baseball parks are not nearly as large as they should be."

Inside, John Philip Sousa led the Seventh Regi-

ment band in military marches, and New York's governor, Al Smith, threw out the first ball. Before the game, Ruth had told a reporter, "I'd give a year of my life if I can hit a home run in this first game in this new park." In the bottom of the fourth, he broke a scoreless tie with a homer into the right field bleachers. The *New York Times* story began:

> Governors, generals, colonels, politicians, and baseball officials gathered solemnly yesterday to dedicate the biggest stadium in baseball. . . . In the third inning with two team mates on the base lines, Babe Ruth smashed a savage home run into the right field bleachers, and that was the real baptism of Yankee Stadium.

In his account for the *Evening Telegram*, Fred Lieb called the stadium "the House That Ruth Built," and the name stuck. The Yankees had the biggest park, the greatest player, and an attitude that brought the team twenty-two championships. After being bested by the Giants in the 1921 and 1922 World Series, the Yankees came out on top in a 6-game Series in 1923, 4–2. For the third time in fourteen years, a team newly blessed with "the biggest stadium in baseball" became world champions.

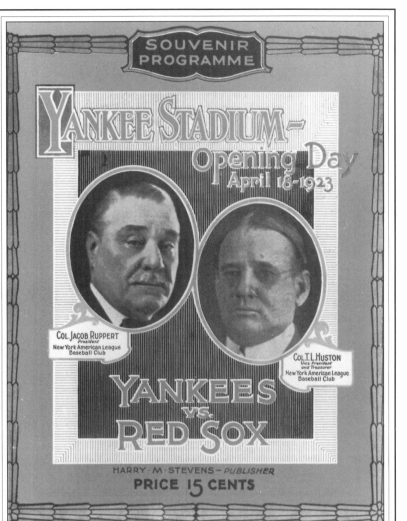

When Yankee Stadium opened, its exterior (below) projected solidity, as befitted a superstadium. The Opening Day program (left) featured the two colonels who owned the club. Four days after the opening, the *New York World* Sunday magazine ran a photo of the stadium (foreground) and the Polo Grounds across the Harlem River (far left). Hilltop Park would have been aligned with the other two parks along the Hudson River had it not been torn down and replaced with evangelist Billy Sunday's tabernacle.

THIRTYSOMETHING: THE GREAT DEPRESSION

On "Black Tuesday," October 29, 1929, 16 million shares were traded on the New York Stock Exchange. By 1932, the stock of General Motors was selling for just 8 percent of its value before the Crash. In 1932, according to *The Glory and the Dream*, "the average weekly wage of those who had jobs was $16.21." For the second time in fifteen years, matters weightier than baseball spoiled its prosperity. On March 8, 1930, Babe Ruth signed a two-year contract at $80,000 per annum. When it was pointed out that he was outearning President Herbert Hoover, the Bambino quipped, "I had a better year than he did."

Commissioner Landis announced in January 1933 that he was taking a 40 percent pay cut to set an example; Ruth signed a few months later for $52,000, down from $75,000 the year before. The clubs pared expenses, often with comic results. On July 10, 1932, Connie Mack sent only reliever Eddie Rommel and starter Lew Krausse to Cleveland. After yielding 3 runs in the first inning, Krausse took a shower, and Rommel turned in one of the weirdest relief jobs in major league history. Despite giving up 29 hits and 14 more runs, he got the win in a seventeen-inning, 18–17 slugfest.

Baseball did better during the early days of the Depression than the economy as a whole. In 1929, attendance for both leagues was 9,588,183 and actually rose in 1930 to 10,132,262; however, in 1931, it was off 16 percent and dropped 17.7 percent in 1932 and another 13 percent in 1933 before rebounding by roughly the same amount in 1934. The table below, from material created for *Total Baseball* by Pete Palmer, shows that many teams followed that pattern.

Attendance During the Depression

National League

CITY	1930	1931	1932	1933	1934
Boston	464,835	515,005	507,606	517,803	303,205
Brooklyn	1,097,329	753,133	681,827	526,815	434,188
Chicago	1,463,624	1,086,422	974,688	594,112	707,525
Cincinnati	386,727	263,316	356,950	218,281	206,773
New York	868,714	812,163	484,868	604,471	730,851
Philadelphia	299,007	284,849	268,914	156,421	169,885
Pittsburgh	357,795	260,392	287,262	288,747	322,622
St. Louis	508,501	608,535	279,219	256,171	325,056
Total	5,446,532	4,583,815	3,841,334	3,162,821	3,200,105

American League

CITY	1930	1931	1932	1933	1934
Boston	444,045	350,975	182,150	268,715	610,640
Chicago	406,123	403,550	233,198	397,789	236,559
Cleveland	528,657	483,027	468,953	387,936	391,338
Detroit	649,450	434,056	397,157	320,972	919,161
New York	1,169,230	912,437	962,320	728,014	854,682
Philadelphia	721,663	627,464	405,500	297,138	305,847
St. Louis	152,088	179,126	112,558	88,113	115,305
Washington	614,474	492,657	371,396	437,533	330,074
Total	4,685,730	3,883,292	3,133,232	2,926,210	3,763,606
Both leagues	10,132,262	8,467,107	6,974,566	6,089,031	6,963,711

When the Cubs traveled to Shibe Park in Philadelphia for the 1929 World Series, the Twentieth Street Irregulars decided that the haphazard, homemade seats they'd made previously just wouldn't do and hired professionals to provide rooftop seating. Note the pipe-smoking foreman overseeing the job on the roof.

The shadow cast by the light stanchion at right is an apt metaphor for the eventual importance of night games in major league baseball. This is minor league Oriole Park in Baltimore on September 4, 1930, when the minors adopted nocturnal baseball as a way of fighting the deepening Depression. The majors wouldn't follow suit for nearly five more years.

When Lakefront (Cleveland) Stadium was unveiled for baseball in 1932, it marked the outer reaches of the superstadium movement and also set a new standard for long-range major league viewing. This fish-eye view makes it abundantly clear that fans sitting in deep center field might just as well have been in suburban Parma.

CLEVELAND STADIUM: THE MISTAKE BY THE LAKE

From July 1932 through the end of the 1993 season, the Indians played most of their home games at what was originally Lakefront Stadium, later Municipal Stadium, and finally Cleveland Stadium. When the Cuyahoga River burst into flames on June 22, 1969, the city became known as "the Mistake by the Lake" (Erie). By extension, the name was attached to the stadium, which by that time richly deserved it. Phil Seghi, the Indians' general manager from 1973 to 1984, said of his park, "The good news is we're entered in the Indianapolis 500. The bad news is we're driving a Volkswagen." Things hadn't changed by 1992, when the New York Times called Cleveland Stadium "a dreary, cavernous edifice."

One of the reasons it is cavernous is the slim attendance. To say Cleveland fans don't support their club is an understatement, The Indians trailed all American League teams in attendance in 1983, 1984, 1985, 1987, 1990, 1991, and even 1992, despite the presence of at least half a dozen outstanding young players. Clearly, it wasn't the team but the park that was depressing attendance.

Since at least 1903, Clevelanders had been planning to develop property along the shoreline of Lake Erie, the city's northern boundary, by turning water into land. In 1923, the year Yankee Stadium was built, Floyd Rowe, a physical education supervisor for Cleveland's public schools, proposed a stadium by Lake Erie which would seat between 20,000 and 25,000 for high school football teams.

Samuel Hopkins, Cleveland's first city manager, asked the Osborn Engineering Company, which had served as architect for the rebuilt League Park as well as Braves Field and Yankee Stadium, to draw preliminary plans. As time went on, however, the proposed stadium gradually became a concrete panacea.

After checking the legality of funding such a building through municipal financing, the City Council in 1928 approved submitting to the electorate a $2.5 million bond issue to construct a stadium. Cleveland Stadium was not built as a ballpark at all but as a track and field emporium, because the city had an outside chance to hold the 1932 summer Olympics. (The games wound up instead in the Los Angeles Coliseum.)

On November 6, 1928, in the middle of a seemingly endless economic boom, Clevelanders approved the bond issue by a 3–2 margin, and the groundwork for baseball's original sin — funding ballparks with public money better earmarked for schools, hospitals, and highways — was laid (although the first municipally owned stadium specifically built for baseball wasn't erected until 1953; see Chapter 8).

The site for Lakefront Stadium had to be extended north into the lake. Since the landfill of crushed cars and old tires wasn't solid, a 200-foot-long bulkhead was built along a 1,300-foot east-west stretch of land and eventually stood 8 feet above the water line of Lake Erie. To level the site, 100,000 cubic yards of fill were added, and work began on the foundation. Given the marshy land, it was necessary to drive 2,521 piles into the landfill as deep as 65 feet. According to James Toman in *Cleveland Stadium,* "The piles were positioned in clusters and then tied together with a concrete cap, each cap serving as a base for the structural steel which would follow."

To understand the scope of the project, consider that in 1915, Braves Field required 750 tons of steel. Combining reinforced and structural steel, Lakefront Stadium required 5,100 tons, nearly seven times as much.

Lakefront Stadium had more individual seats than any ballpark in the world, and they came in three different sizes. Box seats were, as one might expect, the widest — 20 inches. Reserved seats in front of the pillars on the lower deck were 19, and

all the rest were 18. (Some seats have been as narrow as 16.) There were 37,896 seats in the main deck (more than all the seats in Wrigley, Fenway, or Ebbets alone), 29,380 in the upper deck, and 10,913 in the bleachers — 78,189 in all.

At the last minute it was decided to add lights, a sound system, and a scoreboard, which the voters had not approved. The overrun was $535,245, a pittance compared to the rebuilt Yankee Stadium, earmarked at $24 million but eventually reaching nearly six times that amount (see Chapter 9). When completed, Cleveland Stadium, for all the talk, didn't have a baseball tenant, putting a decided crimp in the expected revenues. Although city officials always "assumed that a deal could be struck," it was a full year later that big league baseball came to Lakefront Stadium. On July 31, 1932, Philadelphia's Lefty Grove outdueled the Tribe's Mel Harder, 1–0, before a record crowd of 80,184.

The rest of the year was not so successful, and attendance fell, as noted above, then nosedived another 100,000 in 1933. The Indians, who had been known as the Wanderers when they moved from park to park in 1899 (see Chapter 3),

An aerial view of Braves Field, taken on September 1, 1933, during a Labor Day doubleheader against the Giants, gives an excellent view of the park in its urban surroundings. One can easily spot the ticket booth on Gaffney Street (at left), streetcars just beyond it, the uncovered bleachers in left and right fields, and the tracks of the Boston and Albany Railroad.

repeated history, splitting their time between old League Park and Municipal Stadium. Unlike the Braves, who happily abandoned the cramped South End Grounds in 1915, the Indians left spacious Lakefront Stadium for the cozier confines of League Park.

The division of a major league team's home schedule into two separate parks was unspoken testament that bigger was not necessarily better and ended visions of superstadiums in the minds of baseball's owners and would-be owners. From 1934 to 1946 the Indians played weekdays at League Park, which was never retrofitted for lights, and nights, weekends, and holidays at Municipal Stadium, which had lights in 1931 that were never used for baseball; modern lighting was installed in 1939, adding more dates to Municipal's part of the Indians' schedule. In all, the Indians used two home parks for more than twelve full seasons.

According to Toman, the park made a profit in only one year of its operation, 1948, when the Indians rolled up a pennant and a World Series. Even so, the profit was one measly dollar, a cautionary figure that many city councils, city managers, and mayors have managed to ignore in their rush to be "major league," hence "big time."

Sadly, the fans who came to see the Indians often froze in April and May and were not nourished by intimate contact at any time of the year. Babe Ruth once said of Municipal Stadium, "You'd have to have a horse to play the outfield here." Having a horse might also have moved one a bit closer to the action. Fans sitting at the top of the bleachers in center field are "paying money," in Michael Benson's words, "to sit farther from home plate than any other baseball fans in the world."

The stadium was a mistake in yet another way. With its phenomenal capacity, there was never any last-minute rush to buy seats; fans knew they could always get in at Municipal, no matter how late they showed up. Former manager Jeff Torborg said, "The stadium can be depressing because you can have a pretty good-sized crowd and not notice it. And if you have a crowd of 6,000, it feels like no one's there. It feels like a B game in spring training."

Fortunately, the Mistake by the Lake was retired as a major league ballpark following the 1993 season. The Indians' new ballpark had no official name until the beginning of the 1994 season and was named Jacobs Field by Indians owner Richard Jacobs, after his late brother, David.

MAJOR ADJUSTMENTS

Even though the Depression became more manageable during the late 1930s, thoughts of superstadiums no longer danced in the heads of club owners. Rather than build new parks, they fixed up the old ones on a triage basis:

1. Wrigley Field and Fenway Park were completely redone; Navin and Redland fields became Briggs Stadium and Crosley Field.

2. Griffith Stadium and Ebbets Field remained relatively untouched until after World War II.

3. Cleveland's League Park and Philadelphia's Baker Bowl were never retrofitted for lights, effectively ending their usefulness.

Of course, League Park and Baker Bowl were left over from 1891 and 1895 respectively. In addition to being just plain old and old-fashioned, Baker Bowl was particularly run down. Chicago sportswriter Warren Brown called it "the major league ball park with the atmosphere of a rundown powder room." In a series on ballparks, Ed Burns of the *Chicago Tribune* wrote, "What a ballpark! There are at least 18 better ones in the American Association, the Pacific Coast League, and the International League."

Little had changed at Baker Bowl since it was rebuilt, and attendance was dismal, leaving little money for capital improvements and leading to an accident; when part of the upper deck in right field collapsed in May 1927, the Phillies had to play several home games at Shibe Park.

Rather than use lawn mowers, Phillies groundskeepers kept costs down by letting sheep graze in the outfield. Outfielder Ethan Allen said, "The stands were so rusty that some spectators preferred to stand, to avoid getting covered with debris which would come down . . . as a result of foot-stomping overhead." One sportswriter commented in the 1930s, "National League players will be pleased to learn that the visiting dressing room at Baker Bowl is being completely refurbished for next season — brand new nails are being installed on which to hang their clothes."

While Baker Bowl was never modernized, the coming of the long ball gave owners an opportunity to design a second set of their parks for specific sluggers. Babe Ruth had changed the fans' view of the park as well as of the game. Having seen the Bambino smack prodigious drives out of the premises in the movie newsreels that appeared in the mid-1920s, fans began clamoring for towering

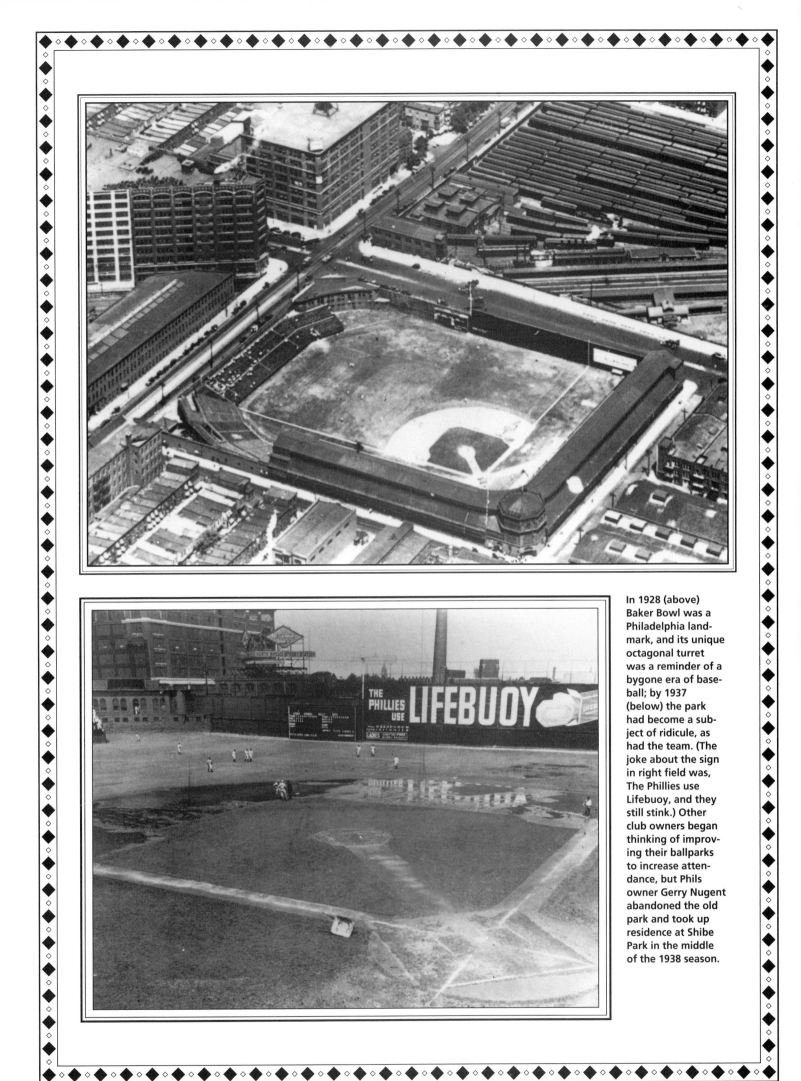

In 1928 (above) Baker Bowl was a Philadelphia landmark, and its unique octagonal turret was a reminder of a bygone era of baseball; by 1937 (below) the park had become a subject of ridicule, as had the team. (The joke about the sign in right field was, The Phillies use Lifebuoy, and they still stink.) Other club owners began thinking of improving their ballparks to increase attendance, but Phils owner Gerry Nugent abandoned the old park and took up residence at Shibe Park in the middle of the 1938 season.

On October 2, 1936, Yankee second baseman Tony Lazzeri hit only the second grand slam in World Series history at the Polo Grounds, leading the Yanks to an 18–4 win over the Giants. This picture, which captures that moment, was featured in an exhibition of World Series photos that toured banks in the Northeast. The ballpark changed very little after this, the only notable addition being advertising signage on the clubhouse in center field. An exterior view from the same time shows the water tower, the tracks of the New York Central Railroad, and, across the river (top left), Yankee Stadium.

blasts hit out of the park rather than the more challenging inside jobs.

Purists can rant all they want, but the fact is that the public likes offense. As noted in *The Bill James Historical Baseball Abstract*, "Throughout the history of the game, almost every significant increase in offense has been accompanied by an increase in attendance." Owners soon understood that they could add seats and create more out-of-the-park dingers at the same time by putting the seats in front of the existing fences, cutting down

the distances for potential home run balls. As things turned out, not one of these maneuvers — aimed at helping such sluggers as Al Simmons, Ted Williams, and Hank Greenberg — ever panned out.

The first attempt was designed for a corpulent catcher, the Braves' Frank "Shanty" Hogan, who weighed 240 pounds. After the 1927 season, left field at Braves Field was moved in 83 feet by adding 26 rows of bleacher seats. To make the effect less noticeable, the diamond was shifted toward right and the scoreboard was moved from the top

The Evil Genius: Emil Bossard

By playing home games in parks with contradictory characteristics, the Indians might have wasted any inherent advantage a home team has, considering the layouts of League Park and Municipal Stadium when the Indians first used them. In League Park, left field was a hefty 374, right field a cozy 290, despite the 60-foot fence. At Municipal Stadium, the foul lines were both 322, giving right-handed pull hitters a significant edge and penalizing left-handers, who complained bitterly. Yet the Indians proved to be an incredible home team regardless of which park they called home:

YEAR	HOME	ROAD
1936	49–30	31–44
1937	50–28	33–43
1938	46–30	40–36
1939	44–33	43–34
1940	51–30	38–35

The answer lay not in the parks but rather in their groundskeeper, Emil Bossard. "The evil genius of groundskeepers" joined the Indians in 1936 and pulled off a ground rule double by making the Indians the favorites no matter which home park they were playing in.

In the process, he started a groundskeeping dynasty that is still active in baseball. The morning after the last game was played at the original Comiskey Park, Emil's grandson Roger Bossard supervised the moving of the infield to the new Comiskey. Roger had learned the tricks of the trade from the ground up, so to speak; when the White Sox had a run of knuckleballers, notably Wilbur Wood, he deadened the area around the plate to make grounders easier to field.

Forgetting the achievements of his descendants, however, Emil Bossard is considered baseball's greatest single groundskeeper. He adapted both Cleveland parks to the talents of individual Indians at any given time. The Bossards attended spring training every year to see how many pull hitters the Tribe featured, how many beat the ball into the dirt (when there *was* only dirt), how many good bunters were around, how many pitchers threw their fastball directly overhand. Then, when the season started, it was the Bossard clan's practice to "custom-build the infield," in Hal Lebovitz's phrase, "to give the Indians the edge percentage-wise." Emil Bossard said, "This is a game of inches. An inch is often the difference between a base hit and an out. We try to have the inches go our way."

Bossard learned his craft in the minors. Business at his father's St. Paul hardware store was slow in 1910, so he walked over to where Lexington Park was being built. "They put me to work carrying lumber. I'd never seen a baseball diamond before." A few weeks later, he was working with the head groundskeeper. When the groundskeeper got sick on Opening Day, Bossard got his job. Twenty-six years later, he went to Cleveland on the recommendation of Steve O'Neill, who had managed against St. Paul in the American Association.

When Bossard arrived, the Indians had Earl Averill hitting, Mel Harder pitching, and not much else. Bossard speeded up the field one day, slowed it down the next, built the foul lines up to aid the Indian bunters, and slowed down hard grounders along third base to make the hops easier to field — whatever it took to give the Indians an edge. He learned that the key to doctoring a diamond is the first bounce the ball takes. He said, "If the first bounce is quick and sharp the ball has a better chance of getting through the infield. [This is even truer of AstroTurf.] So we work on the area where the ball first hits. That's usually in the dirt circle between home plate and the infield grass."

Word of Bossard's wizardry got around and eventually helped other teams as well. When the American League decided to standardize all eight pitching mounds in 1946, a group of veteran hurlers were consulted about the best model. They simply said, "Copy Cleveland's." In September 1953 the Yankees paid Bossard to get rid of their diseased grass and get the field in shape before the start of the World Series. A year later, the Tigers were complaining about bad hops in the infield, and Bossard solved the caking of the skin part of the infield with a new rolling process.

Not all of Bossard's stratagems worked to perfection. In Game 4 of the 1954 World Series, at Municipal Stadium, the Giants led, 2–0, going into the top of the third inning. With one out, Alvin Dark and Don Mueller singled, and Willie Mays hit what looked like a perfect double play ball down to Rosen at third; the ball took a kangaroo hop over Rosen's head, scoring Dark and putting Mays on second. Bob Lemon retired the next two batters, but the Giants won, 7–4, to sweep the Series.

Bossard told Lebovitz, "With Lemon pitching, we tried to make the ground very soft. But we were afraid to soak it too much; there isn't much sun in October to dry the excess water, and the ground might have become too muddy. So we didn't use enough water and the ground got too hard."

One Bossard tactic could never go wrong, as explained by Bill Veeck, Jr., the Indians' owner during the late 1940s. Discussing how the club treated rain delays, Veeck revealed that the Tribe had *two* sets of canvas covers. "We roll one out when we're ahead and time is called for rain. It takes our ground crew two minutes to put it in place. But when the Indians are trailing we get out the second set. It's more unwieldy. Twenty minutes is the time for laying it."

of the left center field wall to right field. Unfortunately, the fans never got a chance to see how great
Hogan might have been because he and outfielder
Jimmy Welsh were traded to the Giants for Rogers
Hornsby before the season started. (Hogan hit only
48 homers in five seasons for the Giants, returned
to Boston, and managed just 9 more in three years
as a back-up catcher.)

The second attempt occurred at Comiskey Park
in Chicago; built as a pitcher's park, it was never a
home run haven. Nevertheless, the punchless
White Sox bought Al Simmons from the Athletics at
the end of the 1932 season and moved home plate
14 feet toward the center field fence. Simmons
managed to hit just 14, 18, and 16 homers in three
seasons before being dealt to Detroit. (He hit 21
homers as a Senator several years later.)

Even Ted Williams, the second Hall of Famer to
get a park retrofitted for his talents, was unsuccessful. In 1939, the rookie hit 14 homers at home.
Attempting to increase his home run production,
the next year the front office installed a bullpen in
front of the right field bleachers, bringing the fence
in a cozy 23 feet. The bullpen was quickly dubbed
"Williamsburgh," and Sox fans foresaw homers by
the carload. It was not to be; the Splendid Splin-
ter's home run production actually dropped from
14 to 9 at Fenway Park that year (and from 17 to
14 on the road).

After World War II, the ploy was tried one more
time, in Pittsburgh. On January 18, 1947, the
Pirates paid the Tigers $75,000 for Hank Green-
berg's contract. The Buccos proceeded to honor the
man who had threatened Ruth's single-season
home run record (58 in 1938) by building "Greenberg Gardens." This time, 30 feet were lopped off
the 365-foot distance from home to the left field

wall by installing a chicken-wire fence. Despite the
change, the number of Pirate and visitor homers
decreased sharply thereafter.

YEAR	PIRATE HOMERS	VISITOR HOMERS
1947	95	87
1948	69	64
1949	77	75
1950	81	79
1951	72	84
1952	45	72
1953	53	88

The left field fence was renamed Kiner's Korner,
and Ralph Kiner became a home run champ seven
times but clearly did lots of damage on the road as
well; when he was traded to the Cubs in 1953, the
fence was removed.

YAWKEYIZING FENWAY

One of the most important dates in Red Sox
history is February 21, 1933, the day Thomas A.
Yawkey turned 30 and inherited $7 million; four
days later, he bought a team that in the previous
decade had finished in the cellar every year save
1924 (seventh) and 1931 (sixth). Like other cash-
poor owners, Joseph Lannin had done nothing to
update Fenway Park, and it was showing signs of
age. That fall, while the Boston Redskins were
playing other NFL opponents at Fenway, its renovation began.

The park's most distinctive feature, Duffy's Cliff,
the 10-foot-high embankment in left field which

had bedeviled outfielders for twenty years, was dug up and hauled away, leaving only a subtle rise as an early warning track. The wooden left field wall was also dismantled and replaced by a concrete base and a wooden frame of railroad ties covered by a tin structure destined to become famous on its own. (See Chapter 8.)

After the football season, construction spread to the rest of the outfield, and the wooden seats in center and right were ripped out and replaced by concrete stands. The foundations were also reinforced to provide support for a second deck that was promised from time to time but was never installed.

The grandstand was enlarged and topped with a 4-foot fence to prevent foul balls from bounding off the roof to the street. A total of 15,708 new seats were installed and, allowing for the outfield seats removed, net capacity was increased from 27,642 to 37,500.

The new seats changed the park's playing dimensions drastically. Left field was reduced from 320 to 315, the figure printed on the wall. (The blueprints say 308, and, in 1975, the *Boston Globe* said 304 feet-plus, using aerial photography.) The big change came in center field, which went from 468 to 420, while right was scaled back from 358 to 334.

In the midst of reconstruction, a fire on January 5 destroyed the center field bleachers, which had to be rebuilt. Insurance covered the $250,000 loss, and as many as a thousand union laborers a day worked double shifts to get the park ready. One of the final jobs was painting the entire exterior green.

On Reopening Day, April 17, 1934, George Wright, who had played at South End Grounds for Boston in 1871, was on hand, but Joe Cronin's

Washington Senators spoiled the party by winning, 6–5, in eleven innings. It was a testament to Yawkey's success that attendance at Fenway increased dramatically — from 268,715 in 1933 to 610,640 in 1934. On September 22, 1935, a doubleheader against the Yankees drew 47,627, which will never be equaled under Fenway's current dimensions because of more stringent fire laws.

THE WALLS OF IVY

If Fenway was renovated out of failure, Wrigley Field was rebuilt due to success. One of the first clubs to reconfigure a park built between 1909 and 1915, the Cubs double-decked their park late in 1927, drew a million fans a year from then until 1931, and won pennants in 1929, 1932, and 1935.

During the 1937 season, a 23-year-old named Bill Veeck, Jr., the same man who would create the first exploding scoreboard, was Wrigley's assistant and had ordered another innovative scoreboard for the field. Instead of light bulbs that flashed on and off, this model had "brightly painted eyelids which were pulled up and down magnetically."

The day before the scoreboard was to be delivered, Veeck called the inventor and got no answer. Driving over to his plant, Veeck learned that he had panicked about assembling it and had disappeared. Veeck called in his grounds crew and recruited electricians from the Kellogg Switchboard Company:

I drilled the frames. The grounds crew put the frames together and the Kellogg electricians wired them. We built the whole scoreboard in that loft during the night, carting it to the park unit by unit. . . . It worked perfectly. It is the scoreboard still being used at Wrigley Field.

The 27-by-75-foot scoreboard remains the only one in the major leagues without artificial lighting, and it is operated mostly by three men inside the three-story-high board. The scores and pitchers' numbers are made of steel and weigh five pounds apiece. The eyelids signaling the batter, ball, strike, and out click when they're changed electronically from the press box behind home plate.

In addition to technology, Veeck was also interested in horticulture. He'd seen and admired the ivy on the walls at Perry Stadium in Indianapolis (now Bush Stadium, for Donie Bush). Knowing that Wrigley was redoing the center field bleachers, Veeck suggested that trees and ivy be planted on the center field wall outside the park; instead, Wrigley wanted trees "*in* the bleachers, on the steps leading up to the scoreboard, and he wanted them planted full-grown." The bleacher stair step was created to allow huge potted plants and eight Chinese elm trees to grow, but there were problems.

In *Veeck as in Wreck*, the promoter writes, "What he got were the most expensive tree plantings in the history of the world." He continues,

> Chicago, you see, is situated on Lake Michigan. A strong wind comes off the lake. Someday, a poet is going to give Chicago some kind of appropriate nickname like, say, the Windy City. We planted all of Mr. Wrigley's giant trees, and a week after we were finished, the bleachers looked like the Russian steppes during a hard

cold winter. Nothing but cement and bark. The leaves had all blown away.

Veeck had also mentioned ivy to Wrigley and had planned to install it at the end of the season; however, when the tree experiment failed, Wrigley wanted the ivy immediately — before the Cubs returned for their final home stand. When Veeck discovered that ivy wouldn't take that quickly, he ordered 350 Japanese bittersweet plants and 200 pots of Boston ivy:

> Bob Dorr, the groundskeeper, and I strung light bulbs all along the fence to enable us to work through the night. When the morning sun broke over the grandstand roof, it shone upon a bleacher wall entirely covered with bittersweet. We had planted the ivy in between, and, in time, the ivy took over.

(The ivy not only became a signature of the park but also produced revenue. In 1979, the Cubs sold 2,500 pots of ivy cuttings for $1.50 apiece.)

Following the 1937 season, the boxes and grandstand seats in the lower left field stand were rebuilt and turned at a 30-degree angle so that the spectators faced home plate rather than center. Surprisingly, one change wasn't made then: lights were not added to Wrigley and wouldn't be for more than fifty years. Wrigley said in explanation, "In deference to people living around our ball park, we will install lights — only if the standards can be disguised as trees."

In 1913, the Ohio River flooded, and Redland Field survived (left). Twenty-four years later, history repeated itself and Crosley Field was buried under more than 20 feet of water (right). Four years later, the Reds had become world champs, and a local radio station celebrated their achievement with a special brochure (below). Outwardly, the area around Western and Findlay had withstood the flood with no ill effects. But some families moved out, and the neighborhood began to deteriorate.

366 FT.

R.F.

328 FT.

L.F.

C.F.

387 FT.

CINCINNATI REDS' HOME GROUNDS

has been baseball grounds since late '70s. First concrete stand in history of baseball was erected here. In 1937, during flood, there was 20 feet of water over Home Plate. Largest capacity crowd was in 1929 . . . 35,770 fans. Present seating capacity is 30,000. Park is located on Findlay Street at Western Avenue. **HOW TO GET TO THE PARK FROM DAYTON:** Drive to Cincinnati on Route No. 25, or No. 48 and No. 42, to 1 mile south of Sharonville. Turn right on No. 126 to Junction of No. 4W. Take No. 4W (Spring Grove Avenue) to Western Avenue. Left on Western Avenue to Crosley Field.

During the Depression, the Reds' attendance nosedived from 356,950 in 1932 to 206,773 in 1934, when the team finished last. General manager Larry MacPhail shrewdly used the poor gate to convince his fellow owners to allow night games in the birthplace of professional baseball. The first major league night game was played on May 24, 1935, and gradually other owners followed suit.

NIGHT GAMES

Phil Wrigley wasn't the only major league owner to drag his heels on night baseball. In his authoritative book, *Lights On!*, David Pietrusza describes what major league baseball has never acknowledged: that the minor and the Negro leagues did the pioneering in night baseball while the big leagues mostly sat on the sidelines.

Indeed, the father of modern night baseball wasn't a Mack, a Comiskey, or a Griffith but rather E. Lee Keyser, the president of the Class A Western League's Des Moines Demons. Keyser, who had bought the concession rights when the Federal League Terriers moved to St. Louis, announced that he would install permanent lights at a cost of $19,000 and scheduled the big night for May 2, 1930.

Although the owner of the Class C Western Association Independence (Kans.) Producers beat Keyser to the punch and played the Muskogee Chiefs on April 28 under temporary lights, Keyser got the coverage he deserved. With Commissioner Landis in the stands and fans listening nationally on NBC radio, the Demons lit up the Wichita Aviators, 13–6. The *New York Times* said, "In the opinion of many fans, the contest was viewed as clearly as a game played under daylight conditions."

Many minor league teams immediately adopted nocturnal play, and the more progressive major league teams scheduled exhibition games against minor leaguers with lights. The Reds played in Indianapolis, the Phils in Baltimore; the Giants played in Bridgeport and Houston and even arranged a night game at the Polo Grounds between two semi-pro teams.

The view developed that night ball was all right for the provinces but wasn't ready for the big city. Will Wedge of the *New York Sun* wrote that transients in big cities "must be amused . . . only on afternoons on the diamond, for in the evenings their preference is for theatrical entertainment." A second drawback was that night games excluded kids. "One of the arguments against night ball is that knotholers can't be present." In a comment made ironic by the all–night game World Series of the 1980s and 1990s, Wedge continued, "Organized baseball, *with a proper view of its future*, [italics added] must always remember the kids, and welcome them as often as possible."

Players and owners alike lobbied against night baseball. Senators owner Clark Griffith said, "There is no chance of night baseball ever becoming popular in the biggest cities. . . . High-class baseball cannot be played at night under artificial light." Giant boss Charles Stoneham said, "With pitchers like Dizzy Dean, Roy Parmalee, and Van Mungo throwing at night, we may have serious injuries to batsmen." The redoubtable Floyd Caves "Babe" Herman announced, perhaps self-consciously, that "it would give outfielders a new alibi. They'd lose the ball in the light instead of the sun."

Some baseball men tried to sell lights to their colleagues but were unsuccessful. Sam Breadon, the Browns' tenant at Sportsman's Park, wanted to install lights, but his landlord refused. Bill

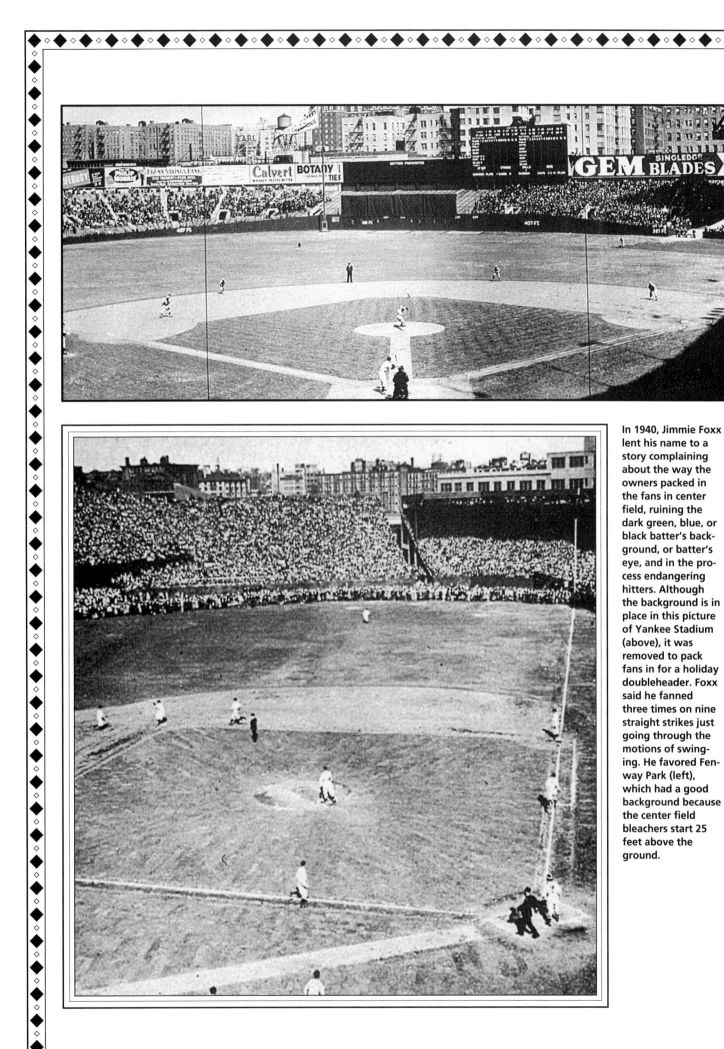

In 1940, Jimmie Foxx lent his name to a story complaining about the way the owners packed in the fans in center field, ruining the dark green, blue, or black batter's background, or batter's eye, and in the process endangering hitters. Although the background is in place in this picture of Yankee Stadium (above), it was removed to pack fans in for a holiday doubleheader. Foxx said he fanned three times on nine straight strikes just going through the motions of swinging. He favored Fenway Park (left), which had a good background because the center field bleachers start 25 feet above the ground.

Night baseball spread to Ebbets Field in Brooklyn in 1938, and Larry MacPhail decided to mark the occasion by printing a special diecut ticket. Unfortunately, Reds pitcher Johnny Vander Meer decided to celebrate the occasion in his own way and pitched his second consecutive no-hitter. The photo below shows his first pitch. The lighting at Ebbets was no great shakes, but things had improved just a year later when night baseball came to Comiskey Park in Chicago (right).

ENTER GATES
22 TO 26 ROTUNDA

LOWER STAND
6   3   2
SEC.   ROW   SEAT

EBBETS FIELD
BROOKLYN
EST. PRICE $1.50
FED. TAX   .15
TOTAL $1.65

NIGHT GAME
1

Veeck, who'd succeeded with the ivy and the score-board, tried to get Phil Wrigley to install lights in Chicago, as he had at Wrigley Field in Los Angeles. Veeck was told that lights were "just a fad. A passing fancy."

Night baseball needed a champion, and it turned out to be Larry MacPhail, the man who had attempted to kidnap Kaiser Wilhelm during World War I. After investing in real estate and refereeing Big Ten football games on weekends, MacPhail bought the American Association Columbus Senators from the Reds in 1930 and secured a working agreement with the Cardinals. He sold season passes to women for $3 and admitted children free on weekdays; the renamed Redbirds were the only AA franchise to make money in that first year of the Depression. On June 17, 1931, MacPhail introduced night baseball to 21,000 fans; he wound up outdrawing the Cardinals that year by more than 30,000.

Despite this success, he was fired two years later for lavish spending and was fined for manipulating player contracts and arguing publicly with fans. Soon, however, the directors of Cincinnati's Central Trust bank asked MacPhail to run the Reds, and

he was able to convince the millionaire broadcaster Powel Crosley, Jr., to buy a controlling interest in the team.

One of his priorities was bringing night ball to the majors. According to Pietrusza, however, Commissioner Landis informed him, "Young man, you can write this down. Not in my lifetime or yours will you ever see a baseball game played at night in the majors." Moreover, the National League had specifically passed a rule outlawing night baseball. Nevertheless, Crosley and MacPhail made a forty-page presentation that concentrated on economics; by noting that 70 percent of the Reds' 1934 gross had come from fifteen dates — Opening Day, Sundays, and holidays — they ultimately won the right to install lights at Crosley Field.

General Electric installed eight 130-foot towers above Crosley Field which held 614 1,500-watt bulbs; they cost $4.75 apiece and provided 921,000 watts of light, about three times more than any minor league field. On May 24, 20,422 paid their way in on a bitterly cold evening to see history being made. At eight-thirty, President Roosevelt pressed a button in the White House which illuminated Crosley Field. The Reds and Phils were given

World War II delayed the changeover to night baseball due to security considerations. Ballpark illumination had become good enough to illuminate military installations, so night baseball was suspended along the East and West coasts. When this postcard of Municipal (Cleveland) Stadium was issued, military censors complained about the planes an artist had added; they were airbrushed out of future editions.

fifteen minutes of practice before the game, won by Cincinnati's Paul Derringer, 2–1.

The initial reviews were mixed. One avowedly anti–night game paper commented, "The game became a strangely colorless, synthetic affair. . . . The consensus was clear: night baseball would never last." But Red Barber said, "As soon as the lights came on, I knew they were there to stay."

Frank Navin, the Tigers' owner, said, "This night game is baseball's ruination. It changes baseball players from athletes to actors. . . . I am sure it hasn't helped much in Cincinnati." But it *did* help in Cincinnati: the Reds pulled 123,991 customers to 7 night games versus only 324,256 for their 69 other games in 1935.

The next team to adopt lights was the Brooklyn

First Night Games at the Original Major League Parks

DATE	PARK	HOME TEAM	VISITOR	RESULT	ATTENDANCE
May 24, 1935	Crosley Field	Reds	Phillies	Won, 2–1	20,422
June 15, 1938	Ebbets Field	Dodgers	Reds	Lost, 6–0	38,748
May 16, 1939	Shibe Park	Athletics	Indians	Lost, 8–3 (10)	15,109
June 27, 1939	Municipal Stadium	Indians	Tigers	Won, 5–0	55,305
August 14, 1939	Comiskey Park	White Sox	Browns	Won, 5–2	30,000
May 24, 1940	Polo Grounds	Giants	Bees	Won, 8–1	22,460
May 24, 1940	Sportsman's Park	Browns	Indians	Lost, 3–2	25,562
June 4, 1940	Forbes Field	Pirates	Bees	Won, 14–2	20,319
May 28, 1941	Griffith Stadium	Senators	Yankees	Lost, 6–5	25,000
May 11, 1946	Braves Field	Braves	Giants	Lost, 5–1	35,945
May 28, 1946	Yankee Stadium	Yankees	Senators	Lost, 2–1	48,895
June 13, 1947	Fenway Park	Red Sox	White Sox	Won, 5–3	34,510
June 15, 1948	Briggs Stadium	Tigers	White Sox	Won, 4–1	54,480
August 9, 1988	Wrigley Field	Cubs	Mets	Won, 6–4	36,399

Dodgers, who got a new general manager in 1938 — Larry MacPhail. Once again, night baseball's Johnny Appleseed sprinkled luminous beams from his pockets and — behold! — there was light at Ebbets Field on June 15, 1938. Even Johnny Vander Meer's second consecutive no-hitter that night didn't quell the optimism for night baseball. That year, the Dodgers drew an average of 30,000 at night games versus 4,000 at day games.

Why didn't other owners clamor to convert? The answer is economics; lights cost roughly $100,000 to install, and cash was scarce. Nevertheless, the A's, Indians, and White Sox added lights in 1939 (see box). Excepting League Park, which never had lights, nine of the fourteen major league parks had installed lights by 1941, and previous naysayers such as Clark Griffith had jumped on the bandwagon. Even Phil Wrigley had ordered lights, but the day after Pearl Harbor was attacked, he donated them to Uncle Sam.

Night baseball lost some momentum during the war. With the lights turned on, German and Japanese submarines could easily see the American ships silhouetted against the night sky. A committee conducted tests off New York Harbor confirming this suspicion, and night games were banned at Ebbets Field and the Polo Grounds as well as in the Pacific Coast League. However, night ball was restored in May 1944, and after the war, even the Yankees adopted it at the urging of their new co-owner — Larry MacPhail.

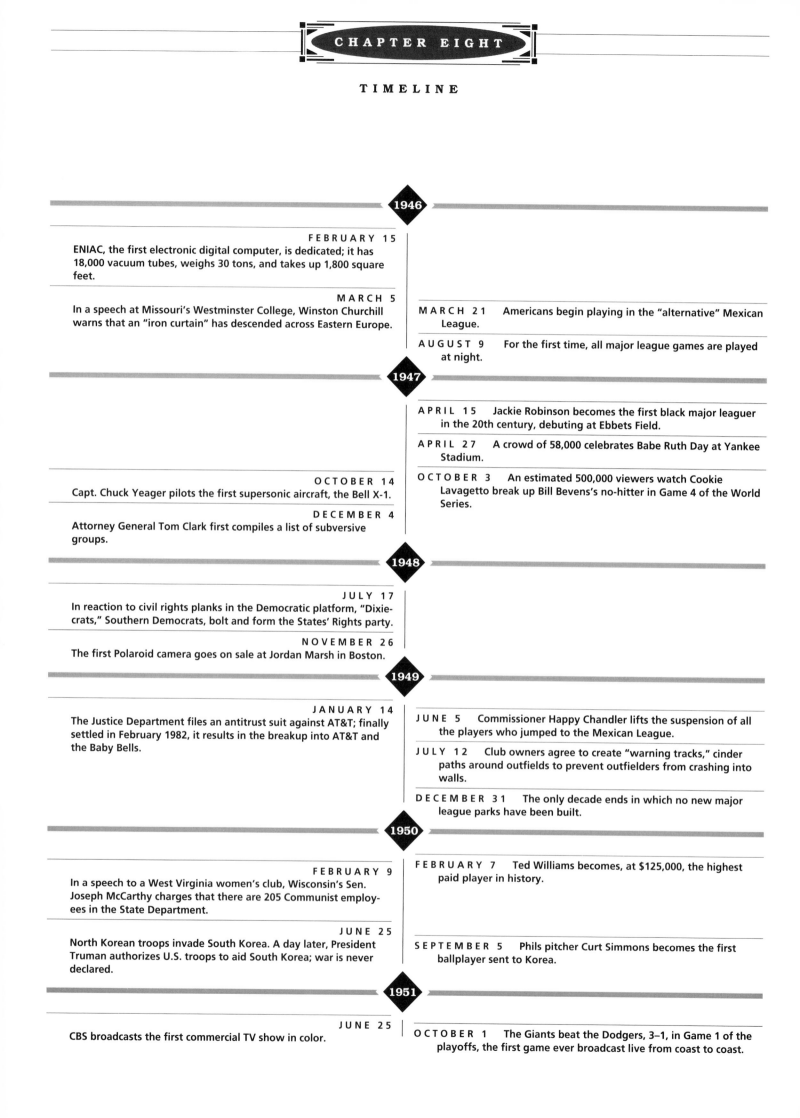

1946

FEBRUARY 15
ENIAC, the first electronic digital computer, is dedicated; it has 18,000 vacuum tubes, weighs 30 tons, and takes up 1,800 square feet.

MARCH 5
In a speech at Missouri's Westminster College, Winston Churchill warns that an "iron curtain" has descended across Eastern Europe.

MARCH 21   Americans begin playing in the "alternative" Mexican League.

AUGUST 9   For the first time, all major league games are played at night.

1947

APRIL 15   Jackie Robinson becomes the first black major leaguer in the 20th century, debuting at Ebbets Field.

APRIL 27   A crowd of 58,000 celebrates Babe Ruth Day at Yankee Stadium.

OCTOBER 14
Capt. Chuck Yeager pilots the first supersonic aircraft, the Bell X-1.

OCTOBER 3   An estimated 500,000 viewers watch Cookie Lavagetto break up Bill Bevens's no-hitter in Game 4 of the World Series.

DECEMBER 4
Attorney General Tom Clark first compiles a list of subversive groups.

1948

JULY 17
In reaction to civil rights planks in the Democratic platform, "Dixiecrats," Southern Democrats, bolt and form the States' Rights party.

NOVEMBER 26
The first Polaroid camera goes on sale at Jordan Marsh in Boston.

1949

JANUARY 14
The Justice Department files an antitrust suit against AT&T; finally settled in February 1982, it results in the breakup into AT&T and the Baby Bells.

JUNE 5   Commissioner Happy Chandler lifts the suspension of all the players who jumped to the Mexican League.

JULY 12   Club owners agree to create "warning tracks," cinder paths around outfields to prevent outfielders from crashing into walls.

DECEMBER 31   The only decade ends in which no new major league parks have been built.

1950

FEBRUARY 9
In a speech to a West Virginia women's club, Wisconsin's Sen. Joseph McCarthy charges that there are 205 Communist employees in the State Department.

FEBRUARY 7   Ted Williams becomes, at $125,000, the highest paid player in history.

JUNE 25
North Korean troops invade South Korea. A day later, President Truman authorizes U.S. troops to aid South Korea; war is never declared.

SEPTEMBER 5   Phils pitcher Curt Simmons becomes the first ballplayer sent to Korea.

1951

JUNE 25
CBS broadcasts the first commercial TV show in color.

OCTOBER 1   The Giants beat the Dodgers, 3–1, in Game 1 of the playoffs, the first game ever broadcast live from coast to coast.

TIMELINE

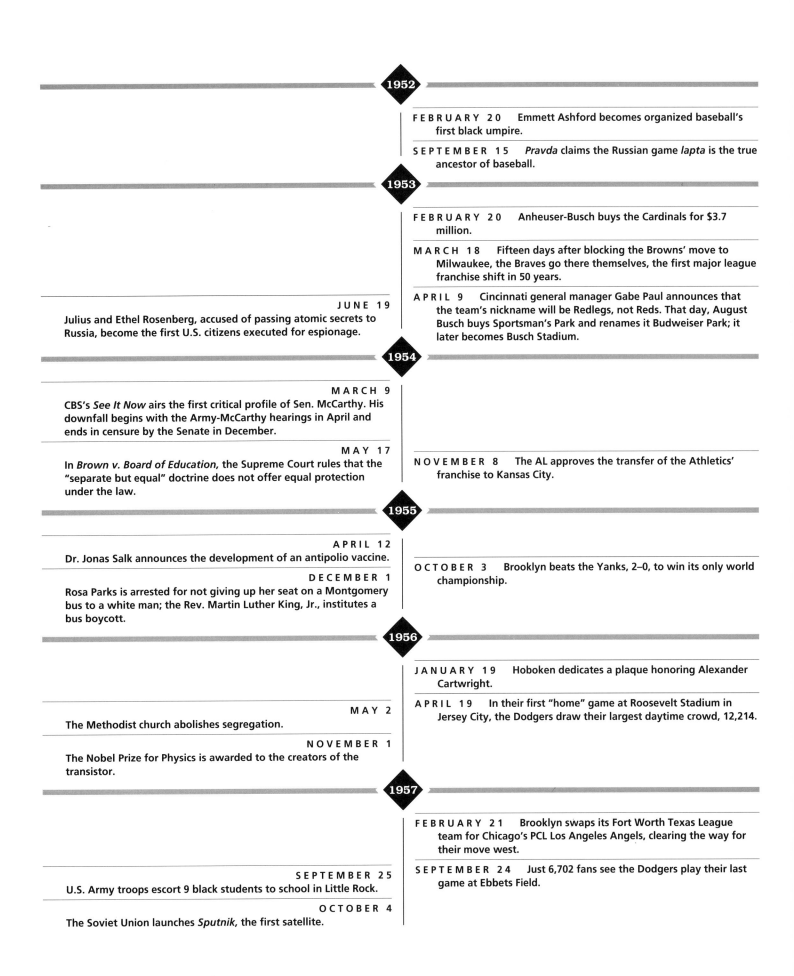

1952

FEBRUARY 20   Emmett Ashford becomes organized baseball's first black umpire.

SEPTEMBER 15   *Pravda* claims the Russian game *lapta* is the true ancestor of baseball.

1953

FEBRUARY 20   Anheuser-Busch buys the Cardinals for $3.7 million.

MARCH 18   Fifteen days after blocking the Browns' move to Milwaukee, the Braves go there themselves, the first major league franchise shift in 50 years.

JUNE 19
Julius and Ethel Rosenberg, accused of passing atomic secrets to Russia, become the first U.S. citizens executed for espionage.

APRIL 9   Cincinnati general manager Gabe Paul announces that the team's nickname will be Redlegs, not Reds. That day, August Busch buys Sportsman's Park and renames it Budweiser Park; it later becomes Busch Stadium.

1954

MARCH 9
CBS's *See It Now* airs the first critical profile of Sen. McCarthy. His downfall begins with the Army-McCarthy hearings in April and ends in censure by the Senate in December.

MAY 17
In *Brown v. Board of Education,* the Supreme Court rules that the "separate but equal" doctrine does not offer equal protection under the law.

NOVEMBER 8   The AL approves the transfer of the Athletics' franchise to Kansas City.

1955

APRIL 12
Dr. Jonas Salk announces the development of an antipolio vaccine.

DECEMBER 1
Rosa Parks is arrested for not giving up her seat on a Montgomery bus to a white man; the Rev. Martin Luther King, Jr., institutes a bus boycott.

OCTOBER 3   Brooklyn beats the Yanks, 2–0, to win its only world championship.

1956

JANUARY 19   Hoboken dedicates a plaque honoring Alexander Cartwright.

MAY 2
The Methodist church abolishes segregation.

NOVEMBER 1
The Nobel Prize for Physics is awarded to the creators of the transistor.

APRIL 19   In their first "home" game at Roosevelt Stadium in Jersey City, the Dodgers draw their largest daytime crowd, 12,214.

1957

FEBRUARY 21   Brooklyn swaps its Fort Worth Texas League team for Chicago's PCL Los Angeles Angels, clearing the way for their move west.

SEPTEMBER 25
U.S. Army troops escort 9 black students to school in Little Rock.

SEPTEMBER 24   Just 6,702 fans see the Dodgers play their last game at Ebbets Field.

OCTOBER 4
The Soviet Union launches *Sputnik,* the first satellite.

TIMELINE

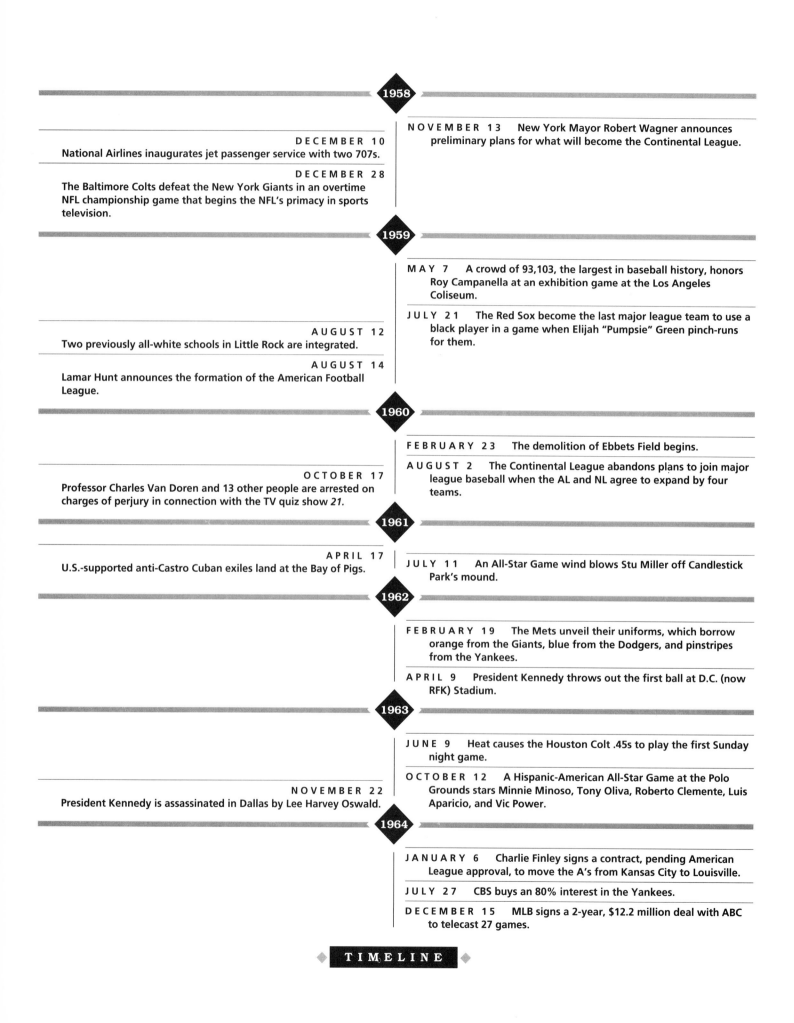

1958

NOVEMBER 13 New York Mayor Robert Wagner announces preliminary plans for what will become the Continental League.

DECEMBER 10
National Airlines inaugurates jet passenger service with two 707s.

DECEMBER 28
The Baltimore Colts defeat the New York Giants in an overtime NFL championship game that begins the NFL's primacy in sports television.

1959

MAY 7 A crowd of 93,103, the largest in baseball history, honors Roy Campanella at an exhibition game at the Los Angeles Coliseum.

JULY 21 The Red Sox become the last major league team to use a black player in a game when Elijah "Pumpsie" Green pinch-runs for them.

AUGUST 12
Two previously all-white schools in Little Rock are integrated.

AUGUST 14
Lamar Hunt announces the formation of the American Football League.

1960

FEBRUARY 23 The demolition of Ebbets Field begins.

AUGUST 2 The Continental League abandons plans to join major league baseball when the AL and NL agree to expand by four teams.

OCTOBER 17
Professor Charles Van Doren and 13 other people are arrested on charges of perjury in connection with the TV quiz show *21*.

1961

APRIL 17
U.S.-supported anti-Castro Cuban exiles land at the Bay of Pigs.

JULY 11 An All-Star Game wind blows Stu Miller off Candlestick Park's mound.

1962

FEBRUARY 19 The Mets unveil their uniforms, which borrow orange from the Giants, blue from the Dodgers, and pinstripes from the Yankees.

APRIL 9 President Kennedy throws out the first ball at D.C. (now RFK) Stadium.

1963

JUNE 9 Heat causes the Houston Colt .45s to play the first Sunday night game.

OCTOBER 12 A Hispanic-American All-Star Game at the Polo Grounds stars Minnie Minoso, Tony Oliva, Roberto Clemente, Luis Aparicio, and Vic Power.

NOVEMBER 22
President Kennedy is assassinated in Dallas by Lee Harvey Oswald.

1964

JANUARY 6 Charlie Finley signs a contract, pending American League approval, to move the A's from Kansas City to Louisville.

JULY 27 CBS buys an 80% interest in the Yankees.

DECEMBER 15 MLB signs a 2-year, $12.2 million deal with ABC to telecast 27 games.

◆ TIMELINE ◆

C H A P T E R   E I G H T

Minor Adjustments and Expansion

When Johnny came marching home from World War II, America had sixteen teams in the same eleven cities they'd been in for nearly fifty years.

By 1958, however, New York — which, with Brooklyn, was actually a three-team city — and the three two-team cities — Boston, Philadelphia, and St. Louis — had only one team. As of 1962, six respected minor league cities — Baltimore, Houston, Kansas City, Milwaukee, Minneapolis, and San Francisco — had become major league; Los Angeles got not one but two major league teams, and "expansion" franchises had been granted to two abandoned cities, New York in the National League, Washington in the American League.

Except for Baltimore, the nation's sixth-largest city in 1945, all the moves were to the Midwest and West, in line with the movement of America's population. In 1790, the center of U.S. population was 23 miles east of Baltimore; by 1870 it was 48 miles east of Cincinnati, and by 1950 it had leapfrogged Indiana entirely to rest 8 miles north-northwest of Olney, Illinois.

Other things had changed, too. Americans used new words like "McCarthyism" and "fission" and learned of such exotic places as Dienbienphu and Saigon. High-speed highways began connecting America; motels replaced roadside rests, and speed limits were raised over time from 35 to 60 miles an hour.

Amid the turmoil brought by these changes and the Cold War, television, and the first moves toward gender and racial equality, there was baseball, unchanged and unchanging. After all, in 1945 a fan could still take a trolley to the ballpark with $2 in hand, buy a bleacher seat, scorecard, frank, and a Coke, and get plenty of change.

Going to the ballpark also meant seeing a familiar friend in a threatening new world. Unfortunately, most of these old friends were past their prime. No big league park had been built for baseball since 1923 (Municipal Stadium had been built for the Olympics); the great ballpark building boom (1909–1915) was thirty years in the past; Sportsman's Park, Crosley Field, and Briggs Stadium had only been patched and painted since the turn of the century.

Worse still, the parks were trapped in the inner cities, where it had once been eminently logical to build them. But the parks and cities had been declining for years. Decay had been ignored out of necessity during the Depression; in the 1940s, the cities suffered from a shortage of resources, as metal, rubber, and concrete were used almost exclusively as weapons against Hitler's war machine.

Other events took their toll in specific cities. The 1937 flood in Cincinnati had caused people to move from the neighborhood of Crosley Field.

Faced with a choice of using Wrigley Field or the Coliseum as a temporary home for the Dodgers, O'Malley chose the Coliseum, which quickly became known as O'Malley's Chinese Theater. This double pun recalled not only Grauman's Chinese Theater in Hollywood but also referred to Chinese home runs, now rightly considered an ethnic slur but then a reference to cheap homers, like pop flies arched over the left field fence.

161

Sportsman's Park, St. Louis, Missouri

Dick Miller described how the Superior Linen and Towel Company beyond the left field wall affected the park:

> Following the 1960 season, the laundry was torn down. Soon more buildings in the area were torn down in the city's "urban renewal project," and the neighborhood concept began to fade away. . . . The park was rapidly becoming an object. No longer was it a part of the urban fabric that had given it character.

Urban centers in the Northeast were unraveling even more quickly. Those who could moved to Newton, Scarsdale, Bryn Mawr; those who could not followed Horace Greeley's advice: "If you have no family or friends to aid you, and no prospect opened to you . . . turn your face to the great West, and there build up a home and fortune."

A TALE OF THREE CITIES: MILWAUKEE, BALTIMORE, & KANSAS CITY

The first club owner to take this advice was Lou Perini, who, along with his partners, was having trouble making money with the Braves. After building attendance by adding lights and refurbishing Braves Field, Boston had won a pennant in 1948. But the Braves' attendance had plummeted as quickly as it had grown (see table, right). Perini had explored selling Braves Field to raise cash and reducing his operating costs by splitting

time at Fenway Park with the Red Sox; Tom Yawkey had always turned a deaf ear to such proposals. Consequently, the Braves owner was stuck with having the second most popular baseball team in town, a condition that also afflicted the A's in Philadelphia and the Browns in St. Louis. All shared stadiums with more popular teams; Perini competed with a legendary ballpark that only grew in stature as time went on.

Like Connie Mack in Philadelphia and Bill Veeck in St. Louis, Perini was faced with a declining population. In 1950, Boston ranked tenth in population among U.S. cities and St. Louis was eighth; by 1988 Boston ranked nineteenth and St. Louis was thirty-fourth. Unlike Veeck, however, Perini had an escape hatch, a thriving city with a long baseball history. In 1946, he and his partners had bought the Milwaukee Brewers of the minor league American Association. Under Bill Veeck, they had won pennants in 1943, 1944, and 1945.

As part of the deal, Perini got the Brewers' ballpark, Borchert Field, which had such narrow foul

Braves' Attendance, 1943–1952

1943	271,289	1948	1,455,439
1944	208,691	1949	1,081,795
1945	374,178	1950	944,391
1946	969,673	1951	487,475
1947	1,277,361	1952	281,278

In May 1944, with both the Browns and Cardinals headed toward winning pennants, Sportsman's Park became the last major league ballpark to integrate; blacks could now sit in the grandstand instead of exclusively in the bleachers, which ran from right to right center (and were screened in so that home run balls could not be caught). Seventy years after it had opened as a National League field, Sportsman's Park hosted the 1946 World Series, when this illustration was done (left). The park, unremarkable despite its longevity, was often identified by its outfield signs. Forty-seven years after the photos were taken, Harry Caray was still announcing baseball, albeit from Chicago.

The Green Monster

The Green Monster, the left field wall at Fenway Park, is a little bit like that changeable girl in the nursery rhyme:

> There was a little girl who had a
> little curl,
> Right in the middle of her fore-
> head.
> When she was good, she was very,
> very good,
> And when she was bad she was
> horrid.

Players who think the wall is horrid are called pitchers; players who think it very, very good are called hitters, particularly right-handed ones.

All too often, of course, hitters are lured by the wall's siren song, imagine themselves more powerful than they actually are, and pop up pitch after pitch to the second baseman. Veteran Soxwatcher George Sullivan says that "rookies drool when they see the Wall. . . . It kindles a twinkle in the eye of banjo hitters, instant mental spinach to make them feel like sluggers." On the other hand, a banjo hitter named Bucky Dent won a pennant for the Yankees on October 2, 1978, by arching a routine fly ball over the wall.

Baseball's most famous architectural feature, as fabled as barriers in Jericho, Jerusalem, China, and Berlin, has gone through four distinct phases:
1. The Cliff (1912–1933)
2. The Monster (1933–1946)
3. The Green Monster (1947–1975)
4. The Monster Gentrified (1976–present)

When Fenway opened in 1912, the most important thing about left field was not the wall itself but rather the 10-foot rise that led up to it. Baseball's most prominent "fielder's mound" stretched from the left field foul pole to the flagpole in center. Its first patrolman, George "Duffy" Lewis, was, with Hall of Famers Harry Hooper and Tris Speaker, a member of the Sox "Golden Outfield," which won championships in 1915, 1916, and 1918. Lewis was so adept at running up and down the declivity that, in his honor, it was known as Duffy's Cliff.

The Wall behind the Cliff required a considerable poke during the era of the dead ball. When Bosox outfielder Hugh Bradley hit one of his two career homers 324 feet over the 25-foot left field fence onto Lansdowne Street, the *Boston Globe* exclaimed, "The scene that followed was indescribable. Players came bolting from the dugout to take a look at the mighty blast. They could not believe their eyes."

When Tom Yawkey bought the Red Sox, he put in a new scoreboard (green for balls, red for strikes) and replaced the original fence with an 18-foot concrete barrier topped by a 19-foot wooden frame of railroad ties bolted together and covered with a skin of tin. This covering added an element of uncertainty; learning how to play caroms off it became a family secret passed on from generation to generation of Sox left fielders.

Ted Williams, the sentry from

1939 to 1960 (with time out for military service), got to know its quirks like few visiting outfielders. He once said, "Any ball down the line meant the shortstop had to come out [to make a relay throw]. If it hit the tin, it dropped straight down; if it hit the cement, it would bounce back hard. If it a hit a bolt, anything could happen."

Carl Yastrzemski, to whom the torch was passed in 1961, became, with Harry Hooper, Williams, and Babe Ruth, the fourth Hall of Famer to guard the Wall. Yaz said, "Every ball comes off at an angle. Williams taught me that. You've got to play every ball three to five feet to the right of where it hits." He also mastered the decoy. "I knew that ball so well I knew if a ball was going to be off the Wall or be catchable. A runner on first base can't tell if it's going to hit."

Balls began booming over the Wall with regularity, so a 23-foot net was erected in 1936 to protect the store windows on Lansdowne Street. Later, a ladder was provided so that the grounds crew could retrieve batting practice home runs. Unfortunately, the ladder was in play and caused the home team grief when a fly ball hit by Jim Lemon struck it and bounded into center field for an inside-the-park home run.

In 1947, Fenway underwent a flock of changes. The initials of Tom Yawkey and his wife, Jean, were added to the scoreboard in two vertical strips of Morse code (TAY and JRY); the park finally got lights, and

lines and oddly placed seats that it was impossible to see the entire field from any single vantage point. AA founder Mike Kelley once said, "You have to pay two admissions to see one game at Borchert Field. The first day you see what happens in right field. The next day you come back to see what happens in left field."

Local boosters aware of Borchert's drawbacks had begun plumping for a new multipurpose stadium as early as the 1920s in hopes of attracting a major league team again. Milwaukee had been a one-year wonder four times, representing four different leagues: the National League (1878), Union

Association (1884), American Association (1891), and American League (1901).

The Depression slowed the momentum for a new park, but Perini's buying the Brewers revived it. On February 24, 1947, the county board approved building a park in the Story quarry section. Wisconsin Senator Alexander Wiley pushed a bill through Congress that allowed the 120-acre site to be sold to the county for parking. Although the voters rejected a 1948 bond issue to finance improvements on the lot, a revised version passed in 1950 and ground was broken, albeit with no assurance of attracting a big league team.

the Monster became the Green Monster. The ads on the left field wall — Gem Blades ("Avoid that 5 o'clock shadow") and Lifebuoy ("The Red Sox use it") — were torn down, and the Wall was painted a distinctive dark green.

With the billboards gone, it was easier to follow the flight of the ball. The coats of paint also seemed to add new energy, as baseballs skittered merrily off eight different wall angles in fair territory, two doorways, and the ladder. The result was crowd-pleasing unpredictability, what poet Donald Hall called "a huge pinball machine designed by a mad sculptor."

According to *The Hidden Game of Baseball,* the Green Monster produces 13 percent more offense than

other parks; it also bothers pitchers, even Hall of Famers like Bob Feller. He said, "The damned thing is so close I scrape my knuckles on it every time I throw a sidearm curve." Johnny Pesky, who played, coached, and managed at Fenway for many years, thinks the Wall teaches patience. He says, "If the other team jumps off to a 2- or 3-run lead, you can't get panicky and have your bullpen up and throwing. You'll wear 'em out. You've got to figure you'll hit the Wall a few times yourself and get back into the game."

After Boston's pennant-winning 1975 season, Sox management cut the heart out of the Green Monster. The tin was cut into thousands of 2½-by-4½-inch rectangles, which were mounted on polished wood and sold

in exchange for contributions to the Jimmy Fund, the department of the Dana-Farber Cancer Institute devoted to children.

The Wall was resurfaced with a material like Formica. Yastrzemski said, "It's mostly fiberglass now." After Fred Lynn crashed into it during the 1975 World Series, it was padded. The Red Sox came close to a championship that year and closer still in 1986, but they still haven't won a championship since 1918. Why? They can't take the Wall on the road.

The Green Monster dominates Fenway Park, even at night, but remains a bit of a mystery because no one agrees on exactly how far it is from home plate. The 325 figure remains official, but sportswriter George Sullivan measured it at 309 feet 5 inches in 1975, the year the new, improved wall went up. The Red Sox have prolonged the intrigue by no longer allowing it to be measured.

Meanwhile, Veeck had bought the Browns and wanted to move *them* to Milwaukee, where he was a proven success; he offered Perini $750,000 to leave, but Perini declined. (Had he gone along, it's doubtful that the other American League owners would have okayed Veeck's move. They wanted to get rid of him altogether for using the 3-foot, 7-inch midget Eddie Gaedel as a pinch hitter and "making a travesty of the game.")

Ultimately, Perini was as motivated to keep Veeck from moving the Browns as he was to move the Braves. On March 11, he proposed a rule change to baseball's executive council, a group of

club owners from both leagues which rules on matters affecting leagues rather than clubs. Perini's proposal would have prohibited the transfer of any major league team to a minor league city before October 1 of a given year. His idea was to prevent Veeck from moving for a year and then to proceed with his own plan. Unfortunately, the council could not officially consider the proposal because one of its members was conspicuously absent — Tom Yawkey, who relished the chance of having a monopoly in Boston.

Perini's hand was forced. On Friday the thirteenth of March, 1953, with Opening Day less than

In the 1940s, Brooklyn fans were still taking the trolley (see sign above) to see the Dodgers play. On April 15, 1947, major league baseball was integrated for the first time in sixty-three years when Jackie Robinson had his first official at-bat at Ebbets Field. That fall, Robinson was an onlooker (right) when Joe DiMaggio blasted a ball to left field in Game 6 of the World Series at Yankee Stadium. The ball was photographed as it started heading for Al Gionfriddo, whose catch near the 415-foot sign saved the game. At this time, center field had just two monuments, for Miller Huggins and Lou Gehrig.

a month away, the Braves owner announced his intention of moving his team to Milwaukee. The next day Yawkey put on his most accommodating civic manner and announced that he'd be delighted to rent Fenway to the Braves if that would keep them in town. His grandstand play was too little and too late; four days later, the other National League owners okayed the move to make Milwaukee National League territory, an astonishingly short amount of time considering the months of machinations involving the Giants and Tampa Bay in the 1990s.

Milwaukee County Stadium, the second to be built with public money, was a success from the outset. Milwaukeeans treated the Braves to free gas, free dry cleaning, and offered huge discounts on real estate, automobiles, and appliances. Hall of Famer Eddie Mathews said, "I don't think any city has ever gone as crazy over a baseball team as the city of Milwaukee." Ernie Johnson, once a Braves pitcher and later their broadcaster, said, "When we got there, I'll never forget how the people put up a Christmas tree — in April — inside the Schroeder Hotel. . . . They said since we'd missed Christmas with them, they wanted to celebrate it with us now."

On Sunday, March 15, the stadium was opened to the public. Despite frosty temperatures and a steady rain, 10,000 trooped in and saw a round, double-decked grandstand that stretched to first and third base with bleachers in left field and left center. The park was designed originally to seat 35,911; the outfield dimensions were symmetrical: 320 down the foul lines, 376 up the power alleys, and 404 in deep center.

Details didn't matter, however. Fans arrived three hours before a game just to watch batting practice. Long before tailgating became a national pastime, fans familiar with Green Bay Packer traditions were grilling kielbasy in the parking lot and making a day of it. The Braves drew 1,826,397, setting a major league attendance record their first year, and broke it again each of the next two years.

The Braves won a championship in 1957, a pennant in 1958, and lost a playoff in 1959. Gradually, enthusiasm waned and attendance slumped. In 1964, Mayor Ivan Allen, Jr., of Atlanta, a city weaned on carpetbaggers, announced, "I have a verbal commitment from a major league team to move here if we have a stadium ready by 1966." It turned out to be the Braves.

While it's true that the Braves had a good club and might have prospered in Boston as easily as in Milwaukee, the reaction of the fans made for a new

After the Pirates acquired Hank Greenberg from the Tigers in 1947, they modified Forbes Field to create Greenberg Gardens (above). Kansas City A's owner Charlie Finley made the most outrageous changes in 1964. Convinced that the Yanks won pennants because of Yankee Stadium's short right field fence, Finley reduced the right field distance from 338 to 296 feet (the same as the Stadium's) with his curved Pennant Porch. When commissioner Ford Frick ruled that it be taken down after two exhibition games, Finley responded with a One-Half Pennant Porch, 325 feet from the plate, which remained in place for the 1964 and 1965 seasons.

The first modern American League franchise shift transformed the St. Louis Browns into the Baltimore Orioles. On Opening Day, April 15, 1954, when the picture at left was taken, 46,354 Baltimoreans crowded into what had been Municipal Stadium and was now Memorial Stadium. Thirty years later, the park had changed dramatically. Although there was no disguising its origin as a football stadium, the steep-seating bowl (above) beckoned invitingly. The first major league park constructed entirely of reinforced concrete, Memorial Stadium was ideally suited to serve a team built on pitching and defense.

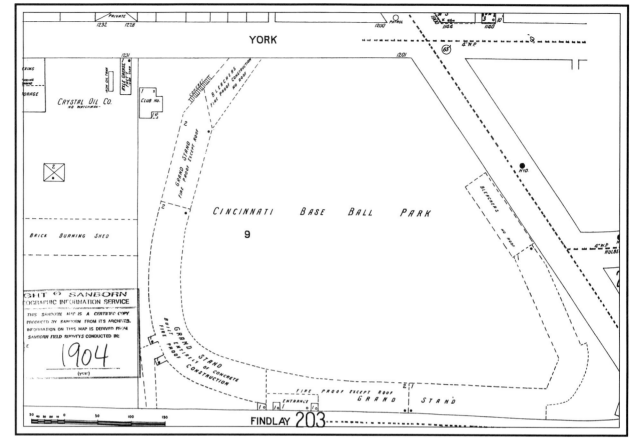

The Sanborn Map Company has been making detailed maps of American cities since the 1870s to give insurance companies an accurate way of assessing potential fire damage. Its maps of the area around what was the Palace of the Fans in 1904 (right) and Crosley Field in 1950 (far right) say much about the way the neighborhood expanded. Note also that home plate was moved to keep the sun out of the batter's eyes.

equation in baseball: if you build it, we will come — in droves. Move to a city with a lot of pent-up enthusiasm for major league baseball, stir in people willing to love even a bunch of also-rans, and novelty alone might attract people to the ballpark in profitable numbers.

Such a formula held great appeal, as noted, for Veeck, who owned the lowly St. Louis Browns. Usually locked in battles for the cellar with the equally inept Washington Senators, the Browns had finished seventh or eighth every year since 1946, save for a dizzying rise to sixth in 1948. In another era and a more forgiving city, they might have had the charm of, say, the early Mets; viewed next to the Cardinals, who finished first or second every year from 1941 to 1949, the Browns were an embarrassment.

The American League owners had three aims: (1) get rid of Veeck; (2) move the losing Browns; and (3) expand into new territory, as the National League had in Milwaukee; they accomplished all three by returning major league baseball to Baltimore.

When the AL became a major league, Baltimore was a franchisee (see Chapter 4). In 1903, the franchise was moved to New York and became baseball's most successful, the Yankees. Passed over, Baltimore had to settle for being the breeding ground for Babe Ruth and Lefty Grove and the haven of the International League Orioles.

In *House of Magic,* produced by the Orioles in 1991, James Bready explains what being a "minor league" city feels like to the inhabitants:

> For half a century, Baltimore along among the five principal cities of the Northeast bore the

stigma, the unfairness of minor-league existence. A city thus degraded suffers psychologically. While its old rivals undertake big construction projects . . . the minor league city retreats into insularity and defensiveness. . . . Such a city thinks, finances, builds, dares small.

Such labeling was laughable considering how the Orioles drew. On October 9, 1944, 52,833 fans, a minor league record, paid their way into what was then Municipal Stadium to see Game 4 of the Little World Series. The same day, only 31,630 paid to see Game 6 of the World Series between the Browns and Cardinals at Sportsman's Park in St. Louis. Sportswriter Grantland Rice commented on the disparity:

> What are big league and what are minor league cities? The situation is something of a joke. . . . Baltimore has no big league team and St. Louis has two. . . . It doesn't make any sense. The time isn't very far away when you'll see a very decided change.

The change came, but it took ten years and involved another sportswriter, Rodger Pippen of the *News-Post.* Municipal Stadium had been built for football in 1922; when Oriole Park, formerly the Federal League park, burned down in July 1944, Municipal of necessity housed the International League Orioles, too. Pippen, unwilling to be rained on in football season, wrote column after column about putting a roof on the stadium.

Inevitably, his ranting about the accommodations fed the debate over "Why is Baltimore still a minor league city?" After the war, the voters

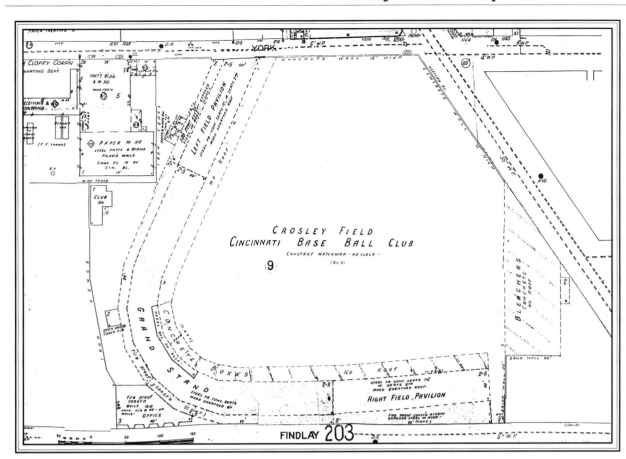

Fifteen years after Tony Lazzeri hit a World Series grand slam at the Polo Grounds (see p. 146), another Yankee second baseman, Gil Mc-Dougald, duplicated the feat. In the intervening time, advertising had been removed from the outfield walls, but the extension above the clubhouse entrance had become a huge Chesterfield sign.

The first city to get a major league franchise in fifty years was Milwaukee, which had accepted Borchert Field's faults since the Brewers had been pushed out of the American League in 1901. This split-view postcard compares Borchert with what was supposed to be the Brewers' new home, County Stadium. Instead, the Braves announced that they were moving to Milwaukee. On Opening Day, April 14, 1953 (below), the park had just 27,982 permanent seats; nevertheless, 53,357 saw the Braves beat the Cardinals, 3–2, in 10 innings. The 7,500 additional seats in left and left center were later replaced by concrete stands, and more seats were added along the first base line (far right).

okayed a $2.5 million bond issue to improve Municipal Stadium, and Pippen enlisted a powerful ally who could have put the kibosh on Baltimore's baseball ambitions for territorial reasons; he got a written promise from Senator owner Clark Griffith not to oppose an American League team's moving to Baltimore.

From 1944 to 1949, Municipal Stadium was rebuilt while the Orioles were still playing there. Briefly renamed Babe Ruth Stadium, it got a single-decked concrete grandstand in 1950 when a $2.5 million bond issue passed, and yet a third bond issue passed when the voters got two pieces of news: the football Colts were replacing the NFL's bankrupt Dallas Texans, and Mayor Thomas D'Alesandro, Jr., was talking with Veeck about bringing the Browns to Baltimore.

When Veeck sold Sportsman's Park to Busch in April 1953, excitement increased, peaking on September 29 when a syndicate bought the Browns for $2.475 million. The American League approved the shift to Baltimore only after Veeck had sold out. (That same day, the AL also adopted a constitutional amendment to expand to ten teams.)

Three months later, in a 1950s scheme to avoid

taxes, an entrepreneur named Arnold Johnson bought the land under Yankee Stadium and sold it to the Knights of Columbus, which immediately leased it back to the Yankees; ultimately, as a result of the transaction, Kansas City became a major league city.

Johnson was a "bottom fisher," a person schooled in the art of revitalizing distressed companies and selling them at a profit. He worked his magic with real estate deals gone bad, then purchased the Automatic Canteen Company and made it a leading manufacturer of vending machines. In the fallout of the Yankee sale-and-leaseback, he also became the owner of Muehlebach Field and the AA Kansas City Blues.

Like Milwaukee and Baltimore, Kansas City had a long history with major league baseball, beginning in the Union Association and continuing with the National League Cowboys (1886), American Association Blues (1888–1889), and Federal League Packers (1914–1915). None played at Muehlebach Field, however. Brewer George Muehlebach bought the Blues from former major leaguer George "White Wings" Tebeau in 1923 and built his team a 17,000-seat park.

Municipal Stadium's size finally became a plus on October 10, 1948, when it contained a record 86,288 fans rooting for the Indians to end the World Series against the Braves. They were disappointed, as Bob Feller pitched poorly, but the record stayed intact until the 1959 World Series, thanks to the even larger seating capacity of the Los Angeles Memorial Coliseum.

It had a single deck but still cost $400,000. Part of the figure was dictated by the park's generous dimensions, large for a minor league park and particularly noteworthy in the era of the lively ball. Muehlebach was 350 down the lines and 450 to deep center; Yankee Stadium, built the same year, measured 490 to deep center but only 280 in left and 295 in right.

The dimensions shrunk over the years, and there were other changes. Former catcher Johnny Kling bought the Blues and integrated the park, which subsequently became the home of the Negro League Monarchs and such black stars as Leroy "Satchel" Paige, Jackie Robinson, and Ernie Banks; however, in the summer of 1937, the Yankees bought the franchise and the park for $230,000, reinstituted segregated seating, and renamed the park Ruppert Stadium after the Yankees' owner; when he died, two years later, it became Blues Stadium.

Ernest Mehl, the longtime sports editor of the *Kansas City Star*, saw Johnson as a man who might bring big league ball to town and stressed to him the publicity value of major league ownership. In July 1954, Johnson began negotiations to buy Connie Mack's Philadelphia A's. When Kansas City voters okayed a $2 million bond issue in August to enlarge Muehlebach Field, it appeared as if the deal were concluded, and the announcement was made that the A's were moving; when the American League voted on the proposed sale, however, it failed under pressure from Mack's sons and the owners who were not convinced that the city would support the A's.

In response, the Merchants Association of Kansas City asked residents to write to the *Star* with requests for season tickets; 10,000 letters arrived the first day. Faced with tangible evidence, the American League approved the sale. But, days later, the league reneged on its commitment when a syndicate, Save the A's, pledged $2 million to cover the A's debts and keep them in Philadelphia. At this point, the American League had approved, at least briefly, *two competing bids* to buy the A's.

Johnson made noises about suing, and there seemed to be no easy solution to the deadlock. Finally, Connie Mack asked representatives of both groups to meet him by noon on a specific Saturday morning. Johnson, who had befriended Mack's chauffeur, got the jump by arriving at 9 A.M. The chauffeur led him up a back stairway to Mack's apartment, and the two quickly agreed on a little more than $2 million for the club. Once Mack was assured that Johnson's check for $604,000 was good, he signed the contract; members of the syndicate arrived at noon only to discover they were too late.

Muehlebach Field was rebuilt in six months, using Detroit's Briggs Stadium as a model. A roofed second deck expanded the seating capacity from 17,000 to 31,000 and the grandstand to the right field foul pole, then wrapped around home to just past third base; uncovered single-decked bleachers continued on down the left field foul line. Observant fans noticed that the big new scoreboard in right center was a holdover from another franchise move; it had been left at Braves Field when Boston became Milwaukee.

THE DEATH OF EBBETS FIELD

When the Dodgers won a second straight pennant in 1953, Brooklyn fans were delirious, but Dodger president Walter O'Malley was very unhappy; his champs had been badly outdrawn by the freshly transplanted Braves, 1,826,397 to 1,163,419. When the Browns and A's moved and prospered, too, the evidence became even clearer; moving a major league team resulted in a 400 to 600 percent increase in attendance (see table, right).

O'Malley couldn't talk about the deterioration around Ebbets, because there hadn't been any. The pennants were still arranged daily to reflect the National League standings, and the hot dogs on McKeever Place smelled just as good. The gate in deep right-center was still opened after every game so that the fans could walk on the same grass as their heroes and go right through the gate onto Bedford Avenue.

In 1947, the scoreboard in right center had been enlarged, and a Schaefer beer sign divulged scorers' decisions, "H" for hit, "E" for error. Jackie Robinson also arrived that year, and new fans helped set an attendance record of 1.8 million.

While attendance never again hit that peak, it also never dropped below 1 million, even when the Dodgers weren't in the race. On the other hand, the team that won five pennants in the next nine years never exceeded 1.3 million in paid admissions due to its puny capacity (32,000).

On March 6, 1952, the *New York Times* said that architect Norman Bel Geddes had been approached about creating a new stadium in Brooklyn which would have a retractable roof, foam rubber seats (to be automatically heated in cold weather), automatic hot dog vending machines, and "a synthetic substance to replace grass on the entire field which can be painted any color." It turned out that Bel Geddes had been working on the plan for four years.

Collier's ran a drawing (illustration, p. 192) which informed fans that all seats "will face the pitcher's box" and be made of "cushioned foam rubber and wider — 28 inches against the standard 22 inches." There were other wonders: "A shopping center is planned for the area under the stands, utilizing what is now waste space in most ball parks. . . . Under the stands will be playgrounds for children so mothers can place their youngsters in the hands of trained young men and women while they shop, or visit the doctor or dentist."

In December 1953, O'Malley announced that the Dodgers planned to build a $7.2 million stadium

Attendance of Relocated Teams

OLD CITY	FINAL YEAR	NEW CITY	FIRST YEAR
Boston	281,278	Milwaukee	1,826,397
St. Louis	297,238	Baltimore	1,060,910
Philadelphia	304,666	Kansas City	1,393,054

and, in 1955, asked Buckminster Fuller to design a stadium with a geodesic dome. Shortly thereafter, O'Malley announced they would play one home game in 1956 against each National League team at Roosevelt Stadium in Jersey City, New Jersey.

On August 20, 1955, O'Malley told New York Mayor Robert Wagner that the Dodgers and Giants might both leave town: "It's unlikely that one club or the other will move. You'll find that the two will move." If the Dodgers moved, the Giants could not survive. In 11 games at the Polo Grounds in 1959, the Dodgers had drawn 350,000 people, an average of 31,818. In 48 games against the rest of the league, the Giants drew 390,000, an average of 8,125.

O'Malley rejected the offer of a stadium in Queens financed by the city. Instead, he wanted the city to help buy land at the Long Island Rail Road's Brooklyn terminal at Flatbush and Atlantic avenues; in that scenario, the Dodgers would invest $6 million to buy land and build a park. Robert Moses, New York's parks commissioner, was unwilling to endorse the project as a slum clearance project. He said to O'Malley, "What you're saying is that unless a way is found to make a home for the Dodgers in this location, you'll pick up your marbles and take them away." The Dodger owner said testily, "Our fans require a modern stadium with greater comforts. They used to come to Ebbets Field by trolley. Now they come by auto. We can only park 700 cars." (Milwaukee had parking for 14,000.)

In September 1956, the Dodgers announced that real estate developer Marvin Kratter had bought Ebbets Field and leased it back to the team for two years, mirroring Johnson's deal with Yankee Stadium. A month later, on October 31, Ebbets Field could be reached on foot and by subway, bus, and automobile but not by trolley; that day, Brooklyn's last two trolley lines, on McDonald and Church avenues, stopped running forever. The trolleys that had given the Dodgers their nickname had left the borough; less than a year later, the Dodgers were gone, too, fleeing Brooklyn, the City of Churches, for Los Angeles, the City of Angels.

The following February, O'Malley bought the

Fans flocked to Ebbets Field in the 1950s, as this day game between the Dodgers and Cubs attests (right). (See pennants.) But owner Walter O'Malley lobbied for a new city-financed stadium in Brooklyn, threatened to move the franchise, and put teeth in it by playing seven home games at Roosevelt Field in Jersey City, New Jersey, in both 1956 and 1957 (far right). After the Dodgers moved to Los Angeles in 1958, Ebbets rapidly went downhill, as shown by the broken windows in this photo from 1960 (below right).

Los Angeles Angels of the Pacific Coast League and their park, Wrigley Field, for $3 million and the Dodgers' Texas League Fort Worth team. The Dodgers played their last game at Ebbets on September 24. In time, the infield was dug up, trucked to Greenwood Cemetery, and used to freshen gravesites, including that of Dodger owner Charles Ebbets, who had turned the first spade of earth at the park that bore his name. Ebbets's eight light tower stanchions were moved to Downing Stadium on Randall's Island, and the Bulova clock that Bama Rowell of the Braves broke with a drive on May 30, 1946, now sits on top of the outfield fence scoreboard at McCormick Field in Asheville, North Carolina.

When Duke Snider was inducted into the Hall of Fame in 1980, he said of the move to Los Angeles, "We wept. . . . When they tore down Ebbets Field, they tore down a little piece of me." In *Nice Guys Finish Last*, Leo Durocher says, "Something went out of baseball when the Dodgers left Brooklyn, and not all the king's horses or all the king's horses can ever put it back."

Baseball suffered; Brooklyn died. Its identity, pride, cohesiveness, and revenue were gone — like that; the area around Ebbets became a slum that spread to nearby Flatbush Avenue, which became more war zone than shopping district. When the Dodgers left, one fan said, "It was the disruption of a social pattern. There was no more sense waiting up for the *Daily News*. The life went out of the street corners. What were you going to stand there and talk about?"

The wreckers' ball made short work of Ebbets, and Marvin Kratter turned the site into the Jackie

Robinson Apartments. In 1974, Jeff Pugh of the *Los Angeles Times* did a follow-up story on Ebbets and reported that the building had put up a sign to discourage tie-ups in street traffic. It read: THIS IS THE FORMER HOME OF EBBETS FIELD: PLEASE NO BALLPLAYING.

THE GOLD RUSH

A hundred and nine years after Alexander Cartwright went west in search of gold, O'Malley and Giant boss Horace Stoneham headed west in search of diamonds . . . with lots of parking.

Although both moved with promised municipal aid to build their own ballparks, they needed temporary shelter. The Giants played in the old PCL park, Seals Stadium; the Dodgers went from the sublime to the ridiculous, playing in the Los Angeles Memorial Coliseum, where organized baseball had not been played before (and, with any luck, will never be played again).

Used to stage much of the 1932 and 1984 Olympics, the Coliseum is imposing. The center arch of the Grand Entrance is framed by two blocks of stone, one brought from the ruins of the ancient Colosseum in Rome, the other from the Altis Olympia, the site of the original Olympic games in Greece. For all its grandeur, though, it's a football stadium, the nation's largest in terms of permanent seating with many 100,000-plus crowds.

Such a scale dwarfs baseball players used to the intimate dimensions of Ebbets Field. As Michael Benson pointed out, "The Olympic playing surface

Continental Divide

Two months after the Dodgers sold Ebbets Field, Mayor Wagner created a civic gang of four to highjack an existing major league team from another city. The group included department store mogul Bernard Gimbel, former Giant pitcher and real estate magnate Clint Blume, and former Postmaster General James Farley; the key man was Bill Shea, perhaps the most influential lawyer in New York.

In addition to his many connections, Shea also had a sports background and did a stint as a law clerk in the Brooklyn Trust Company, which held the mortgage on Ebbets Field. (One of his fellow clerks was Walter O'Malley.) According to sportswriter Jack Lang, the Dodgers were in financial trouble before World War II; George V. McLaughlin, the head of Brooklyn Trust, had to appoint one of his clerks to oversee the operation and chose O'Malley. Later, when O'Malley moved the Dodgers to Los Angeles, Shea was incensed and personally relished the chance of replacing them with a new NL team.

His first efforts were directed toward the Reds, who were mildly interested; however, owner Powel Crosley had other business interests in Cincinnati. Any small chance Shea had of landing the Reds disappeared when National League president and former Reds boss Warren Giles was quoted as saying, "New York? Who needs New York?"

Shea started talking to the Phils' Bob Carpenter, then had an insight that killed his enthusiasm for raiding. He said, "When I'm talking to him, I begin to see that I am placing myself in the position of asking him to do the very thing I would never do. Pull out of your town. That cured me. From then on I stopped bothering the teams."

Instead, he decided to start a new league.

That may sound ludicrous, but remember that one of the conditions that created the American Association (see p. 28) was no major league representation in sizable cities. According to the 1960 census, Houston had become the seventh-largest city, with nearly 200,000 more citizens than San Francisco or Milwaukee; New Orleans and Dallas now had larger populations than Pittsburgh; Seattle, San Antonio, and San Diego were more heavily populated than Cincinnati. There was an obvious hole for the National League in New York, and Mayor Wagner could dangle a new stadium in Queens before prospective franchisees.

Shea made his new league seem even more impressive when he announced that Branch Rickey, the man most responsible for reintegrating major league baseball, would be involved. Rickey said,

> The traditional concept of "major league" and "minor league" cities is now changing. Houston, Dallas, Minneapolis, Toronto, Buffalo, etc. are not going to accept the "minor league" label any longer. . . . This is the basic reason for the sports revolution that is now under way.

As word of Shea's efforts spread, major league baseball grew alarmed, particularly because, at the same time, Brooklyn Congressman Emanuel Celler was threatening baseball with antitrust action. In May 1959, baseball's bigwigs met to discuss expansion. Commissioner Ford Frick acknowledged that there was "no existing plan to expand the present major leagues." He said the two leagues would consider an application for major league status of an "acceptable group of eight clubs which would qualify under ten specifications."

It was standard stuff — no city smaller than Kansas City (opening the way for Indianapolis, Atlanta, Denver, and Memphis), eight parks with a minimum capacity of 35,000 each, and adoption of the uniform player

at the base of the bowl was the same size as the whole plot of land that held Ebbets Field, stands and all." Despite this, foul territory was smallish along first and immense along third and behind the plate. Arthur Daley said, "The Coliseum made a travesty of a once noble sport. It was — and is — a great football field. . . . But there was no way a baseball diamond could be fitted into its warped dimensions."

Those dimensions — the Coliseum's unyielding oval shape — demanded placing the first base line parallel to either the east or west end. Positioning home plate equidistant from the two long sides would have resulted in a shape like that of the Polo Grounds and foul lines even shorter than those on Coogan's Bluff. People called it "O'Malley's Chinese Theater," in mock honor of Grauman's Chinese Theater, and said that "it's the only place that can hold almost a hundred thousand people and two outfielders."

O'Malley objected to having home plate at the east end because the sun would be in the eyes of the batter, catcher, and umpire. (Van Harris, a contractor from Arcadia, helpfully suggested that a hot air balloon, 150 feet in circumference, be hoisted during day games to cast a shadow around home plate.) Ultimately, the Coliseum's football tenants okayed using the west end for baseball — once their rent was halved from 10 to 5 percent of the gross.

O'Malley also had to install $200,000 worth of lights at the west end to help illuminate the infield. He agreed that "all wiring be taken down each time an event other than baseball was scheduled," at a cost of $2,600 per event. The 40-foot fence in left field, erected to make 250-foot home runs gain in height what they lacked in distance, was movable; in 1958, when the Dodgers played on one Friday night, the screen came down for the Rams on Saturday night, then went up again for the Dodgers

contract. The sticking point was "responsibility for . . . financial obligations, *including those involving territoriality* [italics added]. In other words, a new league had to pay off club owners in minor league cities (some of which were owned by the big league teams themselves). Owners in large cities asked seven-figure prices; Jack Dunn III, the owner of the International League Orioles, had received $48,000 for the territorial rights to Baltimore a mere six years earlier.

Despite this drawback, Shea unveiled the Continental League (CL) on July 27 and announced that franchises had already been granted to New York, Houston, Minneapolis–St. Paul, Toronto, and Denver. Each deposited $50,000 and pledged another $2.5 million. When reporters asked where Shea would find players, he answered, "No one heard of an atomic scientist fifteen years ago. Now they're coming out of the woodwork. You can't tell me that a nation of a hundred and sixty million people can't produce two hundred more big league ballplayers."

The CL also had hopes that the antitrust legislation being introduced by Senator Estes Kefauver of Tennessee would open baseball's talent pool. On June 28, the bill came to the Senate floor. Senator Wiley of Wisconsin, who had helped Milwaukee buy a stadium, offered an amendment that gave baseball limited immunity from antitrust action; it passed by a 45–41 vote, and the full Senate then overwhelmingly voted down Kefauver's bill.

Nevertheless, the closeness of the vote concerned major league baseball. Lou Perini convinced CL backers to give up the fight if four of their number joined the majors; on August 2, 1960, the CL agreed. The National League admitted Houston and Shea's New York group, but the American League doublecrossed the new league and admitted a new Washington team (allowing Clark Griffith to move to Minneapolis) and a new Los Angeles franchise willing to pay Walter O'Malley, the man who had deserted Brooklyn, indemnification for his "territory."

The upshot was that the National League returned to New York City in 1962. The Mets played at the Polo Grounds for two years, then moved to what everyone insisted should be called Shea Stadium. When it came time to christen the new park, Shea let fly with two champagne bottles, one filled with water from the Harlem River, which flowed alongside the Polo Grounds, the other from the Gowanus Canal in Brooklyn.

on Sunday and was removed again that night for a rodeo.

In 1959, Ohio State and USC played football on a Friday night in October at the Coliseum; the pitcher's mound, left field screen, and right field fence — removed before the game — were replaced an hour after it was finished, and new foul lines were drawn for the first World Series game played in California. The Dodgers and White Sox drew a record 92,394 (which was broken each of the next two days). Despite the improvised mound, Chicago's Dick Donovan and Los Angeles's Don Drysdale pitched shutout ball for six innings.

No discussion of the Coliseum would be complete without mentioning the effect its dimensions had on home runs. In its first year, left field was 250 feet from home plate, center was 425, and right ranged from 301 down the line to 440 in right center. A total of 193 home runs were hit — 8 to right, 2 to center, and 183 to left. Adapting, lefty Wally Moon learned to loft balls over the screen with an inside-out swing; they became known as "Moon Shots," the only home runs celebrated for their height rather than distance.

Despite the Coliseum's unsuitability for baseball, Los Angeles fans — many of them transplants from the New York area — supported the team vigorously, and the move-a-team, reap-a-harvest, syndrome continued to work. The Dodgers drew 1.8 million in their first year, 2 million each of the next two years.

When the Giants left New York, cartoonist Willard Mullin wove the names of the team's great — Christy Mathewson and Willie Mays — and not-so-great — Sal Yvars and Lou Chiozza — into a uniform. Despite the wave from Father Knickerbocker, New Yorkers didn't spend much time pining for their former heroes. Dodger and Giant games televised in New York drew low ratings and were quickly canceled.

Griffith Stadium was photographed for this team-issue postcard on Opening Day in 1951. Looking carefully, one can see the famous tree and surrounding houses that gave center field at Griffith its distinctive character (lower right). It's equally possible to look at the left field foul line (407 feet from the plate) and understand just how joyful right-handed hitting Senators must have been at the prospect of playing on the road.

BLOWIN' IN THE WIND: CANDLESTICK PARK

In the top of the ninth inning of the first All-Star Game in 1961 (there were two each year from 1959 through 1962), the National League was leading, 3–2, at Candlestick Park. With one out, Roger Maris on first, and Al Kaline on second, 165-pound Giant reliever Stu Miller told Ron Fimrite of *Sports Illustrated*, "I took my set position into the wind, and just then a 65-mile-an-hour blast hit me." Plate umpire Stan Landes called a balk, and Miller said, "Stan, the wind pushed me. He said, 'I know that, Stu, but rules are rules.' "

Candlestick instantly became "the Cave of Winds." It was a sad commentary on the first modern ballpark built with a franchise in place and the second made entirely of reinforced concrete. On the downside, it was built hurriedly, by novices, in the midst of civic recriminations, and in the wrong place. In *Pennant Race*, pitcher Jim Brosnan says,

> Candlestick Park is the gross error in the history of major league baseball. Designed at a corner table in Lefty O'Doul's, a Frisco saloon, by two politicians and an itinerant ditchdigger, the ball park slants toward the bay — in fact, it slides toward the bay and before long will be under water, which is the best place for it.

Other players are equally antagonistic toward Candlestick. As a Met, Keith Hernandez hated Candlestick so much, he had a clause in his contract preventing his being traded to the Giants. Describing catching fly balls at Candlestick, catcher Bob Brenly said, "It would be kind of like dropping an aspirin tablet in a toilet, then flushing, and trying to grab it with a pair of tweezers." Asked what would improve Candlestick, Jack Clark answered simply, "Dynamite."

Candlestick was born in 1954 when the voters authorized a $5 million bond issue to build a ballpark — with a contingency: the money would be spent only if San Francisco got a major league team within five years. Giant boss Horace Stoneham had been interested in Minneapolis, where the Giants owned the AA Millers; he moved instead to San Francisco when the city promised to build a 40,000-seat stadium with 12,000 parking spaces.

Such a project required at least 75 acres, a tract six times as large as Braves Field in 1915. Under those conditions, the choices were limited. One proposal would have put a ballpark downtown, but department store owners feared that traffic congestion would hurt business, and the city's newspapers had to support their major advertisers.

Then there was Candlestick Point, the fingerlike feature that overlooked San Francisco Bay and had

The Giants played at Seals Stadium for two seasons. Known as "the Queen in Concrete," it originally had three dressing rooms, because the Pacific Coast League Missions also played home games here. In 1945, Paul Fagan, a wealthy San Franciscan, bought the Seals and equipped the clubhouse with draft beer, a soda fountain, a barber chair, and a shoeshine stand. The glass backstop he installed (baseball's first) was taken down long before the Giants moved in.

Fans sitting in the original Candlestick Park had a great view of San Francisco Bay but paid for it by having to confront the wind, which blew regularly at 30 to 50 mph in the late afternoon. The park was enclosed in 1971, and while fans are a bit more comfortable, a concrete baffle installed to tame the wind has been largely ineffective; it still swirls around, dropping temperatures and affecting the flight of the ball.

the same attractions as Shibe Park in Brewerytown and Ebbets Field in Pigtown: a cheap site, far from ideal but with potential. A reporter described it as a "breezy track of wild grass, red rocks, chaparral and torn trees . . . all strewn with whiskey bottles and beer cans."

On the plus side, one person, construction magnate Charles Harney, owned 41 acres on Candlestick Point. Getting him behind the project would immediately supply more than half the land needed. There was some concern about wind, but engineers did a test in the morning, and Mayor George Christopher announced, "At no time has a wind sock recorded a velocity of more than fourteen miles an hour. This wouldn't be enough to blow a peanut pack from first to second." (It was later discovered that the wind blows hardest from 1 to 5 P.M.)

Besides, the clock was ticking on the $5 million bond. The Giants had announced their move west in 1957, and the money had to be spent before 1959. Harney sold the land for $2.7 million — $66,000 per acre — although it had been assessed at $26,730 an acre two years earlier. On July 24, 1958, he signed a contract to build a stadium, which he'd never done before, to be designed by John Bolles, a rookie at stadium architecture.

Harney made the deal convinced that "the stadium would be named after him" because he'd provided the land and was building the park. Instead, when the city held a contest to name the field, an overwhelming number of people picked Candlestick Park; Harney fumed.

The project was shaky from the beginning. A month after work started, a grand jury ordered a probe of the financing, and another grand jury investigated the awarding of a parking contract. In November, Harney barred the Giants from the park because they wouldn't accept his work; the voters had agreed to $5 million, but costs were expected to be $15 million.

The park was not finished in 1959 as scheduled and mandated by the bond issue. When it was dedicated on April 12, 1960, Vice President Richard Nixon told the *Sporting News*, "This will be one of the most beautiful baseball parks of all time." On Opening Day, Cardinal center fielder Bill White had trouble tracking Orlando Cepeda's fly ball, which went for a triple, offering a preview of baseball in the Cave of Winds. Some fans came by boat; at the end of the game, they discovered that the tide had gone out, so they had to wade through mud to get back aboard.

There were other problems. In the original blueprints, a radiant heating system, 35,000 feet of three-quarter-inch wrought iron pipe, was to be installed in the concrete floor to heat half of the original 42,553 seats with natural gas. Instead of installing the pipes an inch down, as required, the builders put them 5 inches deep, rendering them useless. Attorney Melvin Belli sued the city in 1962 and got the cost of his season tickets back by insisting that they had come with a temperature guarantee.

The park deteriorated quickly. Wells Twombly wrote, "By the time the Giants played the Yankees in the 1962 World Series, Candlestick was already starting to look like the world's oldest new stadium." In 1968, former mayor Joseph Alioto said, "Putting $7 million into improving Candlestick would be perpetuating a mediocrity." Nevertheless, $16.1 million was spent after the 1971 season double-decking and enclosing the park to seat 60,000. Synthetic turf was installed, movable seats were added in right field to accommodate the NFL 49ers, and escalators were built to take fans from the parking lot to the stadium. Bolles, who had designed the original park, said, "An enclosed stadium will completely eliminate gusting and swirling winds."

It just wasn't so, and in 1983 the Giants tried to make a positive of a negative. Fans who stayed for extra innings during night games were awarded the Croix de Candlestick; it read "I came. I saw. I survived." So has Candlestick, but just barely.

THE CLASS OF '61

Expansion made major league parks out of minor league parks in Los Angeles and Bloomington, Minnesota, a Minneapolis suburb, in 1961. Minneapolis's search began in 1953 when the city created a major league baseball committee called the Minute Men and ended in May 1955 when a site was selected for Metropolitan Stadium — a farm on which Paul Gerhardt grew melons, onions, sweet corn, and radishes. Local businessmen bought it for $478,899 and broke ground in June; by September, Matty Schwab, part of the groundskeeping dynasty that tended Redland Field, the Polo Grounds, and Ebbets Field, was working out the landscaping.

Metropolitan Stadium opened on April 24, 1956, without costing the taxpayers a dime. Exhibition games were arranged to showcase the park for curious major league teams and demonstrate Minnesota's fan support. The Tigers and Reds drew 21,000 and so did the Giants, but Stoneham decided to move to San Francisco. In 1958, the

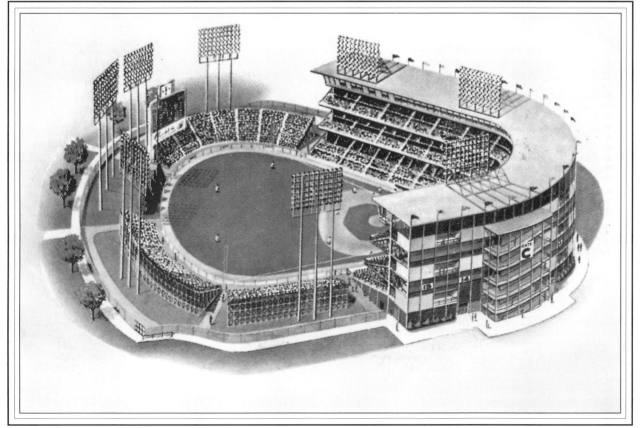

When Metropolitan Stadium opened in 1956, it was the home of the American Association Minneapolis Millers. The sight of a triple-decked ballpark sitting in the middle of a cornfield (above) struck some as comical until the Washington Senators decided to make Minneapolis big league territory. A proposed addition (left) made the field look more like a hot-air balloon rather than the familiar outfield. When the addition was done, the outfield was far more angular and eventually became a flattened hexagon, like other converted minor league parks.

Senators played the Phils, and owner Calvin Griffith got a tour of the area within a 50-mile radius of Bloomington; he liked what he saw and promised the city's baseball committee first crack if his team moved.

The opportunity came when the American League met in 1960 to consider bids for expansion franchises from Los Angeles, Dallas–Fort Worth, and the Twin Cities. Griffith said he'd move if seven conditions were met, including expanding Metropolitan Stadium to 40,000, arranging bank credit, and guaranteeing 2.5 million admissions in the first three years; the committee agreed to all seven, and the league approved the move on October 26, 1960.

The Met grew like Topsy during its lifetime. Minneapolis sportswriter Joe Soucheray compared it to "a solid cottage to which has been added wings as

the family has grown." A curved triple-decker grandstand that ran from first to third was the original park. In 1961, when the Twins took over, permanent bleachers were added along third, a temporary bleacher was installed in left, and the first and second decks were continued down the right field line; the double-decked left field pavilion, underwritten by the Vikings in exchange for a rent reduction, was completed for the 1965 All-Star Game.

When the Met became a big league park, fans and sportswriters feared that the prevailing northwesterly winds could help right-handed hitters imperil Babe Ruth's record for home runs in a season. Angelo Giuliani, an American League catcher for seven years, said, "It could be just the thing that will get someone like Mickey Mantle over the hump. That record of 60 homers is going to go, and

Thirty-six years after it opened, the other Wrigley Field finally became major league (left). A proposed second deck for possible use by the Dodgers was never built, so Wrigley looked like this in 1961, the only year it was used by the Angels. The clock used the park's name instead of numerals, and the president of the Pacific Coast League once used the tower as an office. The diagram gives a clue as to why more home runs were hit here (248) in one season than at any other major league park — the power alleys that are just a body's length farther from home than the foul lines.

an American Leaguer is going to do the breaking." Giuliani was right, but the breaker was not a right-handed hitter; Roger Maris hit 61 homers that year, only one of them at Metropolitan Stadium.

Like the Met, Wrigley Field was a home run paradise, but the one in Chicago is only homerville when the wind is blowing out toward Lake Michigan. For one shining season, there were *two* major league Wrigley Fields, and there was an easy way to distinguish between them; the Wrigley Field in Los Angeles had lights and had had them since July 22, 1931, when 17,000 fans saw the Los Angeles Angels play.

The Angels were owned by Phil Wrigley and shared the park with the Hollywood Stars. It was not uncommon for the two PCL teams to draw well; in 1930, they attracted 850,000 fans while the Browns and Cardinals drew 660,000.

In 1921, Phil's father, William K. Wrigley, Jr., the owner of Wrigley Gum and the Cubs, had bought the Angels. When city officials refused to let him build underground parking at Washington Park, at Washington and Hill, he decided to build his own park at 42nd and Avalon. Wrigley Field cost well over $1 million to build and, according to San Francisco sportswriter Art Spander, "may have been the finest minor league baseball park ever." It was double-decked, a rarity for minor league parks, and seated 18,500 in the grandstand; an uncovered bleacher in right center, very much like the Jury Box at Braves Field, held another 2,000. Left field had no seating, just a 15-foot wall that was covered with ivy, like its Chicago namesake.

It was built on a nearly square lot, and the outfield fences were angled toward the infield, the real reason Wrigley was a home run palace from the

Dodger Stadium opened on April 10, 1962, with an innovation in ballpark seating, a field-level row of special box seats between the dugouts. Two years later, the same wrecking ball used to demolish Ebbets Field began to level the Polo Grounds, seen here in 1964, the year Shea Stadium opened.

beginning. Left field was 340, center was 412, right was 339, seemingly normal dimensions; what was different about Wrigley West was the power alleys; where most bow out toward the outfield, Wrigley's were just 345 feet from home. (In 1959, the park was the site for *Home Run Derby*, the TV show that matched home run sluggers against each other, now popular on cable TV.)

The park opened on September 29, 1925, to 18,000 enthusiastic customers and has the distinction of being the first Wrigley Field in organized ball. (Cubs Park wasn't renamed until 1926.) That January, Commissioner Landis dedicated the tower attached to the park as a memorial for the soldiers who fought in World War I. The tower became a Los Angeles landmark, and when W. C. Tuttle, a well-known writer of western potboilers, became president of the Pacific Coast League, in 1936, the tower held his office and the league offices until 1941.

The franchise became so valuable that Browns owner Don Barnes decided to move his franchise to Los Angeles and had agreed to buy Wrigley Field and the Angels for $1 million. Barnes polled the other American League owners and had oral approval to move. The transfer question was the first item on the agenda at the winter meeting, scheduled for December 8, 1941; the attack on Pearl Harbor changed everything, and the proposal was voted down unanimously.

The last PCL game was played at Wrigley Field on September 15, 1957, and the park stood empty until 1961 when another millionaire, former cowboy star Gene Autry, bought the American League expansion franchise. The Angels and their oppo-

nents hammered 248 homers at Wrigley, a major league record, but the team finished its only season at the park 70–91, then moved to Chavez Ravine, O'Malley territory.

TAJ O'MALLEY: DODGER STADIUM

When Walter O'Malley extracted the Dodgers from Brooklyn, he had a vision of how his new stadium should look and feel. In addition to lots of parking, good sightlines, and more challenging dimensions than those in the Coliseum, he wanted the fans to be comfortable. Despite his overweening greed and shocking lack of social conscience for the citizens of Brooklyn, O'Malley is due credit as the first modern owner with a clear picture of what the public expected from a ballpark.

The core of it was not very different from what the public expected from a fast food restaurant: clean surroundings, fast service, reasonable prices, and a quality product. In baseball, the product is the team. Charles Ebbets, Wilbert Robinson, Larry MacPhail, and Branch Rickey tried but never did bring the Dodgers a championship in Brooklyn; the O'Malley family won the borough's only title and five more in Los Angeles.

Dodger Stadium has maintained its excellence even though it is thirty-one years old at this writing. When it was built, baseball was under heavy competition from television (see Chapter 9), football, and other leisure activities. In 1958, Bob Cobb, the former owner of the PCL Hollywood Stars, told the *Sporting News*, "A modern ballpark

would be one offering the fan the convenience you find at the race track . . . fine food, music, comfort, relaxation. You can't operate any business without thinking of the woman customer. . . . The big league owners must make their parks smart, fashionable places to go." O'Malley built a park that was a haven for both hard-core purists and occasional fans — but not without a fight.

The controversy was over Chavez Ravine, one of five Los Angeles ravines bounded on the north and on the east by the Los Angeles River, by Sunset Boulevard on the south, and on the west and northwest by Elysian Park. Named for landowner and city council member Julian Chavez, the area was settled in 1900 by Mexican Americans and a smaller number of Chinese Americans.

When O'Malley bought the PCL Angels and Wrigley Field in 1957, Los Angeles Mayor Norris Poulson and other city officials flew to Vero Beach, Florida, to clinch the Dodgers' move. Their gift was 315 acres of Chavez Ravine, which the city had just acquired from the Federal Housing Authority when a low-cost housing project went bust; condemnation proceedings had largely cleared it of homes. If the Dodgers agreed to swap centrally located Wrigley Field and build a 50,000-seat stadium and a youth center in the ravine, the city would give up title to the land and spend $2 million on site improvements and another $2.7 million to improve the access roads. On October 7, 1957, the City Council passed an ordinance accepting the Dodgers' contract, and the next day the team announced its move.

Meanwhile, several families in Chavez Ravine

refused to accept the court-approved appraisals of their land, which had been set during condemnation proceedings, and continued to live tax-free for several years. On May 8, 1959, the sheriff's office went in with trucks and bulldozers to "nudge them along." Members of Manuel Arechigas's family forced deputies to carry them out bodily, set up tents in the ravine, and received a flood of donations from the public; reporters from the *Los Angeles Mirror-News* then discovered that the Arechigas family owned eleven other houses and were actually a front for groups that had filed taxpayers' suits.

The last squatter's homes were torn down, and on June 3, 1959, the city and the Dodgers formally signed a contract. With three appeals to the U.S. Supreme Court pending, ground was broken anyway on September 17, 1959; the high court upheld the contract on October 15, 1959, and the building of Dodger Stadium proceeded.

Not that there weren't other complications. The city had been unable to buy out several families who were outside the boundaries of the failed project but within the Dodgers' acreage. It cost O'Malley $500,000 to compensate them. Then it was revealed that the Bureau of Public Works was going to charge $400,000 to move the water mains affected by the grading of the land. O'Malley was running out of cash; according to sportswriter Harold Rosenthal, he made Union Oil pay for the first ten years of the Dodgers' broadcasting rights in advance.

Even in the sleek new facility, Daffy Dodger tradition was upheld. When Dodger manager Walter

Alston and Angel boss Bill Rigney inspected the park three months before its opening, they discovered that it was impossible to see home plate from certain seats. Accordingly, home was moved out 10 feet from the stands, leaving center field just 400 feet away. It was also discovered that the foul lines had been installed completely in foul territory, contrary to baseball's rules. The Dodgers received special dispensation from the National League for the 1962 season. Ebbets Field had opened without a press box; the new park opened on April 10, 1962, without water fountains.

Dodger Stadium, the first park built with private capital since Yankee Stadium, has its detractors. Roger Angell compared it to a suburban supermarket:

It has the same bright, uneasy colors . . . turquoise exterior walls, pale green outfield fences, odd yellows and ochres on the grandstand seats. And there is a special shelf for high-priced goods — a dugout behind home plate for movie and television stars, ballplayers' wives, and transient millionaires.

Others loved it. Third baseman Jim Lefebvre said, "Sometimes I'd go into Dodger Stadium just to be alone. The game might start at 8 and I'd get there at 1 and sit in the stands and look at the field. It was that beautiful."

After all the turmoil, it was also beautiful financially. The Dodgers have returned to Los Angeles billions of dollars in revenue and rewarded fans with five championships. The fans responded by making Dodger Stadium the first ballpark to exceed 3 million in attendance, in 1978, and have matched the number many times since.

Exactly a hundred years after William Cammeyer had enclosed a Brooklyn skating rink, his spiritual descendants were thriving 3,000 miles away. In 1962, Dodger Stadium was the last word in palatial stadiums; three years later, it had been eclipsed by a pleasure dome not even Kubla Khan could have decreed.

TIMELINE

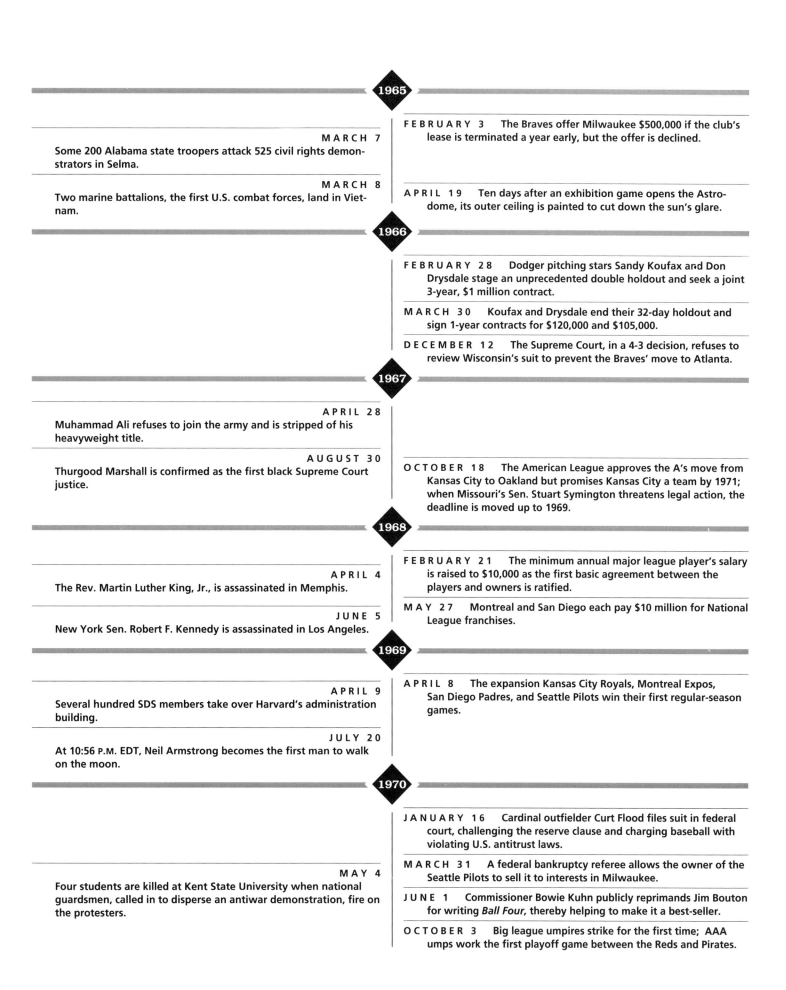

1965

MARCH 7
Some 200 Alabama state troopers attack 525 civil rights demonstrators in Selma.

MARCH 8
Two marine battalions, the first U.S. combat forces, land in Vietnam.

FEBRUARY 3   The Braves offer Milwaukee $500,000 if the club's lease is terminated a year early, but the offer is declined.

APRIL 19   Ten days after an exhibition game opens the Astrodome, its outer ceiling is painted to cut down the sun's glare.

1966

FEBRUARY 28   Dodger pitching stars Sandy Koufax and Don Drysdale stage an unprecedented double holdout and seek a joint 3-year, $1 million contract.

MARCH 30   Koufax and Drysdale end their 32-day holdout and sign 1-year contracts for $120,000 and $105,000.

DECEMBER 12   The Supreme Court, in a 4-3 decision, refuses to review Wisconsin's suit to prevent the Braves' move to Atlanta.

1967

APRIL 28
Muhammad Ali refuses to join the army and is stripped of his heavyweight title.

AUGUST 30
Thurgood Marshall is confirmed as the first black Supreme Court justice.

OCTOBER 18   The American League approves the A's move from Kansas City to Oakland but promises Kansas City a team by 1971; when Missouri's Sen. Stuart Symington threatens legal action, the deadline is moved up to 1969.

1968

FEBRUARY 21   The minimum annual major league player's salary is raised to $10,000 as the first basic agreement between the players and owners is ratified.

APRIL 4
The Rev. Martin Luther King, Jr., is assassinated in Memphis.

MAY 27   Montreal and San Diego each pay $10 million for National League franchises.

JUNE 5
New York Sen. Robert F. Kennedy is assassinated in Los Angeles.

1969

APRIL 9
Several hundred SDS members take over Harvard's administration building.

APRIL 8   The expansion Kansas City Royals, Montreal Expos, San Diego Padres, and Seattle Pilots win their first regular-season games.

JULY 20
At 10:56 P.M. EDT, Neil Armstrong becomes the first man to walk on the moon.

1970

JANUARY 16   Cardinal outfielder Curt Flood files suit in federal court, challenging the reserve clause and charging baseball with violating U.S. antitrust laws.

MARCH 31   A federal bankruptcy referee allows the owner of the Seattle Pilots to sell it to interests in Milwaukee.

MAY 4
Four students are killed at Kent State University when national guardsmen, called in to disperse an antiwar demonstration, fire on the protesters.

JUNE 1   Commissioner Bowie Kuhn publicly reprimands Jim Bouton for writing *Ball Four,* thereby helping to make it a best-seller.

OCTOBER 3   Big league umpires strike for the first time; AAA umps work the first playoff game between the Reds and Pirates.

TIMELINE

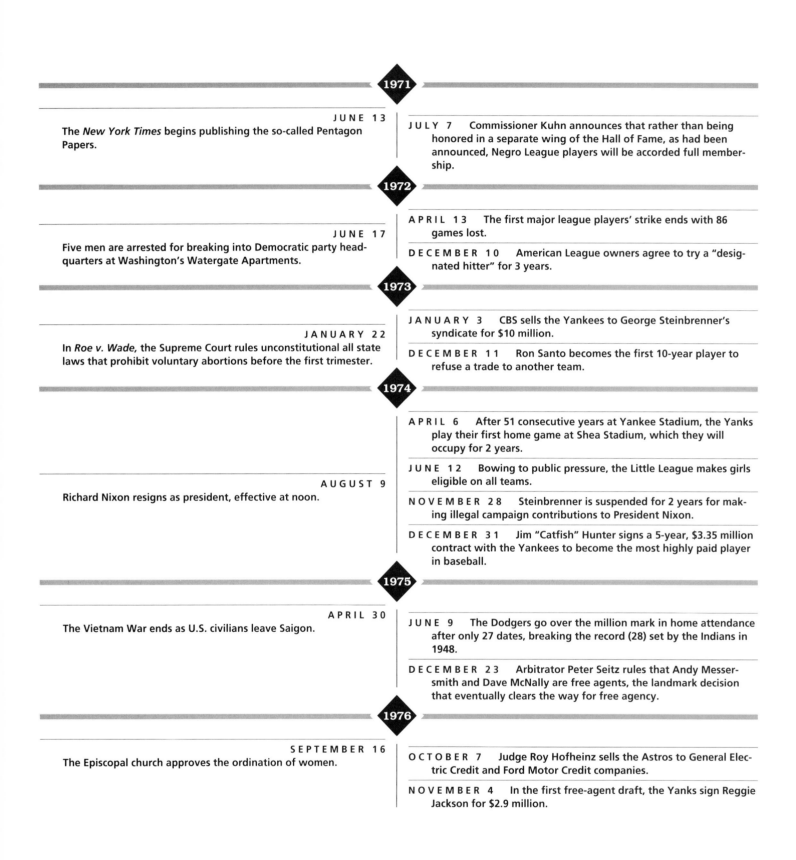

1971

JUNE 13
The *New York Times* begins publishing the so-called Pentagon Papers.

JULY 7   Commissioner Kuhn announces that rather than being honored in a separate wing of the Hall of Fame, as had been announced, Negro League players will be accorded full membership.

1972

JUNE 17
Five men are arrested for breaking into Democratic party headquarters at Washington's Watergate Apartments.

APRIL 13   The first major league players' strike ends with 86 games lost.

DECEMBER 10   American League owners agree to try a "designated hitter" for 3 years.

1973

JANUARY 22
In *Roe v. Wade,* the Supreme Court rules unconstitutional all state laws that prohibit voluntary abortions before the first trimester.

JANUARY 3   CBS sells the Yankees to George Steinbrenner's syndicate for $10 million.

DECEMBER 11   Ron Santo becomes the first 10-year player to refuse a trade to another team.

1974

APRIL 6   After 51 consecutive years at Yankee Stadium, the Yanks play their first home game at Shea Stadium, which they will occupy for 2 years.

JUNE 12   Bowing to public pressure, the Little League makes girls eligible on all teams.

AUGUST 9
Richard Nixon resigns as president, effective at noon.

NOVEMBER 28   Steinbrenner is suspended for 2 years for making illegal campaign contributions to President Nixon.

DECEMBER 31   Jim "Catfish" Hunter signs a 5-year, $3.35 million contract with the Yankees to become the most highly paid player in baseball.

1975

APRIL 30
The Vietnam War ends as U.S. civilians leave Saigon.

JUNE 9   The Dodgers go over the million mark in home attendance after only 27 dates, breaking the record (28) set by the Indians in 1948.

DECEMBER 23   Arbitrator Peter Seitz rules that Andy Messersmith and Dave McNally are free agents, the landmark decision that eventually clears the way for free agency.

1976

SEPTEMBER 16
The Episcopal church approves the ordination of women.

OCTOBER 7   Judge Roy Hofheinz sells the Astros to General Electric Credit and Ford Motor Credit companies.

NOVEMBER 4   In the first free-agent draft, the Yanks sign Reggie Jackson for $2.9 million.

C H A P T E R   N I N E

Domes and Concrete Doughnuts

Domes obliterated the concept of the traditional ballpark. Instead of evoking blue sky, green grass, and sunshine, structures like Seattle's Kingdome were likened to ashtrays, warehouses, and missile silos.

Except for Royals Stadium in 1973, no new parks were built solely for major league baseball between Dodger Stadium in 1962 and the new Comiskey Park in 1991. Instead, there was a proliferation of "multipurpose facilities," stadiums meant to attract everything from soccer, football, rodeos, and boxing matches to conventions, kennel club shows, and franchising seminars.

Minor league parks (Sick's Stadium, Arlington Stadium), football stadiums (Exhibition Stadium), and former major league parks (Milwaukee County Stadium, Municipal Stadium in Kansas City) were pressed into service, and one was even totally rebuilt (Yankee Stadium). But there were only two kinds of new buildings to house baseball: airless, translucent domes — the Astrodome, Kingdome, and Metrodome — and concrete doughnuts, characterless and interchangeable — Riverfront Stadium, Three Rivers Stadium, Atlanta–Fulton County Stadium, Veterans Stadium, which is, technically, an octorad, or superellipse. Pirate third baseman Richie Hebner once said, "I stand at the plate in Philadelphia and I don't honestly know whether I'm in Pittsburgh, Cincinnati, St. Louis, or Philly. They all look alike."

The names all sounded alike as well and represented a corporate sensibility new to baseball. The names of cities and counties do not celebrate teams (Braves, Yankee) or individuals (Wrigley, Ebbets) as parks had in the past. Baseball families with strong roots began disappearing from the mid-1950s to the late 1980s; the Macks, Stonehams, and Griffiths gave way to breweries (Labatt's), media companies (CBS), pizza millionaires (Tom Monahan of the Tigers), and car dealers (the Brewers' Bud Selig and Marge Schott of the Reds).

These changes reflected an insecure world in which franchises moved nearly at will; having a team name on a stadium could be bad business if the team moved, as the Braves and Athletics did (each for the second time) during this period; lionizing waterways, cities, and counties was far safer. Besides, cities and counties were now the only entities building ballparks; even though Walter O'Malley was given land by the city of Los Angeles, he raised every penny for Dodger Stadium in 1962. (Thirty-one years later, it remains the last privately built ballpark.)

Safety and security were the watchwords for these new parks. F. Scott Fitzgerald once described baseball as "a boys' game . . . bounded by walls which kept out novelty or danger, change or adventure." These parks, built in an age of anxiety, were designed to minimize uncertainties of all kinds — bad hops in the infield, crazy bounces in the outfield. In place of uncertainty there was "entertain-

The idea of putting a ballpark under a dome preceded the Astrodome. Two prominent architects had submitted designs for domed stadiums in Brooklyn before the Dodgers left. The first, proposed at O'Malley's urging by Norman Bel Geddes in 1952 (right), envisioned heated seats, automatic hot dog vending machines, and a design that made the ballfield the most prominent part of a shopping center, like the Sky-Dome. The second (far right), created by geodesic dome inventor Buckminster Fuller, along with Princeton graduate students, was less futuristic but much closer to the actual form baseball's first dome took.

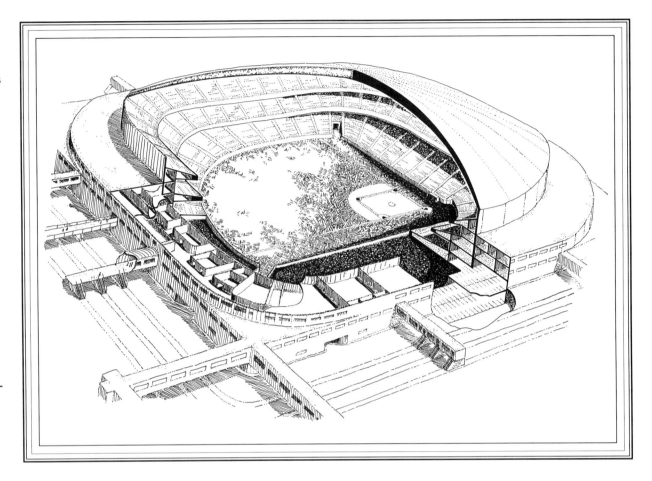

ment" — gigantic scoreboards that featured blowups of players' faces, sing-alongs, and exhortations such as "Chaaaarge!!!!!" Hall of Fame pitcher and broadcaster Waite Hoyt said, "The moment you enter Riverfront Stadium or Three Rivers Stadium . . . you feel like you're witnessing an exhibition, a spectacle. It's like a giant coliseum. You feel alone."

DOME ON THE RANGE: THE ASTRODOME

The stadium that became synonymous with spectacle was the Astrodome in Houston. The prototypical multipurpose facility, it is a place where the Houston Astros play baseball; the Houston Oilers play football; the place Elvin Hayes outplayed Kareem Abdul-Jabbar in 1968, Billie Jean King dispatched Bobby Riggs in a winner-take-all Battle of the Sexes tennis match, and Evel Knievel established a world indoor record for a motorcycle jump.

Billed as "the Eighth Wonder of the World," the Astrodome opened in 1965, when baseball was rapidly losing to football its position as the nation's most popular sport. Houston, a football town,

already had the AFL Oilers but longed for major league status. They got it, as noted, in 1960, and in January 1962, ground was broken for the Astrodome; Harris County officials celebrated by shooting Colt .45s into the air for their team, the Colt .45s, later the Astros.

Other burgeoning cities had become major league, but the majority didn't have the same problems as Houston — heat and mosquitoes. The city's average temperature in July is 83 degrees; New York's is 76, Chicago's is 73, San Francisco's is 62. When the Colts began playing at open-air Colt Stadium, it was clear that the heat would do in both players and fans; during one Sunday doubleheader, a hundred people required first aid. Original Colt Rusty Staub said, "You know how Ernie Banks is always saying, 'Great day for two'? Well, we had one doubleheader in the afternoon, and they had to carry him off the field on a stretcher."

The mosquitoes? Two-time batting champ Richie Ashburn said, "Houston is the only city where women wear insect repellent instead of perfume." The field was sprayed nightly, but some mosquitoes were so big that in Sandy Koufax's opinion, they were "twin-engine jobs." The Colts had gotten per-

mission to stage Sunday night games, but in 1962 the idea of a team's playing mostly or all night games was unappealing. The only feasible solution was to make the weather a nonfactor, cut baseball off from its natural medium — oxygen — and substitute conditioned air.

Most people accepted the realities imposed by the climate but didn't accept (and may have never accepted) the way they were handled by the Astrodome's mastermind, the brash, bumptious Roy Hofheinz. In building the first sports dome and, later, introducing AstroTurf, Hofheinz brushed aside a hundred years of baseball tradition and had a more lasting effect on the game than nearly any nonplayer before or since.

Lyndon Johnson's campaign manager in his race for the U.S. senate in 1948, Hofheinz was a Harris County judge at 24, a multimillionaire at 35, and mayor of Houston at 41. He was originally interested in building a shopping mall on the chosen site and, envisioning a geodesic dome, contacted Buckminster Fuller. The project fell through, but Hofheinz kept the domed mall in mind. Three months after the Colt .45s were granted a National League franchise, voters approved a $22 million

bond issue to build Harris County Domed Stadium near South Main Street.

The stadium that gave new meaning to the phrase "inside baseball" stands as high as an eighteen-story building, cost $35.5 million to build, and was compared breathlessly by publicists to the Colossus at Rhodes and the Roman Colosseum. But the Astrodome revealed its tragic flaw the first time it was used for baseball by the Colts and their Oklahoma City farmhands. Outfielders chasing fly balls, said *Time*, "staggered like asphyxiated cockroaches." The panels were translucent, not transparent, and the sunlight was diffused into a glare so intense that a player was blinded when he looked up. Astro general manager Paul Richards said, "Sure, somebody will win and somebody will lose. But who's kidding whom? This isn't baseball."

An exhibition game against the Yankees on April 9, 1965, the first public event, featured a first ball thrown by Governor John Connally, a Mickey Mantle home run, and a visit from President and Mrs. Johnson.

Nevertheless, the National League played at the Astrodome during the regular season and focused attention, instead, on its "features." The dugouts

The Ten Best Quotes About the Astrodome

1. "It reminds me of what my first ride would be like in a flying saucer." — Mickey Mantle
2. "When I managed there I always felt like I was in a stage show." — Sparky Anderson
3. "Like most of Texas, it owes its existence to a lot of hot air." — Sportswriter Jim Murray
4. "I have no complaints about the synthetic grass. What they need is some synthetic dirt." — Wes Parker
5. "It's the world's biggest pool table." — Leo Durocher
6. "God is still the only one who can make a tree, but Judge Roy Hofheinz bears close watching." — Sportswriter Wells Twombly
7. "This here's the kind of building where from the outside you can't tell where first base is." — Casey Stengel
8. "It's the first infield you could dribble a baseball on." — Jerry Grote
9. "Goldfinger tried to knock off Fort Knox. Hofheinz built his own." — Anonymous
10. "We were surprised at the reaction of the couple behind us. They said the cheering inspired by the scoreboard reminded them of a football game. In Texas you can't get a higher compliment than that." — Johnny Temple

were 120 feet long, nearly twice the length of regular ones, to give more fans "seats behind the dugout." There was a two-story Presidential Suite and a Tipsy Tavern, where the floor tilted and beers sliding down the bar were stopped by a hidden magnet. High above right field, Hofheinz built living quarters that included a barber shop, bowing alley, beauty salon, children's room, gazebo, sidewalk café, and a medieval chapel. When his wife died, the apartment became his permanent home. (The apartment and much of its contents have since been removed.)

The ballpark had once been a place of boisterous companionship, leather-lunged rooting, singing, conversation, worrying, and second-guessing, but that spirit was about to change. Sportswriter Melvin Durslag wrote, "As the standard of living is raised in this country, people become more sensitive to surroundings. They live in comfort. They want to watch sports in comfort." Hofheinz understood completely and gentrified the ballpark by reintroducing the skybox eighty years after Albert Spalding, a luxury suite where people could display their wealth if they had it (and most in Texas did), talk business and gossip, drink fine wine, eat elegant food, track the Dow-Jones ticker on oversize TV screens, and now and then also watch baseball.

But the comfort and spectacle couldn't cure the Astrodome's problem. When outfielders insisted they couldn't see the ball and several players called the conditions dangerous, Hofheinz handed out orange sunglasses. In self-defense, the outfielders began wearing batting helmets during games. The Astros tried ten dozen balls dyed several colors — yellow, orange, red, and cerise — to no avail. Manager Luman Harris ordered his left fielders to cover balls hit to center and vice versa, a practice that was dropped when the fielders' tongues began hanging out.

Ten days after the exhibition game, Hofheinz bowed to reality and had a translucent acrylic coating applied to the roof's panels. It did stop the glare; however, daylight entering the dome was reduced by roughly 30 percent, causing the grass to fail and eventually die. A stopgap measure, painting the dead grass green, only made things worse.

Although baseball had never been played on an artificial surface, Hofheinz commissioned the Chemstrand division of Monsanto to send experimental artificial grass to Houston, and he tested it in the empty Colt Stadium. Members of the Houston sheriff's posse rode horses on it, cars ran over it, and the University of Houston football team scrimmaged on it. When the synthetic lawn passed tests for wear and durability, it was dubbed Astro-Turf and the green plastic was duly installed at the Astrodome. (Hofheinz originally wanted to color the foul lines blue, the infield red, and the outfield yellow but changed his mind.)

A year after the Astros played the first major league game inside an anonymous round building, they played the first on an artificial surface, severing baseball's link to its pastoral beginnings of fresh air, sunshine, green grass. Instead there was merely spectacle. When someone homered, an electronic message board that, Hofheinz said, "put the Aurora Borealis to shame" exploded with flashing lights, skyrockets, gongs, and whistles; two cowboys appeared, firing six-guns, followed by a steer with an American flag on one horn and the Lone Star on the other. At the end of the 45-second show, Hofheinz announced, "Nobody can ever see this and still think that Houston is bush."

The Astrodome became the first stadium that offered guided tours. In its first year of operation, a million people paid $1 each to glimpse its wonders, but the hoopla did little for baseball. After Red Smith saw a game at the Astrodome, he wrote, "Thus, the game of rounders completed its evolution from a Cooperstown cow pasture [sic] to an air-conditioned, floodlighted, weatherproofed greenhouse on the Texas plains."

Originally Harris County Domed Stadium (left), the Astrodome still had grass in this photograph (below), and the gondola was not yet attached to the roof. The dome taped out at 208 feet from the floor, 642 in diameter, and publicists assaulted the public with irrelevant tidbits. While having enough plumbing to accommodate 40,000 people washing their hands simultaneously is impressive, management never built a team good enough to come close to meeting that eventuality.

ABC, AFL, CBS, NBC, NFL

When the Astrodome opened, the AFL Houston Oilers were playing at a high school stadium called Peddesen Field; nevertheless, they were known nationally because their games were regularly shown on network television.

Pro football had a history of good TV ratings even before Pete Rozelle became commissioner of the National Football League in January 1960. At that time, the NFL faced competition from the AFL and had only a handful of employees, but it was a staple on TV. Part of that popularity stemmed from reaction to a single telecast, the 1958 championship game. On December 28, 1958, the Baltimore Colts beat the New York Giants, 23–17, in overtime. The game (sometimes called "the greatest football game ever played") got reams of publicity and firmly established football's "draw" on television.

Ironically, the media attention that did so much to establish football as the country's most popular sport was made available, indirectly, by baseball. In *Voices of the Game,* Harold Rosenthal of the *New York Times* says that the excitement about pro football

> started in New York. And it started after the Dodgers and Giants left town . . . the newspapers, radio, and television stations had always been baseball, baseball, baseball. Now there were only the Yankees left — not nearly enough to write about or to fill their sports pages . . . pro football, which baseball would come to fear so greatly in the sixties and seventies, had its

birth, really, in baseball's abandonment of New York.

A former publicist, Rozelle understood viscerally that television was the way to sell football to the American public. He made the networks promote their football telecasts aggressively and got players, coaches, and announcers to appear on other TV shows, at youth clinics, at meetings of network affiliates, and at corporate sales meetings. Pro football formed a link with national advertisers, and corporate product managers and marketing VPs could now "hang out" with bona fide macho sports heroes. Even Americans who had previously had no interest in sports whatsoever were intrigued by provocative phrases like "ball control," "blitz," "soft coverage," and "penetration." (In an earlier era, Ely Culbertson had promoted bridge with a similar strategy, coining terms like "demand bids," "vulnerability," and "forcing passes.")

The lingo made pro football sound new and exciting when, in fact, it had been around since 1920, when the NFL was formed in a Hupmobile showroom in Canton, Ohio. No one much cared about the straight-ahead running game despite the brief vogues of players like Red Grange and Bronco Nagurski.

After World War II, however, exciting teams like the Cleveland Browns and Los Angeles Rams opened up the game with deep passes — "the long bomb" — football's home run. The game grew in popularity, and curious fans could see what the shouting was about at their ballparks. In 1961, for instance, there were twenty-two pro football teams, and half of them played in ballparks.

In person, football and baseball have their own kind of drama. On television, however, football looks more exciting, like a movie star "the camera loves." The ball is bigger, and both lines, the linebackers, and the backfield can easily fit into the same camera shot because they're bunched close together. In contrast, a shot of nine men on a baseball field makes them look like pygmies because they're so far apart.

Distance forces the television director to focus on only one small part of the field at a time, which has interesting ramifications for the viewer. In *Voices of the Game,* announcer Ernie Harwell analyzes the difference between baseball on TV and in person:

> Say you're sitting in the park and a guy lines a double to left-center and a runner scores from first. At the ballpark, we see it all at once — the runner tearing around the bases and the batter going for two, the fielder chasing the ball, the

Football in Ballparks

CITY	PARK	FOOTBALL	BASEBALL
Baltimore	Memorial Stadium	Colts	Orioles
Chicago	Wrigley Field	Bears	Cubs
Cleveland	Municipal Stadium	Browns	Indians
Detroit	Tiger Stadium	Lions	Tigers
Los Angeles	Memorial Coliseum	Rams	Dodgers
Milwaukee	County Stadium	Green Bay Packers	Braves
Minneapolis	Metropolitan Stadium	Vikings	Twins
New York	Yankee Stadium	Giants	Yankees
Pittsburgh	Forbes Field	Steelers	Pirates
San Francisco	Candlestick Park	Oakland Raiders	Giants
St. Louis	Busch Stadium	Cardinals	Cardinals

Earlier parks were built at the intersections of city streets. The Harry S. Truman complex, which housed Royals Stadium and Arrowhead Stadium, was located at the interchange of an interstate highway (Interstate 70). Its innovative design proved that baseball-only parks could still progress architecturally.

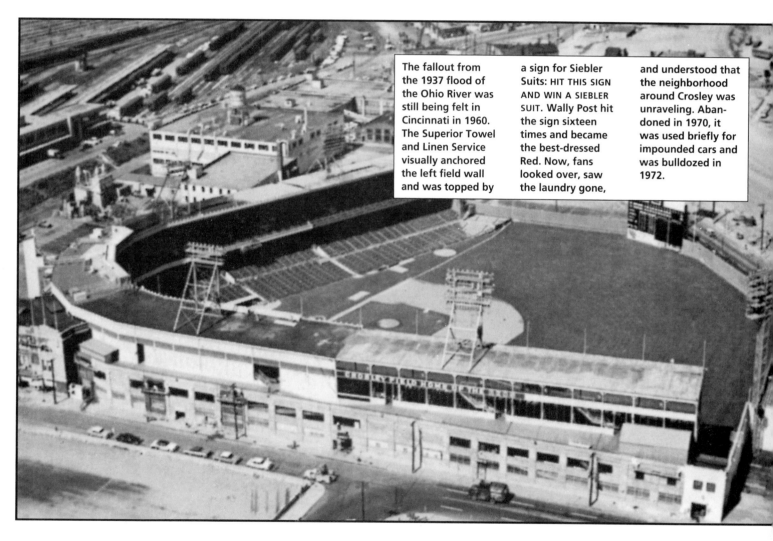

The fallout from the 1937 flood of the Ohio River was still being felt in Cincinnati in 1960. The Superior Towel and Linen Service visually anchored the left field wall and was topped by a sign for Siebler Suits: HIT THIS SIGN AND WIN A SIEBLER SUIT. Wally Post hit the sign sixteen times and became the best-dressed Red. Now, fans looked over, saw the laundry gone, and understood that the neighborhood around Crosley was unraveling. Abandoned in 1970, it was used briefly for impounded cars and was bulldozed in 1972.

shortstop going for the relay throw, the catcher getting ready for the peg — you see it as it's happening. But with TV, all you see are an individual succession of shots. It reduces baseball, makes it smaller than life, less exciting than it is.

Despite this drawback, baseball was initially a huge success on television. On June 6, 1953, the *Game of the Week* began on ABC, the first series of regular-season games televised nationally. Although the Yankees had blacked out New York, 51 percent of all the TV sets in use tuned in to

announcers Dizzy Dean and Buddy Blattner. Even more incredible, outside major league cities, *75 percent* of the sets turned on the baseball game.

But the owners were blind to the implications of these figures. Baseball continued to pursue a piecemeal approach until 1964; by then, the damage was done. From nowhere, football had slowly become the nation's favorite televised sport. In 1968, respondents to a Lou Harris poll said for the first time that they preferred football to baseball, 39–32, on or off TV.

When the next stadiums were built, they were

no longer ballparks — for baseball only. Now, football had a big say in stadium design, with television increasingly becoming involved so that its cameras could be positioned most effectively, its labyrinthine cables within easy reach. As the Coliseum had shown, oval stadiums could not comfortably accommodate baseball without distorting it; the shape of things to come, then, was not square or rectangular for baseball or oval for football but a compromise — round.

Round stadiums could showcase both sports, particularly with movable seats, and give a city sports revenue from April through December, making it easier to pass the bond issues needed to build them. In one case, a round stadium saved professional baseball from leaving its birthplace, Cincinnati.

FROM CROSLEY TO RIVERFRONT

When moving franchises became both chic and profitable, Reds owner Powel Crosley, Jr., threatened to relocate the team rather than try to make do in Crosley Field.

Crosley, built on an abandoned brickyard, seated fewer than 30,000 people in "a part of town where you paid a kid to watch your car and still worried about slashed tires." Bill DeWitt bought the club in 1962 and put teeth into the threat to relocate; after prolonged negotiations, the city of San Diego promised to build a 50,000-seat stadium if the Reds joined the Dodgers and Giants in California.

Cincinnati needed a new stadium whether the Reds were moving or not. Eugene Ruehlmann, elected mayor in 1967, said, "We soon became convinced that baseball alone was not enough to provide the financial base. We would also need a professional football franchise." In 1965, Ohio's Governor James Rhodes met with the Cincinnati Chamber of Commerce and said if the city built a multipurpose stadium, he "would make sure we got a new franchise headed by Paul Brown . . . This really lit a spark."

A feasibility study recommended four possible sites: (1) Maketewah Country Club, north of Cincinnati; (2) an empty lot near Crosley Field itself; (3) the northeastern suburb of Blue Ash, and (4) acreage by the Ohio River. Blue Ash was ruled out because it was rural and had only a small airport; building on Maketewah would have destroyed a residential community of older homes, and Crosley was deemed more appropriate for an industrial park. The Ohio River was the logical place.

On June 8, 1966, Rozelle announced the merger of the AFL and NFL, effective with the 1969–1970 season, and Cincinnati saw Rhodes' promise of an NFL franchise as a way of ensuring a stadium. According to *Reds Report,* Rozelle called Mayor Ruehlmann in October 1967 and said, "I can't give you anything in writing. You're just going to have to take my word for it that you'll be getting a franchise."

Reds owner Bill DeWitt opposed a stadium on the Ohio because of flooding, which had wrought such havoc in 1937; however, he was willing to be bought out if the new owners signed a forty-year lease to stay in Cincinnati. Frank Dale, the publisher of the *Cincinnati Enquirer,* headed a syndicate that bought the club with the understanding that the city would build a stadium; construction began in February 1968, and Cincinnati was promised the 1970 All-Star Game.

On June 24, 1970, the Reds trailed the Giants, 4–3, in the bottom of the eighth when Johnny Bench and Lee May homered off Juan Marichal to give the fans at Crosley Field a happy ending. Seconds after the final out, a helicopter from radio station WLW carried home plate to its new home. Riverfront Stadium opened on June 30, 1970, the first time major league baseball was played on "wall-to-wall carpeting" with cutouts for home plate, the pitcher's mound, and approaches to the other bases.

The Reds sold Crosley Field to the city; after serving as a lot for impounded cars, it was converted into the Queensgate II industrial park in 1972. Next door stands the Phillips Supply Company, its address 1 Crosley Lane. A dozen seats, a miniature AstroTurf diamond (!), and a bronze home plate commemorate the old park; as it turned out, however, Crosley was resurrected.

A WHOLE NEW BALL GAME

When the Pirates moved into Three Rivers Stadium, manager Danny Murtagh said, "I'll have to readjust my thinking and my spitting." Noting that chewing tobacco stains synthetic turf, Murtagh asked, "Do I have to switch to bubble gum or do I attach a spittoon to my belt? I'm a victim of progress."

Progress, in the form of the changes made by Hofheinz and slavishly followed by others, changed ballparks and baseball far more radically than Babe Ruth had. The most obvious difference was that the dimensions of the field became

As tastes changed and the need to satisfy football clients increased, even traditional baseball cities like St. Louis abandoned the traditional rectangularly sited oval or ovoid ballpark. An early version of Busch Memorial Stadium followed the traditional model (right), but architect Edward Durrell Stone made the park harmonize with the nearby Gateway Arch by echoing it in his circular design (below). In its final version, the arches were toned down and appear only at the top of the stadium (bottom).

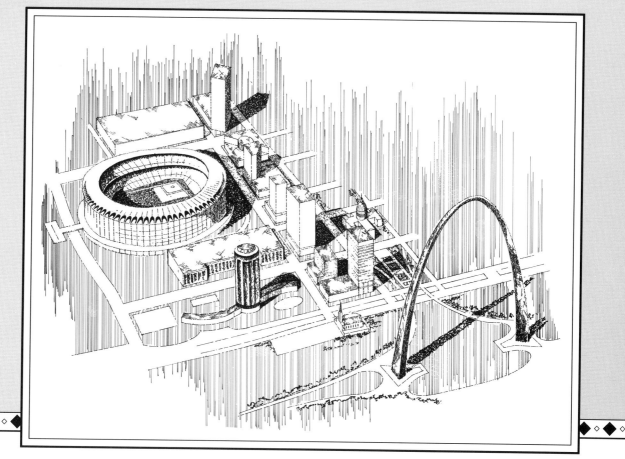

Since they were unavoidably round, domes inevitably popularized the circular shape for multipurpose stadiums. The idea goes back to at least the Colosseum (top left), built in Rome in A.D. 70 by the Emperor Vespasian, although, technically speaking, it is elliptical in shape. Viewed alone, these concrete doughnuts can be numbingly bland, as in this photo of Riverfront Stadium in Cincinnati (left). Yet, in context with the Suspension Bridge, built by John Roebling, creator of the Brooklyn Bridge (above), Riverfront seems a more natural part of its surroundings. Roundness has its limits, however. Fortunately, this design for a stadium across the Monongahela River in Pittsburgh (right) made its way onto a postcard but was never built.

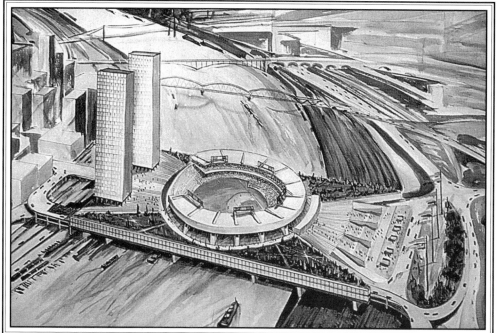

Field of Dreams

Crosley Field is the only major league ballpark to be brought back to life, and it happened twice, in two different states. The first time it was resurrected by Larry Luebbers, a ham salesman and real estate broker from Union, Kentucky. When parts of Crosley were auctioned off in 1970 by King Wrecking Company, Luebbers, a lifelong Reds fan, went to buy two seats as souvenirs, but, he said, "I got kind of carried away . . . Before I knew it, I had the walls and the scoreboard too."

Fortunately, Luebbers had a 206-acre back yard to hold his treasures. Before the wreckers arrived to dismantle Crosley, he took exact measurements of the 40-foot terrace, which made outfielders backpedal

uphill, and the left field (328) and right field (366) lines. He then spent $8,000 bulldozing his meadow, raising it 6 feet, and leveling it off. Over a two-year period, he
• had the 65-foot scoreboard repainted.
• rebuilt the 60-foot flagpole after it cracked into three pieces.
• sawed the ticket office in half so that it could be moved across an Ohio River bridge and nailed back together.

Luebbers also liberated the old popcorn stand, the Reds locker room, the WCKY-WLW broadcast booth, a sign advertising "the new 1970 Dodge," the bat rack, and the pitching rubber. The bartender at a saloon called the Dugout, just across from

Crosley II (Luebbers's name for the park), said, "Well, there's some that likes to collect old cards. Larry, there, he just likes to collect old ball fields." Not only collect but use. Spectators sitting in the 400 seats he salvaged saw Union's Knothole League team play, and those interested in becoming patrons could have their names inscribed on specific seats for $25.

That would have been it except that Crosley II mysteriously disappeared. In 1987, Luebbers took an extended trip before retiring to Arizona. He told the *Cincinnati Enquirer*, "The property was sold when I was out of town . . . when I came back, it was torn down."

The mystery might never have come to light except that Marvin

uniform. These fifteen major league parks are nearly identical.

Where ballparks were once interesting because of their differences, sameness became a virtue. When the new stadium opened in Philadelphia, president Bill Giles proudly characterized it to the

Sporting News by saying that the seats would be identical to those in Anaheim, the center field background would be similar to that in Shea Stadium, the scoreboard would look like the one in Pittsburgh, and there would be skyboxes à la the Astrodome. It even had a name that sounded like the others' — Veterans Stadium.

The great running catches once made by Willie Mays, Tris Speaker, and Roberto Clemente were no longer possible, because any fly ball hit at least 415 feet in the new stadiums — never mind 430 or 450 — is a home run. Also, playing on artificial turf, fewer outfielders attempted diving catches; if they missed, the ball could roll to the wall for a triple or an inside-the-park home run; conversely, bona fide on-the-fly triples and inside-the-park home runs nearly disappeared, because there were no right field walls at Baker Bowl or League Park that made balls bounce crazily.

Managers playing on turf could no longer afford to attempt sacrifice bunts; too often they became double plays. There were no bad hops in the infield, no grounders hitting infielders in the Adam's apple (Tony Kubek in 1960) or kangarooing over the third baseman's head (Fred Lindstrom in 1924) to decide a World Series. Dave Concepcion and Ozzie Smith learned to bounce their throws to first on artificial surfaces. Left-handed slap hitters like Rod Carew, Wade Boggs, and Tony Gwynn learned that, stroked down an AstroTurf third base line, routine grounders became doubles. With artificial turf, groundskeepers like the Bossards and Schwabs could no longer "customize" a park, making it impossible to prolong the career of a local favorite.

Original Dimensions of Modern Ballparks

YEAR BUILT	PARK	LF	LC	CF	RC	RF
1962	Dodger Stadium	330	385	400	385	330
1964	Shea Stadium	338	371	410	371	338
1965	Anaheim Stadium	333	370	404	370	333
1965	Astrodome	330	378	400	378	330
1966	Arlington Stadium	330	380	400	380	330
1966	Atlanta–Fulton County Stadium	330	385	402	385	330
1966	Busch Memorial Stadium	330	383	414	383	330
1968	Oakland–Alameda County Stadium	330	372	400	372	330
1969	Jack Murphy Stadium	329	370	420	370	329
1970	Riverfront Stadium	330	375	404	375	330
1970	Veterans Stadium	330	371	408	371	330
1970	Three Rivers Stadium	335	375	400	375	335
1973	Royals Stadium	330	385	410	385	330
1977	Kingdome	324	362	410	352	314
1991	Comiskey Park	347	383	400	383	347

Thompson had a dream, much like the one Ray Kinsella has in the movie *Field of Dreams.* Thompson is the city manager of Blue Ash, the small town northeast of Cincinnati which had been a possible site for the Reds' new ballpark; while it lost out on the new one, it wound up getting the old one.

In 1985, Blue Ash was planning a baseball and soccer complex, and Thompson remembered hearing of a proposed softball field that would have recreated two major league parks. Thompson got the idea of reconstructing Crosley, and Blue Ash quickly put together a committee that raised $100,000.

Mark Rohr, an intern in Thompson's office, worked diligently to find out exactly what of Crosley remained. Inevitably, he looked up Luebbers and discovered that the only thing left was a ticket booth, which had been sold to the town by Luebbers's mother. Rohr pressed on and eventually located more than 600 of the original seats with the distinctive wishbone "C." According to *Sports Illustrated,* he found 350 underneath the Butler County Fairgrounds in Hamilton, Ohio, another 100 at a softball complex in northern Kentucky, and 100 more at a skating rink in Loveland, Colorado. Most important, Matty Schwab's grandson donated the original architect's drawings; Blue Ash raised another $350,000 and began rebuilding Crosley in earnest.

The Reds, who had nothing to do with Luebbers, got behind the Blue Ash project and created an Old Timers Game to dedicate it on July 11, 1988. Former Cincinnati pitcher Jim O'Toole was involved from the beginning. He says, "It was built as a reminder of the past. Any father from around here enjoys watching his kid play at this Crosley because he remembers his father taking him to the real Crosley as a kid."

THE HOUSE THAT STEINBRENNER REBUILT

In the rush to uniformity that characterized this period, the Dark Ages of Ballparks, the most fabled park of them all, Yankee Stadium, was reduced to a caricature of itself in the name of urban renewal.

Mike Burke ran the Yankees for CBS, which had purchased the team in 1964. Early in 1971, Burke had talked to New York's Mayor John Lindsay about the possibility of the Yankees' fleeing the Bronx for New Jersey or some other location. Lindsay, anxious to avoid losing another valuable asset like the Dodgers, announced in March that, as part of a program to revitalize the Bronx, the city would condemn and purchase Yankee Stadium, renovate it at a cost of $24 million ($3 million for the land and $21 million for the building), and lease it back to the Yankees. (Unimpressed with talk of a new stadium, the football Giants announced they would move to the Meadowlands of New Jersey.)

Yankee Stadium had been built in 284 days in 1923 for $2.5 million; it remained unchanged except for the extension of the triple-decked stands into left field in 1928 and into right field in 1937. Lights were installed in 1946, the scoreboard modernized in 1959, and the stadium cleaned and painted in 1967.

The park was showing its age, and so was the neighborhood around it. When the stadium was built, middle- and upper-middle-class families had moved into smart, new Art Deco apartments along the Grand Concourse, the Bronx's main thoroughfare; now, they were moving to Westchester in increasing numbers. The team was also changing for the worse. After an unprecedented period of dominance, the Yankees won a pennant in 1964, tumbled to sixth the next year, and ended up last in 1966, the first time a Yankee team had hit rock bottom since 1912.

In March 1972, New York's Board of Estimate agreed to buy and improve Yankee Stadium at any cost. By August the city had signed a thirty-year lease with Burke; renovation was to start immediately after the 1973 season, and the Yanks would play at Shea Stadium for two years, alternating home stands with the Mets.

Cleveland shipbuilder George Steinbrenner, who had earlier made an unsuccessful bid to buy the Indians, put together a syndicate in January 1973 to buy the Yanks from CBS. Demolition plans were made, and the dismantling of Yankee Stadium began. On April 6, 1973, Mayor Lindsay announced that a park built for $2.5 million was going to cost nearly $30 million just to tear down.

Although the renovation wouldn't begin until the end of the season, the three red granite monuments in deep center field that had symbolized the stadium were removed on September 13, 1973, because club officials feared that vandals might damage them while the Yankees were on their last road trip. The first had been dedicated to former manager Miller Huggins on Memorial Day 1932, shortly after his death; tablets were added posthumously for Lou Gehrig in 1941 and Babe Ruth in 1949.

By November, the departing Lindsay administration announced that the cost had ballooned

As ballpark design changed, scoreboards, formerly functional elements, were spiffed up to appeal to advertisers and engage casual fans with quizzes, highlight films, and the like. Through the 1983 season, Arlington Stadium, home of the Texas Rangers, had a scoreboard shaped like Texas with the lineup of the team at bat as well as the balls, strikes, and outs. An even more spectacular example is the Big A that gave Anaheim Stadium its name (below). When it opened on April 19, 1966, the park featured a 23-story, $1 million A topped by a halo. After it was enclosed in 1979, the Big A was moved to the parking lot, where it advertises upcoming events.

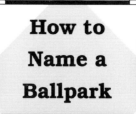

How to Name a Ballpark

All the new stadiums built from the mid-'60s to the mid-'80s needed names but couldn't fall back on cities' or people's names, as noted earlier. One suggestion or another would be debated for months with no resolution; when the Reds moved into their new stadium in 1970, it remained unnamed for five weeks.

Many Ohioans wanted to honor a hero from nearby Wapakoneta — astronaut Neil Armstrong, who had become the first man to walk on the moon the previous summer. Senator Robert Taft, Governor James Rhodes, Powel Crosley (again), and manager Fred Hutchinson, who lost his life to chest cancer a month after the 1964 season ended, also had their supporters. Other possibilities included Red Bengal (after the resident pro teams), Buckeye Bowl, and Queen City Stadium; Riverfront finally won out.

Earlier, when San Francisco agreed to finance a park for the Giants, the City Recreation and Parks Commission held a "Name That Park" contest and received 20,000 entries. The fans submitted 2,000 separate names, including Golden Gate Stadium, Seven Hills Stadium, Argonaut Field, and Zephyrs' Cove. One woman suggested Naismith Stadium. Asked why, she harrumphed, "Why, he's the father of baseball, of course!" (James Naismith did invent a game with a round ball, but it was basketball.)

Perhaps inevitably, naming stadiums became embroiled in politics, and the naming of Philadelphia's new park was intertwined with resistance to the Vietnam War. After the Athletics moved to Kansas City, the

city of Philadelphia began discussing a new stadium with the Phillies and Eagles. The voters approved a $13 million bond issue in May 1967 and construction began in October; the only problem was what to call it.

In November 1968, when the war had become a flashpoint with hawks and doves, the American Legion wrote to Mayor James Tate suggesting the name Philadelphia Memorial Stadium. Four months later, two bills were introduced in the City Council; one suggested War Veterans Memorial Stadium, the choice of council president Paul D'Oronta, the other General Dwight D. Eisenhower Stadium, favored by the Republican minority.

The bills were sent to the Recreation Committee, which was headed by John B. Kelly, Jr. Kelly favored the name Philadium at a time when public opinion was turning against the war; D'Oronta stuck to his guns and, though Kelly suggested holding a referendum on the issue, insisted that it was the council's job to name the facility.

The *Philadelphia Bulletin* muddied the already murky waters with a readers' poll, which drew 1,650 entries comprising 550 different names. Traditional suggestions like Independence Stadium, Philadelphia Stadium, and William Penn Stadium mixed with frivolous choices like Boo-Bird Park, the Gridmound (!), Losers' Paradise, the Playpen, and the Topless Terrace (because the park wouldn't be under a dome).

When a hearing was finally held to consider D'Oronta's bill, Kelly

argued that it was not the people's choice. Townsend Munson, the president of the Western Savings Bank, decried the name, now Philadelphia Veterans Stadium, as "part of the old dull Philadelphia syndrome." Nevertheless, on March 10, 1970, the name was sent to the council for a vote.

As the Philadium–Veterans Stadium struggle intensified, there was a final arresting suggestion. City Controller Thomas J. Gola suggested that the park be named for a specific person to defray the $45 million cost. Citing Wrigley Field and Busch Stadium, Gola estimated that the city could realize $10 million to $30 million over thirty years and endorsed the notion of selling the name to the highest bidder. (As noted, this is how Cleveland will name its stadium.)

According to a Monsanto ad in the *Sporting News,* the Phillies were taking no chances. Around the organization, "it's just called THE NEW STADIUM. That avoids controversy with most of the town's sports buffs who wanted to call it the Philadium." The final City Council vote was held on March 13, 1970. With an estimated 500 people in attendance (many of them wearing veteran's hats), the vote was 11–5 for Veterans Stadium. When it was dedicated, Red Smith made fun of the furor by suggesting that the park had been named "out of respect for [39-year-old] Jim Bunning," who pitched and won the first game; one fan had the last word, displaying a bedsheet reading CALL IT PHILADIUM.

to $49.9 million. When bids for reconstruction were let in December, the price had risen by another $5 million, according to *New York Affairs.* The costs of improving access to the Major Deegan Expressway and building new parking garages made the price skyrocket even more, and neighborhood revitalization, the original motive for the project, was being softpedaled.

When reconstruction began, major structural changes were made to eliminate posts and other visual obstructions. The columns supporting the upper deck and roof were removed, and a new can-

tilevered structure carried a new upper deck and roof. The playing field was lowered 5 feet to improve the sight lines from the lower deck, which was pushed forward to compensate for the change in field level. Installing plastic seats, up to 22 inches wide in the field boxes (versus the old 18- and 19-inch wooden ones), reduced capacity by some 11,000 seats to 54,000.

Other changes altered the park beyond recognition. The scalloped copper frieze, the stadium's signature, was removed from the top of the upper deck and replicated in plastic at the top of the

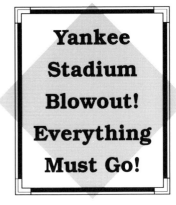

Yankee Stadium Blowout! Everything Must Go!

If there had been any doubts that the original Yankee Stadium was hallowed ground, they were removed when the firm hired to dismantle it, Cleveland's Cuyahoga Wrecking Company, began selling off mementos of the park. The fire sale attracted lots of attention, and 60,000 of the faithful made pilgrimages in search of relics in the first five weeks.

In addition to the fans, some of the men who had helped fill "the House That Ruth Built" wanted souvenirs. Stan Musial bought bleacher seats for his restaurant in St. Louis, and Whitey Ford and Yogi Berra bought box seats; Billy Martin got two stairs and a banister from the dugout; Jim Bouton, who had ruffled Yankee tradition with his tell-all book, *Ball Four,* had enough "pinstripe pride" to spend $500 for box seats, a clubhouse stool, and an enlarged Nat Fein photo of Babe Ruth on Babe Ruth Day at the stadium. Some Yanks were too upset to buy anything. Phil Rizzuto said, "I was sick when they dug the first hunk of dirt out of the infield. . . . I have spent half my life in this stadium."

Many items were donated. The Smithsonian Institution got the Yankee bat rack and bullpen steps, the Museum of the City of New York received a box seat, and John Lindsay donated his to Gracie Mansion, the mayor's official residence. Home plate was given to Babe Ruth's widow; Mrs. Lou Gehrig was given first base and later donated it to the Baseball Hall of Fame, which also got Ruth's locker, the red ticket booths, and a section of an ancient wooden staircase. Joe DiMaggio's #5 uniform was auctioned off for charity, while a cache of 20,000 unanswered letters to Mickey Mantle went unclaimed.

Cuyahoga's pricing policy resulted in some giveaways. The person who bought a sheet of unused World Series tickets from the Yankees' near miss in 1972 paid $3 for an item worth perhaps $1,000 today. Other items were wildly overpriced; only the most wild-eyed partisan would shell out $50 for Joe Pepitone's old duffel bag. Some other auction prices were:

Gate A sign	$300
Huge picture of a young Joe DiMaggio	$200
Blowup of Don Larsen making the last pitch in his perfect game	$150
Turnstiles	$100
Locker room scale	$75
Box seats	$20
Groundskeeper's uniform	$10
Hot dog vendors' trays	$5
The IN sign from a men's lavatory	$3
Brick	$1
Sign, SCOUT ADMISSION 50 CENTS	$.50

The Osaka baseball team in Japan paid $10,000 for the foul poles and $30,000 for the lights. An employee of Japan's Daimaru department store spent $4,000 on memorabilia he intended to resell in Japan, even the box of diapers left behind by one of the players' wives. (It turned out that the Japanese were crazy about the Yankees because of Babe Ruth's visit in 1931.)

On May 12, 1974, the *Daily News* ran an ad: "Get Your Yankee Stadium Seat — only $7.50 plus tax and 5 empty Winston crush-proof boxes while the supply lasts." Reserved seats weighing 45 pounds and 40-pound bleacher benches were made available at twenty-three E. J. Korvette's stores. In all, the proceeds from the memorabilia sale exceeded $300,000, an eighth of what it cost to build the stadium originally.

---

mammoth new scoreboard that ran from center field to the right field grandstand. Before the renovation, fans could pay a subway fare on the Lexington–Jerome Avenue No. 4 line and see part of the field; placing the plastic frieze at the top of the scoreboard, like Shibe Park's spite fence, shut off the view, killing the last "renegade bleachers" in New York.

The exterior fared no better. Architect Kyle Johnson wrote:

> The monumental entrance facades were obliterated by new escalator towers, and a thick coat of gray paint covered the frieze of decorative tiles [just above the first level]. Only the expensive arched openings with their louvers recalled the famous facade of "the house that Ruth built."

In place of past grandeur there were new concession areas, a private club, a public cafeteria, and a section of new V.I.P. boxes on the mezzanine level (for which the Yankees paid). By October 1975, costs had escalated to $66.4 million, and the $2 million earmarked for improving the area around the stadium was now sunk into the building itself. Some of the money was spent on a security system, structural supports for the scoreboard, and toilets for the V.I.P. boxes.

When the park reopened on April 15, 1976, Robert Lipsyte noted in *Sports Illustrated* that "the Stadium, which was renovated to enhance the chemistry of the city, will best serve motorists from the suburbs. Suburban drivers will be able to sweep down an expressway ramp . . . into a recently completed multilevel garage. After parking their cars, they can cross a multicolored plaza and

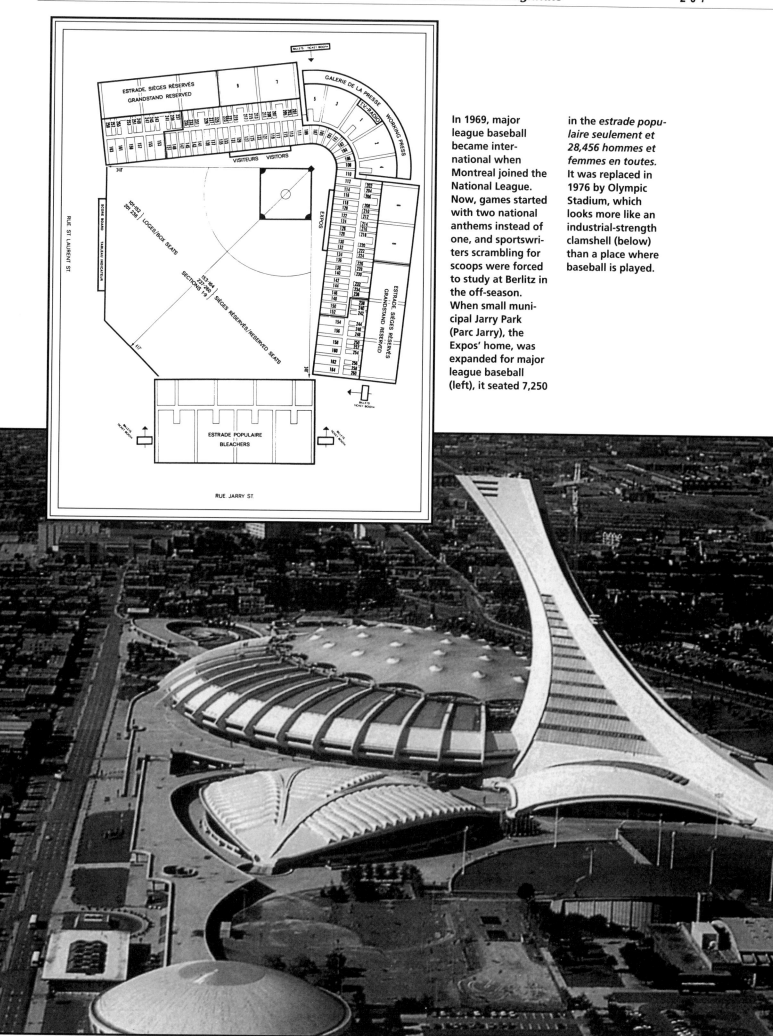

In 1969, major league baseball became international when Montreal joined the National League. Now, games started with two national anthems instead of one, and sportswriters scrambling for scoops were forced to study at Berlitz in the off-season. When small municipal Jarry Park (Parc Jarry), the Expos' home, was expanded for major league baseball (left), it seated 7,250 in the *estrade populaire seulement et 28,456 hommes et femmes en toutes.* It was replaced in 1976 by Olympic Stadium, which looks more like an industrial-strength clamshell (below) than a place where baseball is played.

enter the park. New escalators and elevators will whisk them to their seats."

Suburbanites could marvel at a 138-foot stainless steel and fiberglass smokestack shaped like a Louisville Slugger, which provided an exhaust for the boiler, heater, and air conditioner, but they couldn't see the monuments of Death Valley; those had been moved just beyond center field into "Monument Park," a small narrow enclosure with the sense of place experienced in an alleyway. The scope and drama one felt seeing the monuments on the field had been surgically removed from the House That Steinbrenner Rebuilt.

On March 19, 1978, a *New York Times* story

pegged the cost of rebuilding Yankee Stadium at $95.6 million, of which $48.8 million was used to build the stadium; however, with debt service, the figure was due to climb substantially in the future. Lindsay, no longer mayor, defended his decision in the *Times:* "If the Yankees had left it would have been a disaster for the city and particularly for the Bronx. If inflation and delays boosted the costs of rebuilding the stadium that's regrettable. I think it was the right thing to do. Brooklyn never recovered when the Dodgers left the city."

In 1986, *New York Post* columnist Jerry Izenberg pegged the cost of the stadium at $120 million, five times the original estimate. The neighborhood that

Old ballparks began to look out of place in updated surroundings as cityscapes changed. Some were spared this indignity because of the way they were built in the first place, like Comiskey Park. Surrounded by nothing but cars (left), the park survived until 1991. But Forbes Field, which had been somewhat isolated in 1909 (below), looked anachronistic in 1969 beside the three cylindrical glass and steel towers of the University of Pittsburgh (right).

The first steel and concrete park, Shibe Park, held on through the 1960s. In this aerial view (below), it's easy to see the spite fence at the bottom. The Phillies moved to Veterans Stadium in 1970; Shibe Park was badly damaged by fire in 1971 (right) and was totally demolished in 1976.

The majestic House That Ruth Built in 1923 was replaced in 1976 by the House That Steinbrenner Rebuilt at the public's expense. The original estimate had been $23 million; the final cost was more than $160 million, but what was lost was more than money. The distinctive copper frieze was gone, remembered in plastic out in center field, and the monuments were moved to Monument Park. In Joni Mitchell's phrase, Steinbrenner had paved Paradise and put up a parking lot.

was supposed to have benefited was worse than ever. Fans routinely sang cynical new words to a charming old tune:

Buy me some peanuts and Cracker Jack,
I don't care if I ever buy crack.

The neighborhood was worse, costs kept mounting, eventually topping $160 million, Yankee tradition evaporated bit by bit, and the park had been trivialized beyond repair. Mike Lupica said in the *Daily News,*

It is such a sad baseball thing to see Yankee Stadium getting smaller somehow with each new season, the whole idea of the Stadium and the Yankees getting smaller. There was a time

you could stand at home plate and look out at the monuments and they would be so far out there it seemed like the next stop on the No. 4 train . . . it hasn't been that way for a long time . . . it's as if they keep moving the fences in.

A month later, George Vecsey of the *Times* wrote in language strikingly similar:

The new breed of players feel like tourists visiting a temple in Egypt or an amphitheater in the old Roman empire or a giant Chan Dynasty statue in Vietnam, only able to wonder what it was like when the warriors and the high priests and the performers and the people were in their glory years.

TIMELINE

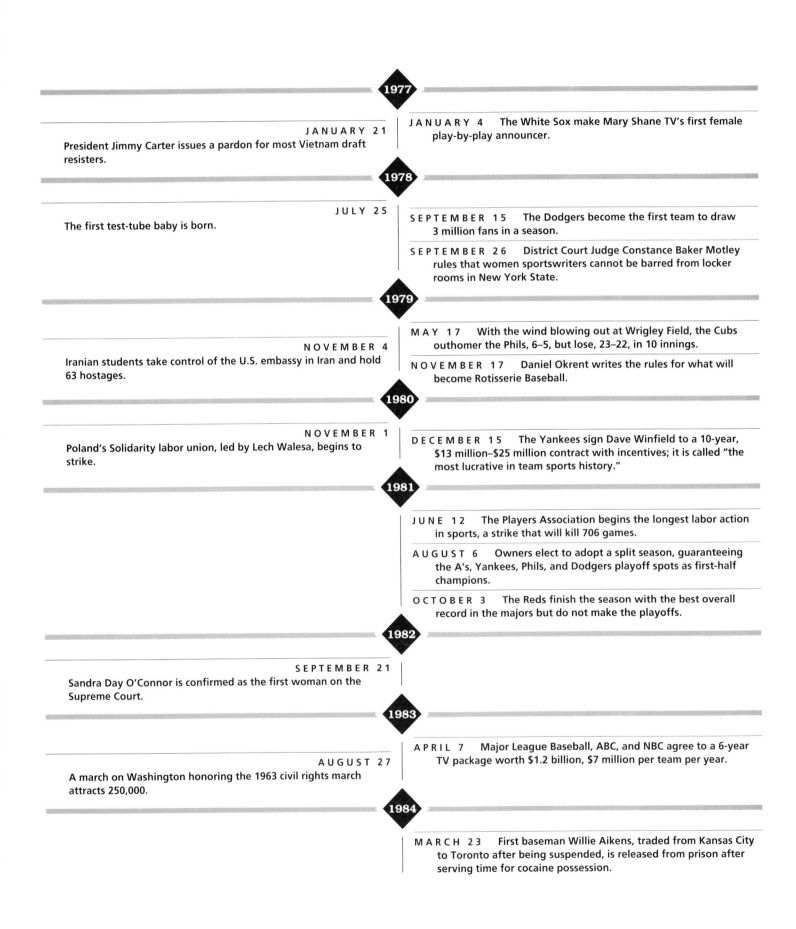

1977

JANUARY 4   The White Sox make Mary Shane TV's first female play-by-play announcer.

JANUARY 21
President Jimmy Carter issues a pardon for most Vietnam draft resisters.

1978

JULY 25
The first test-tube baby is born.

SEPTEMBER 15   The Dodgers become the first team to draw 3 million fans in a season.

SEPTEMBER 26   District Court Judge Constance Baker Motley rules that women sportswriters cannot be barred from locker rooms in New York State.

1979

NOVEMBER 4
Iranian students take control of the U.S. embassy in Iran and hold 63 hostages.

MAY 17   With the wind blowing out at Wrigley Field, the Cubs outhomer the Phils, 6–5, but lose, 23–22, in 10 innings.

NOVEMBER 17   Daniel Okrent writes the rules for what will become Rotisserie Baseball.

1980

NOVEMBER 1
Poland's Solidarity labor union, led by Lech Walesa, begins to strike.

DECEMBER 15   The Yankees sign Dave Winfield to a 10-year, $13 million–$25 million contract with incentives; it is called "the most lucrative in team sports history."

1981

JUNE 12   The Players Association begins the longest labor action in sports, a strike that will kill 706 games.

AUGUST 6   Owners elect to adopt a split season, guaranteeing the A's, Yankees, Phils, and Dodgers playoff spots as first-half champions.

OCTOBER 3   The Reds finish the season with the best overall record in the majors but do not make the playoffs.

1982

SEPTEMBER 21
Sandra Day O'Connor is confirmed as the first woman on the Supreme Court.

1983

AUGUST 27
A march on Washington honoring the 1963 civil rights march attracts 250,000.

APRIL 7   Major League Baseball, ABC, and NBC agree to a 6-year TV package worth $1.2 billion, $7 million per team per year.

1984

MARCH 23   First baseman Willie Aikens, traded from Kansas City to Toronto after being suspended, is released from prison after serving time for cocaine possession.

TIMELINE

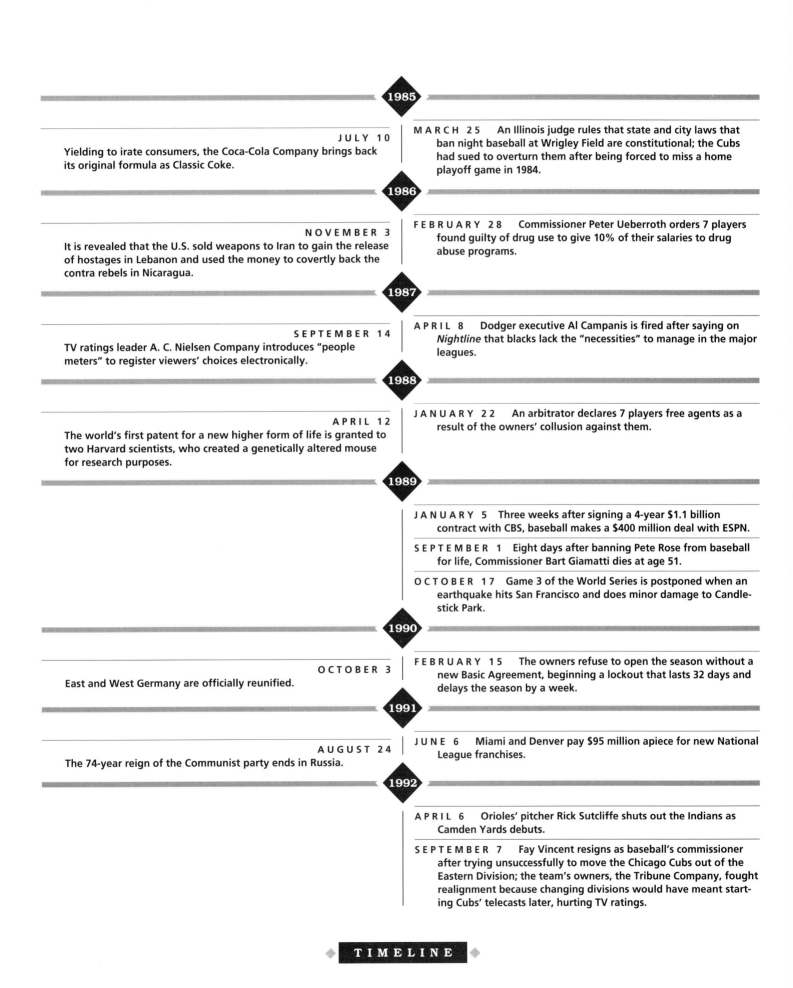

1985

JULY 10
Yielding to irate consumers, the Coca-Cola Company brings back its original formula as Classic Coke.

MARCH 25   An Illinois judge rules that state and city laws that ban night baseball at Wrigley Field are constitutional; the Cubs had sued to overturn them after being forced to miss a home playoff game in 1984.

1986

NOVEMBER 3
It is revealed that the U.S. sold weapons to Iran to gain the release of hostages in Lebanon and used the money to covertly back the contra rebels in Nicaragua.

FEBRUARY 28   Commissioner Peter Ueberroth orders 7 players found guilty of drug use to give 10% of their salaries to drug abuse programs.

1987

SEPTEMBER 14
TV ratings leader A. C. Nielsen Company introduces "people meters" to register viewers' choices electronically.

APRIL 8   Dodger executive Al Campanis is fired after saying on *Nightline* that blacks lack the "necessities" to manage in the major leagues.

1988

APRIL 12
The world's first patent for a new higher form of life is granted to two Harvard scientists, who created a genetically altered mouse for research purposes.

JANUARY 22   An arbitrator declares 7 players free agents as a result of the owners' collusion against them.

1989

JANUARY 5   Three weeks after signing a 4-year $1.1 billion contract with CBS, baseball makes a $400 million deal with ESPN.

SEPTEMBER 1   Eight days after banning Pete Rose from baseball for life, Commissioner Bart Giamatti dies at age 51.

OCTOBER 17   Game 3 of the World Series is postponed when an earthquake hits San Francisco and does minor damage to Candlestick Park.

1990

OCTOBER 3
East and West Germany are officially reunified.

FEBRUARY 15   The owners refuse to open the season without a new Basic Agreement, beginning a lockout that lasts 32 days and delays the season by a week.

1991

AUGUST 24
The 74-year reign of the Communist party ends in Russia.

JUNE 6   Miami and Denver pay $95 million apiece for new National League franchises.

1992

APRIL 6   Orioles' pitcher Rick Sutcliffe shuts out the Indians as Camden Yards debuts.

SEPTEMBER 7   Fay Vincent resigns as baseball's commissioner after trying unsuccessfully to move the Chicago Cubs out of the Eastern Division; the team's owners, the Tribune Company, fought realignment because changing divisions would have meant starting Cubs' telecasts later, hurting TV ratings.

The scoreboard is the focal point of Camden Yards, and even the corny HIT IT HERE sign doesn't ruin the visual blend of scoreboard and warehouse. Notice that the lights in right field are mounted on the warehouse roof, a subtle way of bringing it into the ballpark.

C H A P T E R   T E N

The End of the Dark Ages

Between 1977 and 1989, baseball added five new parks, four of which were domes. In *Once There Was a Ballpark*, Joe Soucheray observes, "Every single game in a domed stadium is by necessity identical to every preceding game played there. No rain. No wind. No sun. No moon. No shadows. No snow. No mud. No ice. No sleet. No hail. No clouds."

Domes reflected a need to shut out the unpleasant realities of the 1980s: the slow, painful death of the inner cities; the wildfire spread of drugs; the loss of America's industrial superiority to Japan; the steady decline of American education; covert presidential misconduct in the Iran-contra affair; and the cynicism bred by junk bond and insider trading scandals.

These industrial-style buildings shut out the real world and made it possible for baseball to expand to the frozen north. From 1953 to 1976, baseball had expanded west — to Milwaukee, Los Angeles, San Francisco, Houston, and Oakland. All five parks that were built from 1977 to 1989 lay in the northern latitudes — Toronto (the Blue Jays played

in Exhibition Stadium and later moved to the Sky-Dome), the Metrodome in Minneapolis, Olympic Stadium in Montreal, and the Kingdome.

None of these buildings will ever be known for their baseball content or ever give fans the chance to share the baseball experiences of their fathers and grandfathers. The Kingdome, in particular, has attracted negative comment from baseball people. Sparky Anderson, who has managed in the big leagues since 1970, says, "I walk in there and I'm not sure what I'm in. It's just a big ball of cement. There's no color, no nothing. It seems like a big factory."

Speakers are hung from the roof in the King-dome and in others, but they are neither unobtrusive nor neutral; they become part of the game, a game that might be properly called arena baseball. No longer does a hitter necessarily get what he earned, because tremendous drives can be deflected by the speakers and become infield hits. On June 5, 1979, Mariner Willie Horton hit a blast that was heading for the upper deck, his 300th homer; it hit a loudspeaker, giving him a single.

Thirty-five years after it ceased to be a major league park, Ebbets Field retains its power as the symbolic ballpark of memory, the ultimate urban field of dreams. Compare how it looked just after opening in 1913 (left) with the design for a proposed ballpark for the Milwaukee Brewers (below).

Ballparks reeked of humanity until domes came along. From the outside, the Metrodome in Minneapolis looks like a circus tent on steroids.

Sportswriter Dave Anderson commented, "When baseball is played indoors, it really isn't baseball. Under a roof, the game emerges as domeball, a completely different sport."

LOUD FOUL: THE METRODOME

There are speakers in the Metrodome, too, but what's coming out of them can rarely be heard above the fans, who make a din that, in Roger Angell's phrase, sounds like being "in an I.R.T. express car with the Purdue Marching Band during a rush-hour rehearsal of 'The Stars and Stripes Forever.' "

The Metrodome wasn't known for sound when it opened in 1982 because the Twins had given their fans little reason to cheer in recent years. Looking like a half-baked biscuit about to rise, the Metrodome was dedicated on April 6, 1982, by Mrs. Muriel Humphrey Brown, the widow of the vice president for whom it was named. It was expected to be a hitter's park, and lovers of offense exulted the first night, when 5 home runs were hit. Pitcher Matt Keogh said later, "The Metrodome is a travesty for baseball. They turn on the blowers that hold up the roof when the game starts and the ball jumps right out of there."

What was unexpected was the abrupt bounce the balls took off the artificial surface, called Sport-

Turf. Ground balls and sinking liners kangarooed over fielders' heads, making arabesques that Nureyev would have envied. Sparky Anderson said, "I don't like the park because it's not meant for baseball. Balls bounce around like you're playing pool. Line drives become guided missiles."

The roof of the dome was painted and, like the Astrodome before it, caused problems. Some outfielders wore sunglasses to fight the glare, and in 1985, Billy Martin said, "If you win here or if you lose, it's on a Little League field. Major leaguers come in here and they look like Little Leaguers running after a fly ball because they can't see it."

For all its faults, the Metrodome might have been just another dome had it not been for the 1987 World Series. Although domes had existed since 1965, feelings against them seemed to coalesce with the Metrodome, which had been built for a franchise that had prospered for twenty years with an undomed park, Metropolitan Stadium (see Chapter 8).

In 1987 the Twins played .691 baseball at home (56–25) and .358 baseball on the road (29–52), almost exactly the reverse. According to *The 1987 Elias Baseball Analyst*, "Home teams won 54 percent of all major league baseball games over the past five years." (Similar figures for other team sports are: the NFL, 58 percent; the NHL, 60 percent; the NBA, 64 percent.) Of all the teams tracked in all four sports, the Twins played 15.8 percent

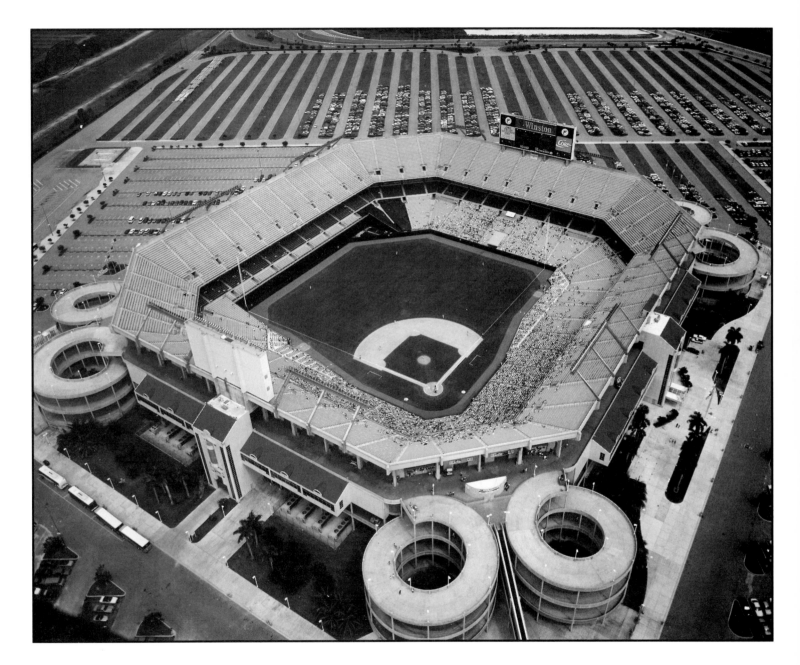

better at home than on the road and, in 1987, 35 percent better.

As it turned out, the Dome had a lot to do with the Twins' edge. In 1987 a Bowling Green researcher concluded, after examining team performance over eighteen years, that, although the Mariners did not benefit, teams based in domed stadiums have a higher winning percentage — by 10.5 percent — at home than on the road. In contrast, teams that play in open facilities do 7.2 percent better than on the road. Keller said the difference boils down to the home field advantage enhanced by the amplified sound of cheering fans under the dome.

Just how loud did the Metrodome's fans cheer during the 1987 World Series? In the April 1988 *Chemical & Engineering News*, Bill Clark, an expert on noise in the workplace, noted that the noise level was 77 to 90 decibels when the Cardinals were ahead but jumped to 95 to 109 decibels when the Twins took the lead. (The federal Occupational Safety and Health Administration sets a 90-decibel limit for unprotected factory noise over an eight-hour shift.)

According to the *Sporting News*, when Dan Gladden hit a grand slam in Game 1, a sound meter read 118 decibels, the noise made by a jet taking off. A letter in the *Journal of the American Medical*

Football teams were once fall tenants in baseball stadiums. In 1993, six-year-old Joe Robbie Stadium, home of the NFL Miami Dolphins, was retrofitted at a cost of $6 million to accommodate the National League Florida Marlins.

Association in January 1988 reported that the noise level in Game 2 ranged from 80 to 125 decibels, the equivalent of a jackhammer ripping up concrete. For the first time in history, a baseball venue had become an offensive weapon. No wonder sportswriters dubbed it the Thunderdome.

NIGHT MOVES: THE ILLUMINATION OF WRIGLEY FIELD

Less than a year after there was thunderous sound at the Metrodome there was sparkling light at Wrigley Field, a mere fifty-three years after the first major league park became outfitted for night games. The story behind the change after so much resistance says much about the devolution of baseball and the ascension of television.

Phil Wrigley and his wife, Helen, died within two months of each other in 1977, leaving their son Bill in charge of the Cubs. The estate, a large one, wasn't settled until December 1980; Bill Wrigley learned then that he owed some $40 million in estate and inheritance taxes to the federal government, California, Illinois, and Wisconsin.

This situation became public knowledge, and the Tribune Company, deciding to go after the Cubs, chose a particularly propitious time to approach Wrigley. There was great uncertainty that the players and owners would reach a new contract in 1981, and the players had raised the possibility of a midseason strike. Wrigley was receptive, and talks began to heat up. On June 12 the players voted to strike; on June 17 the Tribune Company bought the Cubs for $20.5 million.

The Tribune Company wasn't buying the club for ticket revenue, concessions, or licensing but as TV programming. John Madigan, then executive vice president, was asked the company's motivation in *Vineline*, the Cubs' newsletter. He said, "It was the opportunity to control live programming which is the most important thing to a television and radio station [WGN-TV and WGN] — live programming, good programming." In other words, the Tribune Company bought the Cubs in order to install lights at Wrigley Field and then sell the rights to prime time programming — night baseball.

The Tribune executives began talking about lights as soon as the 1981 season was over, but a fan group, Citizens United for Baseball in the Sunshine (C.U.B.S.), successfully fought the change for a while. On May 13, 1982, the Illinois House of Representatives passed a bill that would make baseball after midnight a violation of state noise pollution laws in any facility where night sports had not been played before July 1, 1982.

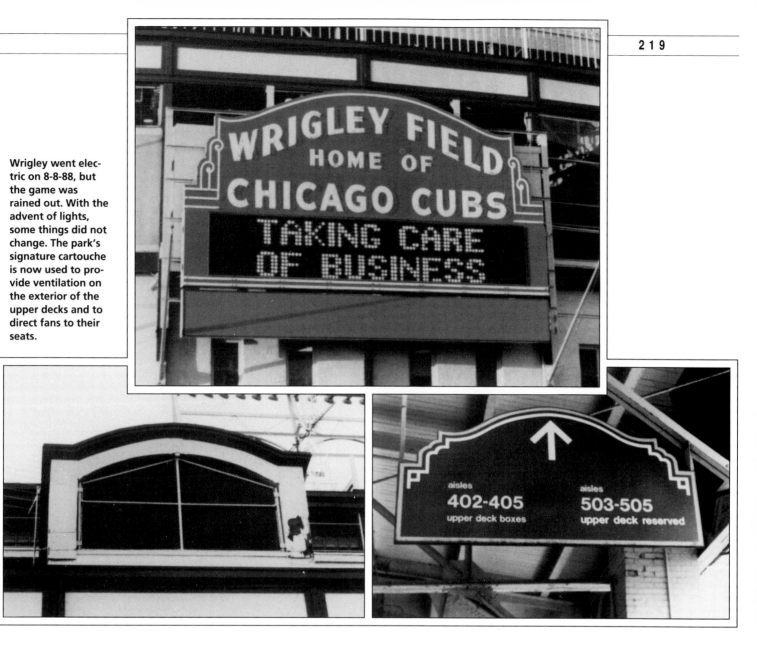

Wrigley went electric on 8-8-88, but the game was rained out. With the advent of lights, some things did not change. The park's signature cartouche is now used to provide ventilation on the exterior of the upper decks and to direct fans to their seats.

When the Cubs made the playoffs in 1984, Commissioner Peter Ueberroth, the shortsighted creator of the all–night game World Series, threatened to move future postseason games to St. Louis unless lights were installed at Wrigley. Using his comments as a wedge, the Cubs filed a suit in June 1985 seeking to repeal the antilights legislation. The team lost its suit. In his opinion, Judge Richard Curry of the circuit court wrote, "Tinkering with the quality-of-life aspirations of countless households so that television royalties might more easily flow into the coffers of twenty-five distant sports moguls is . . . repugnant to common decency."

That wasn't the end of the battle, however. On February 23, 1988, Chicago's aldermen voted to allow the Cubs to install lights, and two days later, the baseball owners voted to hold the 1990 All-Star Game at Wrigley if the park got lights; that same day, the Chicago City Council voted, 29–19, to repeal the antinoise legislation. The new ordinance allowed the Cubs to have 8 night games in 1988 and then 18 a year until 2002.

Of course, the sportswriters had a field day. The *Tribune*'s Bob Verdi commented, "In search of the one man to put them over the hump, the Cubs at long last have added Thomas Edison to their roster." Columnist Roger Simon sniffed, "Putting lights in Wrigley Field is like putting aluminum siding on the Sistine Chapel."

Wrigley's nocturnal premiere was set for August 8 (8-8-88). Before a celebrity audience that included such luminaries as Dabney Coleman, Geraldo Rivera, and Morganna the Kissing Bandit, the Cubs and Phils played night baseball at Wrigley for three and a half innings before rain ended the proceedings. The next night the Cubs beat the Mets, 6–4, in the first real night game at Wrigley. The Dark Ages had officially ended.

Lighting Wrigley wasn't the only change the Tribune Company made. The firm began selling bleacher seats in advance, rather than just on the day of the game, as the Wrigleys had done. Scalpers bought blocs of bleacher seats and resold them at a profit. Thus the long-standing practice of buying bleacher seats spontaneously was made nearly impossible, and the famous Bleacher Bums had to scramble for tickets in advance. (In 1992, the Tribune Company announced that it was selling season tickets to the bleachers for $614.)

Bill Veeck, Jr., boycotted Wrigley when this new policy went into effect, but he never lost his love for the field whose walls he'd personally covered with ivy. He once said of the park, "It's a living thing adapting to its environment. The site was selected because it was the best location for fans to walk or ride the streetcar lines converging on Clark and Addison. When everybody got a car, it no longer was the ideal spot. But Wrigley Field survived because people discovered how lovely it was to come and sit there in the sun and enjoy a game."

BASEBALL ON THE HALFSHELL: THE SKYDOME

It is possible to sit in the sun and enjoy a game at the SkyDome. It is also possible to

♦ dance in the Northern Lights Ballroom.

♦ see a game from the privacy of one's hotel suite.

♦ jog on the world's largest indoor track (2.2 laps per mile).

♦ amble on a Walk of Fame that honors Madonna, Hulk Hogan, and Dave Steib.

♦ view artifacts recovered during the excavation, perhaps a cannon from the War of 1812.

♦ ponder *Salmon Run*, a sculpture of a fountain with "60 oversized salmon swimming upstream."

You would think such a place is not for baseball purists, but you'd be wrong. Former first baseman Bill Buckner said, "That's the perfect park. If I was going to build one, that's the way I'd do it." During the 1992 World Series, Braves manager Bobby Cox exclaimed, "This is a real ball park." And Cub Hall of Famer Ernie Banks paid it perhaps the ultimate compliment: "What a beautiful place. It's almost as beautiful as Wrigley Field."

That an AstroTurf field in a shopping mall covered by a retractable dome can get such respect is a tribute to the talents of architect Roderick Robbie and structural engineer Michael Allen. Robbie, who had never designed a ballpark, saw the proposed field as the centerpiece of "a miniature city" and mortgaged his Toronto home to pay for what became the winning design. He and Allen spent $700,000 of their own money in research and development. They visited numerous ballparks and used as inspirations both Tiger Stadium and Royals Stadium as well as "the opera house in Milan."

Aside from looks, the project would succeed or fail on the concept of a retractable roof. The trick was to make the parts fit together snugly without casting a shadow on the playing field. The two men had sketched removable roofs for a year before Allen scribbled a telescoping roof on a napkin. He divided it into four panels, one of which is permanently fixed over the stadium's north end.

The SkyDome represents the ultimate expression of non-baseballness in ball-park architecture. Yes, a field is visible when the retractable roof is open, but the complex as a whole seems more like a carnival grounds than a platform for athletic competition. Though the roof opens, it is normally closed to the elements. When the stadium was invaded by gnats in 1990, the roof was quickly locked to shut out Mother Nature.

The other three are stacked over it when the roof is open.

Panel one rotates around 180 degrees while the other two telescope straight forward. All three are mounted on a system of steel tracks and 54 drive mechanisms called bogies. The main bogies contain a number of 10-horsepower motors, and the roof, which weighs 11,000 tons, takes 20 minutes to open or close. The flexibility of this roof ends one of the main objections to domes — playing indoors when the sun is shining. There are also no speakers dangling over the field to deflect potential home runs, and the roof is 310 feet high (versus the Metrodome's 156), so noise is not a problem.

The idea that the new stadium should have a retractable roof was suggested by Blue Jays broadcaster and former major leaguer Buck Martinez and financed by Trevor Eyton, the president of

The old B&O warehouse harmonizes nicely with Camden Yards, and spaces in the gates allow fans to see the park every day of the year.

Brascan, a $5 billion holding company with interests in natural resources and financial services. Pressure for a domed stadium mounted as Exhibition Stadium, the Blue Jays' first home, proved more and more inadequate.

Eyton mentioned to Ontario's Premier William Davis that he could raise $5 million each from ten partners to finance the project. He ultimately persuaded thirty corporations to invest $4.3 million each, a total of $129 million; they got the use of a luxury box for ninety-nine years and also received four free parking spaces in the stadium's 575-space underground lot. The city of Toronto contributed $30 million; Ontario Province authorized $30 million and also guaranteed $150 million in bank loans. Ten-year leases on 5,800 Skyclub seats generated another $20 million, and income from 10-year leases on 161 private luxury boxes that cost between $100,000 and $225,000 a year have produced another $40 million.

Although the Blue Jays set major league attendance records (on the basis of tickets sold, not turnstile count) in 1990, 1991, and 1992, exceeding 4 million in each of the last two years, the Sky-Dome *lost* $18 million in 1991, was in debt $275 million, and, according to *Business Week*, could be in debt up to $475 million by the end of the twentieth century.

Despite the cost overruns, the SkyDome opened more or less on time on June 5, 1989. Properly impressed, Malcolm Gray, the editor of *MacLean's*, the Canadian news magazine, said, "We live in secular times, and structures like the SkyDome are the equivalent of the cathedrals that were raised during the Middle Ages." Others were less kind; an anonymous reporter called it "the world's first convertible with 60,000 bucket seats."

The SkyDome has other drawbacks. Like every dome, its field is AstroTurf. A media guide bubbles, "There are 106 rolls of AstroTurf fastened together by 8 miles of zippers — the equivalent of 50,000 pairs of blue jeans."

Speaking of artificial, the SkyDome has the majors' only hydraulic pitcher's mound. It's built on an 18-foot fiberglass dish that resides in a holding chamber. As the chamber fills with water, the mound rises to field level, where it is locked in place. The fans can't see relief pitchers warm up, nor can coaches and managers; the dugout and bullpen communicate by telephone and closed-circuit TV. And, speaking of seeing, there are so many nosebleed seats at the SkyDome that vendors do a thriving business by renting binoculars at $7 a pop.

There are also no bleacher seats at the Sky-Dome, and no park is more expensive to visit. According to an Associated Press survey, a family of four would spend $82 to see a game at Riverfront Stadium, whereas a game here would cost $132.

SOMETHING OLDE, SOMETHING NEW: CAMDEN YARDS

The SkyDome is high-tech, while Camden Yards is the House That Nostalgia Built. The people who built the Orioles' park have seen the future, and it works, all right, but it looks remarkably like the past.

It's impossible to watch a game here without thinking of the jewel boxes that inspired it (see Chapter 6). David Dillon, the architecture critic for the *Dallas Morning News*, said, "From the brick arches to the low-raked grandstands and family picnic area in center field, it evokes Fenway, Wrigley, and Ebbets Field without looking like any of them." Eli Jacobs, the Orioles' owner, grew up in Brooklyn and said, "I wish we could have designed an Ebbets Field without pillars, but I think what we have is even better."

The Name Game

Ballparks ("the House That Ruth Built") and parts of parks ("the Jury Box") have been nicknamed since well before the turn of the century. Here are the best-known — some affectionate, some not:

Ashburn's Ridge. In the late 1940s, Richie Ashburn gave the Phillies a legitimate leadoff hitter with speed and a real bunting threat. To give his taps up third base the maximum chance of succeeding, the foul line at Shibe Park was built up.

Banshee Board, The. See *The Monster.*

Big A, The. The architectural feature that gave Anaheim Stadium its nickname is a 230-foot-high A topped by an equally huge halo. It was put up by Standard Oil of California at a cost of $1 million in exchange for advertising considerations. As high as a twenty-three-story building, it originally stood behind the fence in left and helped support the scoreboard. When the park was enlarged and enclosed in 1980, the giant letter was moved to the parking lot.

Big Owe, The. Built for the 1976 Olympics, Olympic Stadium went way over budget and eventually wound up costing $770 million.

Bloody Angle, The. In 1926, there was a groove between the right field boxes and the old wooden bleachers at Yankee Stadium. Sometimes balls got caught in there, and even the slowest of runners could advance an extra base or two.

Burkeville. The center field bleachers at the Polo Grounds were largely filled with Irish immigrants in the 1890s. See *Corktown.*

Camp Swampy. When the White Sox had a run of sinkerball pitchers in the 1970s, groundskeepers Roger, Gene, and Emil Bossard doused the area in front of home plate at Comiskey Park regularly; the area became saturated and was nicknamed Camp Swampy, or Bossard's Swamp.

Cardiac Hill. Before escalators were installed at Candlestick Park in 1971, walking up from the parking lot was almost as challenging as pitching at Candlestick.

Cave of Winds. When Stu Miller was blown off the mound in the 1961 All-Star Game, Candlestick Park became known as the Cave of Winds.

Chop Shop, The. In 1991, as the Braves approached their first pennant since moving to Atlanta–Fulton County Stadium in 1966, the crowd began using a chopping motion called "the tomahawk chop" as a rallying cry. (See also "the Launching Pad.")

Cigar Boxes, The. In the 1890s, seats were added to the center field bleachers at the Polo Grounds that were wider than they were high. From a distance, the new sections resembled nothing so much as a cigar box, hence the term.

Cobb's Lake. The area around home plate at Detroit's Bennett Park was soaked to keep Ty Cobb's bunts fair, a primitive method later refined by the more subtle tilting. (See *Ashburn's Ridge.*)

Conig's Corner. When Tony Conigliaro was the Red Sox center fielder, in the middle and late 1960s, seats in the triangular Section 34 were withheld from sale to provide a dark background for the hitters.

Corktown. Bennett Park was in Detroit's Sixth Ward, an Irish neighborhood. Similarly, there were predominantly Irish cheering sections at the Polo Grounds in New York and Sportsman's Park in St. Louis called Burkeville and Kerry Patch.

Crow's Nest, The. In 1938, when the Pirates seemed to be on their way to winning the National League pennant, a third deck of seats was built behind home plate to accommodate a surge of fans; however, Gabby Hartnett's "Homer in the Gloamin'" gave the Cubs the pennant instead and put the Crow's Nest on hold for twenty-two years; it was finally finished in time for the 1960 World Series.

Death Valley. From the moment Yankee Stadium was built, its center field was considered one of the places "triples go to die." Death on straightaway hitters, it was originally 490 feet in 1923, 461 in 1937, and 463 in 1967. When the park was rebuilt in time for the 1976 season, it was down to 417 and is 408 as this is written.

Duffy's Cliff. Duffy's Cliff, a 10-foot-high mound that stretched from Fenway Park's left field foul pole to the flagpole in center, was named for Hub left fielder George "Duffy" Lewis. Duffy's Cliff stayed in place until 1934, when it was replaced by another storied part of Fenway — the Green Monster.

Dump by the Hump, The. Philadelphia's Baker Bowl became rundown during the Depression and was never repaired due to penny wise, pound foolish management. Since its most distinctive feature was the "hump" in the outfield caused by the tracks of the Pennsylvania Railroad, it became known as "the Dump by the Hump."

Friendly Confines, The. Wrigley Field, or "Beautiful Wrigley Field," was named the Friendly Confines as part of owner Phil Wrigley's PR campaign to attract fans to the park when his club couldn't do so on its own. The campaign proved brilliant when the neighborhood nearby began to run down. Wrigley was also called Bobby Dorr's House, because groundskeeper Dorr (no relation to Hall of Famer Bobby Doerr) lived in a six-room apartment by the left field corner gate.

Gamblers Patch. The lower right field stands at Shibe Park were so named because gamblers used to congregate there. (Another clique of wagerers sat right above the NO GAMBLING sign in left field.)

Giles Garden. When Warren Giles ran the Cincinnati Reds, fans began to picnic in the area beyond right field in Crosley Field. The spot was also known as Giles Chicken Run and Giles Picnic Grounds.

Grand Old Lady of Lehigh Avenue, The. An affectionate name for Shibe Park, particularly after World War II, when the grand old lady's age began to show.

Green Monster, The. The left field wall at Fenway Park became the Green Monster in 1947 when it was painted green and the ads that had adorned it were removed. (See Chapter 8.)

Greenberg Gardens. In 1947, the Pirates brought in the left field fence at Forbes Field to improve Hank Greenberg's chances of driving balls over it. When Greenberg retired at the end of the year, the fence stayed where it was and was renamed

Kiner's Korner, for Ralph Kiner.

Hefty Bag, The. The 23-foot right field "fence" at the Metrodome consists of "folded up football seats covered with a plastic sheet." Looking like an enormous blue Baggie, it is known as the Hefty Bag or, alternatively, as the Trash Bag.

Home Run Alley. When Frank "Home Run" Baker began peppering drives over the right field wall at Shibe Park in Philadelphia, North Twentieth Street became known as Home Run Alley.

House That Clemente Built, The. A little-used sobriquet for Three Rivers Stadium.

House That Ruth Built, The. Reporter Fred Lieb named Yankee Stadium after Ruth when he homered to beat the Red Sox on the day it opened, April 18, 1923.

Jimmie Foxx Spite Fence, The. Named for a 20-foot-high screen placed on top of the left field fence at Detroit's Navin Field in 1933, it was designed to minimize the right-handed power of Jimmie Foxx.

Jonesville. The left field bleachers at Jarry Park in Montreal became known as Jonesville for outfielder Mack Jones, who drove in 5 runs on Opening Day (April 14, 1969) and stayed with the Expos for three years.

Jury Box, The. One August day, with the Braves well out of the pennant race, the right field bleachers at Braves Field held just twelve fans. A newspaperman noting the dozen diehards dubbed it the Jury Box, and the name stuck.

Kaline's Corner. When Al Kaline joined the Tigers in 1954, his speed dictated the removal of some box seats in the right field corner to give him more room to chase foul flies without crashing into the wall.

Kerry Patch. See *Corktown*.

Kiner's Korner. See *Greenberg Gardens*.

Launching Pad, The. Atlanta–Fulton County Stadium is so named because homers are hit here with great frequency. (*Total Baseball* rates its home run factor as being 39 percent above that of the normal park.) Although it is not thought of as being particularly high in altitude, the park is actually more than 1,000 feet above sea level, higher than any

major league park until the Colorado Rockies began to play in Mile High Stadium.

Lumberville. The "bleacheries" from right to center field at Washington Park were called Lumberville, according to a 1908 *Brooklyn Eagle* clip.

Maury's Lake. When Maury Wills was breaking base-stealing records for the Dodgers, the Schwab family of groundskeepers liberally watered the basepath from first to second at Candlestick Park to impede his progress. (For good measure, they mixed sand in the dirt around first to make it more difficult to get a toehold.)

Mistake by the Lake, The. The cavernous Cleveland Stadium, which squats on the shore of Lake Erie, was built as an Olympic stadium, not a ballpark; its inordinately large seating capacity has proven to be a huge mistake for a perennially under-achieving club.

Monster, The. Bill Veeck's exploding scoreboard at Comiskey Park was also known as "the Banshee Board" and "the Thing."

Oakland Mausoleum, The. A derogatory term for the Oakland Coliseum, it was used in the late 1970s to denote the way the park had been neglected at the end of Charlie Finley's tenure as owner.

Old Lady of Schenley Park, The. An affectionate name for Forbes Field.

O'Malley's Chinese Theater. Outfitting the Los Angeles Memorial Coliseum for baseball necessitated placing left field just 250 feet from home plate. Wits disparagingly compared it to the famous Grauman's Chinese Theater in Hollywood.

Pale House Palace, The. Another name for Comiskey Park.

Parlor Park, U.S.A. Another affectionate sobriquet for Wrigley Field.

Pennant Porch. When Charlie Finley owned the Kansas City Athletics, he was convinced that the Yankees won pennants every year because of their short right field wall. In 1964, he built a crescent-shaped wooden addition that reduced the home run distance in right from 338 feet to 296, the same as the Yankees'. After two exhibition games, it was ordered removed because it conflicted with a

1958 rule mandating that outfield distances must be at least 325 feet from home plate (see Chapter 8).

Pesky's Pole. The right field foul pole at Fenway Park was nicknamed after Sox shortstop Johnny Pesky because Pesky peppered it with line drives several times during his playing days.

Queen in Concrete, The. An affectionate name for Seals Stadium in San Francisco.

Rooters' Row. When Cincinnati's Palace of the Fans was rebuilt in 1902, owner John T. Brush installed ground-level seats from which beer-drinking patrons could razz their heroes. Many availed themselves of the opportunity.

Spite Fence, The. Because the right field fence outside Philadelphia's Shibe Park was only 12 feet high, residents along Twentieth Street built rooftop bleachers and sold tickets, particularly at World Series time. In 1935, Jack Shibe, Ben's son, added 38 feet of corrugated metal to close off the view. Citizens "robbed" of their "rights" began calling the obstacle "the Spite Fence" and also "the Great Tin Monster."

Sun Deck, The. At one time, the rear wall of the right field bleachers at Crosley Field in Cincinnati had a sunburst painted on it, reading SUN DECK. After Crosley got lights in 1935, the wall was renamed MOON DECK.

Sweat Box, The. The Metrodome lacked air conditioning for its first year and a half of operation, hence the name.

Terrace, The. Although the outfield at Crosley Field sloped upward from foul line to foul line, it was most noticeable in left field, which made an uphill climb out of the last 15 feet in front of the left field wall.

Thunderdome, The. The overwhelming noise generated by cheering Twins fans at the Metrodome made this name a natural.

Williamsburgh. After Ted Williams hit 14 homers in his rookie year at Fenway Park, the Red Sox front office installed a bullpen in front of the right field bleachers which was dubbed Williamsburgh.

The Orioles abandoned Memorial Stadium for Camden Yards in 1992. That fall, the NFL staged an exhibition game there (see goalpost) in hopes of heightening fan interest in an expansion franchise.

The dark green slatted seats at Camden Yards are traditional for baseball, and the metal frames at the end of each row are stamped with a stylized emblem of a ballplayer and the lettering of the Baltimore Baseball Club — the Orioles of the 1890s. The park has a curved brick facade with arched openings, and the upper deck and sunscreen are built of steel trusses, making them lighter and more transparent than concrete mausoleums like the Kingdome. Janet Marie Smith, the Oriole vice president who also directed revitalization projects in Los Angeles and New York, said, "We studied the old ballparks to see what made them special. One thing was the use of steel, not concrete."

She continued, "We want people to feel as if they've been there before, even if it's their first visit." Accordingly, right center and right field at Camden Yards are a primer in ballpark nostalgia. The top section of the three-paneled scoreboard features a traditional clock with Roman numerals topped by the Oriole logo. Beneath it, a diamond-patterned lattice is flanked by 8-foot-high oriole weathervanes. (They originally had ornithologically incorrect black feathers on their underbodies but

were repainted orange.) The lattice supports an illuminated ad for the *Baltimore Sun;* large serifed block letters spell out T-H-E S-U-N, and the H and E light up to indicate a hit or an error, echoing the Schaefer beer sign on the right field scoreboard at Ebbets Field.

The middle section is the scoreboard proper, with the line score, indicators for outs and the count, and batters due up. The diamond pattern borders the bottom third, which consists of two colorful ads executed in period style for a beer and a soft drink; they flank a space where league standings, leading hitters and pitchers, and miscellaneous information are flashed. Directly beneath the scoreboard are two sections of seating that recall the Jury Box at Braves Field. Below these seats is the legend HIT IT HERE, a hand, and an enclosed L, which advertises the lottery that helped fund the stadium; inevitably, it evokes the Abe Stark HIT SIGN, WIN SUIT sign at the base of the right field wall at Ebbets Field.

Right field is dominated visually by the 1,016-foot-long B&O warehouse where Abraham Lincoln's funeral train stopped on its way from Washington

Getting to the ball-park is an important part of the experience, and Baltimoreans commute to Camden Yards much as Bostonians of an earlier era took the trolley up Commonwealth Avenue.

to Springfield, Illinois. It runs along Eutaw Street and recalls the warehouse behind left field at Huntington Avenue Grounds in Boston (see p. 69). HOK, the design firm, wanted to tear the warehouse down. Instead, it has become the park's focal point, reinforcing its attachment to urban Baltimore. Although the O's have made arrangements to dedicate plaques to any batters that hit it or break windows, a left-handed power hitter will have to launch a ball 460 feet outside the park in right center to earn a home run or 432 feet down the line, where longtime fans recognize the yellow latticework foul poles from Memorial Stadium.

The warehouse has its detractors, notably John Steadman of the *Evening Sun*. He said,

> That warehouse offers absolutely nothing, and it destroys the vista of downtown Baltimore. And if you buy the best seat in the house, next to the Baltimore dugout, you're going to spend nine innings staring out at a brick wall that reminds me of the Maryland state penitentiary.

The American Institute of Architects disagreed and gave Camden Yards one of seven Urban Design Awards for 1992.

From both an architectural and a baseball point of view, Camden Yards has passed tests that have exposed the new Comiskey Park as a shallow pretender. The White Sox had buildings condemned and businesses moved so that they could surround their park with parking lots and souvenir stands owned by the team instead of independent shops and restaurants that would have added to the neighborhood feeling. It bears no relation to its surroundings and, at first glance, might be a municipal power station or similarly anonymous public building.

It's also the kind of place that belies the White Sox blue-collar heritage, which Charles Comiskey respected and for which he made allowances. It has only 3,500 bleacher seats versus 10,000 at the old park. Several layers of luxury boxes have made the grandstand tall and deep, and the upper deck is nearly twice as high as the old park's. One observer said, "Its perilously steep rake makes one think twice about jumping up and cheering for the home team."

Some homage is paid to the old Comiskey; the signature rounded arches are present as is the exploding scoreboard (see Chapter 4). But, as Dillon said, "Million-dollar scoreboards and spectacular fireworks displays, though entertaining, are secondary . . . Being close to the action is entertainment enough." Ballpark consultant John Pastier, who did precise measurements, says the *best* seat at the front of the upper deck behind home plate at the new Comiskey is farther from the field than the *worst* seat at the very back of the upper deck in the old Comiskey.

This is a ballpark without a heart, a mallpark, a superficially attractive "environment" where fans who decry "the yuppies at Wrigley" are blind to lawyers in uniform gingerly elbowing their way to the taco stand. Even though it's an open-air park with Play-All grass turf, baseball is secondary to chatting and people-watching. At a game here in 1991, I discovered that, in a section of 500 people, I was the only one scoring the game.

In contrast to the symmetrical Comiskey (347 down the lines, 383 in the power alleys, and 400 in center), Camden Yards is asymmetrical — 335 to left, 410 to left center, 396 to dead center, and 321 to right. (This dimension required special dispensation from the American League, which had previously imposed the 330-foot standard that helped make all AL parks look alike.) All the weather elements voided by a dome are present, and the field is Prescription Athletic Turf — grass with improved drainage underneath.

Smith and HOK Sports Facilities made two other decisions that integrated Camden Yards into its neighborhood. By sinking the playing field 18 feet below grade, the collaborators kept the upper deck from looming over neighboring buildings, a subtle and deferential way of fitting the park into the cityscape. Second, by making the outfield walls parallel streets just beyond the park, they turned urban inconsistencies into ballpark idiosyncrasies. Instead of the standard curved center field, Camden Yards has fairly sharp angles in deep left center and right center which provide thought-provoking bounces for outfielders and excitement for fans. Oriole assistant general manager Frank Robinson said, "We have the chance to put the triple back in the game."

Naming the park proved to be as big a headache here as elsewhere (see Chapter 9). There was tremendous sentiment for Babe Ruth Stadium because Ruth was born in Baltimore and the Babe Ruth Museum is a short walk from the park. Support multiplied after a firm hired to do archaeological work on the 85-acre stadium discovered that it included the site of the house that Ruth's father built. From 1906 to 1912, the Ruths lived at 406 West Conway Street, and George Herman Ruth, Sr., operated a saloon one flight down at the same address, which would be in short center field at the park. Smith said, "Ruth made his mark as a New York Yankee, and fans might confuse a Babe Ruth Stadium with the House That Ruth Built, Yankee Stadium."

One Baltimorean proposed calling it Star-Spangled Banner Memorial Stadium, because Francis Scott Key wrote the song when nearby Fort McHenry was besieged during the War of 1812. Jacobs wanted Oriole Park, but Maryland's Governor William Donald Schaefer and nearly everyone else favored Camden Yards. The compromise, for the moment, is the unwieldy Oriole Park at Camden Yards. Jacobs thought he would pull a fast one and put ORIOLE PARK in letters twice as high on the front of the stadium; that sign was changed, but signs on I-95 into Baltimore read CAMDEN YARDS STADIUM.

Oriole officials hope that the fans will choose public transportation to get to Camden Yards. The park is served by twenty bus lines and is easily reached by downtown workers as well as tourists drawn to the Inner Harbor and the Aquarium, six blocks from the park. Camden Yards is also far more accessible from Washington than Memorial Stadium was. Trains run right from Union Station and commuter railways, looking like nothing so much as updated trolleys, and pull right up to the park's back entrance. (As in Brooklyn in 1894, fans have to cross the tracks to get to the ballpark.)

An aerial photograph taken on September 30, 1990, shows the last White Sox game played at the original Comiskey Park and the new Comiskey rising beside it. Side by side, the old and new (unfinished) Comiskey parks have little in common other than Roger Bossard's carefully tended infields. Notice particularly the steepness of the rake of the upper deck and the overall height of the new park compared to the old. It is due to the inclusion of loge seating between the upper and lower decks, a way of gouging a few more dollars from the well-to-do while ignoring the legitimate interests of the average fan. In contrast, the upper deck at Fenway Park (right), shown here in 1985, is about a third as high, and the rake is gradual.

The park was originally supposed to cost $78.4 million, but that figure grew to $106.5 million, with increases for the foundation, facade, and drainage systems as well as the sunscreen for the upper deck and improved sound and lighting. The overall cost of the project was $205.5 million, with $99 million used to acquire the 85-acre site the park occupies. The interest on the revenue bonds is being paid primarily by proceeds from a special baseball-themed lottery — $92.2 million as of March 1992.

A survey undertaken by the city reveals that the economic promise of Camden Yards was more than fulfilled in its first year of operation. In 1991, the O's final year at Memorial Stadium, the fans spent just $13.3 million. In 1992, 80 home games drew 3.6 million fans who spent $38 million at downtown restaurants, hotels, and shops and an additional $14.8 million in the suburbs — a total of $52.8 million, which does not include ticket sales or revenue from food and souvenirs.

There are many things wrong with Camden Yards. There are seats from which it was impossible to see the whole field in 1992; fans at the right edge of the bleachers, for instance, can't see first base. The exit ramps are woefully inadequate to handle the enormous crowds; I sat in the upper deck behind home plate, and after the game, it took me at least half an hour to get outside.

Some of the touches like the HIT IT HERE sign come off as unbearably cutesy, and all the clever repackaging won't turn Camden Yards into Ebbets, Fenway, or Wrigley, at least not for years. As attractive as the park is, it is doubtful that such a modern, multimillion-dollar edifice can ever win the hearts and minds of fans the way the jewel boxes did. It's all too clean, too perfect, too ordered, Walt Disney's version of a ballpark. A good ballpark needs to be mussed up a little, like a pair of sneakers, to develop a patina of hard-won character.

While Pilot Field in Buffalo has been rightly hailed as the park where the "new-old look" was introduced, Camden Yards is clearly the most innovative and influential major league ballpark designed since Yankee Stadium, and it has already influenced parks being built in Cleveland and Texas, which have announced intentions to build what they call traditional ballparks. Nevertheless, Jacobs Field in Cleveland will stack luxury suites three stories high in places and feature pricey club seats as far as 518 feet from home plate. The exterior of the Texas park has many traditional baseball touches — lone stars, outlines of the state of Texas, and heads of longhorn steers.

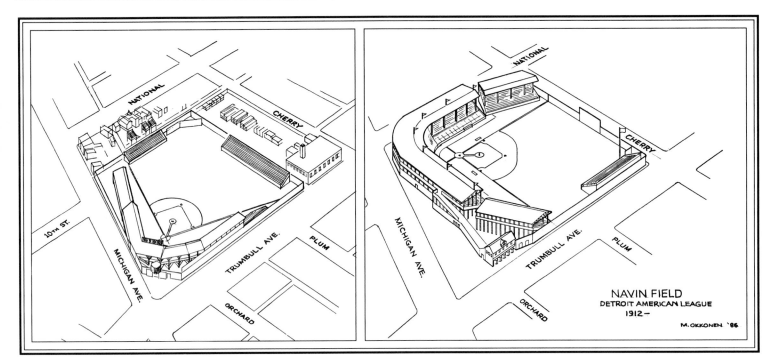

NAVIN FIELD
DETROIT AMERICAN LEAGUE
1912—

M. OKKONEN. '86

Saving Grace: Tiger Stadium

Camden Yards repackages the traditional ball-park in modern dress; at Tiger Stadium, they don't have to repackage what they've had at the corner of Michigan and Trumbull avenues since 1896. In 1976, Richard J. Moss of the Michigan Department of State said, "Tiger Stadium, viewed historically, is like one of those toy eggs that have several similar, but smaller eggs inside. When you peel the years away from the present structure you discover the precursors of the stadium to come."

Although the ground it occupies has changed names — from Bennett Park (1896–1911) to Navin Field (1912–1937), Briggs Stadium (1938–1960), and Tiger Stadium — the site of the ballpark is, as of 1995, the major leagues' longest in terms of continuous service.

In 1912, when Garry Herrmann supervised the building of Redland Field in Cincinnati, it never occurred to him to supply parking spaces or provide for them in the future; only 900,000 cars were registered in the United States. It was different in Detroit. Workers had flooded into his plant once Henry Ford started cranking out Model T's in 1908, and Detroit's population boomed as a direct result of the automobile's popularity: from 285,704 residents in 1900 to 465,766 in 1910. By 1913, Ford had adopted the assembly-line technique favored by meat packers, and, lured by revolutionary wages of $5 per day, workers arrived by the carload. In 1920, Detroit had nearly a million residents.

The Tigers had boomed as well. Their former bookkeeper, Frank Navin, had bought the team from William Hoover Yawkey (the uncle of subsequent Red Sox owner Tom Yawkey) for $40,000 in 1907. Although it never won a World Series, the club proceeded to win three straight pennants, thanks largely to the tempestuous Tyrus Raymond Cobb, "the Georgia Peach," who led the league in hitting (and RBI) all three years.

As Cobb grew more popular, Navin was forced to expand. He spent $300,000 over the winter of 1911, increased the capacity to 23,000 fans, and unveiled the first batters' background — a blank green wall in center field. (Two years later baseball's ruling body, the National Commission, mandated that every park had to have one.) Home plate was moved from the right field corner to its present location, making right the sun field. In the course of tearing down the old park to add seats, Navin was also able to level the houses on the east side of National, finally defeating the entrepreneurs who had operated "wildcat bleachers" there for sixteen years.

Navin Field opened the same day as Fenway Park, April 20, 1912, and the steel and concrete horseshoe stand built then still runs from behind home to the outfield grass. Charlie Bennett was on hand to catch the ceremonial first pitch, and in the bottom of the first inning, Cobb properly christened the park by stealing home on the front end of a double steal with "Wahoo Sam" Crawford, their second of the inning. Cobb also made two spectacular catches, and Detroit defeated Cleveland, 6–5, in eleven innings.

Mickey Cochrane came over from Philadelphia in 1934. Sparked by their fiery player-manager, the Tigers hit .300 as a team, 21 points above the league average, and ran away with the pennant. Soon after the clinching, Navin persuaded the city fathers to tear down the few remaining houses on Cherry Street to make room for a 17,000-seat bleacher section; the left field wall was dismantled and rebuilt in a matter of days.

The upper-deck "overhang" at Tiger Stadium is a product of the Depression. In 1935, Walter Briggs III began to envision Navin Field as a fully enclosed double-decked stadium. In the first phase of his plan, the single-decked first base pavilion was replaced with a double-decked grandstand, but that created a problem in right field; Trumbull Avenue ran right behind it, and there was no way to expand backward.

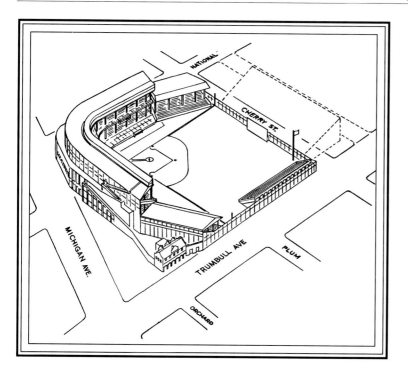

The site on which Tiger Stadium sits has evolved in nearly a hundred years from a wooden enclosure seating 8,500 to a 54,220-seat stadium that has held nine World Series and three All-Star Games. In the Bennett Park era (1896–1911), home plate was at the corner of Michigan and Trumbull (far left); it was reoriented when the steel and concrete Navin Field, which accommodated 23,000, was built in 1912 (middle left).

Owner Frank Navin double-decked the grandstand in 1923, raising the seating capacity to 30,000 (left). After the 1937 season, Walter Briggs redid the entire stadium, adding double-decked wings along the foul lines and into the outfield (below). The only changes since then have been merely cosmetic.

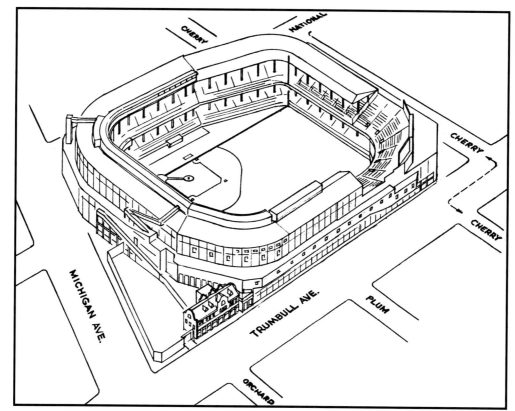

Another problem was that Briggs didn't want to cheapen the home run by moving the wall in any closer than 325 feet. Right field was shortened from 367 to 325 feet, but to compensate, he extended the upper deck 10 feet beyond the lower deck in front and in back. As noted in *Queen of Diamonds*, outside the park "the result is a bulge in the stadium's outer wall. Inside, the upper deck overhangs the lower by ten feet; the effect is one that favors left-handed hitters who uppercut the ball. It is possible to hit a 325-foot line drive that is caught at the fence and hit a 315-foot high-arching fly ball that becomes a home run, adding spice to the game."

Aside from the overhang, fans like Tiger Stadium because they're right on top of the action, some-

thing the players appreciate. Hall of Fame third baseman George Kell said, "I like to hear the people. At Tiger Stadium, I could hear everything that was said . . . One day Hal Newhouser was pitching. He was getting rocked by the Boston club. He came over to back up third base and some fan was getting on him real good. And I said, 'Hang in there, Hal. Don't worry about that guy.' And I heard the guy say, 'You're not doing too good yourself, Kell.' "

When the Detroit Pistons won back-to-back NBA championships, network TV shills made much of their "working-class ethic." They were just plain, simple, blue-collar guys doing a job. Of course, the people who actually saw these blue-collar guys play were white-collar guys and gals who could afford the $20 minimum ticket, not to mention the $50

maximum. In contrast, there are 10,000 bleacher seats at Tiger Stadium; they cost $4 and are filled with real fans who come to see the game, not waterfalls or fireworks, and who hate organ music because it interrupts their conversation.

When new stadiums were sprouting up in the 1960s, sportswriter Melvin Durslag decided that "fifty years is just about the limit for any stadium. Every big city is able to blow itself to a new facility twice a century. A grandfather would not see sports in the same park he did as a child." But Bob Buchta, cofounder of the Tiger Stadium Fan Club, says, "There isn't a single spot in Detroit that carries more associations for the people of this city than Tiger Stadium . . . We like sitting in the same seats our grandparents used."

Such an attitude would be noteworthy anywhere in the United States; it is doubly so in Detroit, America's capital of planned obsolescence, a city whose civic leaders think not in generations or decades but in model years. It was fitting, then, that in 1983, when fast food mogul Tom Monaghan, the founder of Domino's Pizza, bought the team, he lusted for a shiny, brand-new (preferably domed) stadium with luxury boxes, expanded office and clubhouse facilities, and restaurants and concession areas.

Monaghan didn't care about staying in Detroit or seeking a site in the suburbs as long as one or another municipality helped pay the freight. Accordingly, he was able to play two other interested parties against each other. Mayor Coleman Young wanted to keep the Tigers in Detroit to "revitalize" downtown (and also serve as a monument to his stewardship). Wayne County, whose borders include Detroit and Dearborn and which has been mentioned as a possible site, has residual funding authority from an abortive project to build a stadium near the Detroit River (see below) and also enjoys a better bond rating than the city.

These three parties — the Tigers, the city, and the county — have tried to sell Detroit's fans on a new stadium. The tactics have been: (1) "proof" that Tiger Stadium is structurally unsound; (2) renovation estimates in the $85 million range, which make a new $150 million stadium seem a bargain by comparison; (3) threats to move to other cities, such as Phoenix, Washington, D.C., and, inevitably, St. Petersburg, even though the Tigers' lease runs through the year 2008.

Playing the role of civic conscience and David against this Goliath of money and political power is a growing group of concerned citizens, the Tiger Stadium Fan Club. Devoting a fan club to a stadium is a first, although, as noted, neighborhood residents wanted to preserve Washington Park in Brooklyn in 1925. More recently, citizens tried to save Metropolitan Stadium in Bloomington, Minnesota, and Comiskey Park in Chicago; both efforts failed, but Save Our Sox contributed to the Tiger Stadium Fan Club as a show of solidarity.

When the club decided to work against the building of a new stadium, it had ample precedent. Citizen involvement prevented the building of a stadium that has been described in *Queen of Diamonds* as "a half a billion dollar fraud." On September 15, 1971, the Wayne County Stadium Authority announced a plan to build a domed stadium. A forty-year bond issue would raise $126 million: $6 million for parking lots, $85 million for

In the mid-1930s, Detroit won three pennants thanks to the efforts of Mickey Cochrane, Charlie Gehringer, and Hank Greenberg. This view from right center field (left) shows the park near the end of its Navin Field days. After the Tigers won the 1945 World Series, a brochure (right) showed the park in its final incarnation.

Roger Angell once compared Comiskey Park to a docked paddle-wheel steamer, but the metaphor also applies in this 1949 postcard (below), which gives the park a settled air.

the stadium, and $35 million for the land and improvements. Early in 1972, Tiger owner John Fetzer signed a forty-year lease to play there.

A few days before the bonds were to go on sale (without public discussion), two Tiger fans, financial analyst Marc Alan and lawyer Ron Prebenda, met for the first time and began discussing the plan. They made a few phone calls and discovered that, among other things, the Tigers' lease would have given Fetzer *340,000* square feet of office space for nothing. When the two filed an eleventh-hour lawsuit to stop the sale of the bonds, they were joined by B. Ward Smith, the city attorney of Belleville, a Wayne County suburb. Wayne County circuit court Judge Blair Moody scheduled a hearing and later issued a temporary injunction, delaying the project.

Court proceedings soon revealed that fine print in the bond offer had deliberately obscured a point that made Wayne County's taxpayers liable for any shortfalls. The bonds were general obligation bonds, *not* revenue bonds, which would be made good by the stadium itself in case of an overrun. After a nine-day trial, Moody ruled that the lease was too one-sided in favor of the Tigers. Governor William Milliken used a little-known statute to have the case heard immediately by the state supreme court. On June 8, the high court ruled, 6–1, that the project's backers had misled the public, killing the project for good.

With the riverfront scam dead, the state of Michigan spearheaded a multipurpose dome in Pontiac for both the Tigers and the NFL Lions. Construction began in September 1973, using $55.7 million in public revenue bonds; Fetzer had become committed to the idea of keeping the Tigers in Detroit. He said, "This franchise belongs to the inner city of Detroit, and I'm merely the caretaker. I will not move the Tigers." In October 1977, he sold the park to the city for a dollar; the city agreed to make $15 million in renovations by charging a 50-cent ticket surcharge, and the Tigers agreed to a thirty-year lease, ending in 2008.

Major repairs were made to the concrete and steel decking, the plumbing, and the electrical system. The old hand-operated scoreboard in center field was replaced by a computer-controlled model, and the green wooden chairs were replaced by orange and blue plastic seats. New broadcast facilities and two luxury boxes — one for the owner, one for the media — were hung from the upper deck behind home plate. A second renovation, costing $3.6 million and financed by an additional 40-cent surcharge, modernized the clubhouses in 1982,

and the familiar green and off-white stadium was sheathed in blue tile and beige aluminum.

On October 10, 1983, Fetzer sold the Tigers to Monaghan, who vowed publicly that he would never tear down Tiger Stadium. His timing in buying the Tigers was impeccable; they won 35 of their first 40 games, waltzed to the pennant, and blew the Padres away in the World Series. Unfortunately, the celebration got out of hand; new turf laid after a pennant-clinching celebration was ripped up. One fan said, "We were picking up pieces of turf and slinging them over our shoulders like togas."

Fans outside mobbed the streets, and one began throwing bottles and hit a police car, which burst into flames; the next day a picture of a fan waving a Tiger pennant next to the burning car made front pages around the world. The celebration fostered the impression that the area around Tiger Stadium was unsafe. Although it was an isolated incident, Monaghan played on that fear to help justify building a stadium in a different location. Talk of a new stadium filled the newspapers, particularly when the Tigers came from 4 games behind with 7 to play to win the 1987 divisional title.

That September, Buchta, Frank Rashid, Michael Gruber, and other dedicated fans, believing their park was doomed, decided to translate their love into action and started the Tiger Stadium Fan Club to rally support for renovation. Since polls had consistently shown that the fans preferred renovation to a new stadium, the fan club had an advantage if it could mobilize support in Detroit.

On January 5, 1988, the city announced that it would take proposals from architectural firms for plans to renovate Tiger Stadium or build a replacement. The next day, Monaghan aide John McDevitt said an engineering study showed that renovating the park would cost between $45 million and $100 million. (The numbers, which proved to be vastly inflated, were from an engineering study the city had commissioned in November 1987 to estimate the expense of renovating Tiger Stadium; the results were never released.) The cost, two to four times the actual figure, didn't influence the fans; an overnight *Detroit News* poll showed that readers *still* favored renovation by 2 to 1.

At a meeting in February with Buchta and Gruber, McDevitt said, "There was no study." It was just "a conversational estimate," which included putting a fabric roof over the park, quite a difference from making needed structural repairs. When the fan club got press coverage, Mayor Young snapped, "Nobody in their wildest dreams expects

that stadium to last beyond ten years. Most people say it will fall in five." Buchta and Rashid said, "Tiger Stadium is a living, vital connection to our past . . . To baseball fans everywhere, it is a national landmark . . . thus far no studies have been released about the structural integrity of Tiger Stadium. The public has a right to this information before any decision is made about the future of the ballpark."

When media organizations began questioning McDevitt's figures, he invited *Detroit Monthly* to bring in its own structural engineer. In March 1988, Lev Zetlin, an engineer who had been called in to investigate the Hyatt Hotel's collapse in Kansas City, conducted an inspection. He found "no signs of structural weakness . . . no bending of columns, no very large cracks in concrete to indicate underlying problems." The only problem was a section near the visitor's bullpen that had been missed in the last round of repairs. He said, "If you have a loose brick, you fix the brick. You don't tear the whole building down."

Zetlin's report was released on April 20, 1988, the seventy-sixth anniversary of the dedication of Navin Field. The fan club organized a "hug" of Tiger Stadium, and 1,200 people showed up in rainy, 45-

degree weather to celebrate the ballpark in this unprecedented way. Part of the turnout was due to the efforts of a local radio station, WCSX, which had circulated petitions and collected 100,000 signatures in a few weeks.

In July, documents obtained under the Freedom of Information Act revealed that the engineering study the city had commissioned the previous November (and which McDevitt insisted did not exist) destroyed Young's claims that the ballpark was falling down. The Turner Construction Company recommended just under $6 million worth of renovation, only $1.4 million of which was used to repair decking and patch concourses and replace a section of the lower deck in right field. Repairs to plumbing and electricity would cost $1.3 million, and the remainder would be needed for new toilets and concessions, an upgraded pubic address system, and exit signs. (Four years later, Tiger general manager Bo Schembechler told the Economic Club of Detroit that a renovation with cost overruns would cost $100 million.)

Late in 1988, the fan club was successful in placing Tiger Stadium on the National Register of Historic Places, the second ballpark so honored (after Municipal Stadium in Cleveland). As a result,

This view, taken before Reggie Jackson's towering home run against Ferguson Jenkins in the 1971 All-Star Game, affords a splendid view of the right field overhang and a good overview of the park.

federal money cannot be used to tear it down, replace it, or build any new structure at Michigan and Trumbull. Saving Tiger Stadium thus became not only a baseball issue and a Detroit issue but a national preservationist issue. (Although the National Trust for Historic Preservation has put the ballpark on its list of endangered structures, the fan club has not pursued landmark status, which would protect the stadium forever but would not guarantee the Tigers' tenancy.)

Meanwhile, the city asked HOK, which built Three Rivers Stadium and Veterans Stadium, to cost out various options, which the Tigers made public in March 1989:

1. Partial renovation — $57 million. This option would lose 3,500 bleacher seats but would add several tiers of luxury boxes and a new press box.

2. Full renovation — $82 million. Removing all posts from the second deck and building a new one plus two rows of loge seats would lose 8,000 bleacher seats and require the team to play elsewhere for two years.

3. New stadium — $117.9 million.

4. New stadium with a roof — $157 million.

5. New stadium with a retractable roof — $245 million.

Buchta's response was: "It is an insult to destroy a treasured baseball landmark in the name of luxury boxes and more expensive tickets. It is a double insult to ask us as taxpayers to pay for the priv-

ilege." The fan club challenged HOK's figures for renovation and announced a boycott of Domino's Pizza. A public opinion poll showed that fans statewide favored renovation, 61 to 16 percent; the margin in Detroit was 75 to 16 percent.

After the HOK study was released, fan club members began discussing their own renovation plan. Architect John Davids, who had planned Monaghan's private box at Tiger Stadium, did the design with help from club members. For the first time in baseball history, a group of fans commissioned and paid for a plan to keep their favorite ballpark alive.

Called the Cochrane Plan, it calls for three additions outside the stadium, and it enjoys wide support from architects and construction engineers. The largest addition would close little-used Cochrane (formerly National) Avenue; a second along Michigan would provide more walkways behind home plate. Together, they would double the restrooms, concessions, and home clubhouse and triple the visitor's clubhouse and area for food storage. A third addition would more than double the space for offices and the ticket department. A new building along Michigan would house a Tiger museum (which Monaghan had moved to his corporate offices in Ann Arbor). New elevators would rise to a new third deck holding 73 luxury suites for 1,200 people.

The Cochrane Plan was unveiled on January 22, 1990, but Tiger management refused to review it. On October 2, Schembechler was a guest on *Late Night with David Letterman*, and Letterman's first question was, "Are you going to tear down Tiger Stadium?" Schembechler hesitated. Letterman said, "Uh-oh! It's gone! It's gone! It's a cloud of smoke now!"

The Tigers have attracted at least a million fans a year from 1965 through 1992, an American League record. As Betzold and Casey point out, cities that did away with their classic parks showed a large increase in the first decade they were built; however, over the long haul, cities that retained their classic parks show greater long-term growth in the next decade while the replacement parks are flagging.

Turning to legal matters, the fan club learned that a city statute allowed voters to propose an ordinance, put it to a public vote, and have it remain in force for twelve months. Gathering support from church, educational, and social action groups, the fan club formed the Common Ground Coalition on September 14, 1991, and launched a petition campaign to give Detroit voters the power

Cities That Replaced Classic Parks

CITY	1960S	1970S	1980S
St. Louis	1,395,775	1,530,987	2,200,752
Philadelphia	883,500	1,929,529	2,103,880
Cincinnati	895,488	2,145,247	1,731,054
Pittsburgh	1,001,453	1,263,385	1,201,015

Cities That Kept Classic Parks

CITY	1960S	1970S	1980S
New York (AL)	1,333,458	1,598,637	2,273,656
Boston	1,150,469	1,814,588	1,965,188
Detroit	1,282,476	1,518,351	1,908,942
Chicago (NL)	879,671	1,356,673	1,853,352
Chicago (AL)	1,083,043	1,105,387	1,500,180

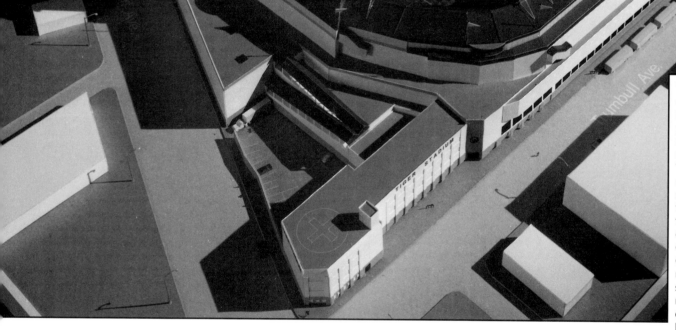

The Cochrane Plan, created by the Tiger Stadium Fan Club, provides for (1) an addition at the corner of Michigan and Trumbull to increase space for administration and selling tickets; (2) an addition on the corner of Michigan and Cochrane (formerly Cherry) to allow for new concession space, more restrooms, and the expansion of clubhouses, offices, and storage areas; (3) a new building on Michigan west of Cochrane to house marketing operations and the Tiger Hall of Fame, which previous owner Tom Monaghan moved to Ann Arbor; (4) an optional new level of luxury suites and press facilities to replace the existing third deck and make it feasible to remove 40% of its supporting posts.

to enforce the city's lease with the Tigers and Tiger Stadium. The proposed ordinance was placed on the ballot, and on March 17, 1992, 67 percent of the voters supported the measure. For at least a year, no city funds could be spent on a new stadium.

Then, in August, Mike Ilitch, the owner of Little Caesar's pizza, bought the Tigers from Monaghan. Since Ilitch has been a supporter of downtown Detroit (he rebuilt the Fox Theater there and moved Little Caesar's headquarters in from the suburbs), there is less of a possibility that the Tigers will move. Members of the fan club have met with Ilitch to discuss the Cochrane Plan and have pointed out that, given the ballpark's status on the National Register, 20 percent of any renovation costs could be written off as repairs on a historic building.

For the moment, then, all is calm at the corner of Michigan and Trumbull and will hopefully remain so. Whether the fan club wins its battle or not, it has clearly earned a "save" and is already influencing other fans to organize and fight, in the best American tradition, to keep what they hold dear.

The Fan Club has translated into action a frustration with municipally financed stadiums that Ralph Nader had sensed in 1977. Nader formed a new consumer group called FANS (Fight to Advance the Nation's Sports) and said, "The arrogance of the owners and their lack of sensitivity toward their fans is accelerating. They never ask the fans what they think of the policies and rules these owners set. And the fans have a right to know the full costs they are paying, as taxpayers, for the municipal stadiums most of them can't get into, even if they could afford a ticket."

Nader's national effort was unsuccessful, but the Tiger Stadium Fan Club has become a formidable force in Detroit, proving once again that, from April through September, baseball is America's *local* pastime. Given their geography and networks, local conservation groups can indeed change the face of history. In fact, a new group has been formed, the Fenway Park Fan Club, amid rumblings that the Red Sox may move to the suburbs.

The ballpark has evolved since William Cammeyer's time, slowly and steadily from a grandstand perpendicular to the diamond to the half-hexagon, the rounded half-hexagon, the round park, and, finally, the enclosed round park — the dome. The pendulum is now swinging back to the traditional ballpark, either in new clothes (Camden Yards) or pre–World War I garb (Tiger Stadium).

Bill Veeck once said, "Baseball's unique possession, the real source of our strength, is the fan's memory of the times his daddy took him to the game to see the great players of his youth . . . If the memories of our youth disappeared, we would look upon baseball as a rather dull game . . . The secret ingredient is what the customer brings into the park with him."

The first time I entered Ebbets Field I brought with me nothing but uncertainty. Walking through the tiled rotunda, uncertainty turned to curiosity. Emerging from a concrete runway, I experienced for the first time what W. P. Kinsella has knowingly called "the thrill of the grass." Seeing all that greenery, I felt at that moment as if I were in the land of Oz. When I walk into Fenway Park and Wrigley Field and Tiger Stadium, I still do.

ACKNOWLEDGMENTS

When I first became convinced that a book was needed to put America's major league ballparks in some historical context, I had no idea the project would take two and a half years to research and write. Many times along the way, I turned to old friends and acquaintances and made new ones using only a shared enthusiasm for ballparks as a common language.

Ballpark lovers are a special breed. Their passion for the places of baseball transcends a single player, a team, a city, and takes in all ballparks of all eras. It can also involve literary and photographic research, with side trips into architecture, transportation, communication, social history, real estate, and politics. This book could not have been done without the generosity of numerous FOBs — Friends of Ballparks. These acknowledgments, then, are a way of remembering — piece by piece — the enormous pile of information they have contributed.

John Thorn, my partner in Total Baseball, was gracious about reviewing the chapters on nineteenth-century baseball and made a number of improvements. He also generously loaned photographs from his collection for inclusion and put me in touch with members of the Society of American Baseball Research, such as Joseph Overfield and Ed Doyle, who supplied photographs of parks in Buffalo and Philadelphia. Richard Puff made me aware of the bird's-eye views of various cities that contained ballparks.

Bob Bluthardt, a fellow member of SABR and the chairman of the Ballparks Committee, reviewed the manuscript and made a number of helpful suggestions along the way. Of course, any mistakes that remain are mine alone.

Two ballpark postcard collectors — Eliot Knispel and Elias Dudash — also reviewed the manuscript and supplied many of the images in the book. Three publishers of ballpark postcards — Ray Medeiros, Vic Pallos, and Gordon Tindall — also allowed me to use their copyrighted material.

Michael Frank loaned items from his extensive collection of ballpark memorabilia for photography as did Dick Miller, a columnist for *Sports Collectors Digest.* Bob Morse shared with me a 1911 book that contained several interesting ballpark pictures, and Christopher Paluso was kind enough to photograph them. John Bunting and Ian Cook also contributed their photographic talents, and Andrew Bartalotta's architectural background made his illustrations particularly pertinent.

Pete Palmer, the coeditor of *Total Baseball,* made available his research on attendance figures, and David Pietrusza shared unpublished material about night baseball. Marc Okkonen, an authority on baseball uniforms, helped me date photographs and also provided illustrations of the evolution of Tiger Stadium.

As usual, Bill Deane of the National Baseball Library answered many of my questions or filled holes with his extensive knowledge of baseball rules, players, and awards. Likewise, Steve Gietschier of the *Sporting News* helped me dig through the publication's extensive text and photo archives, and George Hobart helped me navigate through the Library of Congress's extensive print collection.

Jim Bready provided background on the ballparks of Baltimore, and Millard Mack shared several early photos of Redland Field. Ted Heinecken and Patrick Quinn of the Northwestern University library were helpful on the ballparks of Chicago, and Bill Loughman and Mark Rucker were generous with information on photographs and illustrations. Unasked, Joe Wyszynski provided useful information about the Astrodome, and Doug Donahoe loaned a rare shot of the Polo Grounds for photography.

On a more personal level, baseball friends proved inexhaustible resources for various aspects of the book. Larry Ritter displayed his usual patience with my many questions about economic matters, and Lee Lowenfish was a fount of information on labor-management issues. Dick Johnson of the New England Sports Museum and Glenn Stout provided vital background information on "Nuf Ced" McGreevy, Fenway Park, and the Braves' move to Milwaukee. John Brooks was also exceptionally helpful on the subject of Braves Field.

Publicists for several major league teams went out of their way to be helpful, particularly Vickie Pietryga of the Cubs, Barb Kozuh of the White Sox, Laurel Prieb of the Brewers, Rick Vaughn of the Orioles, Jim Samia of the Red Sox, Jeff Wehling of the Cardinals, Dave Aust of the Mariners, and John Mulroon of the Indians.

Ed Walton reviewed information on the ballparks of Boston, and family friends Ed Lebowich, Edna Grace, and Ron and Jane Scheff provided accommodations during several road trips. Raymond Shaw was a great help on the graphics end, and Carol LeKashman proved to be a great source on modern ballpark architecture.

The men and women at Houghton Mifflin were unfailingly helpful and accommodating. Over the course of seven years, Steve Lewers, Luise Erdmann, Becky Saikia-Wilson, and Jim Lindquist have made publishing a pleasure. Marnie Patterson, the newest member of the team, proved to be an energetic, enthusiastic, and capable editor throughout, and is my unanimous selection for Rookie of the Year.

My wife, Suzy, and son, Aaron, helped with words of encouragement and tolerated stretches of neglect so that I could finish the book. I'm very fortunate to have two such supportive people on my home team.

Westport, Connecticut
May 1993

CHRONOLOGY OF MAJOR LEAGUE BALLPARKS

Compiling a chronological list of all the major league ballparks and their dimensions can be compared to hitting a knuckleball. As Willie Stargell once said, "It's like trying to eat Jell-O with chopsticks."

There are no dimensions worth speaking of before the turn of the century; accordingly, they have been omitted. With the birth of the American League in 1901 the problem changes; dimensions were recorded in the *Reach* and *Spalding* guides as well as the *Sporting News, Sporting Life*, and other periodicals, but they are not necessarily correct. Information was picked up from year to year without much checking, and many authoritative sources are contradictory. What follows,

then, is a best approximation of the dimensions of each park in its original incarnation and its final—or, when applicable, its current—state.

Dimensions at certain ballparks changed at a maddening rate. Center field in the Polo Grounds was 483 in 1923, 505 in 1930, 448 in 1945, 483 (again) in 1949, 483 (again) in 1952, and so on.

To avoid clumsy numbering (Polo Grounds I, II, III) or the use of the often equivocal New and Old, some parks are noted as (Original), although that designation was never part of their names. Thus, (Original) Comiskey Park (1910), Comiskey Park (1991). Also, when parks of long standing changed drastically,

they are listed separately in each incarnation. (The same park in Cincinnati is listed separately as League Park, Palace of the Fans, Redland Field, and Crosley Field.)

The twenty-eight current major league parks are noted in bold. Although a given park may have been used in several leagues (Bank Street Grounds, County Stadium Exposition Park), it is listed only the *first* time it was used for major league games. Sunday-only ballparks are not included here but are listed on p. 34. Also, only parks actually used as *home* parks are included; neutral fields are omitted.

FIRST USE	NAME OF PARK (ALTERNATE NAMES)	CITY	LEAGUE
1871	South End Grounds	Boston	NA
1871	Union Grounds	Brooklyn	NA
1871	Union Base-Ball Grounds (Lake Park)	Chicago	NA
1871	National Association Grounds	Cleveland	NA
1871	Hamilton Field (The Grand Duchess)	Fort Wayne, Ind.	NA
1871	Athletics Park (Jefferson Street Grounds)	Philadelphia	NA
1871	Fairgrounds Park	Rockford, Ill.	NA
1871	Rensselaer Park	Troy, N.Y.	NA
1871	Olympic Grounds	Washington	NA
1871	Maryland Avenue Grounds	Washington	NA

CHRONOLOGY OF MAJOR LEAGUE BALLPARKS

FIRST USE	NAME OF PARK (ALTERNATE NAMES)	CITY	LEAGUE
1872	Newington Park	Baltimore	NA
1872	Capitoline Grounds	Brooklyn	NA
1872	Fort Hill Grounds (Mansfield Club Grounds)	Middletown, Conn.	NA
1872	Haymakers' Grounds	Troy, N.Y.	NA
1873	Madison Avenue Grounds (Monumental Park)	Baltimore	NA
1873	Waverly Fairgrounds (Weequahic Park)	Elizabeth, N.J.	NA
1874	23rd Street Grounds	Chicago	NA
1874	Hartford Baseball Grounds	Hartford	NA
1875	Perry Park	Keokuk, Iowa	NA
1875	Brewster Park	New Haven	NA
1875	Sportsman's Park (Grand Avenue Grounds)	St. Louis	NA
1875	Athletic Park	St. Louis	NA
1875	Red Stocking Base Ball Park	St. Louis	NA
1876	Lincoln Park Grounds	Cincinnati	NL
1876	Avenue Grounds	Cincinnati	NL
1876	National League Park (Louisville Baseball Park)	Louisville	NL
1878	Lake Front Park	Chicago	NL
1878	South Street Park	Indianapolis	NL
1878	Milwaukee Base-Ball Grounds	Milwaukee	NL
1878	Messer Street Grounds	Providence	NL
1879	Riverside Park	Buffalo	NL
1879	National League Park (Kennard Street Park)	Cleveland	NL

1879	Newell Park	Syracuse	NL
1879	Putnam Grounds	Troy, N.Y.	NL
1880	Bank Street Grounds	Cincinnati	NL
1880	Worcester Driving Fields (Agricultural Grounds)	Worcester	NL
1881	Recreation Park	Detroit	NL
1882	(Original) Eclipse Park	Louisville	AA
1882	Oakdale Park	Philadelphia	AA
1882	Exposition Park	Pittsburgh	AA
1882	Troy Ball Club Grounds	Troy, N.Y.	NL
1883	Recreation Park	Columbus	AA
1883	(Original) Polo Grounds, West Diamond	New York	AA
1883	(Original) Polo Grounds, East Diamond	New York	NL
1883	Recreation Park	Philadelphia	NL
1884	Columbia Park (Fourth Avenue Grounds)	Altoona, Pa.	UA
1884	Dartmouth Street Grounds (Union Park)	Boston	UA
1884	(Original) Washington Park	Brooklyn	AA
1884	(Original) Olympic Park	Buffalo	NL
1884	South Side Park (Chicago Cricket Club Grounds)	Chicago	UA
1884	League Park	Cincinnati	AA
1884	Bruce Park	Indianapolis	AA
1884	Athletic Park	Kansas City	UA
1884	Wright Street Grounds	Milwaukee	UA
1884	Keystone Park	Philadelphia	UA
1884	Recreation Park (Union Park, Colosseum)	Pittsburgh	UA
1884	Virginia Park (Allen Pasture)	Richmond, Va.	AA
1884	Palace Park of America (Union Park, Lucas Park)	St. Louis	UA
1884	League Park	Toledo, Ohio	AA
1884	Athletic Park	Washington	AA

CHRONOLOGY OF MAJOR LEAGUE BALLPARKS

FIRST USE	NAME OF PARK (ALTERNATE NAMES)	CITY	LEAGUE
1884	Capitol Grounds (Capitol Park)	Washington	UA
1884	Union Association Grounds (Wilmington Grounds)	Wilmington, Del.	UA
1885	West Side Grounds (Congress Street Park)	Chicago	NL
1885	Vandeventer Lot	St. Louis	NL
1886	St. George Cricket Grounds	New York	AA
1886	Swampoodle Grounds	Washington	NL
1887	Spider Park (National League Park)	Cleveland	AA
1887	Baker Bowl (Huntingdon Grounds)	Philadelphia	NL
1888	(Original) Association Park	Kansas City	NL
1889	Association Park	Kansas City	AA
1889	Exposition Park	Kansas City	AA
1889	Polo Grounds (Manhattan Field)	New York	NL
1890	Congress Street Grounds	Boston	PL
1890	Washington Park	Brooklyn	PL
1890	Olympic Park	Buffalo	PL
1890	South Side Park	Chicago	PL
1890	Brotherhood Park	Cleveland	PL
1890	Brotherhood Park	New York	PL
1890	Brotherhood Park (Forepaugh Park)	Philadelphia	PL
1890	Culver Field	Rochester	AA
1890	Star Park	Syracuse	AA
1890	Speranza Park	Toledo	AA
1891	Union Park	Baltimore	AA
1891	Eastern Park	Brooklyn	NL
1891	Pendleton Park	Cincinnati	AA

1891	League Park	Cleveland	NL
1891	Borchert Field	Milwaukee	AA
1891	Polo Grounds (Brotherhood Park)	New York	NL
1891	Boundary Field	Washington	AA
1893	West Side Grounds	Chicago	NL
1893	Eclipse Park	Louisville	NL
1893	Robison Field (New Sportsman's Park)	St. Louis	NL

Year	Park	City	League	ORIGINAL DIMENSIONS			FINAL (CURRENT) DIMENSIONS		
				LF	CF	RF	LF	CF	RF
1901	Lloyd Street Grounds (Milwaukee Park)	Milwaukee	AL	–	–	–	–	–	–
1901	Oriole Park (American League Park)	Baltimore	AL	–	–	–	–	–	–
1901	American League Park	Washington	AL	–	–	–	–	–	–
1901	Columbia Park	Philadelphia	AL	–	–	–	–	–	–
1901	South Side Park	Chicago	AL	–	–	–	–	–	–
1901	Huntington Avenue Grounds	Boston	AL	440	635	280	440	635	280
1901	Bennett Park	Detroit	AL	–	–	–	–	–	–
1902	Palace of the Fans	Cincinnati	NL	–	–	–	–	–	–
1903	Hilltop Park	New York	AL	365	542	400	365	542	400
1904	National Park (American League Park)	Washington	AL	–	–	–	–	–	–
1909	Shibe Park	Philadelphia	AL	360	515	360	334	410	329
1909	Forbes Field	Pittsburgh	NL	360	422	376	365	400	300
1910	(Original) Comiskey Park	Chicago	AL	362	420	362	347	409	347
1910	League Park	Cleveland	AL	385	460	290	375	420	290
1911	Griffith Stadium	Washington	AL	407	421	320	388	421	320
1911	Polo Grounds	New York	NL	277	433	257	280	475	258
1912	Redland Field (Crosley Field)	Cincinnati	NL	360	420	360	328	387	366+
1912	**Navin Field (Tiger Stadium)**	**Detroit**	**AL**	**345**	**467**	**370**	**340**	**440**	**325**
1912	**Fenway Park**	**Boston**	**AL**	**321**	**488**	**314**	**315**	**420**	**302**

CHRONOLOGY OF MAJOR LEAGUE BALLPARKS

Year	Ballpark	City	League	Original Dimensions			Final (Current) Dimensions		
				LF	CF	RF	LF	CF	RF
1913	Ebbets Field	Brooklyn	NL	419	450	301	348	393	297
1914	**Weeghman Park (Wrigley Field)**	**Chicago**	**FL**	**310**	**440**	**356**	**355**	**400**	**353**
1914	Terrapin Park	Baltimore	FL	300	450	335	300	450	335
1914	Washington Park	Brooklyn	FL	300	400	275	300	400	275
1914	Federal Field	Buffalo	FL	290	400	300	290	400	300
1914	Greenlawn Park	Indianapolis	FL	375	400	310	375	400	310
1914	Gordon & Koppel Field (Federal League Park)	Kansas City	FL	–	–	–	–	–	–
1914	Exposition Park	Pittsburgh	FL	375	450	375	375	450	375
1914	Handlan's Park	St. Louis	FL	325	375	300	325	375	300
1915	Harrison Park	Newark	FL	375	450	375	375	450	375
1915	Braves Field	Boston	NL	402	550	402	337	370	319
1923	**Yankee Stadium**	**New York**	**AL**	**281**	**490**	**295**	**318**	**385**	**314**
1932	Lakefront Park (Cleveland Stadium)	Cleveland	AL	322	470	322	320	404	320
1953	**County Stadium**	**Milwaukee**	**NL**	**320**	**404**	**320**	**315**	**402**	**315**
1954	Memorial Stadium	Baltimore	AL	309	410	309	309	405	309
1955	Municipal Stadium (Muehlebach Field)	Kansas City	AL	312	430	347	369	421	338
1958	Los Angeles Memorial Coliseum	Los Angeles	NL	250	425	301	252	420	300
1958	Seals Stadium	San Francisco	NL	365	410	355	361	400	350
1960	**Candlestick Park**	**San Francisco**	**NL**	**330**	**420**	**330**	**335**	**400**	**330**
1961	Wrigley Field	Los Angeles	AL	340	412	339	340	412	339
1961	Metropolitan Stadium	Bloomington, Minn.	AL	329	412	329	343	402	330
1962	Colt Stadium	Houston	NL	360	420	360	360	420	360
1962	**Dodger Stadium**	**Los Angeles**	**NL**	**330**	**410**	**330**	**330**	**400**	**330**
1964	**Shea Stadium**	**New York**	**NL**	**341**	**410**	**341**	**338**	**410**	**338**

Year	Ballpark	City	League						
1965	Astrodome	Houston	NL	330	400	330	340	406	340
1966	Anaheim Stadium	Anaheim, Calif.	AL	333	404	333	333	406	333
1966	Arlington Stadium	Arlington, Tex.	AL	330	400	330	330	400	330
1966	Atlanta-Fulton County Stadium	Atlanta	NL	330	402	330	325	402	325
1966	Busch Stadium	St. Louis	NL	330	402	330	330	414	330
1968	Oakland-Alameda County Stadium	Oakland	AL	330	400	330	330	410	330
1969	Sicks Stadium	Seattle	AL	320	420	305	320	420	305
1969	Jarry Park	Montreal	NL	340	417	340	340	415	340
1969	Jack Murphy Stadium	San Diego	NL	327	405	327	330	420	330
1970	Riverfront Stadium	Cincinnati	NL	330	404	330	330	404	330
1970	Three Rivers Stadium	Pittsburgh	NL	335	400	335	340	410	340
1971	Veterans Stadium	Philadelphia	NL	330	408	330	330	408	330
1973	Royals Stadium	Kansas City	AL	330	410	330	330	405	330
1977	Kingdome	Seattle	AL	314	410	324	315	405	315
1977	Olympic Stadium	Montreal	NL	325	404	325	325	404	325
1982	Metrodome	Minneapolis	AL	327	408	343	326	407	344
1989	SkyDome	Toronto	AL	328	400	328	330	400	330
1991	Comiskey Park	Chicago	AL	347	400	347	347	400	347
1992	Oriole Park at Camden Yards	Baltimore	AL	318	400	333	318	400	333
1993	Mile High Stadium	Denver	NL	370	420	335	370	420	335
1993	Joe Robbie Stadium	Miami	NL	335	410	335	335	410	335
1994	Jacobs Field	Cleveland	AL	325	400	325	325	400	325
1994	The Ballpark in Arlington	Arlington, Tex.	AL	325	401	334	325	401	334
1995	Coors Field	Denver	NL	358	415	347	358	415	347

Some books are so crucial to a work of this kind that they receive special mention. In compiling the timelines, I relied heavily on *The Almanac of American History, What Happened When, The Baseball Chronology, Facts and Dates of American Sports,* and the numerous chronological team histories (e.g., *This Day in Dodger History*). The main baseball reference was *Total Baseball,* which has, in addition to voluminous player records and prose sections, useful material on each park's home run potential and attendance. *The World Series* provides play-by-play information and attendance figures for each game.

In addition to the numerous books and articles on ballparks in general and specific parks, I found much useful material in the archives of the *Sporting News,* at the National Baseball Library in Cooperstown, New York, and at the Spalding and Chadwick collections at the New York Public Library. The Map and Geography Division of the Library of Congress was invaluable for placing ballparks in a given time frame, and historical societies in Baltimore, Boston, Brooklyn, Cincinnati, New York, St. Louis, and Wilmington, Delaware, were most helpful in nailing down specific games, fires, and other events.

NEWSPAPER AND MAGAZINE ARTICLES

"Astros' Scoreboard of Every Fan's Eye." *Sporting News,* June 12, 1965, p. 9.

"Baker Bowl." *SABR Research Journal,* 1982, p. 1.

"Bleachers in the Bedroom." *Philadelphia Magazine,* August 1984, p. 83.

"Braves Field." *Baseball Research Journal,* September 1978, p. 1.

"Chi Fans . . . Love Voom Voom Veeck's Noisy Board." *Sporting News,* June 1, 1960, p. 1.

"Colt .45s Blazed into Baseball History." *USA Today Baseball Weekly,* April 8, 1992, p. 53.

"Comiskey: It's Time to Say Soil Long." *Sporting News,* October 1, 1990, p. 29.

"Demise and Pall of the Indians." *New York Times,* July 2, 1981, p. B10.

"Dodgers' Maestro." *New York Times,* September 28, 1947, p. 28.

"The Grand Exalted Ruler of Rooters' Row." *Sox Fan News,* August 1986, p. 18.

"Greatest Baseball Crowd at Shibe Park." *Philadelphia Inquirer,* April 13, 1909, p. 1.

"Groundskeeper Can Be Snake in the Grass." *Baseball Digest,* June 1959, p. 84.

"Groundskeeper Is Oft Tenth Man in Lineup." *Baseball Digest,* April 1952, p. 89.

"Home of the Highlanders." *Yankee Magazine,* 1989, p. 20.

"How Stadiums Are Built." *Chicago Tribune,* January 22, 1978, Sec. 3, p. 2.

"Memories of Ebbets Field." *Modern Maturity,* June-July, 1981.

"Much Activity at Baseball Headquarters." *Pittsburg Dispatch,* March 7, 1909, p. 2.

"No Inside-the-Parkas." *New York Times,* March 22, 1992, Sec. 5, p. 12.

"One Place That Still Hasn't Seen the Light." *Sports Illustrated,* July 7, 1980.

"Play Ball!" *Seaport Magazine,* Summer 1989, p. 16.

"The Red Sox' First Home." *Fenway Park Scorecard,* 1989, 2nd ed.

"The Seductions of Nostalgia and the Elusiveness of Intimacy." *Baseball Research Journal* 21, 1992.

"74,200 See Yankees Open New Stadium." *New York Times,* April 19, 1923, p. 1.

"SkyDome Unique, Expensive Project." *USA Today Baseball Weekly,* July 5, 1991, p. 33.

"Stadiums Enter Era of Luxury." *New York Times,* September 25, 1989, p. C1.

"The Story of Harry M. Stevens." *Traveler's Magazine,* May 26, 1927, p. 15.

"They Doctor the Diamond." *Baseball Digest,* July 1955, p. 31.

"Tigers' Lair Has a Corner on Lore." *Detroit Free Press,* September 13, 1987, p. 9D.

"What's Baseball Without a Beer?" *New York Times,* October 25, 1991, p. B8.

"Wrigley Field's Historic Scoreboard." *Baseball Hobby News,* December 1992, p. 52.

BOOKS

Allen, Lee. *The Cincinnati Reds.* New York: Putnam's, 1948.

Betzold, Michael, and Ethan Casey. *Queen of Diamonds.* West Bloomfield, Mich.: A&M Publishing, 1992.

Carruth, Gordon. *What Happened When.* New York: Harper & Row, 1989.

Charlton, James, ed. *The Baseball Chronology.* New York: Macmillan, 1991.

Cunningham, Laura. *Sleeping Arrangements.* New York: Penguin Books, 1989.

Davenport, John Warner. *Baseball's Pennant Races.* Madison, Wis.: First Impressions, 1981.

DiClerico, James, and Barry Pavelec. *The Jersey Game.* New Brunswick, N.J.: Rutgers University Press, 1991.

Fleming, G. H. *The Unforgettable Season.* New York: Fireside Books, 1981.

Flexner, Stuart Berg. *I Hear America Talking.* New York: Simon & Schuster, 1976.

Frommer, Harvey. *Shoeless Joe and Ragtime Baseball.* Dallas: Taylor Publishing, 1992.

———. *New York City Baseball.* New York: Macmillan, 1980.

Fulk, David, and Dan Riley. *The Cubs Reader.* Boston: Houghton Mifflin, 1991.

———. *The Red Sox Reader.* Boston: Houghton Mifflin, 1992.

Gallagher, Mark. *Day by Day in New York Yankees History.* New York: Leisure Press, 1983.

Gershman, Michael. *The Baseball Stadium Postcard Album* (National League). Dallas: Taylor Publishing, 1990.

———. *The Baseball Stadium Postcard Album* (American League). Dallas: Taylor Publishing, 1990.

———. *The 1987 Baseball Card Engagement Book.* Boston: Houghton Mifflin, 1986.

———. *The 1988 Baseball Card Engagement Book.* Boston: Houghton Mifflin, 1987.

———. *The 1989 Baseball Card Engagement Book.* Boston: Houghton Mifflin, 1988.

———. *The 1990 Baseball Card Engagement Book.* Dallas: Taylor Publishing, 1989.

———. *The 1991 Baseball Card Engagement Book.* Boston: Houghton Mifflin, 1990.

———. *The 1992 Baseball Card Engagement Book.* Boston: Houghton Mifflin, 1991.

Goldstein, Warren. *Playing for Keeps.* Ithaca, N.Y.: Cornell University Press, 1989.

Groat, Dick, and Bill Surface. *The World Champion Pittsburgh Pirates.* New York: Coward-McCann, 1961.

Hershberger, C. A. *Sports Hall of Oblivion.* Windsor, Ont.: Sumner Press, 1983.

James, Bill. *The Bill James Historical Baseball Abstract.* New York: Villard Books, 1988.

Kirsch, George. *The Creation of American Team Sports.* Chicago: University of Illinois Press, 1989.

Kuklick, Bruce. *To Every Thing a Season.* Princeton, N.J.: Princeton University Press, 1991.

Lansche, Jerry. *Glory Fades Away.* Dallas: Taylor Publishing, 1991.

Levine, Peter. *A. G. Spalding and the Rise of Baseball.* New York: Oxford University Press, 1985.

Lewis, Dottie, ed. *Baseball in Cincinnati: From Wooden Fences to AstroTurf.* Cincinnati: Cincinnati Historical Society, 1988.

Lieb, Frederick. *The Detroit Tigers.* New York: Putnam's, 1946.

Lowenfish, Lee. *The Imperfect Diamond.* New York: Da Capo Press, 1991.

Lowry, Philip. *Green Cathedrals.* Cooperstown, N.Y.: Society for American Baseball Research, 1986.

———. *Green Cathedrals.* Reading, Mass.: Addison-Wesley, 1992.

Manchester, William. *The Glory and the Dream.* Boston: Little, Brown, 1973.

Mehl, Ernest. *The Kansas City Athletics.* New York: Henry Holt, 1956.

Menchine, Ron. *A Picture Postcard History of Baseball.* Vestal, N.Y.: Almar Press, 1992.

Miller, John Anderson. *Fares, Please!* New York: Appleton-Century, 1941.

Neft, David, and Richard Cohen. *The World Series.* New York: St. Martin's Press, 1990.

Official 1980 Baseball Dope Book. St. Louis: Sporting News, 1980.

Okkonen, Marc. *The Federal League of 1914–1915.* Cleveland: Society for American Baseball Research, 1989.

O'Neal, Bill. *The Pacific Coast League.* Austin, Tex.: Eakin Press, 1990.

Peterson, Harold. *The Man Who Invented Baseball.* New York: Scribner's, 1973.

Pietrusza, David. *Lights On!* South Bend, Ind.: Diamond Communications, 1993.

———. *Major Leagues.* Jefferson, N.Car.: McFarland & Co., 1991.

Povich, Shirley. *Washington Senators.* New York: Putnam's, 1954.

Reidenbaugh, Lowell. *Take Me Out to the Ball Park.* St. Louis: Sporting News, 1983.

Riley, Dan. *The Dodgers Reader.* Boston: Houghton Mifflin, 1992.

Ritter, Lawrence. *Lost Ballparks.* New York: Viking Press, 1992.

Schlesinger, Arthur, Jr. *The Almanac of American History.* New York: Putnam's, 1983.

Schroeder, Joseph J., Jr. *1908 Sears, Roebuck & Co. Catalogue.* Northfield, Ill.: DBI Books, 1971.

Seymour, Harold. *Baseball: The Early Years.* New York: Oxford University Press, 1989.

———. *Baseball: The Golden Age.* New York: Oxford University Press, 1971.

Smith, Curt. *Voices of the Game.* New York: Fireside Books, 1987.

Soucheray, Joe. *Once There Was a Ballpark.* Edina, Minn.: Dorn Books, 1981.

Stein, Fred. *Giants Diary.* San Francisco: North Atlantic Books, 1987.

Tiemann, Robert. *Dodger Classics.* St. Louis: Baseball Histories, 1983.

Toman, James. *Cleveland Stadium.* Cleveland:

Cleveland Landmarks Press, 1991.

Veeck, Bill. *Veeck as in Wreck.* New York: Putnam's, 1962.

Vincent, Ted. *Mudville's Revenge.* New York: Seaview Books, 1981.

PAMPHLETS, BROCHURES, SOUVENIR BOOKS, AND PROGRAMS

Baseball's First Regular Game. White Plains, N.Y.: General Foods Corp., 1946.

Forbes Field 60th Birthday Picture Album. Pittsburgh: Pittsburgh Pirates, 1969.

House of Magic. Baltimore: Baltimore Orioles, 1991.

Jedick, Peter. *League Park.* Cleveland: Western Reserve Historical Society, 1979.

League Park Pointers. Cleveland: Cleveland Indians, 1914.

Roboff, Sari. *The Fenway.* Boston: The Boston 200 Corporation, 1976.

———. *Chicago Cubs Magazine* 8:1. Chicago National League Ball Club, 1989.

Through the Years. Chicago: Chicago White Sox, 1990.